W9-ABN-314

Critical Essays on

CHARLOTTE PERKINS GILMAN

CRITICAL ESSAYS
ON
AMERICAN LITERATURE

James Nagel, General Editor
University of Georgia

Critical Essays on

CHARLOTTE PERKINS GILMAN

edited by

JOANNE B. KARPINSKI

G. K. Hall & Co. / New York
Maxwell Macmillan Canada / Toronto
Maxwell Macmillan International / New York Oxford Singapore Sydney

G. K. Hall & Co.
Macmillan Publishing Company
866 Third Avenue
New York, New York 10022

Maxwell Macmillan Canada, Inc.
1200 Eglinton Avenue East
Suite 200
Don Mills, Ontario M3C 3N1

Macmillan Publishing Company is part of the Maxwell Communication
Group of Companies.

Library of Congress Cataloging-in-Publication Data

Critical essays on Charlotte Perkins Gilman / edited by Joanne B.
Karpinski.
    p.   cm.—(Critical essays on American literature)
  Includes bibliographical references and index.
  ISBN 0-8161-7315-X
  1. Gilman, Charlotte Perkins, 1860–1935—Criticism and
interpretation. I. Karpinski, Joanne B. II. Series.
PS1744.G57Z65   1992
818'.409—dc20
                                            92–22838
                                                CIP

The paper used in this publication meets the minimum requirements of
American National Standard for Information Sciences—Permanence of
Paper for Printed Library Materials. ANSI Z3948-1984.∞™

10 9 8 7 6 5 4 3 2 1

Printed in the United States of America

Contents

◆

General Editor's Note

◆

This series seeks to anthologize the most important criticism on a wide variety of topics and writers in American literature. Our readers will find in various volumes not only a generous selection of reprinted articles and reviews but original essays, bibliographies, manuscript sections, and other materials brought to public attention for the first time. This volume, *Critical Essays on Charlotte Perkins Gilman*, is the most comprehensive collection of essays ever published on this important writer, who has recently emerged as a subject for intense scholarly investigation. It contains both a sizable gathering of early reviews and a broad selection of more modern scholarship as well. Among the authors of reprinted articles and reviews are Harriet Howe, Alexander Black, Olivia H. Dunbar, Amy Wellington, Annie L. Muzzey, Vernon Lee, and Carol Ruth Berkin. In addition to a substantial introduction by Joanne B. Karpinski, there are also five original essays commissioned specifically for publication in this volume: new studies by Lois N. Magner on the exploration of the relationship between Darwinism and Feminism, Frank G. Kirkpatrick on Gilman's religious optimism, Catherine Golden on S. Weir Mitchell's treatment of "nervous disorders," Shelley Fisher Fishkin on subversion in Gilman's journalism and short fiction, and Gary Scharnhorst on Gilman's poetry. Together they constitute a substantial addition to the growing scholarship on this writer, and we are confident that this book will make a permanent and significant contribution to the study of American literature.

JAMES NAGEL
University of Georgia

Publisher's Note

◆

Producing a volume that contains both newly commissioned and reprinted material presents the publisher with the challenge of balancing the desire to achieve stylistic consistency with the need to preserve the integrity of works first published elsewhere. In the Critical Essays series, essays commissioned especially for a particular volume are edited to be consistent with G. K. Hall's house style; reprinted essays appear in the style in which they were first published, with only typographical errors corrected. Consequently, shifts in style from one essay to another are the result of our efforts to be faithful to each text as it was originally published.

Introduction

◆

JOANNE B. KARPINSKI

At the apex of her reputation and influence, Charlotte Perkins Stetson Gilman was an international celebrity, and not just among feminists. Commentators had compared her favorably to Shaw and to Ruskin.[1] William Dean Howells wrote that in her writing on economics Gilman had anticipated Thorstein Veblen's theory of conspicuous consumption, and that her satiric verse was the best to come along since James Russell Lowell's.[2] The London *Chronicle* said of her best-selling treatise *Women and Economics*, "Since John Stuart Mill's essay ['Subjection of Women'] there has been no book dealing with the position of women to approach it in originality of conception and brilliancy of execution" (the *Nation* made a closely similar observation).[3] *Women and Economics* had been translated into German, Dutch, Italian, Russian, Hungarian, and Japanese. Yet by the time of her death a scant thirty years later, all of her works were out of print. She remained in eclipse until the resurgence of American feminism in the 1960s.

Why did Gilman's star fade in the twenties, just as the achievement of suffrage seemed poised to bring women into the promised land of equality? A major reason is that Gilman herself was not primarily a suffragist. She did not believe that simply obtaining the right for women to vote would be enough to produce the fundamental changes in economic and social institutions that she felt would be necessary to truly liberate the human potential of women. She foresaw that many women would follow their spouse's preferences and vote for the status quo: "The political equality demanded by the suffragists [is] not enough to give real freedom. Women whose industrial position is that of a house-servant, or who do no work at all, who are fed, clothed, and given pocket-money by men, do not reach freedom and equality by use of the ballot."[4]

To the extent that the women's movement after World War I was preoccupied with achieving suffrage and felt that it had fulfilled its destiny with the adoption of a Constitutional amendment, Gilman's more wide-

1

ranging and radical demands for social reorganization ceased to capture the imagination of the movement and appeared peripheral to its historians. In two other important ways Gilman's radical message was out of phase with the modernist mainstream; she rejected the sexual liberation that fueled the roar of the twenties, and disliked most manifestations of the modernist aesthetic.

A central tenet of Gilman's theory of social organization was that since prehistoric times women had been obliged to overstress their sexual allure in order to win sustenance and protection from males, who would not allow females to earn their living by more independent and productive means. Consequently, she had little respect for conventional femininity. Far from finding the Freudian emphasis on the role of eros in civilization a breakthrough in personal understanding or social relations, Gilman referred to Freudianism as a "sexuopathic philosophy" and a "species of biological blasphemy."[5] While she supported the right of women to use contraception, she clearly stated that libidinous activity should be confined to the marital sphere: "the normal purpose of sex-union is reproduction. . . . its continuous repetition, wholly disassociated with this use, results in a disproportionate development of the primary sex emotions and functional capacities."[6] Gilman recognized that her convictions put her at odds with both the traditional opinion concerning the sacredness of marriage, which opposed contraception, and with the practices of the hedonistic social avant-garde.

In her personal life, Gilman was not averse to the sexual aspect of marital relations, even to the extent of briefly entertaining a proposal that she and Charles Walter Stetson should live separately but come together "when the erotic tendency was at the maximum" (his words).[7] Her diary account of her wedding night with Stetson is ecstatically described: ". . . he lifts the crown, loosens the snood, unfastens the girdle and then—and then. O my God! I thank thee for this heavenly happiness!" (quoted in Hill, 121). But early in their marriage, Stetson chastises her for being "too demonstrative in her affections," and thereafter the issue of desire falls into silence. Years later, after she had been divorced from Stetson and was contemplating marriage with her cousin George Houghton Gilman, she wrote to him, using a castration metaphor, about what she perceived as the incompatibility between her vocation to world service and married life: "Great men are by no means the best husbands. And to be a great woman is as yet so painful and sacrificial a task as to shear and cripple the poor female thing most cruelly. By virtue of what I have of greatness I am the less desirable wife even if I were young, beautiful, healthy and no relation!"[8]

Since after her mid-life marriage to Houghton Gilman she wrote to him that sex without pregnancy seemed a "Happy thought—take no precautions—take no treatment—all runs smoothly and nothing happens!!!" it seems likely that her circumscribed attitude toward sexual freedom had much to do with her own catastrophic experience of motherhood as well as her mother's (16 May 1900; quoted in Scharnhorst, 57). These traumatic events alone, however, cannot explain why Gilman's convictions stuck so closely to traditional conventions for sexual behavior, since she did support the use of birth control methods. In her biography of Gilman, Ann J. Lane suggests—but stops short of adopting—another explanation: "Her ferocious commitment to heterosexual monogamy as the highest, the best, and the only acceptable form of intimacy is upheld with such inflexibility, determination and rigor that it inevitably arouses one's suspicions, especially given her deep and loving feelings for several women in her lifetime. . . . Still, she is reported to have said to E. A. Ross, 'I am altogether heterosexual and cannot do my best work unless in love and loved,' a statement which is confirmed by her life's work."[9]

Situating Gilman's views on sexuality in the context of her governing philosophy of behavior, Carl Degler notes that "since the mainspring of her own life had been social service and subordination of the individual to society, she had little patience with the new freedom that stressed individual happiness and satisfaction, whether in sexual relations or in anything else" (*Women and Economics*, xvi).

In her utopian novel *Herland*, Gilman dispenses with the problem of female sexual catering to male power by creating an all-female society that reproduces parthenogenetically. When three male adventurers discover this enclave, their B-movie assumptions that they will be treated as phallic gods are rudely disappointed. Eventually, the three try to develop more enlightened relationships, but continue to be baffled by the Herlanders' notion of love, which excludes physical desire. As the narrator/*raisonneur* puts it, "These were women one had to love 'up', very high up, instead of down." Another member of the male trio describes the Herlanders' lack of erotic interest more primitively: "Sexless, epicine, undeveloped neuters!"[10] When, out of frustration with his new wife's refusal to be sexually submissive, this man attempts marital rape, he is expelled from Herland. This dramatic dichotomy between the desire for love and the fear of sexual conquest is rarely addressed and never resolved in Gilman's other writing.

Like her views on contemporary sexual mores, Gilman's aesthetics did not embrace the innovations occurring after World War I. One theme that seems to run through all her works, fiction and nonfiction, is a desire for order and coherence in lived experience. In the world she constructed through language, Gilman could eliminate the painful paradoxes that separated womanliness and motherhood, and both from full human participation. Perhaps for this reason her verse remained syllabotonic and largely rhymed even in the period of high modernism, when it became fashionable for prosody to mirror discontinuities rather than rise above them. Two other characteristics of her verse were also minority reports in the Age of Eliot; it retained an Augustan impersonality of diction ("Never was poet less given to the luxury of self-expression," wrote Amy Wellington)[11] and an optimistic, positivist approach to such abstract qualities as Beauty and Truth not widely shared by a skeptical postwar generation.

As a consumer of art, Gilman's tastes were conservative. She was "disgusted by the Armory Exhibition of 1913 and the advent of modernism in the plastic arts" (Scharnhorst, 101). Although she wrote a poem in praise of Isadora Duncan, it was for her revival of the high seriousness of classical Greek dance rather than for her innovations that Gilman admired her.[12]

The pioneers of the Gilman revival in the sixties stressed both the intellectual caliber and the artistic quality of her writing in order to reinvent an audience for her work. This aim can be seen both in Carl Degler's introduction to *Women and Economics*, where he describes the eclipse of Gilman's reputation as a "blackout in the history of ideas" comparable to that suffered by the geneticist Gregor Mendel, the artist Vincent Van Gogh, the novelist Herman Melville, and the colonial church/state separatist Roger Williams (*Women and Economics*, i), and in Elaine Hedges's "Afterword" to the 1973 Feminist Press edition of *The Yellow Wallpaper*, where she writes that a separately bound edition of the story was essential in order to highlight its quality: "Tucked away among many other selections and frequently with only brief biographical information about its author, the story will not necessarily find in these anthologies the wide audience it deserves."[13]

Many articles and books about Gilman highlight biographical information, since her life experiences directly inform her writing. It is important to point out that writers on Gilman have interpreted the biographical data quite differently from each other, and that often these differences in interpretation reflect the gender politics prevailing at the time of writing. This politics of interpretation begins with Gilman herself. Her autobiography offers an unfailingly optimistic feminist portrait not infrequently at odds with the struggling and divided woman represented in her diaries and letters.[14]

Only since the renascence of the women's movement in the past three decades has Gilman's writing and thought begun to be assessed in scholarly journals. In her own lifetime, she addressed a general public and was written about in mass-circulation periodicals. The reviews quoted in the first paragraph of this essay are typical of the reception accorded her work in both the popular press and the thick journals: nearly unreserved enthusiasm for *Women and Economics*, and more guarded praise for her later books. Vernon Lee wrote in *The North American Review* that she was "accomplishing the duty of a convert" in recommending *Women and Economics*: "[This book] ought to open the eyes and, I think, also the hearts, of other readers, because it has opened my own to the real importance of what is known as the Woman Question."[15] Annie L. Muzzey in *The Arena* notes that even masculine critics praised the book, citing Harry Thurston Peck's review in *The Cosmopolitan* (December 1899).[16] Gilman herself favored the review of *Women and Economics* published by the London *Bookman* (16 [September 1899]: 163–64).[17] The *New York Times* gave generally positive reviews to *Women and Economics* (*Saturday Supplement*, 5 November 1898, 738), *Concerning Children* (*Saturday Review*, 5 January 1901, 4), and *The Home: Its Work and Influence* (26 December 1903, 783). *The Critic* reviewed *Women and Economics* (35 [October 1899]: 890–93) and

The Home: Its Work and Influence (43 [December 1903]: 568–70). *Human Work*, the volume over which Gilman struggled most, received little critical notice. The *Atlantic* objected that "an impatient habit of generalization compromises the effectiveness of the book both from the literary point of view and as a scientific study."

As noted in the first paragraph of this introduction, William Dean Howells had the highest praise for Gilman's volume of poetry, *In This Our World*. At the other extreme were the disparaging remarks of Harry Thurston Peck, written a year before his admiring review of *Women and Economics*. Horace Traubel wrote that the strength of *In This Our World* lay in its convictions rather than in its verbal felicity.[18] Although Gilman wrote, edited, published, and financially underwrote the journal *Forerunner* for seven years, it was not reviewed by other journals. Gilman attempted to interest Howells in the magazine, sending him two bound volumes, but he did not write about it.[19]

Carl Degler may be regarded as the patriarch of the scholarly Gilman revival. His essay "Charlotte Perkins Gilman on the Theory and Practice of Feminism" in the Spring 1956 volume of the *American Quarterly* provided a retrospective on Gilman's thought in the context of the new wave of feminism precipitated by the writing of Simone de Beauvoir. The article led to a reissue of *Women and Economics*, for which Degler wrote the introduction.

Unlike many of his successors in the field, Degler largely avoided biographical interpretation; the *American Quarterly* article relegates Gilman's vital statistics to a footnote, and the biographical section of his introduction to *Women and Economics* is relatively brief. When writing about Gilman's personal life, Degler prefers balanced to value-laden rhetoric. While he believes that "Gilman's candor, forthrightness, and non-conformity make her seem a 'typical' feminist, strong-minded, aggressive, and somewhat overbearing," he also observes that this typecasting results from an "insistence upon a sharp distinction in appearance, manner, and psyche between the sexes in the nineteenth century," which can "undoubtedly" be seen as "a measure of men's anxiety about their own identity" (*Women and Economics*, xvii, xxi). In his evaluation of Gilman's ideas, at least one commentator has found evidence of a masculinist bias. While Degler does not specifically relate Gilman's weak grounding in the scientific method to her gender, Lois Magner feels that Degler's overall tone toward Gilman's use of the scientific idiom is "condescending":

In the introduction to Gilman's classic work *Women and Economics*, Carl Degler cautions that it is a reform tract, which can easily beguile the reader into thinking it is a scientific study. Degler has also harshly criticized Gilman's use of biological analogies as "pseudo-science" (xxx), as if her extension of biological theories to human culture was uniquely female, trivial and inaccurate; and yet the better-known [male] social Darwinists of her time and many modern ethnologists also use animal models to justify the continuation and

even the "inevitability of the patriarchy." . . . Degler condescendingly assesses
Gilman's method as "neither scientific nor even very convincing"

(xxiv–xxx).[20]

Since a relatively small number of women were active in scholarly life
at the dawn of the sixties, it was inevitable that most of the first participants
in the Gilman revival were male. While introducing a new generation of
readers to an overview of Gilman's thought, which they presented on the
whole accurately and in a positive light, Gilman's male interpreters of the
sixties struggled with the same representational paradox that had afflicted
Gilman's contemporaries: how radical feminism could be reconciled with
male-defined conventions of womanliness.

Robert Riegel's profile of Gilman in *American Feminists* (1963) empha-
sizes the romantic aspects of Gilman's and her mother's relationships to
their respective spouses while de-emphasizing the extent to which the two
men contributed to the demise of their marriages. Erroneously stating that
Gilman's father, Frederick Perkins, never remarried, Riegel opines, "Presumably he also continued to be in love, even though he found himself
either unable or unwilling to contribute to the expenses of the family." Of
Gilman's first marriage to the artist Charles Walter Stetson he notes that
"her life was completely disorganized when she fell in love. . . he was the
most important man she had ever met."[21] Riegel describes Gilman's social
philosophy as "highly derivative" of male predecessors Edward Bellamy and
Lester Ward (without noting that Gilman publicly and often acknowledged
those from whom she drew inspiration), and while allowing that "it had
elaborations of its own," he never singles these out for analytical attention.

William L. O'Neill calls *Women and Economics* "the most influential
book ever written by an American feminist," but concludes that Gilman's
major triumphs related to the traditional woman's sphere:

> Charlotte Perkins Gilman compels our respect first of all by the courage with
> which she overcame her extraordinary handicaps. Her childhood was desolate
> and crippling, her first marriage, for which she took all the blame, a fiasco.
> She failed even to make a home for her only child. Yet she struggled back
> from the edge of insanity, enjoyed a long and useful career in journalism,
> married again, this time for good, and finally regained the pleasure of her
> daughter's company. Her experiences marked her for life, of course. . . . But
> she was a mother, and a heterosexual, unlike some feminists. Thus the degree
> of her sexual maladjustment was probably less than might have been expected,
> given her start in life.[22]

As the women's movement gained momentum in the seventies, and as
women's studies began to challenge the dominant academic voice, female
scholars began to write about Gilman; her life seemed less aberrational and
more inspiring to these biographers. Judith Nies wrote, "Her significance

lies in the integrity of her life, in her acts as much as in her beliefs." Where O'Neill saw a story of pathologies overcome, Nies read instead "the story of her insistence on her right to be treated as a human being, to choose work which defined her, to be a producer rather than a consumer" (Nies, 127). Insofar as there is obsession to be seen in this narrative, Nies finds it in Gilman's rejection of "every social, economic, political, and ethical principle society held up as defining the true nature of woman." While both Degler and Riegel attribute Gilman's erratic education to the impoverishment and frequent moves of her childhood, Nies blames her gender, pointing out that when her brother Thomas was sixteen her father's relatives sent him to MIT.

The first volume-length biography of Gilman, Mary Hill's *Charlotte Perkins Gilman: The Making of a Radical Feminist 1860–1896*, appeared in 1980. Able to take advantage of the purchase of Gilman's private papers in the early 1970s by Radcliffe's Arthur and Elizabeth Schlesinger Library on the History of Women in America, and also able to interview Gilman's daughter, Katharine Chamberlin, before she died, Hill frankly focused on Gilman's scarcely explored private life: "My biography rests on the assumption that the truth and power of many of Charlotte Gilman's theories come from her passion and experience, and that her historical significance stems not only from her brilliance, but also from the way she tried to live her life."[23]

When Hill began her projected two-volume study (as of this writing volume 2 is still in preparation) in 1970, she was "looking for a heroine, for closer contact with a woman who could articulate my own frustrations and explain women's problems in ways relating directly to my life" (Hill, 9). This expectation altered with the decade, as did indeed the whole woman's movement between the seventies and the eighties. What emerged with the times was a more complex portrait, struggling to account for failures as well as successes, and therefore in places unsure of its tone:

> For as is so often the case in women's history, it is not only the instances of societal prejudice that dampen women's spirits, but also the prejudice they direct against themselves. Taught from childhood to accept "feminine" responsibilities, to defer passively to other people's needs, women often find it hard to respect themselves, much less to recognize, accept, and respect authenticity and purpose in their work. Like so many professional women even today, Charlotte was unable to feel consistently the self-assurance she publicly projected. Exceptional though she clearly was, she still had not been able to free herself completely of the "feminine" dilemmas, the "burden of our common womanhood" that she so brilliantly described.
>
> —Hill, 296

Gary Scharnhorst's 1985 biography of Gilman uses more dispassionate language than any of its predecessors, neither identifying with its subject nor attempting to categorize her. Without deploying the specialized language of the postmodern theorists who came to prominence in American literary studies in the last decade, Scharnhorst's volume adopts several premises of deconstruction—most importantly, that the body of Gilman's written work should be read as a continuum without privileging one genre over another (especially not allowing autobiography hegemony over all, a stance for which he faults both Hedges and Hill [Scharnhorst, 18]). Scharnhorst typically critiques and defends Gilman's writing through the writing of others, thus decentering the author's voice from its position of authority. Where a critical opinion does not pre-exist his own, however, Scharnhorst does speak *in propria persona*; for example, comparing Upton Sinclair's later, more successful attack on adulterated foods to Gilman's earlier effort, he writes: "Gilman's essay was designed to persuade individuals to improve their habits. She hoped to effect change by example rather than by law. . . . At the risk of oversimplification, Gilman embraced a utopian solution to the problem of contaminated foods and Sinclair spurred practical reform" (Scharnhorst, 72).

Here and elsewhere Scharnhorst also reveals an affinity with the post-modernists in his foregrounding of the production-consumption relations prevalent during Gilman's era and inscribed in her writing. Despite these forays into the postmodern, however, the volume retains the traditional assumption that an objective representation of its subject can be (indeed, has been) achieved.

Ann J. Lane rejects the prospect of such objectivity in the very first words she writes: "This is the story of my Charlotte. The shape of the personality and the life conform to what is known about her. The record provides the boundaries but does not offer the portrait. The portrait is essentially mine, a product of our dialogue these last years. . . . There are two dialogues embedded in this study, that between author and subject and that between the subject's life and her work" (Lane, xi).

Still, Lane does not simply identify with her subject: "her angle of vision was inevitably very different from mine." Reflecting the growing body of theoretical writing on biography and autobiography, Lane's style is "not a smooth movement from place to place but a complex and multilayered progression," the goal of which is to have the reader participate actively in the process of discovery. Without referring to contemporary French feminist theory any more overtly than Scharnhorst refers to deconstruction, Lane is nevertheless consistent with one aspect of its viewpoint in seeing Gilman herself as a decentered subject, one in whom social relations and social issues are embodied (rather than "inscribed," suggesting that Lane sees reality as separable from language, although she goes on to problematize the relation-ship of current and retrospective evaluation as causes of "mischief for the biographer in reading her subject's autobiography" [Lane, xiii]). Taken to-gether, these biographical readings of Gilman present a figure simultaneously "of her times" and "for all ages"—a canonical figure.

The most complete Gilman bibliography is by Gary Scharnhorst (Met-uchen, N.J.: Scarecrow Press, 1985). This usefully annotated work needs to be updated to account for the torrent of works on Gilman that have been published since its first appearance. Fortunately, on-line searching methods now make it easier to keep track of the rapidly growing field of Gilman studies. The newly launched *Charlotte Perkins Gilman Society Newsletter* lists recent and forthcoming publications on Gilman.

Contemporary scholarly criticism on Gilman's work most frequently concentrates on "The Yellow Wallpaper." So many and so multifaceted are the essays on "Wallpaper" that Elaine Hedges considers this image the white whale of women's literature; her review of two decades of feminist writing on this short story appears in this volume. *Herland* has also received considerable critical attention.[24] Other individual Gilman stories that have been the subject of scholarly articles include "The Giant Wistaria"[25] and "What Diantha Did."[26] Collective consideration has been given to her gothic tales[27] and to her satiric poetry.[28] A variety of articles consider Gilman's relationships to other major thinkers of her era,[29] and evaluate her life and thought in the context of social issues such as women's health and female creativity,[30] architectural feminism,[31] and feminine spirituality.[32]

Although the collection of materials on Gilman presented here belongs to the series *Critical Essays in American Literature*, it makes an effort to represent the breadth of Gilman's writing, rather than focus on her literary output alone. There are three reasons for this choice of wider focus. The first is that the quality of her distinctly literary productions is erratic. She made no bones about their polemical rather than their aesthetic import being their raison d'être. Of "The Yellow Wallpaper" she said, "I wrote it to preach. If it is literature, that just happened" (quoted in Black, 39). Didactic purpose is paramount for her short stories as well: "One girl reads this, and takes fire! Her life is changed. She becomes a power—a mover of others—I write for her."[33] Moreover, since she herself regarded her poems, stories, and plays as illustrations of the social issues she wished to explore and rectify, her nonliterary texts and the social context in which they were produced are important to assessing her accomplishments in literary genres. Finally, just as her theories about gender equality and the changes in social organization required to bring such equality into being inform her poetry, fiction, and drama, so too do these specifically literary forms problematize the theoretical issues she raises. A number of essays specially commissioned for this volume address aspects of Gilman's work inadequately represented in published scholarship. In making a selection of articles to reprint, I tried to avoid duplicating the contents of other anthologies of Gilman criticism.[34]

Carol Berkin's "Private Woman, Public Woman: The Contradictions of Charlotte Perkins Gilman" struck me as the most appropriate biographical essay for this collection for reasons that are probably evident from its title. Berkin treats Gilman's life as a "witness to the difficulties of feminism, not as an ideology or a political commitment but as a personal experience" (a distinction not consistently kept by Hill): "Charlotte Perkins Gilman struggled for intellectual and emotional liberation, hampered through much of her life by an internalization of the very split vision of masculine and feminine spheres and destinies that, in her work, she would expose as artificial. . . . This essay seeks to chart her personal confrontation with feminism, because it is in that experience that she may serve as a model [although not necessarily a heroine] for American women."

Several of the articles presented here are assessments of Gilman by writers who were personally acquainted with her and with the effect she had on contemporary audiences. The earliest of these, "Charlotte Perkins Gilman, a Daring Humorist of Reform," looks forward to the time when "the poet will conclude to remove his analytical microscope from the contemplation of his private emotions," thus situating Gilman's aesthetic between the moribund privacies of romanticism and the as yet unarticulated privacies of modernism.

"A Daring Humorist of Reform" appears in the same issue of the *American Fabian* (January 1897) as a short piece on "The Work and Influence of Charlotte Perkins Stetson in the Labor movement" by Eugene Hough, a California friend (and according to Hill, a former suitor) of Gilman's. Despite this connection, Hough's contribution appreciates "without adulation or sentimentalism" Gilman's achievements on behalf of "he who, by his economic condition, is stunted and deformed and impoverished in every part save aspiration."

"Charlotte Perkins Gilman's Dynamic Social Philosophy" (1906) predicts that *The Man-Made World, or Our Androcentric Culture* will "prove her most important book since *Women and Economics.*" The quotations the article takes from this work demonstrate that in her broad-ranging consideration of ethics, Gilman anticipates the notion of crimes against the ecology. The article also reprints the poem "Birth," which opened Gilman's only published volume of poetry, *In This Our World*, "noting a curious lapse in the opening lines of the first, third and fifth verses, into what Mrs. Gilman would term our androcentric nomenclature."

Alexander Black's aptly titled "The Woman Who Saw It First" points out that by 1923, "so much of her preaching that once was regarded as revolutionary is now a matter of polite consideration, if not of practice, that her total effect is no longer so sharply radical as it was to the generation to which we look back." Black sees it as a wise decision rather than a limitation of Gilman's that she did not take an active role in politics: "The trouble was that politics meant adjustment, concession, trimming. She wanted to move as she thought—straight through."

Gilman cooperated with longtime friend Amy Wellington's preparation of a biographical sketch that appeared in Wellington's *Women Have Told: Studies in the Feminist Tradition* (1930). Wellington seeks to counterbalance Gilman's "dangerous" reputation by situating her ideas in a broader context than feminism: "It is a most suggestive fact that the three outstanding English books on the woman [*sic*] movement, written by women—Mary Wollstonecraft's "Vindication of the Rights of Women," Olive Schreiner's

"Woman and Labor," and Charlotte Gilman's "Women and Economics"—were not sex pleas based narrowly on women's rights, but philosophic arguments securely resting on the wide foundation of human liberties."

In contrast to Amy Wellington's civically oriented account of Gilman's work and indeed to the public persona of Gilman's autobiography, Harriet Howe's memoir "Charlotte Perkins Gilman—As I Knew Her" is frankly personal, describing how her association with Gilman increased her own self-awareness and self-confidence. Howe, like Black, refers to the devastating emotional impact on Gilman of the ghoulish tone taken by the California press concerning Gilman's divorce and child-custody arrangements. Agreeing with Black that such writing, resurrected decades after the fact, represents "the vomitings of a newspaper 'morgue,'" I have chosen not to reprint any in this collection.

A selection of reviews of Gilman's works in journals of her era follows. "The Hour and the Woman" by Annie L. Muzzey presents *Women and Economics* from the viewpoint of a turn-of-the-century feminist partisan, while Vernon Lee's "The Economic Dependence of Women" offers an assessment of the same work by a self-proclaimed convert to the cause. Olivia Dunbar's "Mrs. Gilman's Idea of Home" and the unsigned reviews of *The Home: Its Work and Influence* and *Concerning Children* give a flavor of critical opinion about these works at the time that they were first published.

One of the difficulties that Gilman presents to feminist theoreticians reflects "the profound paradox of [any] feminist speaking in our contemporary culture: she proceeds from a *belief* in a world from which—even the philosophers admit—*Truth* has disappeared." Truth, Beauty, and other capital-letter abstractions clearly do exist in Gilman's world and word, imposing on the contemporary feminist not wishing to be forced into denial, silence, or mysticism "a continual attention to the places from which we [and she] speak"[35] The next group of essays aim at contextualizing Gilman and her writing, at examining interrelationships and intertextualities.

From the outset, commentators have recognized that Gilman's social philosophy was grounded in Reform Darwinism. Amy Wellington pointed out that for Gilman, evolution formed the hypothesis for a "lifetime of original and fearless thinking" (Wellington, 31). In "Darwinism and the Woman Question: The Evolving Views of Charlotte Perkins Gilman," Lois N. Magner compares Gilman's writing on social Darwinism with that of the man she claimed as a major mentor in the field, Herbert Spencer. She asserts that Spencer originally allowed his Law of Equal Freedom to apply to women as well as to men, but in his later writings he rejected these early radical views and distorted his evolutionary concepts as he retreated into a gloomy conservatism. Gilman, in contrast, grew ever more confident in the human capacity to understand and therefore to consciously direct the processes of social evolution. Both Spencer and Gilman were influenced by the now discredited Lamarckian view that behavioral modifications made in one generation would rapidly pass on to subsequent generations.

Frank Kirkpatrick also seeks points of comparison and contrast between Gilman's philosophy and that of a widely known male exponent. In 'Begin Again!'—Charlotte Perkins Gilman's Gentle Religious Optimism and Its Cutting Social Edge" Kirkpatrick contextualizes Gilman's religious views in the historical oscillation of America's religious mood "between deep despair over the depravity of the human condition and unbounded optimism about its potential for perfection," locating Gilman "ironically, within the thought world of late nineteenth century romantic liberal theology . . . which her own great uncle, Henry Ward Beecher, did more to exemplify than almost any other major religious leader of the time." Nevertheless, Gilman "would have found herself very much at odds with Henry's *social* views [emphasis mine] and closer to those of the Social Gospel."

Dr. Silas Weir Mitchell, a foremost nineteenth-century neurologist whose theories were in part adopted by Sigmund Freud, articulated his analysis of and therapy for women's neurasthenic disorders in fiction as well as professional publications. Gilman's most famous short story, "The Yellow Wallpaper," indicts the rest cure to which Mitchell subjected her as a treatment for her postpartum depression. Catherine Golden's essay " 'Overwriting' the Rest Cure: Charlotte Perkins Gilman's Literary Escape from S. Weir Mitchell's Fictionalization of Women" compares the rebellious psychology and course of action taken by Gilman's unnamed narrator to the more compliant or resigned attitudes exhibited by the protagonists of Mitchell's fictions.

Elizabeth Keyser's "Looking Backward: From *Herland* to *Gulliver's Travels*" also examines a piece of Gilman's writing in relationship to a male-composed prototype. Keyser sees Gilman's utopian novel as reinterpreting a literary work that "purports to deal with 'the nature of man' but in fact deals only with men" so that it can serve as a model for women.

Barbara Scott Winkler sees a convergence of Gilman's views with those of another turn-of-the-century feminist as grounded in women's shared conditioning and experiences. "Victorian Daughters: The Lives and Feminism of Charlotte Perkins Gilman and Olive Schreiner" attributes the development of their feminism to rebellion against strong maternal figures who, if unconventional themselves, nevertheless believed in and attempted to enforce Victorian codes of femininity.

Rounding out this section are two essays that examine conscious efforts by male figures to act as mentors for Gilman. The excerpt from Mary Hill's introduction to *Endure: The Diaries of Charles Walter Stetson* reveal the private struggles for mastery in his art and in his life of a man who, while strongly attracted to the independent spirit as well as the physical beauty of Charlotte Perkins, nevertheless assumed that married love would effect her transformation into a more idealized, yielding vision of femininity. After his divorce from Charlotte Perkins, Walter Stetson came to love and marry her closest friend and confidante, Grace Ellery Channing. Grace's editorial notes on Walter's diaries illuminate a heretofore obscure aspect of this triangular relationship.

"When the Marriage of True Minds Admits Impediments: Charlotte Perkins Gilman and William Dean Howells" by Joanne B. Karpinski examines the "intellectual minuet" undertaken by the two writers. Howells initiated a mentorial relationship with Gilman, to whom he had numerous similarities of background and temperament. However, he could not manage to act as her advocate and protector in the same way as he had for other women writers (Sarah Orne Jewett, for example), probably because "the restraint that differentiated the Local Colorists' literary style from Gilman's extended to their professional styles as well." Characterizing him as "sincere but correct," Karpinski finds that "Howells was not suited by temperament or conviction to become the passionate champion" Gilman desired.

The final group of scholarly essays deals directly with Gilman's literary production. The "Yellow Wallpaper" is not only Gilman's best-known literary work but the one that has been most frequently written about. From this diverse and growing body of critical material I have selected Elaine Hedges's overview, "Out at Last: 'The Yellow Wallpaper' After Two Decades of Feminist Criticism." Hedges notes that the Feminist Press edition of the story for which she wrote the afterword has become "one of the best-selling works of fiction by university presses in the United States"; thus, "The Yellow Wallpaper" has achieved for Gilman a posthumous international success on the scale that *Women and Economics* accomplished in her lifetime. In this essay Hedges explores the question, "What do the story's changing interpretations tell us about the trajectory of literary criticism over the last twenty years?"[36]

Shelley Fisher Fishkin's " 'Making a Change': Strategies of Subversion in Gilman's Journalism and Short Fiction" surveys the journalistic prose and fiction that Gilman produced while editing *The Impress* and *The Forerunner*. She concludes that "journalism and fiction for Gilman were two distinct but related tools in her efforts to dismantle the seemingly *a priori* assumptions of patriarchy." While journalism allowed her to "launch frontal attacks on an exploitative ideology," fiction gave Gilman the chance to "delineate alternative ways of organizing the world."

Shortly before her death, Gilman arranged for her friend Amy Wellington to edited a second volume of her verse. Wellington was unable to bring this project to fruition before her own death. In "Reconstructing *Here Also*: On the Later Poetry of Charlotte Perkins Gilman," Gary Scharnhorst offers a speculative assembly of that projected work, based on "a tentative list in Gilman's hand of the poems she wished to collect in this edition" and "several of Wellington's letters to Gilman outlining her plans for the volume." He also suggests that reasons why Wellington could not find a publisher for the new collection can be found in the "radically discordant tones" of the satires and the fact that "Gilman's style of verse was no longer fashionable."

Gilman's desire to make a personal impact on the lives of individual women was not only her own particular goal in speech and writing but also a memorable aspect of her personality.

While Gilman gleefully attacked the socioeconomic and religious manifestations of the Western "master narrative," she accepted the notion of essential as well as acculturated gender differences between men and women: the crux of her argument was that these differences were valuable enough to be fully expressed in every aspect of human interaction, rather than confined to a separate and unequal feminine sphere. Perhaps more importantly in terms of a contemporary feminist critique, Gilman never undertook an examination of the androcentric construction of language, never foresaw the conclusion now central to French feminism that "our ways of understanding in the West have been and continue to be complicitous with our ways of oppressing" (Jardine, 24). This aspect of Gilman studies remains to be developed.

I wish to thank Regis College for providing a summer research grant and course load reductions so that I could accomplish this project. Thanks, too, to the tireless and inventive Richard Hansen and Cathy Goldstone at Dayton Memorial Library, and to Nancy Wilson, Mary Beth Stalp, and Claire Russell for their cheerful help with copy preparation. I especially want to salute Greg, Julia, and Elena for their patience in enduring my "living *with* Charlotte Perkins Gilman"; they "got it" better than poor Walter ever did.

Notes

1. "American Fabians may . . . match Mrs. Stetson against the English free-lance Bernard Shaw, in a war of wits." *The American Fabian* 3, no. 1 (January 1897): 3. "About ten years ago an American editor said of Mrs. Gilman, 'She is the George Bernard Shaw of America, unless we prefer to call Mr. Shaw the Charlotte Perkins Gilman of England.' " Alexander Black, "The Woman Who Saw It First," *The Century Magazine* 107 (November 1923): 28; hereafter cited as Black. "Those, however, who disagree with her often admit that she has Ruskin's quality of suggesting more new truth when she is wrong than commonplace writers do when they are right." *Current Literature* 36 (May 1904): 511.

2. Howells on Veblen quoted by Judith Nies, *Seven Women: Portraits from the American Radical Tradition* (New York: Viking, 1977), 144; hereafter cited as Nies. Howells on Lowell in "The New Poetry," *North American Review* 168 (May 1899): 589–590.

3. Quoted in Black, 39. The list of languages into which *Women and Economics* was translated also appears here. *The Nation* compared *Women and Economics* to "Subjection of Women" on 8 June 1899, 443.

4. Charlotte Perkins Gilman, *Women and Economics: A Study of the Economic Relation Between Men and Women as a Factor in Social Evolution* (1896), reprinted with an introduction by Carl Degler (New York: Harper & Row, 1966); hereafter cited as *Women and Economics*.

5. Charlotte Perkins Gilman, *His Religion and Hers: A Study of the Faith of Our Fathers and the Work of Our Mothers* (New York: Century, 1923), 165–70.

6. *The Forerunner* 6 (July 1915): 179; quoted by Gary Scharnhorst, *Charlotte Perkins Gilman* (Boston: Twayne, 1985), 101; hereafter cited as Scharnhorst.

7. *Endure: The Diaries of Charles Walter Stetson* (Philadelphia: Temple University Press, 1985), 83 (19 March 1883); hereafter cited as *Diaries*.

8. Letter to George Houghton Gilman, 22 May 1898.

9. Ann J. Lane, *To Herland and Beyond: The Life & Work of Charlotte Perkins Gilman* (New York: Pantheon, 1990), 349; hereafter cited as Lane.

10. Charlotte Perkins Gilman, *Herland* (New York: Pantheon, 1979), 141. This is the first publication of the novel in book form. It originally ran as a serial in Gilman's periodical, *The Forerunner*.

11. Amy Wellington, "Charlotte Perkins Gilman," *Women Have Told: Studies in the Feminist Tradition* (Boston: Little, Brown, 1930); hereafter cited as Wellington.

12. Scharnhorst, "Reconstructing *Here Also*: On the Later Poetry of Charlotte Perkins Gilman," in this volume.

13. Elaine Hedges, Afterword to *The Yellow Wall-paper* (Old Westbury, N.Y.: Feminist Press, 1973), 39.

14. *The Living of Charlotte Perkins Gilman: An Autobiography.* Foreword by Zona Gale. (New York: Appleton-Century, 1935). Reissued by University of Wisconsin Press (1991), with an introduction by Ann Lane.

15. Vernon Lee, "The Economic Dependence of Women," *The North American Review* 175, no. 548 (1 April 1903): 71; reprinted in this volume.

16. Annie L. Muzzey, "The Hour and the Woman," *Arena* 22 (August 1899): 266; reprinted in this volume.

17. S. M. F[rancis]., "Books New and Old," *The Atlantic* 94 (August 1904), 275; reprinted in this volume.

18. Howells, as cited in note 1. Harry Thurston Peck, "The Cook-Stove in Poetry," *Bookman* 8 (September 1898): 50–53. Horace Traubel, *The Conservator* (Summer 1898).

19. Letter by Charlotte Perkins Gilman to William Dean Howells, 17 October 1919, quoted by permission of the Houghton Library in Joanne Karpinski, "When the Marriage of True Minds Admits Impediments: Charlotte Perkins Gilman and William Dean Howells," in *Patrons and Protégées: Gender, Friendship and Writing in Nineteenth-Century America*, edited by Shirley Marchalonis (New Brunswick, N.J.: Rutgers University Press, 1989), 213; reprinted in this volume.

20. Lois Magner, "Women and the Scientific Idiom: Textual Episodes from Wollstonecraft, Fuller, Gilman and Firestone," *Signs: A Journal of Women in Culture and Society* 4 (Autumn 1978): 70, fn. 44.

21. Robert E. Riegel, *American Feminists* (Lawrence: The University Press of Kansas, 1963), 165.

22. William L. O'Neill, *Everyone Was Brave: The Rise and Fall of Feminism in America* (Chicago: Quadrangle Books, 1969), 131.

23. Mary A. Hill, *Charlotte Perkins Gilman: The Making of a Radical Feminist 1860–1896* (Philadelphia: Temple University Press, 1980), 9; hereafter cited as Hill.

24. Susan Gubar, "*She* and *Herland*: Feminism as Fantasy," in *Coordinates: Placing Science Fiction and Fantasy*, ed. George E. Slusser, Eric S. Rabkin, and Robert Scholes (Carbondale: Southern Illinois University Press, 1983); reprinted in *Charlotte Perkins Gilman: The Woman and Her Work*, ed. Sheryl L. Meyering (Ann Arbor, Mich.: UMI Research Press, 1989), 191–202; hereafter cited as Meyering; K. Graehme Hall, "Mothers and Children: 'Rising with the Resistless Tide' in *Herland*," in Meyering, 161–72; Patricia Huckle, "Women in Utopias," *The Utopian Vision: Seven Essays on the Quincentennial of Sir Thomas More* (San Diego: San Diego State University Press, 1983); Elizabeth Keyser, "Looking Backward: From *Herland* to *Gulliver's Travels*," *Studies in American Fiction* 11, no. 1 (Spring 1983): 31–46; reprinted in this volume; Lucy M. Freibert, "World View in Utopian Novels by Women," in *Woman and Utopia*, ed. Marleen Barr and Nicholas D. Smith (Lanham, Md.: University Press of America, 1983); Carol Pearson, "Coming Home: Four Feminist Utopias and Patriarchal Experience," *Future Females: A Critical Anthology*, ed. Marleen S. Barr (Bowling Green: Bowling Green State University Popular Press, 1981); Christopher P. Wilson, "Charlotte Perkins Gilman's Steady Burghers: The Terrain of *Herland*," *Women's Studies* 12 (1986): 271–92; reprinted in Meyering, 173–190.

25. Gloria A. Biamonte, " 'There Is a Story, If Only We Could Find It': Charlotte

Perkins Gilman's 'The Giant Wistaria,' " *Legacy: A Journal of Nineteenth-Century American Women Writers* 5, no. 2 (Fall 1988): 3–14; Gary Scharnhorst, "Charlotte Perkins Gilman's 'The Giant Wistaria:' A Hieroglyph of the Female Frontier Gothic," *Frontier Gothic*, ed. David Mogen, Scott Sanders, and Joanne Karpinski (East Rutherford, N.J.: Fairleigh Dickenson University Press, 1992).

26. Sharon M. Rambo, "*What Diantha Did*: The Authority of Experience," in Meyering, 151–60.

27. Juliann Evans Fleenor, "The Gothic Prism: Charlotte Perkins Gilman's Gothic Tales and Her Autobiography," *The Female Gothic*, ed. Juliann Evans Fleenor (Montreal: Eden Press, 1986); reprinted in Meyering, 117–32; Julia Rader, "The Dissolving Vision: Realism in Jewett, Freeman and Gilman," *American Realism: New Essays* (Baltimore: Johns Hopkins University Press, 1982).

28. Carol Farley Kessler, "Brittle Jars and Bitter Jangles: Light Verse by Charlotte Perkins Gilman," *Regionalism and the Female Imagination* 4 (1979): 35–43; reprinted in Meyering, 133–44; Grace Paley, "Of Poetry, Women and the World," *TriQuarterly* (Winter 1986): 107–108; Gary Scharnhorst, "Reconstructing *Here Also*," in this volume.

29. Joanne B. Karpinski "When the Marriage of True Minds Admits Impediments: Charlotte Perkins Gilman and William Dean Howells" (for complete citation, see note 19); Joann P. Krieg, "Charlotte Perkins Gilman and the Whitman Connection," *Walt Whitman Quarterly Review* 1 (March 1984): 21–25; reprinted in Meyering, 145–49; Lois Magner, "Women and the Scientific Idiom: Textual Episodes from Wollstonecraft, Fuller and Firestone" (for complete citation, see note 20); Lois Magner, "Darwinism and the Woman Question: The Evolving Views of Charlotte Perkins Gilman" [Gilman and Herbert Spencer], in this volume; Barbara Scott Winkler, "Victorian Daughters: The Lives and Feminism of Charlotte Perkins Gilman and Olive Schreiner," *Michigan Occasional Papers in Women's Studies* 13 (1980), condensed in this volume.

30. Gillian Brown, "The Empire of Agoraphobia" [Gilman and Melville], *Representations* 20 (Fall 1987): 134–57; Catherine Golden, "Overwriting the Rest Cure: Charlotte Perkins Gilman and the Fiction of S. Weir Mitchell," in this volume; Regina Markell Morantz, "The Perils of Feminist History," in *Women and Health in America*, ed. Judith Walzer Leavitt (Madison: University of Wisconsin Press, 1984), 239–45; Suzanne Poirier, "The Weir Mitchell Rest Cure: Doctors and Patients," *Women's Studies* 10, no. 1: 15–40; Patricia Meyers Spacks, "Finger Posts," *The Female Imagination* (New York: Alfred A. Knopf, 1975), 207–220. Ann Douglas Wood, " 'The Fashionable Diseases': Women's Complaints and Their Treatment in Nineteenth-Century America," *Journal of Interdisciplinary History* 4 (Summer 1973): 25–52; reprinted in *Cleo's Consciousness Raised* (New York: Feminist Studies, Inc., 1974), 1–22.

31. Polly Wynn Allen, *Building Domestic Liberty: Charlotte Perkins Gilman's Architectural Feminism* (Amherst: University of Massachusetts Press, 1988); Dolores Heyden, "Charlotte Perkins Gilman and the Kitchenless House," *Radical History Review* 21 (1979): 225–47.

32. Frank Kirkpatrick, " 'Begin Again!': Charlotte Perkins Gilman's Gentle Religious Optimism and Its Cutting Social Edge," in this volume; Amanda Porterfield, "Science, Social Work, and Sociology" and "Changing the Space Inside a Room," *Feminine Spirituality in America: From Sarah Edwards to Martha Graham* (Philadelphia: Temple University Press, 1980), 171–80.

33. "Thoughts and Figgerings," December 1926.

34. These include Meyering and two casebooks on "The Yellow Wallpaper": *The Captive Imagination*, Catherine Golden (New York: Feminist Press, 1992), and one forthcoming from Rutgers University Press.

35. Alice A. Jardine, *Gynesis* (Ithaca: Cornell University Press, 1985), 31, 32: hereafter cited as Jardine.

36. Following this trajectory with Hedges led me to see a similar pattern in the successive biographies of Gilman, as outlined above.

Private Woman, Public Woman: The Contradictions of Charlotte Perkins Gilman

CAROL RUTH BERKIN

Once upon a time, 10-year-old Charlotte Perkins wrote in 1870, the good King Ezephon and his besieged kingdom were saved by the heroic battlefield performance of Princess Araphenia, only daughter of the king. Araphenia had not vanquished the wicked enemy alone, however; she had magical help from the fabulous Elmondine, beautiful visitor from a distant planet. Bejeweled and bewitching, Elmondine had come to a lonely Araphenia in the palace garden and had offered advice and assistance. To save the king and his kingdom, Elmondine created, out of thin air, an army of a thousand men. And to the young earthly princess, this fairy princess gave a magic sword with which to fight and an invincible horse on which to ride while disguised as a warrior-prince. When victory came, the brave girl threw off her disguise, and her astonished father embraced her.

Tales like this one appear in different versions throughout Charlotte Perkins's diaries.[1] The central characters remain the same in each story; a young woman who can, through some magic, overstep the prescribed boundaries of her life and enter into active participation in the great struggles between good and evil in her society; an older woman, resplendently female yet wise and independent and powerful, who guides the novice's path: and always a grateful father whose respect had been won.

Charlotte Perkins was a young girl with an active fantasy life and a lonely reality when she spun these tales. But as a mature woman of 50, she continued to write stories of wise, older women, strong and independent doctors or philanthropists, who appeared out of nowhere to guide some struggling girl to maturity. The setting was no longer fabulous, but the characters were unchanged.[2]

No Elmondine ever appeared in the life of Charlotte Perkins Stetson Gilman. But for many younger women—in her lifetime and today—she has seemed to play that fabled role herself. Writer, philosopher, socialist, and feminist, Gilman has come to stand for the potentialities of American womanhood. She appears very much the self-made woman, overcoming sex-

Reprinted from *Women in America: A History* (Boston: Houghton Mifflin, 1979), 150–73, with the permission of the publisher.

ual stereotype and social pressures to emerge as a woman of depth and dimension.

Valuable as this Elmondine may seem to those searching for a model, Gilman did not come from a distant planet, free of the conflicts that a woman might have faced at the turn of the century or faces today. Nor was she magically transformed by any fabulous figure into a secure, stable, integrated personality without the marks of a difficult childhood. Her life bears witness to the difficulties of feminism, not as an ideology or a political commitment, but as a personal experience. Charlotte Perkins Gilman struggled for intellectual and emotional liberation, hampered through much of her life by an internalization of the very split vision of masculine and feminine spheres and destinies that, in her work, she would expose as artificial. She struggled later in her life to achieve a balance between independence and an interdependence with others. This essay seeks to chart her personal confrontation with feminism, because it is in that experience that she may serve as a model for American women.

SELF-IMAGES: CHILDHOOD AND ADOLESCENCE

Charlotte Perkins was born on July 3, 1860.[3] Her parents' family trees, rooted in New England soil, were already intertwined, with cousins marrying cousins in discrete confirmation of their pride in association. Her father was a Beecher, grandson of Lyman Beecher, and nephew, as Charlotte put it, of twelve "world servers," a young man nearly smothered in the mantle of reform. Frederick Beecher Perkins's mother had been a rebel of sorts, the odd sister who had never taken any interest in public affairs.

Frederick Beecher Perkins struck a compromise between family tradition and maternal heresy: He dedicated himself to the pursuit of knowledge, thus satisfying his own personal desires in the interest of society. It was his world service to know everything, in case anyone might ask. He was quick tempered, sensitive, with a well-mannered hostility to authority. He was never much of a financial success and never seemed to care. In 1858 Perkins married his 31-year-old cousin, Mary Fitch Wescott of Providence, Rhode Island. As a girl, Wescott had been "the darling of an elderly father and a juvenile mother," a naive, lovely, flirtatious girl who broke hearts and prompted numerous proposals at first sight. Her own branch of the family was known for its strong attachment to one another and its indifference to the outside world.

If Mary Fitch Wescott had been naive and frivolous as a maiden, her marriage cured her of both failings with cruel abruptness. Within less than three years she bore three children. The eldest died. Thomas Perkins and his younger sister, Charlotte Perkins, survived. When the exhausted mother was told that another pregnancy would kill her, her husband abandoned her.

The dissolution of the Perkins family worked upon the consciousness and character of each member differently. Despite the poverty, the humiliating dependence on family charity that kept her moving from home to home and city to city, Mary Perkins never voiced a word of criticism at her abandonment. Thus, her children were left to struggle with its mystery. Their father's motives could only be imagined and their mother's continuing attachment to him only accepted as a reality.

Mary Wescott Perkins kept her silence, but she drew from this marital experience a lesson that surely helped shape her daughter's life. She learned, she said, that affection was a fatal vulnerability. What was true physiologically became for her psychologically true as well: Love could kill. She strove, therefore, with devotion and steely determination to arm her own children against emotional disappointment. She resolved to nurture stoics, immune to rejection because no appetite for love had been developed. This denial of affection to her children was, of necessity, also self-denial: out of love for her children she kept her distance from them. "I used to put away your little hand from my cheek when you were a nursing baby," she once remarked with pride and regret to her adult daughter. But her stoicism was acquired rather than natural, and there were lapses; in secret moments, when she thought her daughter Charlotte safely asleep, she held and caressed and kissed her.

It was Charlotte Perkins—precocious, intensely lonely, isolated from other children by her family's nomadic life, and alienated from her brother by his teasing style and his "bad" behavior—who bore most heavily the burden of her mother's contradictions. From Mary Wescott Perkins she learned the unintended but crucial lesson that there was a public, rational, independent self and a secret, emotional, vulnerable self. The young girl took the public self to be estimable and held the private self suspect. By the age of 10 she had constructed this dichotomy.

Her childhood diaries reveal a self-consciously stoical Charlotte, a character ruthlessly creating itself, always disciplining and reprimanding, always self-critical, trusting in rigorous programs for self-improvement to overcome unacceptable character traits. This was, for her, the real Charlotte Perkins. Yet she indulged a secret self. At night she immersed herself in a rich fantasy life, allowing her imagination to transport her to beautiful and exotic paradises where (as she later remembered) "the stern restrictions, drab routines, unbending discipline that hemmed me in became of no consequence." But allowing free rein to her imagination provided more than an escape from drab situational realities. Her fantasy worlds were never so randomly constructed as she might have believed. Repeatedly she peopled them with open and affectionate maternal figures who provided her with the secrets to winning a father's affection and esteem.

As sustaining as she knew her fantasy worlds to be, Charlotte Perkins felt the need to prove that she kept her imagination under control. Unwilling to relinquish it, she struck a bargain with herself that would preserve it: "Every night," she wrote, she would think of pleasant things that could really occur: once a week, of "lovelier, stranger things": once a month, "of wonders": and once a year, of "anything."

This bargain held until her adolescence. When she was 13, as Gilman recalled in her autobiography, her mother discovered the evening fantasies and ordered her daughter to end them. To this, Gilman wrote, an obedient child instantly acceded. Perhaps, however, Charlotte Perkins demanded of herself that the fantasies be abandoned, or transformed into something less disturbing to her conscious self. Such a transformation did occur, for even as she dissolved the kingdom of Ezephon she began to nurture an absorbing enthusiasm for the "things that could really occur" in the world of science and sociology. Social "wonders," existing and potential, began to preoccupy her: physics, with the power of its absolute laws, made magic pale: and the plausible utopias the social reformer could design were "lovelier stranger things," than the fairy kingdoms had ever been.

The bridge between the old fantasy world and the new scientific one was her own role in them. In either setting, Charlotte Perkins's part was heroic. In the new and less-disturbing secret life that took shape, she dreamed of becoming a renowned world server, a major figure in the reorganization of her society. The shift in focus to the real world offered her a better chance to release her productive and constructive energies. But lost in this transformation was the expression of a desire for intimacy and the frank recognition that loneliness was a negative condition.

Her imaginary worlds had helped her confront her feelings. They were populated by individuals who came to cherish her and to love her and, thus, to end her emotional isolation. But in the new world of social realities, Charlotte Perkins saw herself befriended by no one in particular and a friend to no one but impersonal humanity. In such a self-image, loneliness was elevated to a necessity; it was transformed into the price one paid for the heroic self. Through the prism of her new ambitions, the years of stoical training at last revealed their clear purpose. Her mother had intended to prepare her for survival only; now Charlotte Perkins saw that self-denial and discipline prepared one not simply to endure life, but to perform great deeds in it.

As this perception of her life hardened into an ideology, Charlotte Perkins lost the power to discern genuine interests from defensive commitments. The attraction of social reform became a shield against the appeals and the dangers of personal intimacy. The two modes of living were forced into contradiction. Armed with a rationale for dismissing her feelings, she often refused to probe their meaning. Some emotions she could incorporate into or redefine within her heroic image. Responses and impulses she could not thus account for, she simply denied. Her conscious certainty masked her deep ambivalence.

Her new self-image and its ambitions drew Charlotte Perkins to a closer identification with her father. He loomed in her mind—as figures often do who are not familiar realities—as the embodiment of his ideals rather than his performance. His reputation as a humanitarian was as well known to her as he was unknown. His apparent dedication to public service contrasted, in her mind, with her mother's slavish commitment to her children and the narrow circle of domestic life. Certain that her mother led a "thwarted life," she became equally certain that her father did not.

Thus, attraction to Frederick Perkins increased, even as the key to gaining his attention seemed to be found. Charlotte Perkins had sought that attention before, appealing to him to write to her because she was lonely. Appeals for support and approval now gave way to requests for reading lists in history, anthropology, and science. To these came speedy and lengthy replies. In this manner she reached out to him, speaking of her intellectual isolation, not a personal loneliness but an absence of tutelage and collegiality. No one at home, she wrote, could understand as he could her ambitions to relate to social issues. It was in this shared breadth of vision that she pressed their kinship. But for all her efforts to rise above "personal pain or pleasure," her disappointment at his frequent coolness and distance slipped into the letters. "Should I continue to write," she asked after a long period without response from Frederick Perkins, "for I am anything but desirous to intrude."

Her mother conveyed a sense of danger in the admission of personal needs, and her father seemed simply to dismiss them as trivial. Thus, both parents denied the validity of feelings to their daughter. But without knowing it, mother and father conspired in a second way. The young Charlotte Perkins came to believe that the compensations for self-control and self-negation were real in the public sphere and were only a mean mockery in the circle of the home: that the avenue to satisfaction and the path to despair were as inevitably separated as this man and woman. She must choose between them. And she must be allowed to choose between them. The choice was a demand upon her own resources: the possibility of choice was a demand upon the society in which she lived. The Victorian society she encountered seemed more hostile than receptive to her pursuit of a public life, and this would direct her reformist energies to the place of women in American society.

The new self-image that took shape in the early 1870s may have cushioned Charlotte Perkins while family relationships and economic circumstances disintegrated further. In 1871, after a decade of separation, Mary Wescott Perkins began a suit for divorce. Her motives are unknown, but the decision brought a dramatic alteration in her public image. When the divorce came in 1873, Mary Perkins was no longer a loyal and suffering wife; she had become a scandalous divorcée. Once-sympathetic Beechers and Perkinses closed their doors to her, and she and her children were left entirely on their own.

In 1873 the three moved to Providence, Rhode Island. They spent a brief time experimenting in cooperative living. When this failed, the Perkinses settled into independent poverty. While her mother struggled to support the family, Charlotte struggled for autonomy. At 15 she openly challenged her mother's rule of complete obedience, with ironic success. Free of parental control at last, she promptly disciplined herself. She swore to give total obedience to her mother until she reached age 21.

Superficially the results of rebellion and of defeat were one and the same; in more ways than she yet understood. Charlotte Perkins remained a dutiful daughter. Her real rebellion was not in character but in the uses to which she intended to put the stern self-discipline and the dire vision of a woman's lot in the world that were her inheritance. Mary Wescott Perkins intended to protect her daughter from disappointment, and to prepare her for life. But that protection was situational: It was in marriage, as wife and mother, that Charlotte Perkins was expected to face her tests. Charlotte Perkins intended, however, to escape marriage, to avoid the despair and defeat it guaranteed, and to meet her test in a world her mother could not know or imagine.

The reality of her adolescent years offered few opportunities to test the meaning of her commitment to spinsterhood. Her mother's excessive restrictions on Charlotte Perkins's social life limited her access to men and even to women. Without any real attachments and always desperately lonely, she fell back upon her imagination for relief. She formed a wild and absorbing crush on an actor she had seen perform but had never met. She nursed an adoration of an older woman who had been only casually kind. In her diaries she regularly denounced love and marriage, yet she filled its pages with speculation: "Who will you marry?" "What will be his age?" "What will you wear on your wedding day?"

QUESTIONS OF FRIENDSHIP OR MARRIAGE

At the age of 18 Charlotte Perkins described herself in her diary: "18 years old. 5′6½″ high. Weigh some 120 lbs or thereabout. Looks, not bad. At times handsome. At others, decidedly homely. Health, perfect. Strength— amazing. Character—ah! . . . I am not in love with anybody; I don't think I ever shall be." This was written in January 1879. In February a short diary entry reasserted her lack of attachments. "No Valentines! No Regrets!" Perhaps there were no regrets. But in March of that year, her mother allowed Charlotte to accompany her on a visit to relatives in Cambridge and Boston. Here, suddenly, the 18-year-old found herself the belle her mother had so often been in her own youth. She was surrounded by young college men, courted by Arthurs, Edwards, and Charles Walter Stetson, a "Nice boy . . . but young." She frankly enjoyed the flirtation, and when she returned home in July, her mood grew gloomy.

That fall she returned to Cambridge and then went to Connecticut, and again was faced with a happy embarrassment of beaux. Back home in November, she kept herself busy writing letters to her new male friends, among them a younger cousin from Connecticut, George Houghton Gilman. For several months letters passed between "Dear Ho!" and "Dear Chopkins," and it was to Houghton Gilman that she most openly wrote of the boredom and the tension of living under the heavy hand of her mother. On March 6, 1878, she had chastised herself in her diary: "I must really abolish all desire for comfort or any sort of happiness if I expect to have any peace." But back in Cambridge for New Year's Day 1880, she recorded with pleasure a day of excitement and expectation, the "best day of my life."

Charlotte Perkins was nearly 20 when this brief flurry of social life broke the monotony of her Providence existence. When the excitement ended, she settled once more into biding her time until, at 21, she could embark upon her own life. Even in her impatience, however, she knew that things at home had greatly improved. She had studied art, and recently had enjoyed some independent income through the sale of miniatures and other decorative pieces. She found release for her physical energies—and an opportunity for sorority—at a local woman's gymnasium.

And despite her mother's continuing interference with her life—reading her mail, intercepting and rejecting social invitations—Charlotte Perkins had established her first genuine friendships with other women. One of these women was Grace Channing, daughter of a noted New England clerical family, a girl with a background similar to Charlotte's. Together, Grace Channing and Charlotte Perkins wrote plays and poems to entertain themselves and their families. But most intimate and most important was the friendship formed with Martha Luther, a young girl who for almost four years held Charlotte Perkins's unguarded confidence.

These friendships were hard-earned. Charlotte Perkins was as deeply wary of them as she was eager for them, thinking affection to be a trap and a drain on one's energies, but feeling it as a voluntary vulnerability. To protect herself, she compelled Martha Luther to make a pact, pledging that their affection would be "permanent and safe." Even with such a guarantee, Charlotte worried that she would jeopardize the relationship either by excessive demands for affection or, conversely, by sudden withdrawals of affection. "I was always in a fervor," she later recalled, "that for a time I should want to see her continually, and that there would be spaces when affection seemed to wane."

Sometime before the end of 1881 Martha Luther married and moved from Providence. Perkins felt the separation keenly, experiencing the old isolation and loneliness more intensely after the years of sharing with Luther. She was, by her own account, in a vulnerable state when, in January 1882, Charles Walter Stetson re-entered her life. Like Perkins, Stetson had trained as an artist. Art was an immediate bond between them, though perhaps it involved more competitive tension than either thought to admit. Even deeper was the bond of circumstance. "He was," Gilman later recalled, "a great man—but lonely, isolated, poor, misunderstood." Stetson's state of mind and worldly condition seemed to mirror her own perfectly. The two quickly fell in love and, within a short time, Walter Stetson proposed.

The effect of Stetson's proposal upon Charlotte Perkins was deep and disturbing. It came in her twenty-first year, and thus it set her cruelly at odds with herself. She was, by the terms of her bargain with herself, free at last of parental control. She felt an urgency to give her past meaning by pursuing its heroic dreams. Her self-esteem depended upon an energetic dedication to her social goals. To abandon the pursuit of a life of world service before it had begun, and to embrace instead love and marriage, would be to shatter a self-image that had, despite its problems, been sustaining.

Just when she needed most to understand what she truly desired and what she might realistically work to have, Charlotte Perkins was most completely at a loss. She could not separate her genuine commitment to social reform from the power she had invested in it to justify her emotional isolation; and because she had invested her commitment with that power in order to defend against emotional rejection and disappointment, she could not risk disarming it in the face of a proposal of marriage, with its confusing threats and promises of intimacy. She loved Walter Stetson and wanted to be with him. But she could neither overcome the powerful image of her mother's thwarted life nor separate that image from the institution of marriage itself; the two concepts were merged.

In order to avoid confronting her confusion, Charlotte recast her dilemma. She posed the choice as one between two mutually exclusive duties rather than two strongly felt desires. She faced, she told herself and Charles Walter Stetson, a decision to be made between a duty to life and a duty to love. Thus she distorted her feelings and the issues entirely; she sacrificed any awareness of her positive yearnings for both choices in order to avoid the reasons for rejecting either. In her diaries and her letters to Stetson, she hid behind a rhetoric of obligation and self-sacrifice that not even she could resist in the end. She made no effort to accommodate both duties. She was protected from this approach not simply by her psychic patterns, but also by her sociological perceptions. For women, life and love were not overlapping spheres. Men could have marriage and careers: women, responsible for home and children, could not. A sense of injustice that she could not entirely hide sprang from the fact that it was exactly this social division of labor and duties that she intended to reform.

For months, Charlotte Perkins pleaded with Walter Stetson for delay. This she won in large part simply by her indecision. Although he suffered, she felt she suffered more, because she was torn this way and that, and had, she told him, no peace. "How often one duty contradicts another," she exclaimed when, in the midst of reading in order to acquire a "general notion of how the world worked," she stopped to write him a letter. "And what a world of careful practice it needs to distinguish the highest!" It was the skill required to distinguish the highest duty that she felt sorely lacking. And this, she argued, accounted for her delay.

"I am not a tenderhearted child," she assured him, and herself, "neither am I an impulsive girl: But a clearheaded woman who is weighing a life time in her hands." How could she know what she would lose or gain if she had no experience of either life? On marriage and motherhood there were, she knew, all-too-many voices of authority to guide her. "This is noble, natural and right," said "all the ages." Her own body, she admitted, urged her to yield. Against her independence ran "all the ages" as well, for "no woman yet has ever attempted to stand alone as I intended." The grandiosity of this statement was entirely innocent, although it did not reflect social reality.

In the 1880s American women of her race and region were experimenting with independence. The existing social currents for change had, in fact, suggested to her the role of public woman and reformer; her ambitions confirmed that the struggle had already begun. Of course, the general contours of her society reinforced both her notion of women's segregated sphere and the heretical quality of her career aspirations. But when Charlotte Perkins spoke of standing alone, it was the expectation of emotional isolation rather than the concrete problems of economic support or practical opportunities that gave force to her personal drama.

What did she want to do? She had taken care to bury the answers and could not now plumb her own depths. She tried to clarify her thoughts in letters to Walter Stetson, in soliloquy rather than conversation. But she could not explain—or understand—herself. Why, she wrote, do I hesitate? Life with him promised paradise, she said, but love seemed to ask "more than I can give." Repeatedly, and with an unwitting callousness for his feelings, she pressed for a relationship that was limited, a friendship, like the one agreed upon with Martha Luther, that would free her from the necessity of choice. Companionship and friendship would satisfy her; why must there be love and marriage? "I ought not to complain of being offered the crown of womanhood," she confessed, voicing her own and her mother's tenacious romanticism about all that they feared: but she did not fully wish to accept it.

Slowly the choice crystallized into one of duty to submit and endure, or duty to rebel. Posed in these terms, love lost all its positive potential, and independence had its romance restored. But at the last moment, with frustrating perversity, she denied even her own freedom and responsibility to choose. Instead she bowed to the moral imperative of finding one's "right duty." The "right duty" was surely the more difficult one. As she weighed each choice, her pride—and the hint of pleasure—in her insistence "that my life is mine in spite of a myriad lost sisters before me" made her crucially uneasy with the choice of independence: thus, she chose marriage. On December 31, 1882, she wrote in her diary: "With no pride, with little hope, with uncertain occasional happiness, with no glad energy and living power: with no faith or nearly none, but still, thank God! with firm belief in what is right and wrong: I begin the new year."

A deep nostalgia and a sense of loss showed in her diary for 1883 as she made plans for marriage. Self-pity, wholly shrouded from her own consciousness, marked every page. Dread—equally of unhappiness and of happiness—pervaded this secret record of events.

MARRIAGE, MOTHERHOOD, AND COLLAPSE

On May 2, 1884, Charlotte Perkins and Walter Stetson were married. Despite all her mother's care and preparation, despite her own, Charlotte Stetson entered marriage as an innocent and a romantic: "My Wedding Day . . . HOME. . . ."

> I install Walter in the parlor and dining room while I retire to the bed chamber and finish its decoration. The bed looks like a fairy bower with lace, white silk, and flowers. Make my self a crown of white roses. Wash again, and put on a thin shift of white mull fastened with a rose bud and velvet and pearl civeture. My little white velvet slippers and a white snood. Go in to my husband. He meets me joyfully: we promise to be true to each other; and he puts on the ring and the crown. Then he lifts the crown, loosens the snood, unfastens the girdle, and then—and then. O my God! I thank thee for this heavenly happiness! O make me one with thy great life that I may best fulfill my duties to my love! to my Husband!

May was filled with diary reports of great personal happiness and a total commitment of energy and ego to cooking, baking breads, visiting, and house care. She aimed for perfection and was furious at any domestic failures. Culinary errors made her "disgusted with myself." By mid-June efforts to prove herself a perfect wife were interrupted by an illness that left her weak and bedridden. By June 25 she was miserable, not because of domestic failures, but now because her "old woe"—"conviction of being too outwardly expressive of affection"—had begun to fill her with fears of driving Walter Stetson away. Assurances by her husband could only temporarily ease her mind. In early August she learned she was pregnant.

Through most of her pregnancy, Charlotte Stetson was both sick and depressed. The physical incapacity and loss of the body tone she had acquired through hours in the woman's gymnasium disturbed her, and they no doubt contributed to her sense of unnatural lethargy and of a passivity she held in contempt. Holding herself in ever lower esteem as the months went by, she feared Walter Stetson must share her disgust with herself. But her husband—

almost stubbornly—proved sympathetic and supportive. "He has worked for me and for us both, waited on me in every tenderest way. . . . God be thanked for my husband!"

The pregnancy brought her little pleasure. Still, as the months passed, Charlotte Stetson began to adjust to her child-to-be in the terms she best understood: in the language of duty. Her hopes, she wrote, were that the child she carried would be a "world helper" and that she herself could serve the world by a devotion to the child. "Brief ecstasy, long pain. Then years of joy again," she wrote on the morning of March 23, 1885, when Katherine (Kate) Beecher Stetson was born.

But pain and joy seemed to wage a confusing struggle that left her helpless. Despite desperate efforts to be a perfect mother, Charlotte Stetson had given over the care of her daughter to her own mother by August 1885. Depressed, ill, bedridden, she had few days without "every morning the same hopeless waking." She could not explain her deepening depression. Her child was lovely, her husband was loving; she berated herself for not regaining control over her emotions and carefully shied away from locating in her illness any hostility or anger. She was suffering, she was certain, from a new disease called "nervous prostration," and she came to fear that she had contracted an infection of the brain.

Walter Stetson, however, surmised that marriage and motherhood were his wife's problems. Although he did not understand why this was the case, he accepted it. That fall he offered her a separation. But with desperate insistence Charlotte Stetson refused this relief. "He cannot see how irrevocably bound I am, for life, for life. No, unless he dies and the baby die, or he change or I change there is no way out." The dilemma was once again, if not of her own making, at least one she would not allow to be too easily resolved. She could not permit herself to be relieved or consoled; she was invested in this painful punishment. And, with the unintentional blindness of the determined sufferer, she forced husband, daughter, and mother to participate in her nightmare.

Then, in the summer of 1886, Charlotte Stetson bowed to family urgings and left, alone, for California. She looked forward to a host of reunions, visiting her brother Thomas in Utah, her father in San Francisco, and her good friend Grace Channing in Pasadena. The trip restored her health and spirits almost magically. The lush, rich floral splendor of Pasadena satisfied her childhood dreams of beauty; to her, the city was Edenic.

But her return home brought immediate relapse into illness and despair. That winter her husband took her to the famous woman's doctor. S. Weir Mitchell, for treatment at his clinic. Here, her worst fears that either love or "her driving force" must be relinquished were given confirmation by a representative of that impartial science she had always trusted. Mitchell, famous for his belief that anatomy was a woman's destiny, argued that the passivity of the womb must be echoed in the woman's daily life in order for true health to be hers. He prescribed for Charlotte Stetson a totally domestic life, the constant companionship of her child, and an absolute end to any writing or serious reading. Determined to obey this dictum of absolute domesticity, Charlotte Stetson reached the dangerous edge of insanity.

This total collapse, with its admission of failure and its punishment, seemed to release Charlotte Stetson from her commitment to her marriage. Every effort had been made. Thus, in early 1887 she agreed to a separation from her husband. She had, in significant if shrouded ways, recapitulated her parents' marital history. Her mother's physical danger from childbearing found its counterpart in her own near-insanity. But the Stetsons' separation, unlike that of Frederick and Mary Wescott Perkins, had no taint of a husband's abandonment.

Walter Stetson remained nearby, visiting whenever his wife allowed, some weeks coming to see her every day. He brought her gifts, cared for Kate when his wife or child was sick, and, as Charlotte Stetson frequently recorded in her diary with gratitude, did not press any demands upon her. Yet when she looked at the examples of marriage and motherhood around her, she identified with the despair of vulnerable and abused women. "Talked with Mrs. Smythe," she wrote on February 20, 1887. "She is another victim! Young, girlish, unexperienced, sickly, with a sickly child, and no servant . . . ignorant both, and he using his 'marital rights' at her vital expense."

By the end of the year, Charlotte Stetson had begun to think again of California and its healing effect on both body and mind. In 1888, with her daughter and her mother, she set out once again for Pasadena. She had done her duty to love: now she meant to fulfill her desire "to have my utmost capabilities called out in some necessary work."

The California Years

In this manner, the Charlotte Perkins Gilman known to us through her books, lectures, novels, magazine articles, and poetry began her career. If this were a fairy tale, the woman who left New England "ashamed, degraded and despairing" to become an independent woman and a leading intellectual and social critic of her day would have soon experienced the personal satisfaction and self-esteem her achievements should have brought her. But this woman was who and what she was, and like us all she carried her past into her present.

With her mother (soon to develop cancer) and Kate, Charlotte Perkins Stetson lived a precarious existence, economically and emotionally, in California. She was formally uneducated, and unskilled except in commercial art. This occupation she did not pursue. Her goal was a public life and her career the preaching of a gospel of reform. She tried to support her family by giving public lectures on reform topics, but the proceeds from a passed hat were small. Extra income came from taking in boarders. Debts piled up; soon the triad was moving from house to house in a nomadic pattern reminiscent of her own childhood. If her experience as the head of a husbandless household echoed her mother's years of struggle, Stetson's love life became an odd parody of her marriage.

In 1890 she formed a relationship with another woman writer. The affair was not necessarily sexual; the intensity of emotion did not demand, though it may have included, physical expression. Perhaps Stetson was only seeking a friendship similar to the sustaining one with Martha Luther, but with "Dora" she accepted the subservient and self-negating role she had always associated with "wife." The aspects that had driven her from marriage she now experienced with, even seemed to invite from, Dora. Dora was generous with money, and Charlotte, who would take no financial aid from her estranged husband, accepted assistance from Dora—with every string attached. In return for the money and the companionship. Charlotte provided Dora with her domestic services, "making a home for her," and with intellectual support, cheating her own career by "furnishing material for [Dora's] work."

But the companionship was not so gentle and constant as that she had received from "her dear boy," Walter. Dora was an openly abusive partner. She was "malevolent. She lied . . . she drank . . . she swore freely, at me as well as others. She lifted her hand to strike me in one of her tempers." This affair, begun with the decade, ended when Dora left Charlotte in 1893. From this demeaning experience, Charlotte Stetson refused to learn anything except disappointment. She did not examine her choice of loves or raise any questions about what the affair reflected of her needs and her insecurities. She would only chastise herself in her diary: "Out of it all I ought surely to learn final detachment from all personal concerns."

These private turmoils did not prevent, but coincided with, Charlotte Stetson's growing recognition as a public figure. Her skills at extemporaneous speaking had earned her little money in her early years in California, but they had brought her a reputation, just as her first essays and published articles had brought national notice. Her radical views on the rights of labor and of women, on child care, and other social reforms earned her influential friends in California, as well as the expected enemies. In an essentially conservative state, there were nevertheless several active women's organizations and a few lively communities of intellectuals and writers. These groups welcomed Charlotte Stetson without hesitation, helped her find speaking engagements, and encouraged her to develop and expand her ideas.

Through her work with women's organizations like the Pacific Coast Women's Press Association, she made contact with the national leaders of the women's rights movement—Stanton, Stone, and the settlement house organizer, Jane Addams. To these friends and associates Charlotte Stetson appeared as an energetic, creative, remarkably productive, and admirable woman. But this image contrasted sharply with her own critical sense of herself. In her public life, as in her private life, she seemed determined to demean herself. She was not to be applauded for her raw energy or its constructive channeling, she felt. In reality, she was no better than a cripple: illness, fatigue, and the accompanying mental lethargy that she insisted were the legacy of her married life had permanently damaged her intellectual abilities. She was certain never to realize her potential, and thus she was a disappointment to herself, as she should be to others.

In her first year in California, amid the confusion of establishing a new life, with financial worries and a young child to care for, she had written 33 articles and 23 poems. But this was not enough to bring a sense of satisfaction. In every possible way she seemed to flee the self-esteem her work could and, by her own declared philosophy, should provide. She was hampered by an inability to take her work (rather than herself) seriously. Her speaking and her writing she dismissed as "natural" for her and therefore not to be confused with true work. Work she defined as everything she could not do easily, well, or at all, and she could not hope to do such work because her nervous condition prevented it. Thus, she felt her marriage remained with her: she had not escaped.

It was not the marriage itself that Charlotte Stetson remained wedded to, but rather her concept of her feminine identity. This identity was rooted in disappointment and the thwarted life. As she moved into what she viewed as a masculine sphere, the world of the mind and of action, she would not abandon its opposite. Ironically, though perhaps not surprisingly, the very things she defined as legitimate, enviable intellectual work—"reading, going into a library, learning languages"—were her father's skills, joys, and professional duties as a librarian. And these were, she insisted (and thus it was so), the achievements her past made impossible.

Intellectual Contributions

But Gilman's abilities were extraordinary. Quick, creative, able to grasp immediately the essentials of an argument and to generalize from seemingly disparate particulars, she had trained and tutored herself well during her lonely youth. Her true genius lay in her ability to transform her personal contradictions into valuable and legitimate insights on social problems and on the institutions and ideologies that created and sustained the problems.

In her ability to bridge the gap from personal experience to social understanding, she liberated her intellect from the immobility she protested she suffered. What fueled the process was her conviction that social solutions could be found that would some day obviate psychological dilemmas like her own. In this there was potential irony, for she had committed her energies to the elimination of a source of her creativity.

The intellectual framework of her insight was that of the evolutionary and progressive social analysts of her era. Like Lester Ward, Edward Bellamy, and other social critics of the late nineteenth century, she believed that the always shifting patterns of social organization could be understood, predicted, and to some extent manipulated if the evolutionary laws Charles Darwin had discovered were properly applied to human society. By understanding the laws of sociology, human participation in the shaping of human destiny was possible—and, for the concerned citizen, imperative.

Charlotte Perkins Stetson Gilman, like her peers, wrote and lectured to suggest the appropriate actions. For committed evolutionist reformers like herself, change was synonymous with progress. No matter how dark or regressive they might seem, the past and the present always served as a useful and ultimately justifiable base for a better future. Thus, there was equanimity in her perspective, despite the tone of urgency or impatience in pressing reform or the polemical style of her argument. She was dedicated to prodding for changes she was convinced would eventually come. It was only a matter of when and how smoothly the changes would arrive.

Gilman's own work was devoted to the analysis of the relationship of women to their society.[4] Her ideas were not formally or systematically presented until *Women and Economics* was published in 1898, but they had been formulated many years before and were already introduced in the work of her California days. As a historical social anthropologist, she traced the rise and institutionalization of patriarchy as a necessary step in human growth and progress. Until the development of modern industrial society, this patriarchal structure with its rigid segregation of women into sex-related functions had been essential for race preservation. But modern society no longer required such a segregation, nor its aggrandizement to the male of privilege and power through the monopoly of the social sphere. The laws and customs sustaining male monopoly on socially productive activity were now clearly without legitimacy. This kind of social division of labor was neither permanent nor fixed by nature: permanent sexual differences did not, as social conservatives argued, mean permanent differences in capacity for social productivity.

Women's potential for contribution in the social—or, as Gilman called it, the human—sphere must now be released and realized. This would mean a radical restructuring of the society, which would be resisted by men jealous of their privileges and by women ignorant of their deprivation. But, she wrote in 1912: "Social evolution has never waited for the complete enlightenment of mankind."

Gilman's vision of the future did not eliminate the genuine sex-related functions. Reproduction remained woman's specific natural specialization, essential to the preservation of the race. But she wholly renounced the traditional social institutions and duties that surrounded this sexual function. In books like *The Home* or in her *Forerunner* essays, she entirely dismantled the imprisoning female sphere of home-making and child care.

Astute and direct, Gilman located the institutionalization of women's oppression in the home and the family, and in the conditioned mentality that channeled all love and all sense of responsibility and potential for self-esteem into limited personal relationships rather than social activities and humanitarianism. Women were not merely trapped in the home, but also psychologically crippled so that they must only hope to remain there. Not only was their world too narrow, but they could not hope to master it. The sphere itself, with its multiple and dissimilar duties, its undifferentiated requirements, its mystique that forbade systematic training for what was "natural"—this chaotic agglomeration called home and child care could not be successfully managed by the average woman.

The fault lay with the role, not with the woman, Gilman insisted. Only a total disassembling and rationalization of "women's sphere" would be acceptable, with each component of women's traditional roles transformed into a modern, scientific, and professional activity. Once this process had begun, women could abandon their old tasks with confidence that none suffered as a result. They could release their energies in the larger world. Professional "baby gardens" or nurseries, professional food services, and house-cleaning services—on these Gilman's hopes rested. Woman's role would thus disappear, and she would not be accused of deserting it.

Femininity itself would be redefined and attainable: "As women grow, losing nothing that is essential to womanhood, but adding steadily the later qualities of humanness, they will win and hold a far larger, deeper reverence than that hitherto vouchsafed them. As they so rise and broaden, filling their full place in the world as members of society, as well as their partial places as mothers of it, they will gradually rear a new race of men, men with minds large enough to see in human beings something besides males and females."[5] Gilman's woman of the evolutionary future would be Elmondine, female and independent, at ease with her sex and her work.

Yet, ironically, Gilman's new woman carried with her the crucial social and psychic trappings of the old. Gilman, like many of her contemporary feminists, could not ultimately envision woman liberated from the task of nurturance itself, could not imagine woman pursuing work for her own personal satisfaction or solely for its challenge to her mind and ambitions. Although she was genuinely radical in the surgery she wanted to see performed on society and all its sacred institutions in order to free women from a sex-defined sphere of domesticity, her goal was to expand the area in which women might serve, not be served. Admittedly she placed the same standard of morality upon men; a desire to cooperate with and to contribute to the welfare of the greater society was, if anything could be said to be, the defining impulse of true humanity.

Here was the reform vision of her century, perhaps, but those who struggled to meet its demands with an obliteration of self were too often women like Charlotte Perkins Gilman. Too many of her own psychic struggles were over defining *self*, its boundaries never stable, the distinction between self-fulfillment and selfishness never clear. She had married, driven to a great extent by a repulsion at her *pride* in defining herself as a woman different from others and independent. Her self-esteem was stifled once she achieved that independence because, to take pride in her own creativity and talents, to cherish them for their own sake, could only be understood as selfish. Surprisingly, she would have more success in her private life resolving this dilemma of self and selfishness than her intellectual work incorporated or revealed.

Gilman's feminist ideas were shared by other women of her generation. Although her radical programs, such as dismantling the home, were resisted by feminists and nonfeminists, her central analysis of women and society was embraced. In her thinking and writing, in the realm of ideas, she was not isolated from others, but had found companionship.

THE RETURN EAST

In 1895 Stetson left California. Within those eight years she had established herself as a writer, admired in literary as well as intellectual circles and praised by social reformers across the country. She had lectured for socialist and women's organizations. She had edited a financially unsuccessful but intellectually exciting radical newspaper. She had helped organize and had participated in women's conferences that earned her a place among the leading ranks of international feminists. She had organized a unique employment office, through which "day work" domestics could find temporary jobs. She had written about evolutionary socialism, anthropology, history, and feminism. But at the age of 35, when she left for the East, she judged herself a failure.

Charlotte Stetson returned East alone. Her mother had died in 1894. That same year Walter Stetson had remarried, choosing his ex-wife's friend Grace Channing as his bride. To many people's surprise—and disgust— Charlotte Stetson appeared delighted with this match. Soon after their marriage, she sent Katherine to live with them.

The decision to relinquish Katherine had been characteristically a blend of rational considerations and deep emotional ambivalence. Her relationship with Katherine was so complicated by fears of failure to be a good mother, by self-conscious and rigid pursuit of a program of "good mothering," and by doubts about its success, that her daughter made her both anxious and guilty. Like her own mother before her, she found it difficult to express directly the love and sympathy she felt for Katherine, often because she feared it would burden the child in some way.

She chose, again as her own mother had, to be useful to her daughter, to protect her by building in her a "right character." She substituted the doctrines of "understanding and self-control" for Mary Wescott Perkins's "obedience and discipline," and she produced a perfectly behaved, sober, responsible, emotionally distant young girl. When in 1894 Charlotte Stetson decided to send her daughter to the more stable home of the Stetsons and thus to the care of Grace Channing, she refused to let Katherine see that the separation would hurt her. In this way, she said, she protected Katherine from any uneasiness at deserting her mother. The cost of this denial Charlotte Stetson thought only she had to absorb.

Nothing she ever did raised such hostility or brought her such notoriety as this act of voluntary separation from her child. She was labeled an unnatural mother, accused not of failing as a mother but of renouncing her duty to be one. Duty and self-indulgence seemed to reverse themselves in the public eye, like a reflection in the mirror: She thought she was helping Katherine by giving her up; the newspapers said she was freeing herself. Her critics' insight was only semantic: The freedom they spoke of, a self-conscious self-interest, was not yet within her reach.

The year 1895 was spent in Chicago, with Stetson working for Jane Addams in the Chicago settlement-house projects. In January 1896 she attended a suffrage convention in Washington, D.C., where she met and befriended the famous pioneer in American sociology, Lester Ward. Between January and July of that year she took to the road, lecturing and giving guest sermons at 57 different churches or meeting halls in the Corn Belt.

In the midst of a hectic schedule she found time in April to visit New York City where her father, now remarried, had settled. Stetson liked her new stepmother and her grown daughters. Her father seemed content, their meeting was warm, and she allowed herself the sweet contemplation of a home at last—with her father. But by November 1896, when she returned to New York, Frederick Perkins had been moved to a sanatorium. He was helpless, growing rapidly senile as the arteries in his brain hardened. Her own intellectual powers were on the rise; his had ebbed. He would not be there to welcome or commend her to the larger world he had so long symbolized.

The next two years were important ones in Stetson's life. Free entirely of personal ties, she devoted herself to her work. She kept up an extraordinary pace, traveling for months at a time, lecturing, attending feminist meetings and conventions, and in her uncommitted hours, reading and writing. Everywhere she went she was confronted by the tangible evidence of her success. Men and women greeted her in each town, receptive to her ideas and eager to be near the energy she radiated. Younger women confessed that she was their model of independent womanhood. Her litany of self-doubt and self-criticism was weakened by this daily routine confirmation that she was indeed what she had wished and worked to be.

Reality thus seemed to catch up with Stetson during these years, and the passage of time seemed to make her more comfortable in her chosen role as spokeswoman for reform. Yet surely this maturation process pointed to a new receptivity to self-esteem. Perhaps the loss of both her parents freed her from the need to view her life in the old pattern of dichotomous loyalties and aversions, a duality that allowed her no victory without its companion, defeat.

One thing is clear: The acceptance of her success changed her understanding of her personal loneliness. Loneliness lost its heroic quality and she came to feel it not as a necessity or a punishment or the price of success, but simply as an emptiness. This changed perception influenced the course of her renewed friendship with Houghton Gilman.

MARRIAGE AND WORK: RESOLUTION

On March 8, 1897, Charlotte Perkins Stetson visited Houghton Gilman's New York office for advice on a legal matter. It had been almost 20 years since "Ho" and "Chopkins" had exchanged letters, yet Houghton recognized her at once. "This," she later wrote, "was the beginning of a delightful renewal of an earlier friendship."

George Houghton Gilman was seven years his cousin's junior, a handsome, courtly, intelligent man. He was gentle, steady, generally likable. He had for most of his life been burdened with responsibility that had tied him down, emotionally and financially, for his mother was an invalid, his brother Francis a dwarf. These family obligations, heavy enough to oppress others, seemed not to embitter Houghton Gilman or to produce in him any debilitating sense of lost opportunities. He may have lived a circumscribed life, but he nevertheless found enjoyable moments and interesting pastimes. He was modestly ambitious and honorable: he liked his work as an attorney. He was not politically active or much attuned to the issues that so engrossed Charlotte Stetson. But he very much enjoyed her company.

Charlotte Stetson was obviously pleased with the new friendship and could not stay off the subject of Houghton Gilman, even in a letter to her daughter. "Last week I made a delightful discovery! Found a cousin! . . . This cousin is Houghton Gilman . . . he is now a grown man nearly thirty, but when I remember him he was just your age." Then, only a few sentences later, she found herself writing: "To return to my newly discovered cousin: he is in the 7th regiment, and is going to take me to see them perform next Tuesday."

By March 18 the cousins were corresponding again, as they had decades ago. Charlotte, full of things to say and feelings to show, chose to write them to "Ho" even though they were both in New York City. "In some ways," she explained, "paper is freer than speech." The paper served her well, for the letters are frank and intense. "What a good time I did have the other night!" she wrote on March 18. "You now float and hover in my brain in a changing cloud of delectable surroundings."

Enjoying Houghton Gilman's company and his confidence seemed to reinforce Charlotte Stetson's awareness of how carefully she had repressed her feelings over the last several years and had escaped dealing with them by a frenzy of activity. "These years, when I stop doing things and my mind settles and things come up into view, most of these are of so painful a nature that I have to rush around and cram them back into their various (right here I have to stop and write a poem on 'Closet Doors' . . .)." But Gilman had created a mental space for her. "Now when I am quiet," she wrote, "there's a pleasantest sort of feeling—warm and cosy and safe."

Although her friendship with Gilman had allowed her room to test her capacity for affection once more, and helped her come to terms with its long absence, she was still wary and insecure. She often insisted that the relationship was platonic, familial, with herself the idiosyncratic but interesting older cousin and him the elegant and courtly young boy who found her educational and amusing in a maiden-aunt fashion. "I am looking ahead and wishing most earnestly and tenderly that you may have such a house as you deserve and one of the very charmingest of wives." Charlotte Stetson typically included in a long and effusive letter, using her pose as "Aunt Charlotte" like a talisman against disappointment.

As the odd courtship continued, these letters became—as those to Walter Stetson had once appeared to be—an open battleground for her conflicting emotions. But Charlotte Perkins Stetson had grown. There may have been defensive cul-de-sacs and charades, but there was nevertheless a true effort to discover her feelings, to know her desires, and to act as she wanted to act rather than as she ought. She knew that Houghton Gilman made her feel good about herself, good enough for her to admit how very low her self-esteem had always been. "Truly Houghton, for all the invulnerable self-belief and self reliance which I have to have to live at all, you have no idea how small potatoes I think of myself at heart, how slow I am to believe that anyone's kindness to me is other than benevolence."

Houghton Gilman could not help but know. She had revealed her insecurity in every letter, in a transparent flippancy that was too earnest to be coy. "It won't surprise me in the least when you get over liking me as they all do," she had written, and in a hundred different forms she repeated the same fears over the next years. It was an appeal for reassurance woven into the letters with others. "Do [my letters] annoy you? I couldn't write for a week cause this fear depressed me," she wrote while in Kansas: "*Say* you like me if you do—often!" she added to a letter that summer.

For four years Charlotte Stetson confided her present and her past to Houghton Gilman, in a dialogue largely with herself. And, although much of the content was self-denigrating and self-pitying, there were moments of a new comfortable feeling about herself. She began to treat herself well, to buy clothing, and to indulge in gratuitous touches of luxury. She had begun to celebrate herself. Although this delight in self would previously have repelled her, now she began to accept personal pleasures that harmed no one by their fulfillment. Most important, she re-examined the very basis of affection.

Duty, she discovered, could not always promote or sustain love. "I have loved many people, in various ways, mostly because they needed it," she wrote Houghton, "but . . . the way you make me feel is different. It is not merely in the nature of wanting you—in the sense of a demanding personal affection, or even of—well, any kind of hungriness. And it is not at all in the sense of wishing to serve . . . the uppermost feeling is of pure personal gratification because you are so!"

What surprised Charlotte Stetson most was that the frank commitment to love did not destroy the sense of commitment to her life's work. Self-denial and self-satisfaction were not after all mutually exclusive rulers of character and destiny; there was room in her to accommodate both states. Her work improved, she told Houghton, her energies increased, her desire to write was not diminished but intensified. She had moments of genuine optimism. "The new charmed being now accepted by Madam Conscience, who has been struggling violently to choke it up for some time past, works admirably and I begin to see my way to let out more love towards Kate, too."

In truth, Charlotte Stetson was at the peak of her career when she wrote these letters to Houghton Gilman. *Women and Economics* was published in 1898 and won instant international acclaim. Even before it was published she was at work on a second book. In the summer of 1899 she returned to England, a star among equals at the international women's conference. Her lecture tours at last showed a profit, with Houghton Gilman acting as her agent and adviser. Her personal philosophy, equating living with growing, had once located growth in the soil of pain, denial, and disappointment. Now she conceded a growing that was expansive and inclusive. What could be a clearer sign of the changes in Charlotte Perkins Stetson than that she had at last developed a sense of humor. The heroic figure could now laugh a little at herself.

In June 1900 Houghton Gilman traveled to the Midwest to meet Charlotte Stetson. She was in the midst of a speaking tour: he had taken the summer away from his law practice. They had not seen each other for almost a year. On June 11 they were married. Of this wedding day, Charlotte Perkins Gilman, now 40, wrote:

Monday . . . Our Day . . . the end of waiting, not to let the happiness blind and mislead me—dull my sensitiveness, check my sympathy, stop my work. It will not, I know; it has not so far and it will not. On the contrary I shall do more work and better. . . . I suppose I shall get used to love and peace and comfort and forget to be grateful everyday! But I doubt it. The other life has been too long. . . . I have liked as well as loved you from the first. . . . So strong and quiet and kind . . . to your pure and noble Manhood I come humbly, gladly full, bringing all that I have and am—willing to be taken as I am. . . . I am coming to be your happy Wife.

Gilman's new confidence in the harmony possible between her public and private lives proved well founded. For 34 years her personal happiness neither hampered her work nor eroded her feminist perspective. When, on August 17, 1935, she ended her own life to avoid debilitation by cancer, she was no longer an influential figure in the world of ideas or politics. The war and the decade that followed had destroyed the world she knew. The era of optimistic reform had passed: and the search in the 1920s by young women for self-gratification and satisfaction without any commitment to public service had made her militant but nurturant feminism obsolete. Despite her eclipse, Charlotte Perkins Gilman continued to write and to advocate the restructuring of society. Her last book, however, was not social anthropology but autobiography, charting an inner odyssey to both independence and interdependence. It was a conscious effort to mark the path for other, younger women.

In the end, Charlotte Gilman's philosophy and her psychic needs seemed, after all, to be one. She sought a social and a psychological androgyny: a full humanity, to be experienced by each individual, that would create harmony among them through shared experience rather than the isolation and dualism of the sexually segregated world into which she had been born. She sought the pride in contribution and participation that ensured self-esteem, and the condition of independence that ensured equality. She sought the integrated self, and even at those moments when she felt it impossible for herself in her own lifetime, she was determined to secure it for future generations of women and men.

DOCUMENTS

Two Callings, by Charlotte Perkins Gilman, 1903

I

I heard a deep voice through uneasy dreaming,*
A deep, soft, tender, soul-beguiling voice;
A lulling voice that bids the dream remain,
That calms my restlessness and dulls my pain,
That thrills and fills and holds me till in seeming
There is no other sound on earth—no choice.

*Published with permission from the Charlotte Perkins Gilman Collection, Schlesinger Library, Radcliffe College, from *The Home: Its Work and Influence*, New York, 1903.

"Home!" says the deep voice, "Home!" and softly
    singing
Brings me a sense of safety unsurpassed;
So old! So old! The piles above the wave—
The shelter of the stone-blocked, shadowy cave—
Security of sun-kissed treetops swinging—
Safety and Home at last! . . .

I shrink—half rise—and then it murmurs "Duty!"
Again the past rolls out—a scroll unfurled:
Allegiance and long labor due my lord—
Allegiance in an idleness abhorred—
I am the squaw—the slave—the harem beauty—
I serve and serve, the handmaid of the world.

My soul rebels—but hark! a new note thrilling,
Deep, deep, past finding—I protest no more;
The voice says "Love" and all those ages dim
Stand glorified and justified in him;
I bow—I kneel—the woman soul is willing—
"Love is the law. Be still! Obey! Adore!"

And then—ah, then! The deep voice murmurs "Mother!"
And all life answers from the primal sea;
A mingling of all lullabies, a peace
That asks no understanding; the release
Of nature's holiest power—who seeks another?
Home? Home is Mother—Mother, Home—to me. . . .

II

A bugle call! A clear, keen, ringing cry,
Relentless—eloquent—that found the ear
Through fold on fold of slumber, sweet, profound—
A widening wave of universal sound.
Piercing the heart—filling the utmost sky—
I wake—I must wake!—Hear—for I must hear!

"The World! The World is crying! Hear its needs!
Home is a part of life—I am the whole!
Home is the cradle—shall a whole life stay
Cradled in comfort through the working day?
I, too, am Home—the Home of all high deeds—
The only Home to hold the human soul!

"Courage!—the front of conscious life!" it cried;
"Courage that dares to die and dares to live!
Why should you prate of safety? Is life meant

In ignominious safety to be spent?
Is Home best valued as a place to hide?
Come out, and give what you are here to give!

"Strength and Endurance! of high action born!"
And all that dream of Comfort shrank away,
Turning its fond, beguiling face aside;
So Selfishness and Luxury and Pride
Stood forth revealed, till I grew fierce with scorn,
And burned to meet the dangers of the day. . . .

"Duty! Unlimited—eternal—new!"
And I? My idol on a petty shrine
Fell as I turned, and Cowardice and Sloth
Fell too, unmasked, false Duty covering both—
While the true Duty, all-embracing, high,
Showed the clear line of noble deed to do.

And then the great voice rang out to the sun,
And all my terror left me, all my shame,
While every dream of joy from earliest youth
Came back and lived!—that joy unhoped was truth,
All joy, all hope, all truth, all peace grew one,
Life opened clear, and Love? Love was its name!

So when the great word "Mother!" rang once more,
I saw at last its meaning and its place;
Not the blind passion of the brooding past,
But Mother—the World's Mother—come at last,
To love as she had never loved before—
To feed and guard and teach the human race.

The world was full of music clear and high!
The world was full of light! The world was free!
And I? Awake at last, in joy untold,
Saw Love and Duty broad as life unrolled—
Wide as the earth—unbounded as the sky—
Home was the World—the World was Home to me!

The Forerunner *Editorial, 1911*

. . . The need The Forerunner seeks to meet is not of a general and popular
sort, but is no less real for all that; being the demand of a rather special
group of people for clear expression of their rather special views.*
    The main ground of appeal of this magazine, is the Near Sure Perfectly

*From *The Forerunner*, 2 (1911), 28–29.

Possible Improvement of Life; offering to that end its quota of thought and feeling, its presentation in fact, fiction, fable, fancy, verse, and prose.

Its view upon the Woman Question is that which sees women as human beings, not merely struggling for freedom, privilege and power, but as heavily behind hand in their duty to the world: holding in their gift a mighty fund of Love and Service which we can no longer do without.

It sees in Socialism the natural evolution of our economic system: long since begun, now already introduced in many lines in varying degree, sure of ultimate adoption, and calling for the intelligent study and recognition of every conscientious citizen. . . .

Excerpt from The Crux, 1911

[Vivian] sat with her shapely hands quiet in her lap while her grandmother's shining needles twinkled in the dark wool, and her mother's slim crochet hook ran along the widening spaces of some thin, white fuzzy thing.* The rich powers of her young womanhood longed for occupation, but she could never hypnotize herself with "fancy-work." Her work must be worth while. She felt the crushing cramp and lonliness [sic] of a young mind, really stronger than those about her, yet held in dumb subjection. She could not solace herself by loving them; her father would have none of it, and her mother had no use for what she called "sentiment." All her life Vivian had longed for more loving, both to give and take; but no one ever imagined it of her, she was so quiet and repressed in manner. The local opinion was that if a woman had a head, she could not have a heart; and as to having a body— it was indelicate to consider such a thing.

"I mean to have six children," Vivian had planned when she was younger. "And they shall never be hungry for more loving." She meant to make up, to her vaguely imagined future family, for all that her own youth missed. . . .

Notes

1. In this essay, all materials from Gilman's diaries and personal correspondence with family and friends are drawn from the Charlotte Perkins Gilman Papers, Schlesinger Library, Radcliffe College, Cambridge. Massachusetts.

2. See, for example, the novelettes serialized in *The Forerunner* (1911–1916), reprinted by Greenwood Press, New York, 1968.

3. Gilman's own account of her family history and her life, from which much of the information in this essay is drawn, can be found in her autobiography, *The Living of Charlotte Perkins Gilman*, D. Appleton-Century, New York and London, 1935.

4. Gilman's books, published between 1898 and 1935, are: *Women and Economics*,

*From *The Forerunner*, 2 (1911), 45. *The Crux* is a serial story.

Small, Maynard, Boston, 1898; *In This Our World*, Small, Maynard, Boston, 1898; *Concerning Children*, Small, Maynard, Boston, 1900; *The Home: Its Work and Influence*, McClure, Phillips, New York, 1903; *Human Work*, McClure, Phillips, New York, 1904; *What Diantha Did*, Charlton, New York, 1910; *The Man-Made World*, Charlton, New York, 1911; *His Religion and Hers: The Faith of Our Fathers and the Work of Our Mothers*, D. Appleton-Century, New York, 1923; *The Living of Charlotte Perkins Gilman*.

    5.   Charlotte Perkins Gilman, "Are Women Human Beings? A Consideration of the Major Error in the Discussion of Woman Suffrage," *Harper's Weekly* (May 25, 1912).

REVIEWS AND
CONTEMPORARY COMMENT
◆

Charlotte Perkins Stetson: A Daring Humorist of Reform

ANONYMOUS

As certainly as new occasions bring new duties, new societies will bring new poets, and Socialists often indulge in speculations as to what form the poetry of the future will take. Greece had her epics, Rome her lyrics of luxury, England her dramas, Scotland her songs, contemporaneous literature has replicas and studies and echoes of all these, and we—this especial American we—well we, I am told, have produced some remarkable "short stories," and certain people say we have Walt Whitman, and then, of course, we have the newspapers. We have our quotum, too, of modern poets, who keep us informed as to how they feel on occasions of all human experiences; what they think of stars and flowers, and how it feels to be lonesome, and what effect the night wind has on one's general estimate of things in general.

But we look forward to the time when—with the growth of the social consciousness—the poet will conclude to remove his analytical microscope from the contemplation of his private emotions. He will find in that day that nothing will satisfy him but to submerge himself in the national life of his people, and feeling its vitality in all his faculties, raise his voice in "full throated ease" to sing for his race what the race feels but cannot itself express. In the meantime social sensitiveness is already latent in sufficient quantity to make the fervor of any strong national excitement sure of finding a more or less adequate articulation. The anti-slavery movement evoked fervent hymns to freedom, and the civil war had its trumpet tones of martial song. And while no great poet has yet appeared for the hour that calls, the social awakening which has been slowly gathering strength during the last decade has not failed of its impress upon sensitive strings. Half a dozen years ago in the far West, where all things are new, there arose a perfectly new figure— a woman armed with the keenest weapons of wit and satire. From the crown of her jet black hair to the tip of her restless foot she quivered with that sort of earnestness which always dodges the sentimentalist's grasp. Playing hide and seek in and out behind the pillars of irony, Charlotte Perkins Stetson mocked at him for his pains. With fierce enthusiasm she threw herself into the Labor agitation around her and was soon speaking in clubs and churches

Reprinted from *The American Fabian* 3, no. 1 (January 1897): 1–3.

throughout California, adding the fire of her zeal to the force of that "Nation-alist" movement which had followed the appearance of Mr. Bellamy's "Look-ing Backward," and which had a phenomenal career in the Pacific States. Her best known poem, "Similar Cases," was published first in their *Nationalist* of Boston in 1890. It is a curious biological satire and has been quoted from one end of the land to the other, appearing now in the lectures of learned professors of natural science, and again furnishing trenchant arguments for the political agitators. In its few verses it shows a panorama of instantaneous photographs of the world-old contention between the spirit of Progress and the sluggish mass of skeptical conservatism. It tells us that among our humble progenitors in the animal world there appeared now and then a radical who experienced the same pangs of progressiveness and sweet pains of discontent that we advanced reformers know. The little eohippus, forefa-ther of the horse, declares his intention to rise in the scale of being; the anthropoidal ape announces "I'm going to be a man;" the neolithic man expresses in turn his confidence of rising to civilization. All these progressives meet the fate of their kind; jeered at for his temerity, each in turn is summarily crushed by the good old argument—"*You would have to change your nature.*" The writer draws a caustic brush over this dictum. What satire could be keener than her demure explanation?

> "That was the way they argued
> In the early Eocene;"
> "*You would have to change your nature*;
> We would like to see you try!"
> They chuckled then triumphantly,
>   These lean and hairy shapes,
> For these things passed as arguments
>   With the Anthropoidal Apes.
> "You must alter Human Nature"
> And they all set back and smiled.
> Thought they, "An answer to that last
>   It will be hard to find."
> It was a clinching argument
>   To the Neolithic Mind.

An instance of the way this poem has touched the mark is the fact that many "last verses" have been added by reformers of all shades and creeds everywhere—each feeling that a further illustration of his own particular conviction was necessary to bring this picture of the march of evolution up to date.

A volume of Mrs. Stetson's poems entitled "In This Our World" has recently been published in San Francisco and republished in England, and has been widely commented upon. It is a collection of singularly fresh and vigorous pieces—not poetry in the lofty meaning of the word, and, indeed, the author lays no claim to the title of poet, but in the trenchant parables she deftly cuts into her page is teaching of the highest order. If it is not poetry it certainly is not prose. A Scotch critic calls her "a Bret Harte with a mission." "She tilts at evil with bantering irony," he continues, "and her audacious analogies are absolutely startling." Another foreign reviewer exclaims: "She is one of the coolest-headed and most daring humorists of her country."

Curiously enough—and yet from another aspect not surprising at all— this strange, passionate, mocking woman comes of long lines of Puritan stock, with a stern ancestry of orthodox deacons and Unitarian "come-outers" behind her. Her grandmother was Mary Beecher, daughter of the redoubtable Rev. Lyman Beecher and sister of the famous Henry Ward and Harriet Beecher. The same reformer's blood that issued in thunder from Plymouth pulpit and in the light of reason and genius in "Uncle Tom's Cabin" runs in her veins. It is not too much to say that the emancipation of the negro slaves was due in larger measure to the fire and power of these American writers, both members of the Beecher family, than to any other single cause, and the same traits, veiled in the peculiar quality of an elusive but poignantly intense personality, are reappearing in their young kinswoman. Mr. Beecher liked to relate, with a little touch of grimness in his delightful humor, that people had used to say that he had helped his sister to write "Uncle Tom's Cabin," but that when his own novel, "Norwood," appeared—they never said so any more.

Mrs. Stetson has shown evidences of possessing both strains of the Beecher talent, humor, pathos and graphic descriptive ability as a writer, combined with the power of the preacher. She has repeatedly filled pulpits in the West and in the East with credit to her cause and to them. Upon a visit to England last summer this American Socialist was warmly received by all the leaders of the reform, and the Fabian Society at once elected her a member—a rare honor nowadays. Her speeches were everywhere received with favor; her view of "Women in Evolution" being by competent critics hailed as a distinct contribution to this somewhat threadbare subject. Keir Hardie's newspaper, "The Labor Leader," devotes a column in a recent issue to an account of her Glasgow lecture.

We have spoken of Mrs. Stetson's work as not taking rank in the annals of true poetry, but there are signs that a further development may place her in that list before long. If the power to concentrate into close, highly-charged rhythmic diction whole areas of human experience and give in a verse the entire atmosphere of some region of human life be real poetry, then Mrs. Stetson's lines called "The Wolf at the Door," secured by Scribner's and published by them in a recent issue of their magazine, are certainly entitled to this rank. We think it far and away the best thing she has yet produced. There is the very still, creeping horror of poverty in the lines:

> "The slow, relentless padding step
> That never goes astray."

And what but genius could sum up the inherited misery of overworked generations in the solemn words:

> "We are born to hoarded weariness,
> As some to hoarded gold."

The analogy of the figure carries a double reflex meaning in the dependence of one of the statements upon the other. The writer is too much of an artist to say it, but the reader hears the undertone of stern reminder that the "hoarded weariness" is because of the "hoarded gold." Here is this remarkable poem in full:

THE WOLF AT THE DOOR.

There's a haunting horror near us
　That nothing drives away—
Fierce lamping eyes at nightfall,
　A crouching shade by day;
There's a whining at the threshold
　There's a scratching at the floor—
To work! to work! In heaven's name!
　The wolf is at the door!
The day was long, the night was short,
　The bed was hard and cold;
Still weary are the little ones,
　Still weary are the old.
We are weary in our cradles
　From our mother's toil untold;
We are born to hoarded weariness,
　As some to hoarded gold.

We will not rise! We will not work!
　Nothing the day can give
Is half so sweet as an hour of sleep;
　Better to sleep than live!
What power can stir these heavy limbs?
　What hope these dull hearts swell?
What fear more cold, what pain more sharp,
　Than the life we know so well?

To die like a man by lead or by steel
　Is nothing that we should fear;
No human death would be worse to feel
　Than the life that holds us here.
But this is a fear that no heart can face—
　A fate no man can dare—
To be run to the earth and die by the teeth

Of the gnawing monster there.
The slow, relentless, padding step
   That never goes astray—
The rustle in the underbrush—
   The shadow in the way—
The straining flight—the long pursuit—
   The steady gain behind—
Death-wearied man and tireless brute
   And the struggle wild and blind!

There's a hot breath at the keyhole
   And a tearing as of teeth!
Well do I know the bloodshot eyes
   And the dripping jaws beneath!

There's a whining at the threshold—
   There's a scratching at the floor—
To work! to work! In heaven's name!
   The wolf is at the door!

Hood's "Song of the Shirt" and Mrs. Browning's "The Cry of the Children" struck pangs of self-reproach into the public conscience. This poem of Charlotte Perkins Stetson's portrays perhaps no less forcibly the ghastly persecutions of the unceasing poverty which hangs over thousands of human beings in our day.

A different but equally pointed arraignment is contained in her little verses on "Charity." In these lines of child-story Mrs. Stetson touches with light satire the whole indictment against the despotism of private property:

CHARITY.

Came two young children to their mother's shelf
   (One was quite little, and the other big)
And each in freedom calmly helped himself
   (One was a pig).
The food was free and plenty for them both
   But one was rather dull and very small,
So the big, smarter brother, nothing loath,
   He took it all.
At which the little fellow raised a yell
   Which tired the other's more aesthetic ears.
He gave him here a crust and there a shell
   to stop his tears.
He gave with pride, in manner calm and bland,
   Finding the other's hunger a delight;
He gave with piety,—his full left hand
   Hid from his right.

He gave and gave;—O blessed Charity!
How sweet and beautiful a thing it is!
How fine to see that big boy giving free
What is not his!

New York Fabians are congratulating themselves on the acquisition of this ardent worker to their ranks, and are basing hopes of strong lectures and widening influence from her contemplated stay in the city. They feel that if her abilities develop according to present promise, American Fabians may begin to hold up their heads in the presence of the London Society, and already they would like to match Mrs. Stetson against the English free-lance Bernard Shaw, in a war of wits.

Charlotte Perkins Gilman's
Dynamic Social Philosophy

ANONYMOUS

For twenty years or more this latest representative of the Beecher family has journeyed through the United States and in Europe. From San Francisco to Budapest, speaking from church pulpits, for woman suffrage and Socialist meetings; heroically formulating an unpopular philosophy and presenting it with the illumination of genius. Perhaps no other living woman can communicate with such a thrill the aspiration for social righteousness. Mrs. Gilman's philosophy is dynamic: it is essentially one of hope, courage, joy: and it is for America today. We must forget, she tells us, Greek and Roman civilizations: study our present-day life in the light of evolutionary science: achieve full social consciousness: and proceed to build that which has never been constructed before—"a social body for the soul of God."

There is a remarkable poem entitled "Birth," the opening one in Mrs. Gilman's book of verse—"In This Our World," which gives the key-note to her whole philosophy. It is as extraordinary a contribution to the religion of evolution as Emily Brontë's famous "Last Lines." We quote in full, noting a curious lapse in the opening lines of the first, third and fifth verses, into what Mrs. Gilman would term our androcentric nomenclature.

> Lord, I am born!
> I have built me a body
> Whose ways are all open.
> Whose currents run free.
>
> From the life that is thine
> Flowing ever within me.
> To the life that is mine
> Flowing outward through me.
>
> I am clothed, and my raiment [sic]
> Fits smooth to the spirit.
> The soul moves unhindered.
> The body is free:

Reprinted from *Current Literature* 51 (July 1911): 67–70.

And the thought that my body
Falls short of expressing,
In texture and color
Unfoldeth on me.

I am housed, O my Father!
My body is sheltered.
My spirit has room
'Twixt the whole world and me.
I am guarded with beauty and strength,
And within it
Is room for still union.
And birth floweth free.

And the union and birth
Of the house, ever growing.
Have built me a city—
Have born me a state—
Where I live manifold,
Many-voiced, many-hearted.
Never dead, never weary,
And oh! never parted!
The life of The Human,
So subtle—so great!

Lord, I am born!
From inmost to outmost
The ways are all open.
The currents run free.
From thy voice in my soul

To my joy in the people—
I thank thee, O God.
For this body thou gavest,
Which enfoldeth the earth—
Is enfolded by thee!

Man's subjugation of woman, which ended the matriarchate, and wherein, according to Prof. Lester F. Ward, woman lost her virtue (that is, her power of free sexual selection) and man his "normal chivalry and respect for the preferences of woman," Mrs. Gilman regards as the most catastrophic change in the evolution of human society. She bases her philosophy squarely on the gynecocentric theory of Professor Ward, which assumes that the female is the true race type—order Mammalia—and the male the sex variant. This theory, "than which," says Mrs. Gilman, "nothing so important to humanity has been advanced since the theory of evolution, and nothing so important to women has ever been given to the world," is not yet accepted even by a majority of biologists. But if ever it becomes a matter of popular belief, human life will be revolutionized. Mrs. Gilman claims that this is precisely what is happening today. Consciously or unconsciously, whether we will or no, the revolution is taking place.

About ten years ago Mrs. Gilman startled the thinking world with "Women and Economics," a book violently disputed, which has been translated into German, Dutch, Italian, Hungarian, Russian and Japanese. "Concerning Children," "Human Work" and "The Home" followed in logical succession; three of these works being used as college textbooks. Their underlying philosophy Mrs. Gilman now presents in a series of lectures— "Man, Woman and Child," and also in the chapters of her latest sociological work, "The Man-Made World, or Our Androcentric Culture," which, we venture to predict, will prove her most important book since "Women and Economics." Here we can only touch upon a few main points.

. . .

Under these newly evolving and more maternal conditions of life, how, Mrs. Gilman asks, shall we finally face the root problems of crime and punishment? "The world's last prison," she believes, "will be simply a hospital for moral incurables." She says further: "Some are morally diseased, but may be cured, and the best powers of society will be used to cure them. Some are only morally diseased because of the conditions in which they are born and reared, and here society can save millions at once. An intelligent society will no more neglect its children than an intelligent mother will neglect her children: and will see as clearly that ill-fed, ill-dressed, ill-taught and vilely associated little ones must grow up gravely injured. As a matter of fact we make our crop of criminals, just as we make our idiots, blind, crippled, and generally defective."

But Mrs. Gilman is considering here only the older, simpler forms of crime. What, she questions, of the new ones—the "big, terrible, far-reaching, wide-spread crimes, for which we have as yet no names, and before which our old system of anti-personal punishment falls helpless? What of the crimes of poisoning a community with bad food: of defiling the water: of blackening the air: of stealing whole forests? What of the crimes of working little children: of building and renting tenements that produce crime and physical disease as well? What of the crime of living on the wages of fallen women—of hiring men to ruin innocent young girls: of holding them enslaved and selling them for profit? . . . And what about a crime like this: to use the public press to lie to the public for private ends? No name yet for this crime: much less a penalty. . . . Or this: to knowingly plant poison in an unborn child?" Which brings her to the conclusion:

> "The whole punishment system falls to the ground before the huge mass of evil that confronts us. If we saw a procession of airships flying over a city and dropping bombs, should we rush madly off after each one crying. 'Catch him! Punish him!' or should we try to stop the procession?
>
> "The time is coming when the very word 'crime' will be disused, except in

poems and orations: and 'punishment,' both word and deed, be obliterated. We are beginning to learn a little of the nature of humanity: its goodness, its beauty, its lovingness: and to see that even its stupidity is only due to our foolish old methods of education.

"It is not new power, new light, new hope that we need, but to *understand what ails us*.

"We know enough now, we care enough now, we are strong enough now, to make the whole world a thousand-fold better in a generation: but we are shackled, chained, blinded, by old false notions. The ideas of the past, the sentiments of the past, the attitude and prejudice of the past, are in our way: and among them none more universally mischievous than this great body of ideas and sentiment, prejudices and habits, which make up the offensive network of the androcentric culture."

But the time has come, Mrs. Gilman claims, when we have reached a stage in human development where both men and women are able to look beyond the distinctions of sex and mutually work for the world's advancement. It is to this great change from the injurious dominance of one sex to the equal power of two that her philosophy looks confidently forward. She writes:

"The effect of the change upon ethics and religion is deep and wide. With the entrance of women upon full human life, a new principle comes into prominence—the principle of loving service. That this is the governing principle of Christianity is believed by many: but an androcentric interpretation has quite overlooked it: and made, as we have shown, the essential dogma of their faith the desire of an eternal reward and the combat with an eternal enemy.

"The feminine attitude in life is wholly different. As a female she has merely to be herself and passively attract: neither to compete nor to pursue: as a mother her whole process is one of growth: first the development of the live child within her, and the wonderful nourishment from her own body: and then all the later cultivation to make the child grow: all the watching, teaching, guarding, feeding. In none of this is there either desire, combat, or self-expression. The feminine attitude, as expressed in religion, makes of it a patient, practical fulfillment of law: a process of large, sure improvements: a limitless, comforting love and care.

"This full assurance of love and of power: this endless cheerful service: the broad provision for all people, rather than the competitive selection of a few 'victors,' is the natural presentation of religious truth from the woman's viewpoint."

One of Mrs. Gilman's poems sets a fitting conclusion on this argument:

> She walketh veiled and sleeping,
> For she knoweth not her power;
> She obeyeth but the pleading

Of her heart, and the high leading
Of her soul, unto this hour.
Slow advancing, halting, creeping,
Comes the Woman to the hour!—
She walketh veiled and sleeping,
For she knoweth not her power.

The Woman Who Saw It First

Alexander Black

About ten years ago an American editor said of Mrs. Gilman, "She is the George Bernard Shaw of America, unless we prefer to call Mr. Shaw the Charlotte Perkins Gilman of England." Superficially, the reference was not much more than a picturesqueness complimentary to Mr. Shaw. The actual intention may have been to characterize certain lively traits in the work of two persons who could not well be more strikingly different. It would have been absurd, for example, to imply that Mrs. Gilman likes to be startling. She *has* been startling, but scarcely in Mr. Shaw's way. She has been quotable, and has, perhaps with less than Mr. Shaw's luck, paid penalties for pungence. To be quotable is to be misquoted. It once seemed that shuttling crippled quotations of Mrs. Gilman was an established indoor sport. So much for being a radical.

The American's theory of keeping a jump ahead, his frequent display of a go-getter complacency, as if he had invented initiative, give a grotesque twist to the fact, never more apparent than it is to-day, that he does not like radicals. He can offer a spirited welcome to a new *thing*, but he continues to give the impression of being less sympathetic than the European toward new thinking. Having called himself a pathfinder, he is likely to be annoyed by any reminder that he has overlooked something. Perhaps the most stubborn stodginess begins with this sort of dismissing gesture. How can the open-minded be wrong? Having started business as a nation with quite satisfying slogans by which all the world might see that we were up and coming, that we were a lusty, high-spirited company, defiant of traditions, quick on the trigger, nervously responsive to new devices, we proceeded politically to become the most conservative nation on earth. In political ancestor worship we are supreme. The most ancient of delusions, that difference of opinion can be stamped out by statute, is seen at its ripest in this country. We are sometimes tolerant of a nice, decently conforming liberalism, but the sheer inconvenience of people who refuse to leave life as it is nowhere meets with more violent resentment.

Naturally, the degree of discomfort in a radicalism is fixed by the degree of its nearness. A radical in a foreign country is permitted to be a prophet.

Reprinted from *Century* 107 (November 1923): 33–42, with the permission of the publisher.

In an adjacent town he can be ridiculed as a visionary. Next door he is a menace. And in a community that is convinced of its special enlightenment and liberality there is a fate for menaces. However, all of our radicals have not landed in jail. Early and late we have found divers ways of expressing disapproval. And we have agreed to differentiate between one sort of radical and another.

We do not adjudge every blow at the established as an assault in the first degree. To be a little too sympathetic toward male laborers, for example, is a very serious matter. Merely to be deeply concerned about female laborers, especially unsalaried female laborers in households, is naturally less serious. A Thoreau or a Walt Whitman will make less trouble than an Altgeld. Even a Thomas Paine could not hurt like a Debs.

All radicals share the chance that civilization will catch up with them. The radical of Nazareth may illustrate the fact that there can be no certainty of such a consummation, but the phenomenon happens often enough to remind any who care to think about it that civilization does at times, perhaps breathlessly, come abreast, or almost seem to have come abreast, of one who has been striding ahead. Civilization can do this without condoning the original offense of being too soon, which gives a peculiar interest to speculation upon the situation of the caught-up-with.

§ 2

It might be a bit reckless to classify Charlotte Perkins Gilman among thinkers who have been overtaken. She is still, in many of her doctrines and convictions, lonesomely in advance of the accepted. The arc of her early challenge ran beyond the visible horizon. But so much of her preaching that once was regarded as revolutionary is now a matter of polite consideration, if not of practice, that her total effect is no longer so sharply radical as it was to the generation to which we look back. She herself is still looking forward. She was never a mere storm. An imitative noisiness is often mistaken for real rebellion. Mrs. Gilman has always been more like an incorrigible current. Her tide seems to have no ebb. She is the poorest compromiser I know. She is never pugnacious. No one could have less interest in conflict for its own sake. Her persistent idealism has often appalled the merely aggressive. I can testify that as partner in a wrangle she is as gentle as a river. When you try an obstruction, she overflows the banks of the argument. She can do this graciously—as graciously as gravitation.

She exemplifies a fact, which we frequently have occasion to notice, that preachers of a better socialization for the world have seldom been aggressively "sociable." It is as if to *see* socialization one must be aloof. We do not look for social idealism in a mixer. The prophet is likely to be an incompetent pusher, perhaps because the all-of-us vision is hard to acquire in contact with the crowd. Yet Mrs. Gilman might seem to have followed Emerson's suggestion with regard to solitude and society by keeping her head in one and her hands in the other. She is no recluse. I am thinking of her congenital inadaptability to the free-for-all. She is more a telescope person than a microscope person, despite her disposition to open every scientific door. She thinks best in terms of constellations, with due respect to the electron as a theoretical detail. To her the individualist represents the great delusion. She sees the human brain as a social product and all separatist efforts as grotesque. She speaks somewhere of an "ex-man" on a desert island. The absurdity of the socially created trying to be *selfish*, of trying to feed a social hunger an ego meal, stirs her sense of the incongruous.

There is plenty of room for quarrel in any such contention, as any strugger in philosophy before or during Bergson well knows. I have, on occasion, joined the mêlée. I belong among the innocents who are ready to admit that the collective comes first. But first considerations are not always most important considerations. It is of first importance to be born. It is of greater importance to be worth borning. Mass is a beginning fact. It may be that it was invented to make possible an individual destination—that it is the mass and not the individual that is a means. Mrs. Gilman holds, adding her own inflections, with the school to which the individual is purely theoretical. Her individual is atomic. He never really happens. When he is being most personal he is simply expressing a unit sign of a collective fact.

No one could offer a profounder illustration of the individual paradox than Mrs. Gilman herself. Before an audience she can seem to prophesy the most perfect participation. Yet her flame is not to be merged. When she preached socialistic ideals in California, the Socialists assumed that they had found a leader. But it turned out that a capital S could not be attached to her. Political Socialism, that is to say, applied Socialism, was unable to enlist her. She could speak before the Fabians in England, beside Bernard Shaw and his compatriots, but they could not make a Fabian of her. To the religion of socialistic effort she was warmly responsive; to the theology of Socialism she was cold. It was the same with the suffrage question. She was one of the strongest of the intellectual forces animating the woman-suffrage movement. With voice and with the printed word she stirred the pulse of progressive opinion, but recoiled from the political implications. It was not that she resented, here or elsewhere, the drudgery of application. She has, indeed, too seldom considered the limits of her strength in throwing herself into any labor of brain or hand, in the forum or in the household, that seemed to make demand of her. We cannot think of her as standing on a chair in the sooty rain of a Liverpool street, holding that British crowd with a voice as slender as her body, but singularly impassioned and penetrating, conquering the ear by the silent attention it could win, without realizing her resources in sacrifice. The trouble was that politics meant adjustment, concession, trimming. She wanted to move as she thought—straight through. The devious strategies of politics always affected her as not only irksome, but immoral. It was useless to argue that all application implied concession; that a search-light might fall straight, but that the journey to the illuminated spot might mean not only fences and wet feet, but certain contentions as to right of way. She held the search-light with a fervent steadiness. Talking to her about expedience was like asking a compass to compromise.

It was in her blood to be a preacher: the Beecher strain was there, the Perkins strain was there. Preacher traditions came to her with the impress of a liberal New-Englandism. Her conscience may have been of New England; her convictions had no geography. Perhaps the West influenced the flowering of her impulses. Inevitably, her trend was affected by conditions of her youth, which had been piercingly unhappy. With her athletic frame came bitter mental struggles. The gestation of a spirit is not completed with the birth of a body. A long and torturing travail brought her face to face with a world in which women seemed to be playing a submerged part. The imaginative excursions of her girlhood were as of dreams in a prison. These excursions were extraordinarily diverse and fantastic. She was only eleven when she worked out a theory of a color concert based upon a rainbow octave, of a symphonic rain of color accomplished with the aid of a piano—and an imagination. There was a sustained fairy-story about a benevolence that carried unhappy children to wonder places. At the elbow of all possible benevolences lurked the fearful figure of Duty. The thing that was right dominated all other things. Beauty and happiness had always to be justified— or was it excused?

No picture could be more disturbing, more profoundly pitiful, than that of a child building a conscious system of ethics. Yet this is the picture I see in the adolescent years of Charlotte Perkins. The brain carried by that energetic body began, before it should have been through with dolls and dryads, to grapple with abstractions, to diagram this duty matter, to piece together an original formula for explaining the world. It seethed with theories. It strove, with a burning earnestness, in school, in what should have been the time of play, in the dark of bed hours, to read the hidden, to answer that strange, too early, questioning cry. As a young girl there was a bit of weirdness in her blending of conscience and adventure, of enormous restraint and a plunging mind. She had ravened among books. She had ransacked the philosophies, halted and fascinated by all sorts of intellectual fantasies, but emerging always into the heights. She had reached a kind of incandescence. And she wanted to be a voice.

Dominating all of her eager perceptions was the notion that women were people. The implications of this idea were vastly complicated, the more so because philosophy had ceased to be contemptuous, and civilization, after merely mouthing the words, had been content to ask, What of it? An honest recognition of the idea involved a rearrangement of the world. Charlotte Perkins set about the job.

§ 3

She began to be the voice. The note defied her own resources of strength, the clutch of personal situation. Poverty and a stricken mother did not stifle her wish or silence her voice. The way opened among common men and women, strugglers, thinkers—the nuisances of a stay-put civilization. She had rapt attention wherever she spoke in those early California days. There was the tipsy man who shouted, "Here comes our little queen!" The little queen had turned for an hour or two from a bedside and a kitchen where, one evening, a delegation of working-men found her. "We have heard," stammered the spokesman, "that you are—indigent." He hated to say "poor," and the elaborate word seemed to soften the suggestion. The business of the moment was to give her money, and it soon appeared that this couldn't be done. He would have been an inspired ambassador to know how to give Charlotte Perkins money. That smile of hers may have been bitter, but it was there. The teeth of facts never frightened her. "It is my purpose to talk to you," began one of her early speeches, "not about what has been said concerning things, but about the things themselves." That has always been her note—things themselves.

There was a harsh reality in the long ordeal ended by her mother's death. The sharp change left her free, on nothing a year, to go forward with the work of changing the world. It was characteristic of the world she sought to change that it should find so many ways of lashing her for the calamities of a marriage.

She was twenty-three when she married Walter Stetson, unquestionably one of the ablest American painters of his time. She had been painting and earning precariously as a teacher of drawing. Stetson thought she could paint still life as skilfully as any one living. But her call was not in that quarter, and all aspirations were engulfed in a physical breakdown such as recurred again and again to threaten all sustained effort. To be a good wife and a good mother—we can readily fancy the ardor of such an aspiration in an idealist of this type. Motherhood was realized. Wifehood crashed. It is not for the outsider to ask why such a relationship came to seem impossible to the two directly concerned. "A good and great man," she has called him. His reverence for her was of no lesser sort. A good man and a good woman; yet the mating which should not have been could not endure, though it was maintained for seven years. Separation was followed by divorce. The fact that, ten years later, she married her cousin. George Houghton Gilman, and that this marriage has been markedly happy, will suggest what it may to confident exponents of newer psychologies. It cannot fail to suggest that in this matter of marriage Mrs. Gilman's life has no fundamental quarrel with her philosophy. Any but an intensive and impudent criticism would have seen the consistency of her attitude toward her child. The welfare of the daughter was more to her than any sentimental tradition. If the daughter's development could be favored, as it was, by a later interval of life with her father, if an inherited artistic talent could be nourished by travel and the associations of European art centers, if her ultimate happiness could be advanced by a time of withdrawal from the independent struggles of her mother, the mother could await the fulfilments of a quite secure affection. The event justified the sacrifices. The mother-and-daughter closeness was unbroken.

It was like Charlotte Perkins that even in the midst of the divorce disaster she should stubbornly hold aloft the ensign of a personal loyalty to the partner in failure. This was against the code. The code was that heart unions might be dissolved by law under legal imperatives, but that social expectations involved a few blackguardly gestures. If there was to be divorce, some one had to be pictured as a monster. The Pickwickian trick would be understood. Such stultifications were impossible to Charlotte Perkins. Her crowning offense came when Walter Stetson, in the following year, married the brilliant granddaughter of William Ellery Channing, and it became known that the first wife recognized the assured beauty of this marriage. Not to hate her friend Grace Channing when she became the second Mrs. Stetson was an eccentricity beyond all atonement.

Since you may think this an intrusion upon private circumstances, let me note a reverberation only a few months old. When Mrs. Gilman recently went to California to visit her daughter, to romp with her grandchildren, and to deliver a lecture, one of the local newspapers, in announcing the public appearance, remarked that this was the woman who thirty years ago gave away her husband. Only a newspaper man could feel to the full the goulish atrocity of such a performance. Only a newspaper man could know that the reference reflected not a surviving recollection, but the vomitings of a newspaper "morgue." Only a newspaper man, aware of blunders in holding up the mirror that inevitably catches dirty and flippant minds, and measuring the offense against the high purposes of a profession, can reach the utter depths of chagrin before an incident of this sort.

§ 4

Ten years of struggle followed the dissolution of the marriage. Out of this period of poverty and abuse shine the first flashes of an extraordinary talent for verse. There had been miscellaneous writing, frequently for "The Impress," the vigorously original organ of the Pacific Coast Women's Press Association (Helen Campbell was among the contributors), but verse seemed to give the most effective vent for a unique irony as well as for an impassioned sense of beauty. "Similar Cases," printed in the "Nationalist" in 1891, had wide echoes. "We have had nothing since the Biglow Papers," wrote Mr. Howells, "half so good in a good cause." Mr. Howells added: "Since then I have read your 'Women of Today' in the Women's Journal. It is as good as

the other almost, and dreadfully true." Europe caught up "Similar Cases."
As a *tour de force* in sarcasm the "evolution poem" gave lively joy to all who
were thrusting into new lines of thought. The picture of the Eohippus who
said, "I am going to be a horse!" of the ape who declared. "I'm going to be
a Man!" and of the chorus screaming, "You'd have to change your nature!"
had the fighting color. The prophecy of the Neolithic Man,

> "We are going to wear great piles of stuff
>   Outside our proper skins!
> We are going to have Diseases!
> And Accomplishments!! And
>   Sins!!!"

and the eternal rebuff, "*You must alter Human Nature*," which was

> "a clinching argument
>   To the Neolithic mind,"

accomplished a merry jab at the stand-patters, of which a glimpse is given
in other verses, called "The Conservative." Here the dejected infant butterfly
weeps over his wings.

> " 'I do not want to fly,' said he,
>   'I only want to squirm.' "

The squirmers have been Mrs. Gilman's mark from the beginning. "In
This Our World" was the title given to a pamphlet edition of the poems, of
which James H. Barry of the San Francisco "Star" and John H. Marble,
printer, brought out a second edition in 1895. In the same year Mrs.
Catherine Helen Spence carried the verses to England, and Fisher Unwin put
them forth. Mrs. Gilman had begun to be known when she made her first
trip to England in 1896. But it was the coming of that amazing document,
"Women and Economics," which established her position in Europe. "Since
John Stuart Mill's essay," said the London "Chronicle" (it was alluding to
Mill's "Subjection of Women"), "there has been no book dealing with the
position of women to approach it in originality of conception and brilliancy
of exposition." It was this book, since translated into German, Dutch,
Italian, Russian, Hungarian, and Japanese, that effected picturesquely Mrs.
Gilman's welcome at the congress of women in London in 1899. She was
ardently sought out as the revealer of a new vision. Although no adept in
being "taken up," as she was by the Duchess of Sutherland and other admirers, her simplicity made as deep an impression as her incorrigible logic.
There was an even greater ardor to the reception in Germany five years later.
Supplementing her formal addresses in Berlin was an impromptu speech in

defense of marriage that created a genuine stir. This lithe American woman, who, when she kindled, seemed to be all eyes, who could blaze without heat, and who had a way of looking like a militant Madonna, may well have puzzled those who had theories of an American type. Doubtless she did not appear to look or act the part. Whether she was lecturing in England, with Alfred Russell Wallace in the chair, or was moving from one meeting-hall to another in Berlin, with crowds following, she was always more absorbed in her ideas than in herself or her hearers. Such an absorption could neither be embarrassed nor be thwarted.

Meanwhile, Europe had taken notice. Lectures in Holland, Germany, Hungary, and England in 1905 brought pronounced reactions. When H. G. Wells came to America in 1906 and was asked about his curiosities, he answered that he wanted to meet Charlotte Perkins Gilman. That meeting, when it happened, was, I fancy, somewhat a fizzle. These two did not hit it off personally; as thinkers they parted with unshaken respect. "Human Work," which appeared in 1904, greatly added to English and Continental interest in the author of "Women and Economics." Its huge lines and its philosophical audacity might well have given Europe an impression of a dynamic figure looming large on the American scene. As frequently happens, the prophet at home faced many obstacles. Yet none of these was more serious than the obstacle of ill health.

It was after consulting Dr. Weir Mitchell, and being told by him that her nerves demanded absolute abstinence from all intellectual work, that she wrote "The Yellow Wall Paper," which Howells gathered into his "The Great Modern American Stories." Weir Mitchell was to be her audience, and it is certain that his reading of the story influenced all of his later methods of treating neurasthenia. When the story, as a work of art, came in for many honors, she remarked: "I wrote it to preach. If it is literature, that just happened."

§ 5

Here you have a hint of her philosophy as a literary workman. There is a good deal the effect of maintaining that, having one's idea, the transmission of it may be left to the grace of God. That the thing might be the other way about—that the idea might be by the grace of God and the expression remain a matter of momentous individual responsibility—would not strike her as tenable if it implied close consciousness in writing. She can fling an idea into an art package without the slightest anxiety as to its possible loss in the mail. To argue that the primary importance of the idea is not contradicted by the integrity of the house in which it is to live, and that certain ideas may really deserve a temple, is never impressive to a believer in the righteousness of free-striding thought. Perhaps success in talking to audiences eye to eye breeds impatience with the technic of the written page, and written pages that have nothing but technic supply arguments enough to literary rebels. They are not good arguments. A literary house out of plumb, a temple with a leaky roof, do not praise impulse. To put it another way, a gorgeous art chariot without a passenger can be ludicrous, but, on the other hand, a noble ambassador deserves something better than a rickety vehicle in which to reach his appointed destination.

Such criticism would be less valid if Mrs. Gilman's resources were not so plainly to be seen. In her early writings, in parody and in analysis, she displayed real artistic virtuosity. She has a deep sense of beauty. This may often be repressed, or held in subjection to the scientific spirit, but its reality is never to be doubted. Her knowledge of verse forms and her use of them, whimsically or emotionally, indicate an uncommon equipment. In all of her writing the frequency with which she is able to bring a stinging clearness to crises of her thought convicts her at other times of a rushing indifference to form and to effectiveness. Thus in the enormous volume of writing she poured into her magazine, "The Forerunner," which for a fertile seven years she wrote from cover to cover, and which included two thought-crammed novels of great significance, "What Diantha Did" and "The Crux," she often sacrificed much to a pace of expression.

When Mrs. Gilman says, "I am not an artist," she is rebuking strictly esthetic expectations. A thing like "The Yellow Wall Paper" (there is many another) proves that she *is* an artist when she chooses. She has interests sterner than esthetics. Even in her most vivid verse she is too intent upon meaning to dally with merely gracious sounds. The whole effect of her work, in every field, is of an intentness, of a seer's intentness, a prophet's passion to say, without hurry, but without lingering. She is nowhere observable as making a *thing*: she is making a case, she is translating a vision. That vision of woman has had an unexampled wideness. It has left suffrage, labor, all sociological detail to seem incidental. She has marked out more inclusively and more audaciously than any other thinker of her time the implications of the new biology as bearing on woman's place in the human game. She saw and described with an unmitigated clearness the obligation imposed by admitted truth as to the position of woman. Concession in theory gave her no comfort. She saw that systems of living had to be made over; that the whole structure of society stood upon a viciously wrong notion of human work and of woman's relationship to that work. She saw life as a verb, work as an expenditure of energy by society in the fulfilment of its organic function: that woman had never really escaped the primordial stigma of labor slavery; that man's place and his work had undergone vast adjustments, but that woman's place and woman's work were supposed to be immutable. Even woman's ignorance was invested with a mawkish glory. A mother who had "buried seven" was subject to no cross-examination as to her fitness for the non-competitive job she had been permitted to fill. She refused to be fooled by the opinion called history. She began by refusing to accept "human nature" as final. She accepts nothing as final, and is chary of "laws." She objected to "piling the dead years on the quivering brain of the child." She dared to insist that children, also, are persons. Her "Concerning Children" was a disturbing and epoch-marking plea. She dared to want "woman's work" professionalized, to wish to emancipate the mother who had need to earn wages. Her advocacy of the expert, specialist care of babies was greeted by cries of horror and pictures of her as one who would tear the child from its mother's breast. It had been bad enough to cast doubt upon the invariable mother capacity of a woman who had happened to bear a child; it was going too far to suggest that any outsiders could help her. Of course day nurseries came in due time; professionalized house service began to happen in due time; real prophecies of some sort of labor justice for women came along with suffrage and other statutory changes.

There have been so many fulfilments of demands made by our women pioneers that reactionary minds often assume that their work is done, and in this respect women are sinners quite equally with men. The grotesque delusion that women have really won an equality because they may go out to work, may hold judgeships and sit in legislatures, meets its startling contradictions. Mrs. Gilman concedes the appearance of vast change since the days when she worked with Jane Addams at Hull House or with the courageous suffrage leaders for a great cause. She still sees women as subsisting in a man-managed and over-sexed world.

She has been skilful in giving a biologist's interpretation of sex. In her new book, "His Religion and Hers," there is a ripe and relentless analysis of the larger sex question as revealed in sex interest. It recalls her picture of woman as the survival of the original sex and of man as the enterprising afterthought, which first elicited for her the special notice of European thinkers. Here again she takes up sex conflict as growing out of the failure to use the human rather than the sex equation. She sees man as primordially a fighter and consumer, if not a destroyer; woman as from the beginning the producer and conserver. She sees man's religion as based upon a postponed heaven; woman's religion as expressing a desire for a heaven here and now. She sees heaven not as a place, but as a race condition. She believes that when women have a greater degree of control of the world they will insist on a greater degree of practical consideration for the needs of immediate living; that the earth will be less a vale of tears when it is regarded less as preparation and more as opportunity. She can say "man-made," here as elsewhere, without giving the phrase a sharp flavor. No champion of the woman side has ever been freer from controversial acidity. No sociologist of either sex (she marks as of a true third sex the women who are childless because they hate children) has written of sex with greater detachment, and detachment in sex controversy is a triumph of ideality (and humor) over instinct. To a man she must always look like a fair fighter. A man may wince in watching her cheery excursions to the matriarchate; he may, indeed, especially when he is reading "Herland" (peopled wholly by women who have only girl children), feel that he has just escaped being negligible. He tritely admits that males have managed the world. He might weakly steal her logic and set up that they have managed it badly not because they were male, but because they were human. It would be a poor bit of shuffling, as poor as admitting that women could scarcely make a worse muddle of things.

Mrs. Gilman's vision of woman, of her rightful place in the world, of her supreme responsibility for race progress, however it may be debated, has strongly influenced the thought and the practices of her time. She was first to see many truths that have won acceptance. She still faces the horizon. As a true radical, she is impregnable to the influence of fashions. Hystericalisms leave her secure in her tower of vantage, without irritation and without concession, serenely intent, unshakably insistent that all arts, all religions, shall bend to the religion of a race ascent to a perfected peace.

I have avoided calling her a "feminist" not merely because the word is foolish, but because her emphasis of woman has been the stressing of an outstanding imperative in a scheme as wide as life, rather than either a class complaint or a specialist infatuation. It might be excusable to call her the prophet of woman, a smiling Isaiah, too good a scientist to be quite a poet, too much a poet to meet the ultimate mechanics of a system; withal one to whom the women of the world will owe a special debt, and to whom all well-wishers of humanity will owe the acknowledgments due a brave, utterly honest, and ever stimulating champion of a larger humanism.

Charlotte Perkins Gilman

Amy Wellington

Mrs. Gilman is "dangerous," said the conservative. Mrs. Gilman is "erratic," said the consecrated radical. Mrs. Gilman is "queer," said the man or woman in the street. America has in Mrs. Gilman a genuine creative thinker, said the European student of her work, and the Americans do not appear to know it! One more expression of opinion. "The various Utopias have fallen wide of the mark," wrote the author of "Pure Sociology," Lester F. Ward. "The difficulty . . . has always been a much too narrow vision, especially the lack of a cosmological perspective. The only person who, to my knowledge, has clearly brought out this cosmological perspective, not merely in things human, but in the vast reaches of organic evolution, is a woman." Professor Ward was writing in 1906, and the woman he so distinguished was Charlotte Perkins Gilman.

.   .   .

Charlotte Perkins saw more clearly, with more imaginative insight, than any other New England girl of her day, the crippled lives of housewives and mothers, their narrow deadening circumstances; above all, their pitiful economic dependence. "In Duty Bound," one of her earliest printed poems, written when she was about twenty-one, expresses eloquently, not only the limitations of her own young life, but of all New England girlhood in that generation.

One counts it, therefore, an historic date when, on New Year's Day, 1887, Charlotte Perkins Stetson, then a young wife and mother, a busy artist and writer, went to the Public Library in Providence, Rhode Island, and, getting a new card, filled it with the names of books on women. The contemplation of women's subordinate and cruel position in life had begun to move her powerfully. Six days later, she started an article on "the distinction of the sexes."

It was not until 1890, however, with the publication of her satirical poem, "Similar Cases," that Charlotte Stetson became widely known as a writer. These original verses, with their singular high power of social satire, were first printed in *The Nationalist*, then copied and quoted wherever English-speaking people had begun to think socially and in terms of organic

Reprinted from *Women Have Told: Studies in the Feminist Tradition* (Boston: Little, Brown, 1930), 115–31.

evolution. Other social satires in verse were quick to follow, equal in wit and forcefulness of phrase—"A Conservative," "Wedded Bliss," bright weapons for the reformer the world over!

Charlotte Stetson could communicate the thrill of horror in both prose and verse, an uncanny art, used infrequently, with a purpose, and finding its most startling expression about this time in "The Yellow Wall Paper," the story of a nerve-sick young mother's hallucination caused by loneliness and inactivity. The figure of a woman creeps from the paper of the room in which the patient is most tenderly confined, and haunts her with a secret and growing power until the day comes when she completely identifies herself with the creeping form and is mad. "The Yellow Wall Paper" has been placed by critics with the weird masterpieces of Hawthorne and Poe; but this is only a lazy classification for a story which stands alone in American fiction. For originality, both as thinker and writer, was Charlotte Stetson's outstanding quality, except, perhaps, the inspirational beauty of her thought and its joyousness, which rose from her profound perception of reality.

In 1891, one finds Charlotte Gilman (still Charlotte Stetson) making this illuminative affirmation in one of her lectures: "I am scientist enough to know that man with all his brain is an orderly product of evolution; I am naturalist enough to know that law rules everywhere, that the subtlest action of the soul is resolvable by long and careful study back to the simplest elements of life; I am poet enough to know that the natural world is divine and the divine world is natural." Her unshakable belief, then as now, (a religion formulated at the age of sixteen) was in that "force which has with slow and constant miracle turned protoplasm into personality." Her dominant desire was "the perception and transmission of applicable truth." Then, as now, she was a philosopher making pure and beautiful poetry out of her vision of the evolutionary processes of life and their continuation into a just world made perfect. Yet in California, in the early 1890's, this brave thinker and dreamer in the sun roused a persistent and even scurrilous hostility.

She had become active in the Nationalist Movement, a political sequel to Edward Bellamy's novel, "Looking Backward." Charlotte Gilman wrote and spoke for the movement, throwing, for a time, her wit and poetry, her whole dynamic power of expression, into its propaganda. Nationalism in California was quickly kindled into a blaze, but as a blaze died down. Only Charlotte Gilman caught and perpetuated its spirit in both prose and verse; and her lectures on different aspects of Nationalism were the beginning of her life-work as a sociological writer and speaker.

When one hears of Charlotte Gilman in the 1890's as a "dangerous" woman, a disrupter of family life and destroyer of the home, one turns to these early lectures which, unlike her later ones, were put on paper, and one reads: "Let me say again, a hundred times if necessary, that I believe in permanent monogamous marriage." Then: "Let me say again, a hundred times if necessary, that housework has nothing to do with love." And so "kitchen-minded" were we that in spite of the former statement, reiterated, probably, many times one hundred times, the later was interpreted as meaning the destruction of marriage. But life has a way of agreeing with Charlotte Gilman, whatever we may choose to think about it. A kitchenless home is rapidly becoming a necessity. Women's energies are thus released for every kind of service, from the preparation of food, scientifically and professionally, to the making of new philosophies; and marriage is not discontinued, the home is not disrupted. Again and again, in those early formative lectures, Charlotte Gilman reached the crux of her argument in "Women and Economics:" "The absolute first condition in the growth of the real woman is economic independence." This was a revolting thought to the majority of both men and women in the 1890's.

Wheresoever Charlotte Gilman went during those years of lonely and courageous thinking, she was a strange dynamic power. Both she and her work were marked "dangerous." She encountered the sinister hostility of a certain section of the American press, led by Ambrose Bierce. Her public speeches were distorted and often made to appear ridiculous. Her personal life was never free from blackguardly intrusion. But fear of misunderstanding, ridicule or insult never held Charlotte Gilman back from saying or doing the thing she once saw clearly ought to be said or done. "Do you expect this to succeed?" she once was asked before a particularly doubtful undertaking. No! came the answer. Yet the thing was done, in the face of almost certain failure, because some one must have the courage to make a beginning, and some day it *would* succeed.

Ever since early childhood, Charlotte Gilman had been writing verses. To her, they were in truth Heine's "divine playthings"—sure joy and recreation in hours of hard won leisure. In 1893, for the first time, she gathered her verses together, and they were printed in a paper-covered edition under the title, "In This Our World." This original contribution to American literature contained scourging civic satire ("the noblest since Lowell," according to W. D. Howells) and poems of living beauty, philosophic and detached. Yet for several years, the book appeared without the imprint of an American publishing house, and the first worthy cloth edition was made in England. Although much of its contents has been reprinted and quoted throughout the English-speaking world—and beyond, American literary criticism, with the fine exception of Mr. Howells, has taken little notice of the book's existence. An English poet, of the stature of John Davidson, was required to appreciate its singular power.

"In This Our World" opens with a poem entitled "Birth," which gives the keynote to Charlotte Gilman's social philosophy. It is as important a contribution to the social and religious thought of the twentieth century as Emily Brontë's "Last Lines" to the religious discovery of the nineteenth. The book also contains two short poems, "She Walketh Veiled and Sleeping" and

"She Who Is to Come," which, brief as they are, will live, crystal clear and shapely, as classics in the poetry of the woman movement. Personal emotions are rare and elusive as in all of Charlotte Gilman's poetry. Never was poet less given to the luxury of self-expression. But the passion for beauty is there, and great warmth of human love and hate—love not of people only, but of cities, world-love, and hatred of social wrong. The inexorable and unescapable logic of her satire is not weakened by a single sneer.

Five years after the publication of "In This Our World" came "Women and Economics." The first setting down on paper of this revolutionary sociological essay required only seventeen days, but back of it were years of study, slowly evolving thought and discussion. So early as 1891, one of its main arguments had been stated in a lecture. "We have pushed sex distinction to such a point that it has reached the very soul," Charlotte Gilman then said, "and we suffer mortally under the consequences without knowing what is the matter. . . . The most important thing for a human creature is to be *human* rather than to be male or female; and yet our course has been to sink our common humanity in our separate sexuality, constantly dividing ourselves where it was most essential to be united." This argument, so familiar to us now and undisputed by many, was first advanced, it is interesting to recall, at a time when a serious writer like Grant Allen was classifying his fellow-women, in a popular magazine, as "a sub-species told off for reproduction only."

It is a most suggestive fact that the three outstanding English books on the woman movement, written by women—Mary Wollstonecraft's "Vindication of the Rights of Women," Olive Schreiner's "Woman and Labor," and Charlotte Gilman's "Women and Economics"—were not sex pleas based narrowly on women's rights, but philosophic arguments securely resting on the wide foundation of human liberties. Charlotte Gilman wrote "Women and Economics" in a fortnight or so of leisure largely because in her agitation for industrial and political betterment she found the economic dependence of women an insuperable obstacle. The subtitle of her epoch-marking book explains its relative intention: "A Study of the Economic Relation Between Men and Women as a Factor in Social Evolution." Shortly after the appearance of "Women and Economics," its author sounded a very significant note of warning against the excessive individualism of women which a misinterpretation of her book might arouse. "The position of economic independence which is opening to women today," she stated, "is not merely an opportunity to 'earn one's living', it is the bringing forward of the last great detachment of primitive individualism into the wide and loving mutualism which is our order." This is a point which she rarely failed to emphasize in both previous and subsequent lectures.

Here was a writer whose one great concern was "the perception and transmission of applicable truth," to whom it was given to see further and suggest more than any other American woman of her day; who, moreover, possessed the art of choosing the inevitable word even in her most hasty propaganda for the "humanization" of women. Yet in New York, as in San Francisco, aside from "the deep interest and conviction" of the discerning few, to quote an older feminist, "she brought down upon herself a storm of criticism, ridicule, caricature and consternation." She and her works continued to be marked "dangerous."

Nothing startles the editor of the usual American magazine (or advertising business) like an original idea—startles and antagonizes, causing him hastily and prudently to reject. He has an almost legal horror of printing anything that is against precedent or liable to form one. Consequently, although Charlotte Gilman is an astonishingly rapid and prolific writer, with an acute sense of timeliness, her articles and verses have appeared in American periodicals only occasionally and under exceptional circumstances. She began, therefore, in 1909, to write, edit and publish a magazine of her own, *The Forerunner*, which was printed monthly for seven courageous years. *The Forerunner* was packed with original ideas from cover to cover. Within its pages, Charlotte Gilman freely expounded her feminist philosophy, in essay, poem, sermon, short story, allegory and review; contributing, also, each year as serials a novel and a sociological study. The last included her most provocative work since "Women and Economics."

"Modern society is no human society," Ibsen had said in his justice to women; "it is merely a masculine society." In "The Man-made World, or Our Androcentric Culture," Charlotte Gilman analyzes our masculine civilization with startling results. "Desire, combat and self-expression" being the "basic masculine characteristics," she postulates, it follows that they dominate a man-made society, shaping industry, politics, religion, and almost every department of human life. The feminine characteristics of "love and service" have found little social expression up to the present. But it is in literature, the chief art of humanity, the art with "the vertical reach" ("Through it we know the past, govern the present, and influence the future.") that Charlotte Gilman finds this predominance of masculine traits most subtly injurious. For men have written and men have read the world's literature. It is only within comparatively recent times that women have done either. And it is this "masculized" record of human life and thought which gives "humanity consciousness."

Twelve years after the appearance of this disturbing and avoided volume, in 1924, Charlotte Gilman continued her analysis of the extent to which masculine concepts have governed and still dominate human life and thought. In "His Religion and Hers," she concentrates on a study of masculine religious creeds and advances a theory of religious development when woman really begins to express herself.

Charlotte Gilman is not the ecstatic discoverer of a "new religion." She is not dogmatic. One of our few creative thinkers, with an extraordinary power of social analysis, her intention is to suggest, to stimulate thought, to present a theory for discussion. How, she now questions, have the man-made religions of the past "modified our conduct in regard to those three laws of living—self-preservation, race-preservation and improvement?" Injuriously again, she finds. For masculine religions are based on the idea of death and a future life. Death was the great crisis in the existence of primitive man, the hunter and fighter. Death was the stimulus to his religious thought. It has so persisted down the ages. Even the teaching of Jesus of Nazareth, the "truth-filled doctrine of 'God in man', of 'Thy kingdom come on earth', of worship in love and service," was soon hurt, Charlotte Gilman maintains, by the "resurgence" of man's "older death-idea." But the great crisis in the life of primitive woman was birth, not death—the child, its nurture and growth. So it remains. The question follows: What, then, might a religion become if based, not on death and a speculative future life, but on birth and our knowledge of human continuity?

Human conduct is examined in its relation to man-made morals and ethics, and the popular philosophies, "so heavily modified by sex," which have contributed to our man-made religions. These philosophies conflict, Charlotte Gilman maintains, with the simplest mother knowledge of the laws of human life and growth. Most hurtful of all is the "perverted sex philosophy of Freud and his followers," this "belated revival of phallic worship," which now distorts our literature. A more normal philosophy of sex will develop, Charlotte Gilman predicts, through "thinking motherhood"—a motherhood free, at last, not only from economic and political, but from sexual subjugation.

In conclusion, it is best to quote Charlotte Gilman's own summing up of her revolutionary hypothesis—the hypothesis not only of this particular book, but of a lifetime of original and fearless thinking:

> "That evolution means growth, not mere combat; that the human race is young and growing and open to measureless improvement; that the female is the race type and her natural impulses are more in accordance with the laws of growth than those of the male; that the race lives immortally on earth, recreated through birth, and so, through love and service, may rise continually; that social development as a conscious process is our chief duty; that God is the Life within us, the Life of the world, to be worshipped in fruition; that religion is the strongest help in modifying our conscious behavior, but that it cannot so help without teaching these truths."

Charlotte Perkins Gilman—As I Knew Her

Harriet Howe

It is with reverence that one who knew her since 1890 opens the volume of her autobiography—reverence for imperishable memories, yet with eagerness to discover how well her memory served her to recall a multitude of events, happenings, and ordeals, great and small, serious or amusing, heroic or commonplace, and to note to which of all those innumerable incidents she had chosen to give the permanency of print. For this would reveal just what values she placed, in perspective, on hundreds of episodes familiar to us both, since time can sometimes turn a crisis into a comedy.

The first time I saw her was at a lecture for a small Nationalist Club in Los Angeles immediately after her name had been flashed across the country by her first success, the publication of "Similar Cases." I was a member of the program committee of that Club, and the committee had decided we must have such a vital person to speak for us. So I wrote to her in Pasadena, and receiving her consent, made the necessary arrangements. I shall never forget those first impressions. A slender woman, seeming on the platform even smaller than she really was, with—Eyes! Such eyes, magnetic, far reaching, deep seeing, nothing could be hid from such eyes, and a Voice, clear, compelling, yet conversational, easily reaching to the farthest end of the hall, entirely devoid of effort.

What a relief, to have, at last, a woman speaker who could be heard beyond the fifth row! But in a moment it was obvious that she was saying things that made people look at each other with varying expressions on their faces. Across the gulf of forty-five years it is impossible to recall exactly what her subject was that day. Whatever it was, it was very much all right, and the audience began to interrupt her with frequent applause, their puzzlement at first no doubt being due to hearing valuable ideas from a woman, a woman who had something to say and knew how to say it devoid of all platitudes. They had never heard such clear statements of plain facts, and they had never heard anything of the kind from any woman. So it took them a while to recover from their astonishment, and then she captured them.

After the lecture, when I had thanked her and paid her all that our meager resources were able, I asked her why women, husky and twice her size, well able to yell loud enough to be heard three blocks, could seldom

Reprinted from *Equal Rights: Independent Feminist Weekly* 5 (September 1936): 211–16.

be heard from a platform beyond the fifth row. "Modesty," was her one word answer, with dancing eyes. Seeing my daze at trying to connect modesty with vocal delivery, she quoted: "A low voice is an excellent thing in woman," and we both laughed.

Hastily I consulted the chairman of the program committee to sound him out to see what were his reactions and if he felt favorably disposed to inviting her to speak for us again. To my delight he was almost as enthusiastic as I was, "Sure," he agreed, "invite her again, soon, she's a mighty smart woman. Ought to be more like her." Wise Mr. Stewart, of blessed memory.

So she spoke for us again and often, always with high appreciation but small pay. So Mr. Stewart and I had a quiet understanding that, after the rent was taken from the collection, we each privately added to the balance intended for Mrs. Stetson (as she then was) whatever we had in our purses. It was, at most, we keenly felt, utterly inadequate as payment, but she was cheerfully unconcerned about it.

The women in the Nationalist Club were treated with the usual condescension with which men treat women in all matters supposed to be over women's heads. The women tired of that treatment, so a woman's club was formed with a small nucleus which grew steadily. The first thing I urged them to do was to study Cushing's "Manual," or Robert's "Rules of Order" and so prepare themselves to speak easily and correctly in public. The next thing was to invite Mrs. Stetson to speak for us, and she accepted with enthusiasm, always glad to help women to realize their individuality. We could pay her still less than the Nationalist Club because housewives have a limited budget, but she fully understood our circumstances.

Then began a series of lectures by Mrs. Stetson which were memorable. Her object was to persuade women to think for themselves instead of accepting what they were told to think. For years I had been harboring heretical thoughts on many subjects, chiefly on the degraded position which women held without seeming to be aware of it, and the inevitable effect this must have on the children born under such conditions and of such unthinking mothers; but I had never dared whisper these views because even a hint of such ideas in those days was regarded as more than eccentric. And now here stood this scintillating soul on a public platform and hurled my very inmost thoughts at a small audience which received it with uneasy, hesitating satisfaction. Uneasy, because it was new to them; hesitating, because they were not awake enough to be quite sure it was "safe," and yet with some sub-conscious satisfaction that they only half recognized. They were hesitant also because women have never yet seen themselves as they really are. If they could see, as a whole, something drastic would happen. Women are taught to see themselves through men's eyes, and so feel that their present status is right, natural, and good. Religion has had much to do with this condition. But religions are all made by men. And since religion is paradoxically a fighting word, no religion can be criticized. But Mrs. Stetson sailed through these choppy seas, skirting the shoals and reefs, without disaster. She was helping these women to begin thinking without startling them. It was magic. It was an EVENT. I sat enthralled. I knew at once that I had met the greatest personality that I had ever seen, or likely ever would see. This was, and still is, true. And she had given me the greatest of all gifts,—the courage of my convictions.

It is needless to say that during all this period I cultivated her acquaintance assiduously and met a cordial response. We told each other our personal histories and found that in certain respects they ran almost parallel and in other ways widely divergent. We wrote letters, we visited at each other's homes. And on one notable occasion I was invited to spend a whole week with her in the little rose-covered cabin on Orange Grove Avenue in Pasadena. . . .

That week's visit with Mrs. Stetson marked an epoch in my life. In the mornings she wrote from 9 to 12, on a writing pad, in her lap, seated in a low easy chair. . . . In the afternoons we sat out on the little porch and talked. She then told me of her strenuous youth, and of her rebuilding her life, of her discovery of God as a working force, available to all, and of the religion that was the result of this discovery. Up to that time I had been an agnostic, and while I could accept her idea of God as Force I could not harness that Force to work out my personal ideas as she could.

The evenings were a revelation. She introduced me to that gem of poetry, a little green book, "Ballads and Rondeaux" collected by Gleason White, and I became fairly intoxicated with the beauty of rhythm and of exquisite words, played upon by masters of language. She could read poetry unlike anyone I have ever heard. She not only brought out all the author's meaning, but gave an added beauty by the magic of her interpretation. Indeed, long later, when she read some of my pastels to some caller, she drew from my own words a beauty I had never known was there. . . .

Later on, much later, she was my guest for another whole week at a summer home at Long Beach, California, Long Beach being then but a small village, and there again I knew the charm of daily, hourly intimacy, filled with wonderful reading and still more wonderful talking. . . .

It was here that she introduced me to another precious book, a mere pamphlet in size, "Three Dreams in a Desert," by Olive Schreiner. And if I had been exulted before, over the poetry, I was now transported; for here was more than beauty, more than glory; here was vital truth, aspiration, reality for the whole human race, in so perfect a setting that no work of human hands could excel it. I cried incredulously, "And this book is in the world, and still the women are asleep? Then what use is it to try further, for this cannot be surpassed." In a reverent tone she answered me, in the very words of the book, "We make a path to the water's edge." And I wept, unashamed, while she walked away a little distance, I think to conceal her own eyes, but I am not sure. From that hour I was dedicated to the work of lifting humanity by awakening women to a knowledge of their power and their responsibility. It was a consecration.

Even now, when recalling that moment, after all this long lapse of years, I think apprehensively—what if I had never known her! What a loss to my life, to my work, to my hopes for humanity. Would Fate have led me, by some other route, to these so necessary guides?

Of all those days, of these two memorable weeks, there is no mention whatever in her autobiography. Probably she had so many such experiences that they overlaid each other in her memory.

Early in our acquaintance her searching gaze had seen that all was not well in my individual life. It did not take long for her to draw forth from me my personal problems which I could not solve. She asked me only a few questions and then announced, "When a situation is hopelessly impossible, walk out of it, but first be sure that it is hopeless." I explained that to walk out was impossible also, and gave valid reasons. Followed more discussion, and in the end she showed me how to solve everything. So that it is perhaps no exaggeration to say that she saved my life. Henceforward, all my time was at her disposal for any service. I could do no less. This prompt efficiency was her prevailing characteristic. Nothing daunted her, nothing could daunt her; there was, in her understanding, only one purpose to live for, humanity; and all obstacles existed only in order to "walk directly through them as if they were not there."

It was probably in March, 1892 (not positively) that certain changes in Mrs. Stetson's personal affairs made it necessary for her to leave Pasadena and go north to Oakland (California) to live. One of the purposes of the change was to assume the care and responsibility of her mother who was ill of cancer. Before she left, I had decided to follow her as soon as I could adjust my own details to do so.

So September of 1892 found me established as paying boarder in the house which she had taken in Webster Street, Oakland, for the purpose of taking boarders to support her dying mother and her own little daughter, then aged 7. This project showed again her dauntless courage, confidence, and faith. There was no other way to support and also to care for her mother and her child without leaving home, except by taking enough boarders to pay the bills. Therefore, according to her religion and her psychology, this had to be done, and consequently, it could and would be done. To support and nurse a dying mother would be enough for almost any woman; to take over a house full of boarders would be more than enough for the majority of women. Yet she cheerfully assumed all three of these responsibilities, because they were necessary. There were no hesitation, no doubts, and no such word as "can't" in her vocabulary.

There were six women of us altogether, not one in robust health, though no one was actually ill, save of course, the mother. The situation looks, at this distance, too formidable to be true, but there it was. Another really incredible item was, that on top of all these features, Mrs. Stetson actually managed to do considerable valuable writing. Nothing could extinguish her creative powers. . . .

In December, Mrs. Stetson became resolved to have a real Christmas tree for the entire household. A tall tree, gayly bedecked, and we were each to buy a tiny gift for all the rest, a "joke gift" not to cost over 15 cents, and we must each write a stanza of verse, appropriate to the gift, and wrap both gift and verse in gay paper, tie with colored ribbon, and fasten a card with names of donors and of recipients respectively on each package. Each recipient must, on receiving her gift, read aloud the verse each contained. For master of ceremonies she invited her father, Frederick Beecher Perkins, then a librarian in San Francisco. To our delight, he accepted and came, and thus I met the father of Mrs. Stetson. He was of portly carriage, serene dignity, kindly, very impressive, of few words, but oozing knowledge unconsciously, at every pore. He did not in the least resemble the photograph of him in the autobiography. Our enthusiasm over this Christmas had led us to invite various neighbors, so when the evening arrived there were seventeen people present. Mr. Perkins officiated beautifully, with a twinkle in his eye, but never once losing dignity. . . .

Long before Christmas, Mrs. Stetson's amazing endurance began to give way under the strain she had imposed on herself, and various kinds of help had been called in to relieve her, until at last a really capable woman was found. But at no time during this heavy ordeal was any member of the household fully aware how seriously it was affecting her, for there was never a word of complaint save that of ordinary fatigue. The autobiography reveals conditions which none of us fully realized. It is difficult to reconcile the gay and gallant courage with which she did all tasks and met all problems, with the serious, even pitiful, conditions described in the book. We all certainly knew that she was grievously overburdened and under great strain, but the dissimulation she must have used to conceal from her sympathetic household her true condition is now proved to have been no less than heroic.

> "Dreamer devout, by vision led
> Beyond our guess or reach—"

It must have been her own idealism, her far vision, that gave her such super-human endurance.

She was at all times a gay companion, although often over-wearied and would change one occupation for another to shift the strain, but always equal, apparently, to any situation. . . .

On March 7, 1893, the delicate, dainty, beautiful, gracious mother passed away. After an interval of readjustments, Mrs. Stetson's creative work, writing and lecturing, was resumed. . . .

One of my greatest delights was accompanying her on her various lecture engagements, sitting in the audience, watching faces and listening to comments favorable and unfavorable, which I repeated to her later to our mutual enjoyment. At the close of each address she always invited questions from the audience. The questions asked her and the skill with which she answered them were always enjoyable. Sometimes the questions were really worth while, serious, and showed an honest effort to learn. These she answered with great care, but frequently they were quite without thought, and it was irresistible not to answer them in a way to expose the questioner's lack. This invariably resulted in roars of laughter from the audience and the discomfiture of the questioner. It was not diplomatic, but perhaps merited. Sometimes she was too caustic and no doubt lost favor with many. Altogether, attending a lecture by Mrs. Stetson was sure to be an unmixed joy. She was a master of repartee.

The various ladies' clubs of the vicinity sought her lectures and she was always glad to comply. It seemed to me that sometimes her talks went completely over their heads, but she did not think so. She usually recited one or more of her poems to emphasize some point. At one lecture she recited a poem called "The Amoeboid Cell." She was, as usual, highly complimented at the conclusion of the talk, and one enthusiastic lady asked permission to call and the request was gladly granted. So a few days later this lady appeared at the house, quite effusive and evidently thrilled at visiting a celebrity. As she was leaving, she asked if she might have a copy of a poem. Mrs. Stetson, quite willing, asked which poem she wanted. "That one you recited so beautifully,—'The Apple-Boy for Sale.' " An interpretation of the "Amoeboid Cell" quite worthy of Mrs. Malaprop. And the subject of that lecture had been "Our Brains and What Ails Them!"

That lecture, though never given twice alike because she spoke extemporaneously, was my first favorite, because it dealt with the most amazing subject in all this amazing world, *viz.*, the spectacle of adult human beings going about their daily work with a measure of success sufficient to keep the wolves from their doors, yet without using one quarter (shall one say?) of their brain power! Some psychologist has said that human beings are not using one-tenth of their brains. If so, certainly "it doth not yet appear what we shall be." What marvels of achievement lie in store for us, we have not yet even the imagination to guess. At present we are each like a person owning a magnificent castle of a thousand rooms full of priceless treasures yet content to live daily in a hall closet under the staircase. "Eye hath not seen, nor ear heard," what is to come, yet she had the Vision. . . .

Along in the year 1893 in the Oakland home she began having "at home" evenings which developed into a sort of salon, but really more of a forum, where various psychological, philosophical, economic, biological, and ethical questions were discussed sometimes heatedly, sometimes descending in rapid cascades of wit to the humorous, in the clash of minds and the flow of words. People of all sorts happened in on these evenings, a local labor leader, a society woman, some friendly newspaper men and women, an poet, a lawyer, and once came a minister who smiled benignly. . . .

One argument that swirled about our heads for several evenings was proposed by Mrs. Stetson, *viz.* "Is a lie ever justifiable?" This was wrangled to a threadbare degree, Mrs. Stetson always firmly taking the negative. At first the discussion was serious, the opposition citing instances of critical illness where it would be fatal to tell the truth; or cases of danger where thousands of lives were at stake and some smooth deception used temporarily would avert a panic. The group labored to break down her opposition. She would not yield an iota; she could not be shaken. Said one newspaper man at last, "See here; if you were invited to lunch with some lady upon whom you wished to make a very favorable impression—for perfectly legitimate reasons" (this phrase in deference to her rigid principles) "and if she served you with a particularly fine looking custard pie, triumphantly announcing that she made it herself, and if you happened to detest custard pie, yet gallantly started to eat your portion anyway, and found there was something definitely wrong about the flavoring, wouldn't you consider it necessary to continue to eat it and to praise its excellence?"

Every one in the room awaited her answer. But she only said, "All that couldn't happen." "Why not?" from all voices at once. "Because I should first praise the fine appearance of the pie, and then confess my personal aversion to custard." "But you would hurt her feelings and fail in courtesy to your hostess." "Not if she valued truth," she stoutly declared.

The middle-aged newspaper man ran his hands through his still luxuriant hair and cried dramatically, "I give up." The battle for truth ended that night, with Mrs. Stetson victorious as usual.

"Will there ever be another war among civilized nations?" was a question that held the attention of the group for two evenings. (In those peaceful gracious nineties we really felt that we had outgrown war.)

Those were fascinating evenings, but there is no mention of them in the autobiography. Mrs. Stetson seemed to thrive and expand on these occasions. The mental duel of strongly contested opinions seemed to be her favorite pastime provided, of course, that she had a foeman worthy of her steel. There was one dear, chubby rosy-faced little lady who invariably fell asleep about 9:30 and peacefully slumbered all through the conflicts until the group began to make their farewells, then suddenly became animated and radiant, declaring with perfect sincerity how greatly she had enjoyed every moment, never knowing that she had been asleep. She was so gentle and innocent that she was lovable.

Just opposite to us on Webster street, Oakland, was the home of Ina Coolbrith, and we visited with her frequently and informally. (Miss Coolbrith was made poet-laureate of California by an act of Legislature in 1915.) Occasionally Mrs. Stetson invited her to dine with us. As Miss Coolbrith and Mrs. Stetson were both masters of repartee, these dinners were so highly enjoyable that we often forgot what we were eating in delight over the shafts of wit that flashed across the dishes. Joaquin Miller was a frequent caller at Miss Coolbrith's, they being close literary friends of long standing, even from early days in California, so she brought him, one evening, to call on Mrs. Stetson, who invited them both to dinner the next week.

They came. Joaquin was already famous for splendid poetry and equally famous for gallantry with the ladies, also for amiable ostentation and affectation in dress. Possibly he fancied himself as a knight of olden time. But to see him, bending low over the hand of a beautiful woman, kissing it ceremoniously, with the well-known bear-skin jauntily festooned across his shoulders, did not produce quite the romantic effect he imagined, on account of the tobacco stained whiskers.

On the occasion of this dinner of the three geniuses, I felt like a molecule and kept silence, that I might better remember the conversation. Apparently Joaquin was in a mood for sympathy, and began to lament his dark and dreary life, with no affection, no understanding, no love, no anything. After some moments of self-pity he paused expectantly, and Mrs. Stetson spoke, gravely, gently, "I am surprised to hear of your great lack, for I had always understood that you were surfeited with devotion."

Miss Coolbrith cleverly bridged the interval and conversation rippled on graciously.

The poems which Mrs. Stetson used to emphasize points in her lectures while not poetry in the true meaning were so pungent and vivid that the increasing requests for copies led her to thinking about having them published in book form. So we decided to have a small edition of her verse printed and bound in paper covers by a local job printer. I felt privileged and honored to be allowed to assist in this plan (as mentioned in the autobiography) and we asked for estimates from various printers of Oakland, finally choosing McCombs & Vaughn to do the work. We did the proofreading and make-up ourselves, with many arguments. These job printers were so unfamiliar with books that the first complete copy sent up for our approval had the fly leaf title page on the left-hand page instead of on the right. My exclamation of shock was profanity. But she saw nothing wrong whatever. In vain I pulled book after book from the book case to prove to her that such a thing was never done. "What of it?" she declared. "It makes no difference whether the title page is on the right side or the left." I was in despair when the bell rang at this psychological moment and I opened the door to a friendly newspaper man. I was never so glad to see him. In great anxiety I called him to view the (to me) tragedy. Instantly he burst into laughter, to her amazement. "What is wrong?" she demanded. "Nothing, nothing at all," said he, between chuckles, "except that if your book goes out like this, it will be ridiculed. Your printer's experience has been limited to hand-bills and circulars evidently." For the first time since I knew her she was subdued. But only for a moment. Then briskly, to me, "Come on; get your hat and we will rush down at once and have this thing put right before any more copies are spoiled." I had the forethought to snatch three books from the table to take with me, as the printer himself might need ocular proof of his mistake. He did need it. He even called in a few witnesses who fortunately agreed that the title page had been set in the wrong place.

It was an eventful day when Mr. McCombs drove up the door with a bundle of the first hundred copies. Eagerly I examined a copy. It was all right. Not perfect, of course, for the printer had not the ideal type for such purpose, but there was nothing really wrong. As soon as Mr. McCombs left, Mrs. Stetson selected six copies of the book, took her pen and wrote a beautiful inscription to me on a fly leaf of one of them and duly presented me with those six copies. I felt honored. I was far happier with that little paper edition of "In This Our World" than I ever was with the various other autographed copies of other important prose books, sent me in later years, that issued from well-known publishers in proper, dignified cloth bindings. Henceforward, whenever I accompanied her to lecture engagements, I could sit by the door and sell copies of the book for her and feel a little bit useful. This edition was soon gone and then another printer, in San Francisco, James Barry, brought out another larger and better edition, of which I was given an autographed copy also. Long later, and after she went East, other editions of "In This Our World," in regular cloth bindings were issued by well-known publishers.

During June or July of 1893 I went to Chicago to the Exposition. On my return to Oakland after six weeks' absence, Mrs. Stetson met me at the station and immediately announced in a completely changed voice, two events; first, the little daughter had been sent East to join her father and his new wife, and second, in her own words, "I have officiated at a funeral." Her voice shocked me, it had such a different quality, a graver, deeper note. Naturally I demanded whose funeral. It was that of the wife of a man we knew, who had met death under peculiarly deplorable circumstances. We had met the woman only once. The husband had begged Mrs. Stetson to officiate on account of the conditions, and her pity made her consent.

Reaching home I found the atmosphere there completely changed. The absence of boarders (now all gone) and the absence of the child partly explained the emptiness, but there was something more—the emptiness in the mother's heart—which made itself felt throughout the silent rooms. By all the facts of reason, wisdom, and common sense it was undisputably best that the child should go, for the period of her school years, where she would have the greatest possible advantages, besides being tenderly and devotedly loved by two people whom the child herself devotedly loved. Yet all this logic, the logic which had always ruled her life, must have been as ashes to the mother-heart. Which is the greater love, the demanding, possessive, clutching love of the average mother, or the self-denying love of this mother which gave and gave and gave, that her child might have the best, better than even her own love could bestow? Yet for this supreme love was she criticized by those who could not fathom its depth.

Nothing but her own drastic training in self-control could have given her strength for this ordeal.

The call which had first brought Mrs. Stetson from Pasadena North to Oakland and San Francisco had come from a gifted woman who was then organizing a band of earnest women writers called the Pacific Coast Women's Press Association. On arrival she had joined this organization and on my arrival she had asked me to join it also. They had been conducting from some time a *Bulletin*, and naturally Mrs. Stetson became a contributor. It was chiefly a report of their work at first, but somewhere in 1893 Mrs. Stetson took entire charge of it, re-naming it The Impress, enlarging it and making it a valuable weekly. This organization, the P.C.W.P.A., was composed of energetic women eager to do something worth while, and it was among their enterprises that the idea of a Woman's Congress to be held in San Francisco took shape. The idea became an enthusiasm. But it was a large enterprise. It entailed a prodigious amount of work without pay. But when did women ever shrink from work without pay? The object of the proposed Congress was to bring together all the women of the entire Pacific Coast who had achieved marked success in any line of recognized work and have each one tell of what she had done. I was "drafted" to be assistant secretary and it took six months of typing letters to arrange the first Congress. The scope grew beyond their furthest expectations. So their ambitions reached eastward and invited our grand leaders, Susan B. Anthony and Anna Howard Shaw. It was my proudest moment to meet these two magnificent women face to face. A large part of the planning of this Congress had been done by Mrs. Stetson, and it was she who arranged the system of programs, which were unlike any other I have ever known. Every moment of time was utilized to get the fullest amount of value. The sessions were crowded and a larger hall had to be found at short notice. The success of the first Congress was so overwhelming that another was held the next year. There was never anything to compare with those Women's Congresses, at least on the Pacific Coast, either before or since, that was done solely by women.

. . . But the Impress failed, not withstanding its real excellence, because of unthinking prejudice. Mrs. Stetson was greatly misunderstood, misjudged, and mistreated in San Francisco. But that is the penalty of greatness everywhere. No great soul can wholly escape it, since some people hate superiority because it hurts their own egos. She carried her standard so bravely always that I never realized how deeply she was hurt by this buzzing of flies until reading her autobiography.

. . . She invited me to join her for a whole summer in Woodstock, New York, at an Arts and Crafts Colony founded by Radcliffe Whitehead, a philanthropic English gentleman who was enthusiastic about the possibilities of the American farm family. It was for me a whole "summer in Arcady." Famous people in all lines of art and craft all busy at their individual works under the benevolence of Mr. Whitehead. It was the most delightful Summer I ever knew. Names known on two continents were walking about in rustic clothing. Mrs. Gilman was busy studying German (she could not be idle) in preparation for going to Germany the next year to attend the Congress of the International Council of Women in 1904. She went, next year, to Berlin and received a greater ovation than she did in London in 1899, on account of a German translation of "Women and Economics" which had a great popularity and a wide sale there.

. . . Whenever her "Women and Economics" had been translated into another language she was delighted. "See, the world is moving. Ideas are growing," she would exclaim with glowing eyes. But there was little or no money from this extended circulation. She must have been robbed of her rights in many instances. But it never troubled her. Her purpose was to do the work, she said, not to seek for pay. Sometimes on these visits she would be full of news about some famous person who had called on her and said— so and so—"which was nonsense," she avowed. Another time, some other famous person would have visited her, "a truly great spirit, a joy and inspiration" would be her comment. Another one might be "splendid, noble, truly worth knowing." A life more full of action, thought, plan, and inspiration that hers can scarcely be imagined.

. . . Someone has said that there are three things a man can pour millions into and never get any returns from—a gold mine, a race horse, and a magazine. No doubt that is true, but I can vouch for the fact that there is nowhere any such satisfaction to be had as in running a magazine, no matter if it never pays a cent in cash. It is an unsurpassed outlet of all energies. Mrs. Gilman's "one-man" magazine, *The Forerunner*, filled most of her time during the years 1909 to 1916, but I know that while its returns were small financially, yet it paid her enormously in satisfaction during the seven years of its existence. Running as serials, there were seven complete novels published in it during that period. With the seven other books on other subjects, this totals fourteen volumes. But she had set herself to write a shelf of twenty-five books.

Work and plans filled each of our lives now so that correspondence dwindled. Once she wrote: "We really don't need to write letters. I know that you are there, and you know that I am here."

I read of her at times in papers and magazines, glad to see her power undiminished by time. Of recent years there were no letters, except a few three years ago, but she did not then tell me that she had cancer. If she had told me, I would have known the result, for when we both watched her slowly dying mother, years ago in Oakland, she whispered to me one day: "If this should come to me, in future years, I will not go through with it. It is needless." I fully agreed with her.

So when the news came to me, one year ago this month, of what she had done,* I understood, yet I was stunned. It is impossible to realize that

---

*Editor's note: Gilman euthanized herself with chloroform when her own cancer had advanced to the point that she feared becoming a burden to her daughter.

so much vigor, purpose, intensity, inspiration, is no longer to be seen or heard.

> "This Power that wrought on us and goes
> Back to the Power again."

Indomitable, valiant, she was never vanquished, she even conquered death. Death did not seize her, an unwilling victim. She went resolutely to meet it, with serene self-determination, as she met all things, gallantly, like a soldier on the field of battle.

The Hour and the Woman

ANNIE L. MUZZEY

A Woman—in so far as she beholdeth
  Her one Beloved's face;
A Mother—with a great heart that enfoldeth
  The children of the Race:

A body free and strong with that high beauty
  That comes of perfect use, is built thereof:
A mind where Reason ruleth over Duty
  And Justice reigns with Love.

A self-poised royal soul, brave, wise and tender,
  No longer blind and dumb;
A Human Being, of an unknown splendor
  Is she who is to come.
        —*Charlotte Perkins Stetson.*

Perhaps to no one more than to the writer herself are these prophetic lines applicable, though she aimed to picture only her ideal woman. To arrive even in a remote degree at the realization of one's ideals is, in itself, a distinction that compels admiration and inspires reverence. The human craving to find in poet and philosopher a living embodiment and exponent of the thought flashed upon one's consciousness, is well satisfied in Charlotte Perkins Stetson, whose word and work are synonymous.

For a number of years the original verse of Mrs. Stetson has been floating about in the newspapers, which, with all their faults, are more or less fair records of the upward thought and movement that show at what point of recognition we are in our march of human progress. It did not matter that the now world-famed poem, "Similar Cases," was first printed in a periodical of limited circulation among a few radical thinkers who dared to aspire to a higher order of life than is possible in the existing state of things. It did not matter that "The Nationalist" itself went down before the adverse winds that have wrecked many other brave crafts setting sail for the port of Freedom.

Reprinted from *Arena* 22 (August 1899): 264–72, with the permission of the publisher.

This poem that first took passage in the ship-of-war,—which by the way, went down only to rise with ten-fold power in other forms—has since made its world voyage on its own strong, bright wings, claiming swift recognition even with the "Neolithic Man," who is sufficiently susceptible to its truth and humor to appreciate the satire on his own "clinching argument," and to give hope that he, too, in the slow evolution of the race, will "have to change his nature."

Other poems of equal force and brilliancy, over the same signature, have, from time to time, appealed to our slumbering sense of truth and justice in respect to common customs which we had accepted without thought; as things to be regretted, perhaps, but still endured. The keen, delicate lance that with one dart pierces to the very center of sores that we have kept covered, has been felt many times through the poems, under various familiar titles, which have come to us in fragmentary ways during the last half dozen years. To find them collected in the first pamphlet editions sent out from San Francisco in 1893 and 1895, was a real delight which lost nothing in flavor to some of her admirers because they could be shared with others for a half dollar. A more expensive, revised, and enlarged edition has been issued within the last year. It is called "In This Our World," and in it Mrs. Stetson's admirers will find new claimants for favor.

But just now our business is with Mrs. Stetson's latest work, "Women and Economics," a philosophic study of the economic relations between men and women—a study which aims, as the author says in her preface—"To show how some of the worst evils under which we suffer, evils long supposed to be inherent and ineradicable in our natures, are but the result of certain arbitrary conditions of our own adoption; and how, by removing those conditions, we may remove the resultant."

The primal evil which Mrs. Stetson points out in our social life, is the economic dependence of woman on the sex-relation. From this false and unnatural position, sanctioned by human law and sustained for centuries as an inviolable custom, has proceeded the multitude of social perversions which the present age has set about eradicating by this, that, and the other so-called reform. While granting that the sexuo-economic relation has had its use in the earlier evolutionary stages of humanity, the time has come, in the view of Mrs. Stetson, for a radical change in the status of woman who can no longer find her sole environment in man.

·　　·　　·

It must not be supposed that Mrs. Stetson's clear and sustained argument militates at any point against marriage in its truer and diviner sense. On the contrary, the whole trend of her reasoning is towards such freedom, such independence, as shall make possible between the individual man and woman a union based on the highest sentiment of love and social use, rather than on the low, common plane of selfish passion and economic dependence. None too scathing is the scorn and shame with which the lower and baser motives of marriage, so-called, are held up to our view by this bold, logical thinker who fearlessly strips the illusion of false sentiment from what passes in the world as love and wedlock. The process may be a little startling, but the flash of light which penetrates and riddles the sham, reveals to us all the more clearly the beauty and perfection of the true.

It is not a fair treatment of "Women and Economics" to give its bald, bare statements, wrested from the chain of argument that harmonizes and shows the logical sequence and consistency of its conclusions. The best that can be done is to ask every reader to lay aside all preconceived views and prejudices on the particular subject in hand, and to bring to the study a calm, impartial spirit of inquiry that does not shrink from admitting truths even when they undermine the long-cherished theories and beliefs of heredity and education.

The conventional thinker will inevitably be shocked by Mrs. Stetson's ungloved handling of a relation which has been from time immemorial regarded as, on the one hand, sacred and beautiful, or, on the other, wanton and unmentionable. But it is sometimes necessary to be shocked before we can be moved to that dispassionate, unbiased consideration which will qualify us to distinguish between the real and the fictitious value of time-honored customs and institutions. A great step is gained by the woman who reads this book, if she catch a glimpse of larger horizons, and begins to realize that any personal love which limits her vision to mere temporal ends and fills her life with doubt, anxiety, anguish, fear, dissatisfaction, and unrest, is unworthy of the name of love, and must either be lifted to a higher plane or be set aside altogether. What Byron calls "the blind necessity of loving" does not compel any human being to merge all individual hopes and aspirations and possibilities in the unsympathetic sphere of another life when from every side comes the appeal of nobler objects for which to live and toil and sacrifice, the demand for the larger good that embraces and benefits all.

In this affirmation there is not a breath of irreverence for love and marriage in the truer sense. Rather is there a declaration of freedom to reject the false and meretricious, and to exalt the real and abiding union of man and woman, founded not on the mere selfish and external relations, but on the deeper spiritual sympathy and purposes that find in each the impelling force of larger inspiration and accomplishment.

No doubt, on this point, the author of "Women and Economics" has yet a further and fuller word to speak. She is too thorough an evolutionist to stop on the threshold of a subject which she has here barely opened to the shocked eyes of the conservative thinker, satisfied with a form that has no in-breathing power of life and substance.

When Mrs. Stetson has waited long enough for the storm of protest against her radical utterance to subside, we shall look for the reconciling and fulfilling word of which this book is but the *avant courier*—a sort of John

Baptist, in wild skins, going before to stir the "Neolithic Mind" which is crying:

This is chimerical! Utopian! absurd!

There is another problem connected with this profound subject which some of us do not find settled by the brilliant argument that makes "Women and Economics" what one of its critics has called "the book of the age," and another has named "a force that must at last be reckoned with."

The question of economic independence for women is one very difficult to dispose of in a day when strong able-bodied men go about the streets begging for work that shall save them from the almshouse or the penitentiary.

It is true that Mrs. Stetson gives us in high light the ideal picture of that kingdom of righteousness in which every member of the human family shall have an equal place and opportunity for the development of individual powers of use and happiness.

This, indeed, is the end toward which all earnest, sincere workers are striving. But not until the industrial world is reorganized and resystematized upon the platform of the golden rule, can woman enter upon her career of absolute economic independence without adding to the accumulated train of evils in the mad struggle, when every hand clutches at both its own and its brother's portion. Possibly, to anticipate the best, the sudden assumption of every woman to economic freedom and industrial rights might precipitate the revolution which is to usher in that reign of "peace and good will" forecast by all the prophets.

Meantime no woman in sexual relations need consider herself a dependent on such relation. The matter is in her own hands. When she makes her own individual law in the sex-union it will be respected. For the rest, if she will follow her highest convictions of right, without too many words about it, she will arrive at a clearer vision of her own place and power. It is certainly not the man's place and power. It is a new insight, a new impulse that we want and not the accumulated force, in the same direction, of women acting as men.

Mrs. Stetson herself, is giving a fine example of free womanhood in following her own high ideals, with a sincerity and directness that wins the admiration of even those who do not agree with her.

As a masculine critic[1] remarks, "No one can easily overpraise the vigor, the clearness, and the acuteness of her writing." And he adds, "She writes, indeed, like a man, and like a very logical and very able man."

This is a mistake. She writes simply like Charlotte Perkins Stetson, a woman who, in the school of experience, has learned her lessons, not automatically from the text-books of custom and tradition, but with spiritual insight and a keen analytical sense that penetrates to the heart of things,—that insists on a reason for existing conditions, as well as upon the logical process of reaching a higher state. If there are errors in her vision she will be swift to acknowledge them when discovered, for truth is what she seeks. Unquestionably she brings to her study of human life the force and vigor and independence derived from the strong ancestral Beecher stock from which she springs; for the powerful influence and direction of heredity cannot be denied even with our higher claims to heredity from God. Added to a noble birthright, a wise training has given to the world a woman of individual character; one free enough and brave enough to speak her honest understanding and judgment on a matter which the world of modern men and women have accepted without thought, or with finger prudishly pressed on lips that murmur secretly over conditions regarded as inevitable and unalterable while nature endures.

To some persons—perhaps to the majority—there appears a certain hardness and rudeness of touch in Mrs. Stetson's treatment of wifehood and motherhood, which is instinctively resented. But a closer study of her attitude toward these relations will reveal an unusual reverence for all that is deepest, purest, and holiest in them. It is only the false sentiment that is riddled and cast out in her keen analyzing process.

．　　　　．　　　　．

So far from undervaluing the vocation of maternity, which has been conceded as the one unquestioned right of womanhood, it must be acknowledged by even her severest critics, that Mrs. Stetson exalts and broadens the office and power of motherhood. But there must be the condition of free, brave womanhood to insure such a race of mothers.

However distant may appear the day when the principles of "Woman and Economics" shall be put to a practical test, we may congratulate ourselves on the impulse to thought which has been given by the book. It is well to consider all possible underlying causes of unhappy conditions which are bewailed, but accepted as the mysterious providences of an inscrutable Law. For the rest each must determine individually in how far he or she may give unqualified support to any radical movement toward a higher social state. It remains to be seen whether women, more than men, will resist this relentless attack on the time-honored institution of marriage as a means of livelihood, vested as it is, with the sacred rites of the holiest of compacts. But all changes from lower to higher levels are pushed by the power of thought, and if the sex relation is lifted, in common perception, from the sensual plane, and made to stand in its true character for something greater than mere worldly considerations, then the author of "Women and Economics," by her bold stroke, will have contributed her share to the upward impetus.

Notes

1. Prof. Harry Thurston Peck, in "The Cosmopolitan."

The Economic Dependence of Women

Vernon Lee

I.

In recommending Mrs. Stetson's "Women and Economics," through the help of this REVIEW, to my Anglo-Saxon readers, I am accomplishing the duty of a convert. I believe that "Women and Economics" ought to open the eyes and, I think, also the hearts, of other readers, because it has opened my own to the real importance of what is known as the Woman Question.

I must begin by confessing that the question which goes by that name had never attracted my attention, or, rather, that I had on every occasion evaded and avoided it. Not in the least, however, on account of any ridicule which may attach to it. There is, thank goodness, a spice of absurdity in every one, and in every thing, we care for in this world; and the dear little old lady in Henry James's "Bostonians," who pathetically exclaims: "And would you condemn us to remain mere lovely baubles?" is the very creature to endear a *cause*; she is the Brother Juniper, so to speak, of the Woman Question.

My vague avoidance of the movement was not even due to the perception of some of the less enjoyable peculiarities of its devotees. For a very small knowledge of mankind, and a very slight degree of historical culture, suffice to teach one that it is not the well-balanced, the lucid, the sympathizingly indulgent or the especially gracious and graceful among human beings who are employed by Providence for the attack and possible destruction of long-organized social evils; nay, that the martyrdom in behalf of any new cause begins, one may say, by the constitution of the individual as an inevitable eccentric, unconscious of the diffidence, the scepticism, the sympathy, the sense of fitness and measure which check, divert, or hamper normal human beings. The early saints, judging by St. Augustine's "Confessions" and the "Legenda Aurea," must have been appalling prigs, indifferent to family affections, higher literature, hygiene, and rational cookery; while the Hebrew Prophets were quite devoid of their historian's—M. Renan's—intelligent indulgence for the administrative passion of, say, Nebuchadnezzar, or the

Reprinted from *North American Review* 175, no. 548 (1 April 1903): 71–90, with the permission of the publisher.

touching pleasure in *toilettes* of Queen Jezebel. And, as to Socialists, who may be considered as the modern representatives of such virtuous tactlessness, we have all seen something of them, and of their well-meant efforts to clash with our habits of dress and manners, and to ruffle our feelings on trifling occasions. So that it does not require the generalizing genius of Dr. Nordau, clapping Tolstoy and Ibsen into his specimen-box of "Degenerates," to tell us that the Woman Question, Femininism, is likely to be taken up by those disconnected and disjointed personalities who are attracted by every other kind of thing in *ism*; whose power consists a little in their very inferiority; and whose abnormal and often morbid "pleasure in saying 'no' " (as Nietzsche puts it) is, after all, alas! alas! so very necessary in this world of quite normally stupid and normally selfish and normally virtuous "pleasure in saying 'yes.' "

All these things I knew, of course, and I do not really think it was any of them which made me thus indifferent, and perhaps even a little hostile, towards that Woman Question. Indeed, when I seek in the depths of my consciousness, I think the real mischief lay in that word "Woman." For, while that movement was, of course, intended to break down the legal, professional, educational, and social barriers which still exist between the sexes, yet, owing to the fact of its necessarily pitting one of these sexes against the other; owing to the inevitable insistence on what *can*, or *cannot*, or *must*, or *must not*, be done, said, or thought by women and not men—women—women—women—always women! there naturally arose a certain feeling, pervading, overpowering, intolerable—like that one suffers from in visiting a harem or a convent—the fact of sex, exclusive, aggressive, immodestly out of place, perpetually obtruded on one's consciousness; while the other fact, the universal, chaste, spiritual fact of *humanness*, of *Homo* as distinguished from mere *Vir* and *Femina*, was lost sight of. And somehow—if one is worth one's salt, if one feels normal kinship not only with the talking and (occasionally) thinking creature around one, but also with animals, plants, earth, skies, waters, and all things past and present; if one be able, as every decent specimen of genus *Homo* must, to join in Francis of Assisi's *"Laudes omnium creaturarum"*—why, then, one feels a little bored, a little outraged, nay, even sickened, by this everlasting question of sex qualifications and sex disqualifications; and (very unjustly, but perhaps therefore very naturally) one gets to shrink from that particular question exactly because it is the *Woman* Question.

Very unjustly. Let me repeat that; and remind the reader that what I am describing is my still unregenerate state.

II.

I was converted by Mrs. Stetson's unpretending little book, because in it the rights and wrongs of *Femina, das Weib*, were not merely opposed to the rights and wrongs of *Vir, der Mann*, but subordinated to those of what is, after all, a bigger item of creation: *Homo, der Mensch*.

There was nothing new in connecting the Woman Question with Economics. If I may judge by myself, the majority of people who know anything of Political Economy must be accustomed to regard such questions as marriage, divorce, prostitution, the legal position of mothers and fathers, and many of the peculiarities of law and custom with respect to the sexes, as hinging upon the facts of wealth production and distribution, tenure of soil, heredity and division of property; upon the whole immense question of the individual's share in the products of nature, of invention and of industry. Indeed, I much suspect that, as in my case, many thinking persons shelve the question of women's abilities and disabilities exactly because it seems to depend almost completely upon the far more important question of the redistribution of wealth; to represent a minor act of social justice and social practicality (bringing much waste energy under cultivation) inevitably involved in the greater act of social justice and social practicality which, through revolution or evolution, must needs take place some day or other.

The originality, the scientific soundness and moral efficacy of "Women and Economics," appear to me to lie in its partially covering this fact; and in its substituting a moral and psychological reason for the rather miraculous mechanicalness which mars every form of the "historical materialism" of the Marxian school. In other words, this book shows that the present condition of women—their state of dependence, tutelage, and semi-idleness; their sequestration from the discipline of competition and social selection, in fact their economic parasitism—is in itself a most important factor in the wrongness of all our economic arrangements.

This main thesis of the book can be summed up as follows:

In consequence of the immense benefit which a prolonged stage of infancy, that is to say of intellectual and moral plasticity, obtained for the human race, all other advantages tended, during the beginnings of civilization, and have tended ever since, to be sacrificed to the rearing of children; and, first and foremost, there has been sacrificed to it that equality in the power of obtaining sustenance, and that consequent mutual independence in such matters, which we find existing between the male and female half of almost every other race of animal. The human race has obtained much of its superiority through the partial replacing of instinct by individual experiment and conscious tradition; but this has meant that the human infant has been born into the world far less mature, far less typically developed, and far less near to independence than the young sheep which can walk within half an hour of its birth, let alone of the chick which can find the right seed almost as soon as it has broken out of the shell. In proportion as the human adult has become rich in original powers, has the human infant required a longer and longer period of tutelage; with the result of requiring of the human mother a longer and longer devotion of her strength, her mind, and, even more, of her time, to the rearing of her offspring. The difference between the female of genus *homo* and the female of other genera has therefore originated not in a longer period of gestation (for that of the horse, for instance, is nearly one-third longer), but in a longer period of education of her offspring. The different position of the female whom we call *Woman* is not due to a difference in psychological, but in sociological functions.

For the longer duration of human infancy, and, even more, the greater helplessness, the greater educability of the human infant, have made it difficult, and in some cases impossible, for the human mother to find food for herself, let alone food for her growing and already weaned child. Hence, the continuance of the human race has called forth a personage who (save among birds, so oddly like human beings in many things) can scarcely be said to exist among animals; the Father—the Father, as distinguished from the mere begetter; the pseudo-father in many stages of primitive life (without ironical references to later stages of existence!), the uncle, the maternal male relative, the head of the tribe, the patriarch: the man who provides food for the child, and food for the woman who rears it; the man who procures, by industry, or violence, a home (cave, cabin, tent, or house) in which the woman remains with the children, while he himself goes forth to hunt, to tend flocks, to make captives, to till the ground, to buy and sell; and in modern times to do those hundred curious things which, producing no tangible product, come under the heading of "making money."

This all seems very simple; but the consequences are complex. The female *homo*, thus left to rear the children (and do what else she can), becomes, what the female of other animals is not, or only (in birds and certain lower creatures) for a very short time, the *dependent* of the male *homo*. The home which she inhabits is *his* home, the food she eats is *his* food, the children she rears become, whether father or only patriarch, *his* children; and, by a natural evolution, she herself, the woman thus dependent upon his activity and thus appropriated to his children's service, becomes part and parcel of the home, of the goods, of the children; becomes appropriated to the nursing, the cooking, the clothing, the keeping in repair; becomes, thus amalgamated with the man's property, a piece of property herself, body and soul, a slave (often originally a captive, stolen or bought), and what every slave naturally is, a chattel. By this process, therefore, we have obtained a primitive human group, differing most essentially from the group composed by the male and female of other genera: the man and the woman, *vir ac femina*, do not stand opposite one another, he a little taller, she a little rounder, like Adam and Eve on the panels of Memling or Kranach; but in a quite asymmetrical position: a big man, as in certain archaic statues, holding in his hand a little woman; a god (if we are poetical, or if we face the advantages of the case) protecting a human creature; or (if we are cynical, and look to the disadvantages) a human being playing with a doll.

.   .   .

IV.

Now the really fine piece of work which Mrs. Stetson has done, has been to demonstrate—to me at least—that, although the exclusion of womankind from the world's active work, and her subordination to man, have been a sociological necessity—the price paid for the lengthened infancy, the increased educability of man, and also for that solid familial organization which alone permitted an accumulation and multiplication of human inventions and traditions; that, although the *regression*, or, at all events, the stagnation of one half of the human race has been inevitable and beneficial in the past, it has ceased to be beneficial, and is ceasing to be inevitable, in the present. A particular automatic arrangement of historical evolution has done its work; like slavery, like servage, like feudalism, like centralization (according to individualists), like competition (according to socialists), it has grown to be an impediment to progress. For the prolonged infancy and youth of genus *homo* can now no longer be endangered; and a large proportion of human education has, since thousands of years, passed from the care of the mother to that of the community as a whole, or of portions—guilds, priesthoods, universities, and so forth—of the community; while, on the other hand, the inventions and traditions have been stored, multiplied, and diffused far beyond the powers of family education. The benefit has long, long ago been obtained beyond all possibility of loss; but the price is still being paid for it.

Now, what is that price? The stagnation or regression, answers M. Durkheim, of the female mind. The removal, answers Mrs. Stetson, enlarging the same thought with a different intention, the removal of womankind from the field of action and reaction called "the universe at large" to the field of action and reaction called "the family circle"; the substitution, as a factor of adaptation and selection, of the preference of the husband or possible husband for the preferences, so to speak, of the whole of creation. In other words, the sequestration of the capacities of one half of the human race, and their enclosure inside the habits and powers of the other half of the human race. Briefly, a condition in which the man plays the part of the animal who moves and feeds freely on the earth's surface; and the woman the part of the parasitic creature who lives inside that animal's tissues. The comparison is exact; but we ought not to push the analogy to the point of considering the parasitism of womankind as the parasitism of a destructive microbe. The mischief lies not in the fact of parasitism, but in the fact that this parasitic life has developed in the parasite one set of faculties and atrophied another; atrophied the faculties which the woman had (or might have had, even if in lesser degree) in common with the man, and developed those which were due to the fact of her being a woman.

We have come to a point where a clear understanding is very necessary.

Even admitting that chastity, devotion to offspring, tenderness, and that peculiar negative quality (called after the domesticated animal) *mansuetude*, let alone certain aesthetic graces which the ancients by no means discovered in womankind, have come to exist in the female as the result of her dependent position, [a theory which is seriously damaged by the coyness in courtship and the maternal passion observable already in animals where the female is not dependent], we must be careful to add this gain to the other advantages, and main advantages, of "feminine stagnation or regression," namely, the prolongation of childhood and the establishment of the family group. And we must not gratuitously argue that these virtues will disappear if the position of women is changed; since, whatever their origin, they have become so far common to both sexes that Christianity and Buddhism have for centuries been taking for granted that chastity, mansuetude, and tenderness are the most essential virtues of mankind at large, the "one thing needful."

But the question arises, What price has been paid for all these advantages?

The first answer which arises in the mind is naturally a direct one: the work which womankind might have accomplished during those hundreds and hundreds of years if she had not had a man to work for her; the work which might have been given by two halves of the human race, instead of being given by one only. But here again we have need for a *distinguo*, though not a casuistic one. The woman did do work throughout that time. Not merely the essential work, direct and indirect, of rearing a new generation and, in a measure, keeping up the acquired standard of civilization; but also the work, less essential indeed to the race, which enabled the man not merely to seek for food away from the home, but also to be as idle as he required (or at least as he liked) while in it. The woman, save among the exceptionally wealthy, has always been a chief domestic servant; and even nowadays she is so, to a greater or lesser extent. The woman, therefore, has worked; but— and here comes the subtle distinction on which the whole economic and sociological part of the subject reposes—she has worked not for the consumption of the world at large, and subject to the world's selection of good or bad, useful or useless, work; but for the consumption of one man and subject to that one man's preferences. The woman has worked without thereby developing those qualities which competition has developed among male workers. She has not become as efficient a human being as her brothers; whatever her individual inherited aptitudes (and, as Mrs. Stetson aptly reminds us, women are, after all, the children of men as well as of women, and must, therefore, inherit some of their father's natural powers), she has not been allowed to develop them in the struggle for life; but has been condemned, on the contrary, to atrophy them in forms of labor which can require only the most common gifts, since they are required equally of every woman in every family.

But this is by no means the whole of the price which the human race has had to pay for the needful "division of labor" between its two halves. Negatively, the position of women has prevented their developing certain of their possibilities; positively, it has forced them to develop certain other of their possibilities; it has atrophied the merely human faculties, which they possess rudimentarily in common with men; it has, on the other hand, hypertrophied the peculiarity which distinguished them from man; hypertrophied their sex.

There is one particular sentence in "Women and Economics" which converted me to the cause of female emancipation: "Women are over-sexed."

V.

Women over-sexed! *Over-sexed!* There seems something odious and almost intolerable in that word. In the fact also—but odious and intolerable in a manner more subtle and more serious than mere scandalized modesty can ever understand. Let me try to explain the extreme importance of Mrs. Stetson's thought. *Over-sexed* does not mean over-much addicted to sexual indulgence; very far from it, for that is the case not with women, but with men, of whom we do not say that they are *over-sexed*. What we mean by *over-sexed* is that, while men are a great many things besides being males— soldiers and sailors, tinkers and tailors, and all the rest of the nursery rhyme—women are, first and foremost, *females*, and then again females, and then—still more females. It is a case for paraphrasing Danton; only that, alas! there is a considerable difference between *"de l'audace, de l'audace et encore de l'audace"* and *"de la femme, de la femme, et encore de la femme,"* which sums up the outspoken views of the Latin races, and the practice, alas! of the less outspoken but more practical Teutonic ones. And here we touch the full mischief. That women are *over-sexed* means that, instead of depending upon their intelligence, their strength, endurance, and honesty, they depend mainly upon their sex; that they appeal to men, dominate men through the fact of their sex; that (if the foregoing seems an exaggeration) they are economically supported by men because they are wanted as wives and mothers of children—that is to say, wanted for their sex. And it means, therefore, by a fearful irony, that the half of humanity which is constitutionally (and by the bare facts of motherhood) more chaste, has unconsciously and inevitably acquired its power, secured its livelihood, by making the other half of humanity less chaste, by appealing through every means, material, aesthetic and imaginative, sensual or sentimental, to those already excessive impulses and thoughts of sex. The woman has appealed to the man, not as other men appeal to him, as a comrade, a competitor, a fellow-citizen, or an open enemy of different nationality, creed, or class; but as a possible wife, as a female. This has been a cause of weakness and degradation to the man; a "fall," like that of Adam; and, in those countries where literature is thoroughly outspoken, man, like Adam, has thrown the blame on Eve, as the instrument of the Devil.

VI.

. . .

Mrs. Stetson has mentioned this aspect of the question, and I have followed her example, because it is certainly an important one. But Mrs. Stetson has taught me to see that there is another aspect, more important by far. The fostering of vices, especially of vices so harmful to the race as those presided over by *La Femme*, is a very grave mischief; but vices, from their very nature, are more or less exceptional and tend to die out. And a far more serious evil consists in the wasting and perverting of virtues, the systematic misapplication of healthy feelings and energies. Now, the chief point made by the author of "Women and Economics," the point which, as it converted myself, ought to convert many others from indifference to the Woman Question, is concerned with the misapplication and waste of the productive energies and generous impulses of men, thanks to the necessity of providing not only for themselves and their offspring, but for a woman who has been brought up not as a citizen, but as a parasite, not as a comrade, but as a servant, or—well, consider the word even in its most sentimental and honorable sense—as a lover. The economic dependence of women (however inevitable and useful in the past) has not merely limited the amount of productive bodily and mental work at the disposal of the community, but it has very seriously increased the mal-distribution of that work and of its products by creating, within the community, a system of units of virtuous egoism, a network of virtuous rapacity which has made the supposed organic social whole a mere gigantic delusion. Virtuous egoism, and virtuous rapacity; for *it is* virtuous on the man's part, husband or intending husband, to sacrifice himself for another human being, and the consciousness of the virtue enables the sacrifice to be extended, with a clear conscience, to the interests of the community at large. A man has to be first a good father and husband, and then, with such honesty as remains over, a good citizen.

"Such honesty as remains over! Sacrifice of the community to the wife and children!" you exclaim. "Why, this accusation of yours against the modern man and the modern woman is far more really dreadful than any of that French rubbish about *La Femme* and her victims!" Exactly so; and a great deal more important, because it is a great deal truer and more sweeping. The very fact of its truth not being recognized merely goes to prove how extraordinarily our moral sense in economic matters has been perverted (or has failed to grow), owing to the fact of the man having to supply the material wants and satisfy the caprices not only of himself, but of that "better"—or worse—self who sees the world only through his eyes, and damages the world only through his hands. It is not a question of cheating or robbing; I am not a collectorist. I believe no more in the rights of labor than in the rights of property, and I have no reason for supposing that the author of "Women and Economics" does so either. Our moral obtuseness is, on the contrary, proved irrefutably by our always connecting the idea of dishonesty with such narrow and crass categories as cheating and robbery— cheating and robbery which can be practised only against individuals, and on very rare occasions; besides being severely, perhaps almost too severely, punished. What cannot be punished (but is on the contrary praised and admired, when successful) is exactly the chronic and all-pervading preference of the interest of the individual as against the interest of the community, the debasing of the standard of work and the quality of products. Now, this kind of dishonesty triumphs not merely in commerce and industry (perhaps almost least there, where most visible), but in all the professions which are exercised, and in many cases (bureaucracies of all kinds, civil and ecclesiastic, and who shall say how large a portion of our supposed necessary military system?) are kept in useless existence merely because men have to make a living. *"Je n'en vois pas la nécessité"*: the minister might make that simple answer to the unmarried parasite, office-seeker, or journalist, or whatever he was; but no minister, however cynical, would dare to question the married man's right—nay, his duty—to support his wife and family, or, more strictly, his wife.

I repeat: *more strictly his wife*; because it is, in reality, not the unborn children, or even the born children, who decide the "standard of living" but the wife, extremely on the spot, and already accustomed both to a certain degree of expenditure as a reality, and, what is quite as important, to a certain expenditure as an ideal in the future. Even the poorest paupers contrive to rear offspring; and, by a melancholy irony, the greater part of the world's most necessary work happens to be done by people "whose dear papa was poor," as Stevenson makes the good little boy express it. No, no, it is not the children who ask for carriage horses, toilettes, and footmen, or (in more sordid spheres) for the Ibsenian "home for happy people," with its one overworked drudge and its preoccupation about the husband's dinner. It is not even the children who clamor for nurse-maids and governesses and expensive schools: it is the wife.

VII.

"Tout cela a été fait pour casser," remarks Nana, after one of her bouts of destruction. Reputable women do not, usually, while away a dull morning like Zola's ingenuous courtesan; they do not set to tearing and smashing. But the only difference, very often, is that while the light lady destroyed in a couple of hours the product of many men's and many months' labor, the

virtuous woman of the well-to-do classes, and of the classes (more numerous and important) aspiring or pretending to such well-to-do-ness, alters, discards, throws away more gradually those objects which are no longer consonant with "what one *has* to have," and whose continued use would therefore suggest the horrid thought that the family was not really well-off; in eminently business countries the thought that the husband's *business* was not thriving. "It is good for trade," remark the more responsible among these ladies, unconsciously echoing a reflexion of that same Nana. It is a good for trade: and so is a town being burnt down, or swallowed up by an earthquake, or washed away by a tidal wave. It makes room for more objects (dresses, crockery, furniture, houses, or human beings); but, meanwhile, you have wasted those that were already there, and all the labor and capital they have cost to produce.

But the spirit of wastefulness is by no means the worst correlative among women of the spirit of rapacity, of "getting wealth, not making it," as Mrs. Stetson luminously describes it, which the economic dependence of the wife develops (as a virtue, too!) in the husband. An enormous amount of the hardness in bargaining, the readiness to take advantage, the willingness to use debasing methods (such as our modern hypnotizing advertisement system), the wholesale acceptance of intellectual and moral, if not material, adulteration of work and its products—correspond in the husband to what is honored as thrift, as *good management*, in the wife. It is more than probable that the time wasted, the bad covetousness excited, the futile ingenuity exercised by the women who crowd round the windows of our great shops and attend their odious "sales," are really the result of a perverted possibility of virtue.

For the man's virtue is to *make money*; the woman's virtue is to *make money go a long way*. And, between the two virtues, we are continually told that a business house cannot give better wages and shorter hours because it would be "crowded out of the market"; and we are told also, by more solemn moralists still, that nations cannot do without war, lest they lose their "commercial outlets," or fail to secure those they have not got.

Who can object? All these people are good husbands and good wives; the home is the pivot of our morality. And the most disheartening thing is, that all this is true.

VIII.

How do you propose to remedy it? By what arrangements do you expect to make the wife the economic equal of her husband, the joint citizen of the community?

I propose nothing, because I do not know. All I feel sure of is, that if people only want a change sufficiently strongly and persistently, that change will work out its means in one way or another. Which way? is a question often unanswerable, because the practical detail depends upon other practical details which the continuance of the present state of things is hiding from us, or even forbidding. And because, moreover, we are surrounded on all sides by resources which become available only in connection with other resources, and only under the synthetic power of desire. The lids of boiling kettles went on rising all through Antiquity and the Middle Ages; but the notion of using that expansive movement of steam could not occur until people had already got roads and mariner's compasses and mechanical mills, and until people were beginning to find stage-coaches and sailing vessels and wind-mills and water-mills a little unsatisfactory. The integration of women as *direct* economic, and therefore *direct* moral and civic, factors in the community, is not a more difficult question than the question of the integration of the laboring classes into the real life of nations; and yet the "social question" will find, some day, its unexpected solution; and the "Woman Question" will, very likely, have to be settled beforehand.

Have to be settled? I would have said "settle itself," for that is more like my meaning, if it were not that I wish to insist that questions do not *settle themselves* satisfactorily, unless we wish and help them to do so. It is for the sake of such increase of wish for a change in the economic position of women, or, at all events, a diminution of the present very strong prejudice against such a change, that the discussion of ways and means appears, to me at least, principally useful. I do not agree with Mrs. Stetson's suggestion of our eventually living in a kind of hotel, or at least dining permanently in a restaurant; but the discussion of such a plan, odious as it appears to me, is infinitely useful in accustoming us to the thought that some arrangement will require to be devised for delivering women from the necessities of housekeeping. I see some similar usefulness even in discussions about the future of women (including the possibility of that famous "third sex" which haunts the imagination of the Latin believers in *La Femme*), such as I. H. Rosny has introduced (I scarcely know whether as a joke or not) into his *"Chemin d'Amour."*

Besides this fact, the one thing certain about the future of women is, surely, that they ought to be given a chance, by the removal of legal and professional disabilities, if not of becoming different from what they have been, at all events of showing what they really are. For one of the paradoxes of this most paradoxical question is precisely that, with all our literature about *La Femme*, and all our violent discussions, economical, physiological, psychological, sociological (each deciding according to some hypothesis of his immature science), as to what women must or must not be allowed to do, and what women must and must not succeed or fail in, we do not really know what women *are*. Women, so to speak, as a natural product, as distinguished from women as a creation of men; for women, hitherto, have been as much a creation of men as the grafted fruit tree, the milch cow, or the gelding who spends six hours in pulling a carriage, and the rest of the twenty-four standing in a stable.

One of the very great uses of Mrs. Stetson's most useful book is to accustom those who *can* think, to think in terms of change, of adaptation, of evolution; to free us from the superstition that the present is the type of the eternal, and that our preferences of to-day are what decide the fate of the universe. *Woman*—even letting alone *La Femme*—is, so to speak, the last scientific survival of the pre-Darwinian belief in the invariability of types; *Woman*, I may add, is almost a relic of the philosophy of the Middle Ages; for has not *woman* an *essence*, something quite apart from herself, an essence like the *"virtus dormitiva"* of opium (not always so tranquillizing), an essential quality of being—well, being a woman?

One word more. There is a notion, founded in the main on the facts of a period of struggle, segregation of interests, and general uncomfortable transition, that if women attain legal and economic independence, if they get to live, bodily and intellectually and socially, a life more similar, I might say more symmetrical, to that of men, they will necessarily become—let us put it plainly, less attractive to possible husbands. Of course they will; if they have changed, they will no longer realize the ideal of gracefulness, beauty, and lovableness of the particular men who like them just as they are; but then those particular men will themselves probably no longer exist. Moreover, there is, undoubtedly, a certain correlation between the qualities of the two sexes, due to the fact, which we are all of us (not only M. Durkheim with his "division of labor") inclined to forget, namely, that the woman is, after all, not merely the *wife* (since that noble word must be put to such mean use) of the man, but also his daughter, his sister, and his companion; and that, as such, he requires her to be not *unlike*, but *like* himself. There is, if we watch for it, a family resemblance, after all, between the men and women of the same country. I was very much struck, while at Tangier, by the fact that the husbands of those veiled and painted Moorish women were themselves so oddly like women in men's clothes, those languid Moors lolling in their shops, with black beards which looked almost as if they had been gummed on to their delicate white faces: the ultra-feminine woman belonged, quite naturally, to the effeminate man. In a similar way, the "masculine" Englishwoman, fox-hunting, Alpine-climbing, boating, is the natural companion of the out-of-door, athletic, sporting, colonizing Englishman; she has been taught by her big brothers during their holidays *"not to be a muff"*; she has learned to be ashamed of the things "the boys" would be ashamed of. And, living as I do equally among Latins and Anglo-Saxons, I have got to guess that, if the Latins see a "third sex" in a portion of Anglo-Saxon womankind, the Anglo-Saxons, on the other hand, have a vague but strong feeling that a corresponding category might be found among the Latin males morally emasculated by belief in *La Femme*. For if *manly* be an adjective denoting certain virtues, and *effeminate* an adjective denoting certain weaknesses, you may be sure that the same civilization, the same habits and preferences, will produce more of the one than of the other in all the members of a race, just because they do belong to the same race.

And let me remind Mrs. Stetson's readers that it is just the most aesthetic, but also the most athletic, people of the past which has left us those statues of gods and goddesses in the presence of whose marvellous vigor and loveliness we are often in doubt whether to give the name of Apollo, or that of Athena.

Mrs. Gilman's Idea of Home

Olivia H. Dunbar

"Shall the home be our world . . . or the world our home?" is the brief preface to this discussion of the one subject in the world that has been immemorially taken for granted. But happily, Mrs. Gilman has the habit of being a pioneer; and she is abundantly equal to the opportunity provided by her unprecedented theme. Although written in "no iconoclastic frenzy," the book does succeed in shattering practically all the domestic furniture that is now in use, and it arrives at conclusions which, if at all generally accepted, would change the popular frame of mind and habit of life to an interesting degree. Indeed, Mrs. Gilman has not intended her book so much as a treatise for the scholar as a surgical operation on the popular mind. Frankly, it is a book that most well-meaning folk will resent, and this in spite of the fact that it cannot candidly be called an "attack on the home."

What Mrs. Gilman has urged is not a universal migration from the home to the boarding-house, or even to the woods, but, seriously, a substitution, in everyday life, of the humanitarian for the more selfish domestic ideal, this chiefly to be accomplished by an alteration of women's social position and by an extension of their field of energy; and by a general relentless house-cleaning which shall eliminate "primitive industries" from the home. Those who regard the home, and particularly the kitchen end of it, as sacred will doubtless object to being told that "home cooking" is merely self-indulgence and that it is arrogance for the average mother, on the theory that mother-love connotes trained efficiency, to act as sole nurse and teacher to her own young children. These two points constitute the most radical features of the book, from the housewife's point of view. The outline of a broader and more rational life for "home-bound women," for which Mrs. Gilman made her first plea in "Women and Economics," may have a less discordant sound to the conservative ear.

From a diverting variety of points of view, Mrs. Gilman has, in characteristically uncompromising fashion, examined the present-day home and in each case found it wanting. Not only, she argues, does it cripple women by giving them life sentences at outgrown forms of hard labor, but it fails adequately to provide for that most important member of the household, the

Reprinted from *The Critic* 43 (December 1903): 568–70.

child, and is furthermore wasteful and extravagant in its economy, and neither clean, hygienic, nor beautiful. The severest and most significant criticism of domestic life is, however, contained in the chapter on "Domestic Ethics," which maintains that almost all the accepted modern virtues originated outside the home and practically have no place there. If indeed it be the case that "in half the race we ask nothing but the domestic virtues" and that "our moral growth is to-day limited most seriously by the persistent maintenance in half the world of a primitive standard of domestic ethics," then one chapter in one book is small space in which to consider it.

Many are the familiar problems upon which this book piquantly touches, and in each case it invites quotation. There is the question, for instance, of the "girl at home."

"What real place has a grown woman of twenty-five and upwards in any one else's home?" "Children are very violently taught that they owe all to their parents and the parents are not slow in foreclosing the mortgage. But the home is not a debtor's prison—to girls any more than to boys." "The girls of to-day, in any grade of society, are pushing out to do things, instead of being content merely to eat things, wear things, and dust things."

In connection with the "servant problem," we are reminded of the absurdity of that "Blessed Damosel of our domestic dreams,—a strong, capable, ingenious woman, not hampered by any personal ties or affections; not choosing to marry; preferring to work in a kitchen to working in a shop; and so impressed by the august virtues and supreme importance of our family that she becomes 'attached' to it for life."

The comment on "housework" is that the effort temporarily to remove the accumulation of waste matter in the home "is one of the main lines of domestic industry; the effort to produce it is the other."

"The fatal inertia of home industries lies in their maternal basis. The work is only done for the family,—the family is satisfied. What remains?"

"We are founding chairs of Household Science, we are writing books on domestic economics; we are striving mightily to elevate the standard of home industry,—and we omit to notice that it is just because it is home industry that all this trouble is necessary."

The point most strongly suggested by such a book as this is the extreme universal disinclination to look plain, everyday facts in the face; otherwise it would have been written long ago. Apart from the conclusions which it draws, it presents facts which it requires no special advantages of study or training to perceive; it has not a paragraph of academic language; it is clouded by no murky adumbrations of theory. It is simply the result of a decidedly uncommon ability to look squarely at familiar facts,—a view that is undoubtedly of rare psychologic value, whether you agree with it or not. It happens to be expressed, however, in a vein of genial satire, an element which, though it makes her book so readable, may not contribute inevitably to the consummation of Mrs. Gilman's ends. If she were roundabout and prosy, one might sleepily persuade oneself that the grievous parting with the cooking-stove and the domestic doughnut might be an act of virtuous self-denial. But to suffer easy, good-tempered ridicule of those awesome institutions is a different sort of test.

But with all its air of high spirits, the book is not flippant; rather, profoundly serious. It commends itself refreshingly for its high degree of honesty and vital force, and is as innocent of mere futile faultfinding as it is of literary self-consciousness. It should be possible, even though not agreeing with its point of view, to concede it not only a witty and original, but a conspicuously notable book.

The Ideal Home

ANONYMOUS

Mrs. Gilman arraigns the home as it is, with an irresistible array of facts
and with not a little pungent wit. She contrasts the home of universal
idealization with the home of reality, and, after the manner of Thackeray as
regards gentlemen, practically invites us to take the fingers of one hand and
count the happy homes we have known. We tried the experiment and found
no need of the other hand! We remember, too, that, whereas the gentleman
or the cad speedily discovers himself, the unhappy home is kept out of the
drawing room, and hides successfully from even its intimates. To how many
men is the home merely a "growlery"? To how many of both sexes is it "a
Heaven-appointed place to be disagreeable in"? Mrs. Gilman's logic and the
logic of fact are at one in pointing out the utter divergence of the dream-
home from the actual home. Nor is she less clear-sighted when she discerns
the terrible economic waste of our domestic methods—a waste not only of
money, but of energy, vitality, all the best attributes of manhood and
womanhood. She shows, too, the imperfect ethics of family life, the injury
resulting therefrom to man and woman, most of all to the child. She is
careful to emphasize again and again that she is not making war upon the
home in its essential qualities, but upon the home of distortion and excrescence that we know at present. Her fine prefatory poem, "Two Callings,"
and her introductory chapter plainly define her purpose to be constructive
and not destructive.

All save the two closing chapters of the book are devoted, however, to
the faults and failings of the home *in esse*. We read with delight the keen,
incisive analysis of "things as they are": we acknowledge the justice of the
knife-edged criticism, but, most of all, we want an answer to the ever-
recurring question, "What shall we do about it?" And here, we think, our
author fails us. If we understand her aright, in her ideal home there is no
kitchen and no dining room. The domesticities are adjusted somewhat after
the fashion of "Looking Backward." So far, so good. Certainly this is "a
consummation devoutly to be wished." Then in the morning each family
separates; the man goes, as always, to his business; the woman has a business
to which she also departs as regularly as the man; the older children go to

Reprinted from *The New York Times*, 26 December 1903, K3, with the permission of the publisher.

their schools, the babies are cared for in a sort of crèche by trained nurses and kindergartners. The home is closed for the day, receiving its inmates in the late afternoon, simply to rest and enjoy life together. Somehow, in spite of all Mrs. Gilman's eloquence and ingenuity of argument, this is not a very appealing picture. It seems open, too, to many objections, of which it is sufficient to note that the very conditions of a woman's being and the child's physical dependence upon her during the first year of its life would prevent her becoming a co-factor with man in the world of affairs. Also, with competition already hot, what would become of the world were this competition doubled?

Truth is the great antiseptic. Much wholesome truth does Mrs. Gilman's book contain. To that extent it is helpful and suggestive, but we think the author shares the illusion common to the thought of the time that perfecting the machinery of life will bring about millennial conditions. The machinery of the home may undoubtedly be greatly bettered, but we are confident that the ideal home is to be achieved from within, not from without. The great need of change is in characters, not in conditions. There is something cold and shivery about Mrs. Gilman's vision of a home. We hardly think that just this is to be the family life of the future.

Nonetheless should her book be read by all homemakers, for it is full of wise criticism and is refreshingly free from cant of any kind.

[Review of *Concerning Children*]

ANONYMOUS

Mrs. Gilman loves children, and observes them with keen and affectionate interest, but much that she writes about them and their educational requirements is strangely deficient in judgment and common sense. She works herself into the hysterical condition which seems to be becoming the normal state of many writers on education. Much of her advice and several of her observations are valuable, but they are lost amidst so much really nonsensical writing that the work is often ridiculous rather than useful. Mrs. Gilman tells us, and quite rightly, that "we have travelled far and deep in scientific study, climbed high in art, and grown through grand religions. Our one great need—a need that grows daily greater in the vivid light of these swift-moving years—is for a better kind of people."

From this it follows that all possible improvement must be made in the individual before parentage, that is, speaking generally, in the "precious ten" years between fifteen and twenty-five. But what is meant by the statement that "a girl of fifteen is quite old enough to see the splendid possibilities that lie before her, both in her individual service to society and the almost limitless power of motherhood," we fail to recognize; nor do we think it would be altogether prudent to inculcate this kind of knowledge into the minds of children of fifteen; and it could hardly be expedient to concentrate young girls' thoughts on the coming responsibility of marriage and burden of maternity. We do not know whether Mrs. Gilman's work is intended for children's perusal or not, but at any rate the chapters devoted to 'Meditations on the Nursemaid,' to the relations between children and servants, and to the discussion of 'Mothers: Natural and unnatural,' would hardly furnish profitable reading for girls in their teens. No doubt many mothers might read, with considerable profit to their families, Mrs. Gilman's classification of themselves. The social conditions described are transatlantic, and the ordinary English reader is not competent to gauge the accuracy of the descriptions; but we are inclined to think that most of the mothers for whom Mrs. Gilman writes will resent being classed with domestic servants. At any rate the "unnatural" mother, fair, vigorous, and beautiful, who has added a honed intellect to a warm heart, entirely wins

Reprinted from *The Athenæum*, no. 3838, 18 May 1901, 628, with the permission of the publisher.

our admiration and sympathy, "and when we have enough of them the rarest sound on earth will be that now so pitifully common—the crying of a little child." In this and much else in the book we cordially agree with Mrs. Gilman; but the book as a whole is likely to do as much harm as good.

Mrs. Gilman's Volume on Children

Anonymous

As one closes Mrs. Gilman's volume of original and illuminating thoughts "Concerning Children," one's first impulse is to exclaim: Wanted—A philanthropist to put it into the hands of all English-speaking parents to whom have been vouchsafed hearing ears and responsive hearts. True, the first effect would be to raise the price of sackcloth and create a "run" upon all banks of ashes; but, once supplied with these useful articles, parents would find the humiliation good for their own souls, and still better in its results upon the souls of their offspring.

Mrs. Gilman has heeded good Dr. Johnson's counsel, and has freed her mind of cant. Her thoughts are her own; they are brightly and deftly put— saving, O shade of Pym, an occasional split infinitive!—and, best of all, she has not only the courage, but the logic, of her convictions.

"The Effect of Minding on the Mind," "Presumptuous Age," and "The Respect Due to Youth" express certain opinions of our own which we have long held in cowardly silence; and, therefore, we naturally find these chapters peculiarly convincing. We wish Mrs. Gilman had added another on "The Descriptive Method of Management." We have known families in which the children were chiefly managed after this fashion—they being present: One grown-up remarks to another or addresses some tutelary genius in the empty air; "Did you ever see such frightful table manners as Tom has?" or, "I do think Susie has the worst temper I ever knew," *Sic*, ad infinitum. Poor Tom and Susie sit red and silent, and the hapless guest takes off his mental hat in homage to their self-control, fervently wishing the while that the fantastic story of "Vice Versa" might at once be realized.

If we cannot find our desired philanthropist, we would urge that "Presumptuous Age" be printed as a tract and strewn throughout the length and breadth of all lands. Has there ever been a family that could not adduce examples of the unconscious assumption and tyranny of its elder members, their futile endeavor to coerce a respect they could not command? What Mrs. Gilman has to say on this subject she might well have concluded with a triumphant "Quod erat demonstrandum."

Reprinted from *The New York Times*, 5 January 1901 (*Saturday Review*), 4, with the permission of the publisher.

Some of her theories are in advance of the age, and, indeed, it may be that they are too radical for even future acceptance—such, for instance, as are set forth in "A Place for Children" and "Mothers, Natural and Unnatural." But we believe that some modification of them must obtain and that the nursemaid must go.

When we observe how marriages are made, the wonder is, not that so few should be tolerably happy, but so many. In like manner, when we observe how children, even the most carefully reared, are of necessity neglected in their earliest and most impressionable youth, the wonder is, not that there should be so few noble and right-minded men and women, but so many.

We are afraid even the full carrying out of Mrs. Gilman's theories would not do away with "original sin." We confess our sympathies are with the mother of "Mary Don't" quite as much as with the child. "See what Johnny is doing, and tell him to stop," is a pretty safe general order under the present system. But such ethical training as Mrs. Gilman advocates would from the beginning foster all that is best in human nature; the virgin soil would be so occupied with useful, healthful growth, that there would be little room for evil weeds, and we might hope that the close of the next century would see not only the many inventions of this but a race as superior to ourselves as the noonday to the struggling dawn.

It is to be hoped that "Concerning Children" will be widely read and thoughtfully considered. It is one of the books that deserve a large and a heedful public.

[Review of *Human Work*]

S. M. F[RANCIS].

Of a far sterner sort [than *Work*, by Hugo Black] is the book by Mrs.
Gilman on the same theme. This, we see at the outset, is to be no mere
literary effusion, no mere product of individual reflection. It represents,
indeed, still another current notion as to what the Return to Nature means.
A glance at the table of contents intimates plainly that such things as
psychology, sociology, and political economy are in the wind. Our noses are
at once applied to the scientific grindstone. We learn what a concept is and
wonder that we have so long been indifferent to it. We have interesting
illustrations of what the concept can do by way of interpreting incidents of
which poets have loosely prated: "An excellent proof of the power of concepts
compared with conditions is given in the heroism of William Phelps, the
Indianapolis negro. Two colored men were at work in a great boiler, riveting.
Some person by accident turned on the steam. Hot steam as a material
condition is quite forcible, and the two men started for the ladder. But
Phelps, who was foremost, was arrested by a concept. He stepped back,
saying to the other, 'You go first—you're married!' Even in that comparatively undeveloped brain, a group of concepts as to Duty and Honour were
stronger modifiers of conduct than boiling steam." The description appears
to be not without humor, whether conscious or otherwise. Elsewhere, an
impatient habit of generalization compromises the effectiveness of the book
both from the literary point of view and as a scientific study. It is all very
well for the lady writer to say, "A flourishing society can maintain more
fools than any savage period could afford." But when she proceeds, with such
dicta for authority, to nudge us toward the conclusion that nothing that is
is right, we begin to surmise that at least there is much to be said on both
sides. There is not a little cleverness in the book, much raw output of
intellect; but so little literary quality that the substance of the work may be
had pretty satisfactorily from the summaries which are methodically prefixed
to the several chapters.

Reprinted from *The Atlantic* 94 (August 1904): 274–75, with the permission of the publisher.

MODERN CRITICISM

◆

Darwinism and the Woman Question: The Evolving Views of Charlotte Perkins Gilman

Lois N. Magner

Although some historians have argued that in the late nineteenth century Darwinism was all things to all men, the question of what Darwinism meant to women has been essentially ignored. However, the feminist response to Darwinism may provide insight into the paths by which those outside the scientific and academic world learned about, interpreted, and in turn taught others about the meaning of science. Analysis of the relationship between feminist ideas and Darwinism may also expose subtle links between prevailing concepts of human nature, assumptions about the special or peculiar nature of woman, and the uses and abuses of scientific theory. Although women's access to direct participation in science has generally been limited, feminist writers like Mary Wollstonecraft, Elizabeth Cady Stanton, Antoinette Brown Blackwell, Charlotte Perkins Gilman, and Eliza Burt Gamble have demonstrated that the use of scientific theories to justify social arrangements may indeed be a two-edged sword. These women did not restrict their interest in science to its use in debating the "woman question," but saw science as a major component of human enlightenment, and of technical and intellectual progress.[1]

In the wake of the Darwinian revolution, science became as powerful as religion in providing a rationale for theories of human nature and the proper arrangement of society. Antoinette Brown Blackwell (1825–1921), the first woman in the United States to be ordained as a minister, argued that science had replaced the Bible as the primary authority in explaining the creation of the world and woman's place within it. Indeed, the answers to all questions of social life and progress were increasingly being found in the deepest strata of scientific studies. Having analyzed the writings of her contemporaries Charles Darwin (1809–1882) and Herbert Spencer (1820–1903), Blackwell warned her readers that women must answer their alleged biological "proofs" of female inferiority by developing for themselves the scientific basis of their pursuit of equality.[2]

This essay is a slightly revised version of a paper presented to the History of Science Society Annual Meeting in New York City, December 1979. It is published here for the first time by permission of the author.

No one took up Blackwell's challenge with greater enthusiasm than Charlotte Perkins Gilman (1860–1935). Therefore, in this essay, I shall use Gilman's writings to illuminate the feminist response to Darwinism and compare her ideas with those of the best-known exponent of social Darwinism, Herbert Spencer. Although Gilman was neither a scientist nor a scholar, her concepts of human nature and social evolution were inspired by the theories of Darwin and Spencer. Thus, both Spencer and Gilman were interpreters and popularizers of science in an era when evolutionary theory was applied to virtually every facet of the human condition. Both Gilman and Spencer saw themselves as "Social Philosophers" building social and philosophical systems upon secure scientific foundations, but like many other interpreters of science they tended to deal more in models and metaphor than in observations and experiments. Basing their prescriptions for social relations, political rights, and economics on what they took to be the "natural laws" of organic evolution, they reached very different conclusions as to the causes of present social disorders and future human evolution.

Gilman and Spencer differed in many ways, besides their obvious differences in sex, age, and nationality. Although neither was a professional scientist, Spencer enjoyed a secure place among British scientists and intellectuals, and could justifiably lay claim to having explored various aspects of evolutionary theory before Charles Darwin had published the *Origin of Species*. When Spencer visited America in 1882 he was lauded as a thinker more capacious, powerful, and profound than Aristotle.[3] After a period of relative eclipse, Spencerian studies seem to be enjoying a minor boom, but his theories have been subjected to close and critical scrutiny.[4] Gilman, born the year after publication of Darwin's *Origin*, worked largely in isolation during much of her "vagabond" life. Even her relationship to the woman's rights movement was ambiguous.[5] Following publication of *Women and Economics*, she became internationally known as a "woman intellectual"; but as Walter Bagehot said of another female phenomenon, "Nothing is so transitory as second class fame."[6]

When Gilman began her career as author, poet, lecturer, publisher, and "social inventor," various forms of social and reform Darwinism had proliferated, but the work of Darwin and Spencer remained the touchstone for disciples and critics alike.[7] For Gilman, the scientific perspective was the key to alleviating individual and social problems and to eliminating obstacles to human progress. From a Darwinian viewpoint, history could be reinterpreted as a record of generally unsuccessful experiments in humanness. Therefore, ascertaining the natural causes of the "sorrows and perplexities of our lives" would enable us to overcome them.[8] In her time of greatest personal suffering, Gilman says, she turned to what she thought she had learned from Herbert Spencer: "Wisdom and how to apply it."[9] Such generous praise for the lessons taught by the British philosopher suggests that we might find the inspiration for many of Gilman's ideas in the work of Herbert Spencer.

However, if we examine Spencer's writings it becomes obvious that whatever Gilman might have learned from this source had to be transformed into a new feminist vision of human evolution.

Spencer's most radical views of the scientific and moral basis for the rights of individuals in society appear in his first major work, *Social Statics, or the Conditions Essential to Human Happiness Specified and the First of Them Developed*, which was published in 1851. In *Social Statics*, Spencer argued that a "true system of morality" could be found only by analyzing the attributes of human beings just as physicists studied atoms. Although Spencer insisted that his "Synthetic Philosophy"—with its prescriptions for the conduct of individuals and society—was firmly grounded in biological science, critics have argued that it is riddled with inconsistencies and ambiguities concerning the relationship between his social and biological theories.[10] Though Spencer claimed that evolutionary science provided the basis of all true social theory, he never came to terms with a fundamental defect in his system: if human form and behavior were both the substrate and product of evolution, they could in no way be treated as constants. Only by assuming that evolution proceeds in a defined path through the Lamarckian mechanism of inheritance was Spencer able to create even a very precarious bridge between his two major articles of faith: evolution and individualism.

Though he later rejected some of his radical ideas, Spencer never lost his conviction that a general acceptance of "evolutionary views of mind and society" was the necessary foundation for "right guidance" in politics, ethics, education, psychology, and biology. In more mature reflections, Spencer regretted that the truths contained in his first book had been mingled with and disfigured by crude ideas and "illegitimate corollaries."[11] Presumably, from Spencer's mature perspective, the most disfiguring ideas were his early views on the rights of women and children. The heart of the *Social Statics* was the "Law of Equal Freedom," which stated that: "Every man has freedom to do all that he wills, provided he infringes not the equal freedom of any other man." In this argument "man" was used in the generic sense, and applied to the species as a whole, female as well as male. The rights that were deducible from the law must belong equally to both sexes because the Moral Sense was innate in both men and women. Therefore, the restricted position of women in both the political and the domestic sphere was a relic of barbarism contrary to scientific ethics (Spencer, *Autobiography*, I, 365, 353).

Social Statics, published only three years after the Seneca Falls Convention (1848), might have given members of the nascent women's rights movement hope of finding an ally in a man with credentials as both scientist and philosopher. Unfortunately, Spencer's later writings were to provide antifeminists with a powerful rationale for a view of human nature, human society, and social evolution that specifically excluded women. The reason for this profound change of mind with respect to the rights of women remains obscure, and because the subject has been outside the mainstream of Spencerian and evolutionary studies, has been dismissed as an example of how the ultraconservative Spencer could maintain radical ideas on "incidental themes." However, after following Spencer's views on the nature of the sexes through the increasingly weighty volumes of the Synthetic Philosophy, Antoinette Blackwell concluded that in his obsession with evolving a *system*, Spencer had abandoned any serious investigation of women's place in nature (Blackwell, 15).

Having expunged all traces of supernaturalistic interpretations from his mature works, Spencer claimed that the remaining conclusions were exclusively naturalistic, that is, evolutionary. Evolutionary ethics required strict interpretation of the "Law of the Species"; the stern biological law that enjoyed untrammeled operation among subhuman species must also govern human society. In Spencer's concept of evolutionary law, the biological imperatives of the "survival of the fittest" and the "apportionment of commensurate benefits" even applied to the cells of the body. For example, blood was apportioned to each cell according to its function. The organism as a whole was thus fitted to its existence by competition among its constituent parts. Spencer concluded that the same arguments applied to the relationship between society and individual human beings: just as the cells within the body prospered and suffered in accordance with the law of fitness, so too did the "cells" of the "social organism" receive just reward and punishment.

Since a balance of functions was needed for the health of the social organism and its members, according to Spencer, rewards and power must be distributed according to functions rather than to the number of functionaries. Therefore, an unwise distribution of political rights must inevitably have evil—that is, anti-evolutionary—consequences. The biological function of the female in the social organism was the bearing and rearing of children; therefore, women, as wives and members of families, had no *interests* of their own and should not be granted representation as individuals.[12] This line of argument illustrates the kind of mental gymnastics by which Spencer strove to reconcile his commitments to evolution, individualism, and the social *status quo*. The attributes of childhood and motherhood were incompatible with the human image demanded by a model of social evolution in which the "struggle for existence" was the essential motor.

In his examination of "The Constitution of the State," Spencer argued that the primary reason for the organization of the state was the need to prevent military takeover by other states. Therefore, the Law of Equal Freedom could not apply to women because men had the obligation to defend the state through military service. During a period of permanent peace it might be *possible* to make the political positions of men and women the same, but it still might not be *desirable*. Obviously, the "test" of military service is simplistic and superficial when placed in the context of the complete Synthetic Philosophy. It was useful for its very simplicity, but more sophisticated reasons for denying political rights to women could be mined from various layers of the scientific and philosophical strata of the Spencerian system.

If men and women were regarded as independent members of a society, no restraints could equitably prevent women from participation in any occupations, professions, or careers they might wish to adopt. However, a difference in the rights of men and women was unavoidable because evolutionary ethics applied even to the marriage relationship. Before marriage, men and women had an equal claim to certain liberties. After marriage they retained those liberties that did not interfere with the marital relation. In practice, Spencer concluded, the Law of Equal Freedom cannot work within the domestic sphere because authority belonged to the husband since his struggles supported the family.

Abandoning his position of strict individualism, Spencer concluded that the loss of women's rights in marriage was just and reasonable. Reciprocity in maintaining the family, although theoretically possible, was actually negated by biology in the form of the "onerous functions of the female," which incapacitate her for "active life." Therefore, Spencer proposed a compromise, generally known as the "domestic equivalence theory": the discharge of the domestic and maternal duties by the wife could be considered a fair equivalent for the earnings of the husband. The fact that not all women were mothers, or that the "burden" would vary with the number of children was irrelevant; motherhood existed in women as a class and the amount of it per woman need not be measured.

Not only did the "onerous burden" of reproduction provide a biological obstacle to female activity, it also produced a more subtle mental disability that rendered women unfit for the struggle for existence. Caring for the young and helpless, females came to see all social problems through the distorting medium of maternity. The maternal instinct caused women to manifest a tendency to foster "the worse at the expense of the better." Obviously such a female instinct would be disastrous to the body politic if women had the vote. The parental role and the condition of the young represent an area where Spencer's fundamental individualism came into conflict with his ostensibly primary commitment to evolution.

Essentially, Spencer solved the problem by equating the species with the adult and focusing his study of human society on intraspecific competition between males. But since evolution necessarily proceeds through succeeding generations, Spencer needed to find some means of incorporating the young into the system. Turning to a survey of "animal ethics," Spencer determined that without some degree of self-subordination by adults, losses among the young would cause the species to disappear altogether. For the welfare of the species, some of the adults must be called upon for partial or complete self-sacrifice. Extrapolating from animal ethics, Spencer concluded that evolutionary ethics demanded a similar sacrifice from the human female.

Spencer found the most convincing scientific argument for denying equal rights to women to be based on the biological "evidence" that women were less highly evolved than men. Although he considered men and women to be members of the same species, his "development hypothesis" assumed that whatever was put into reproduction was taken away from individual life.[13] Because of woman's burdensome role in reproduction, the female sex had evolved for both earlier cessation of physical development and lesser mental power than men.

Spencer denounced those misguided reformers who called for education as a panacea for social and political evils. Ironically, he thought that intellectual functions, the most human of human traits, were also the least capable of deliberate, safe, and healthy individual development. Moreover, education was a danger to female health and the vitality of the species. Evolution had created quantitative and qualitative differences between the male and female mind because of a physiological necessity that no amount of culture could obliterate. When the body and brain were challenged, energy set aside for reproduction would be used up *before* the energy used for individual life. If expenditures for cerebral activity were excessive, there would necessarily be losses in the energy needed for race-maintenance. The human male was not exempt from the law of limited energies. Just as higher education of the female posed a danger to reproduction, overwork among men produced the specter of ill health and weak offspring. Therefore, men must avoid physical overwork and women must avoid brain work or they would transmit disease, feebleness, and stupidity to their descendants instead of health, strength, and intelligence.

The mechanism that would drive the race to the "ultimate state" was evolution via the "struggle for existence." Because this mechanism was equally applicable to both organic and social evolution, the advance of society required allowing its fittest members to assert their fitness with the least hindrance and avoiding all artificial attempts to prevent the unfit from dying out. Initially, Spencer held that because man was an organized being subject to evolutionary law, natural modification would eventually make him so perfectly fit for the social state that human beings would spontaneously adapt to the moral law. The approximation of the ideal state of relationships within marriage would be a sensitive index of the approach of human evolution to a stage of perfection. Approaching the ideal state of society would require eons of evolutionary time, however; no shortcuts were possible, despite the naive claims of philanthropists and educators. In the "ultimate state" of society, morality would become "organic" so that even the anomaly of the child's primitive character would disappear. The infant, presumably in the manner of a newly hatched reptile, would spontaneously unfold into a form fitted for the requirements of society.

Further reflection convinced Spencer that his assumptions about the eventual perfection of social evolution had been in error. Adaptation would always remain incomplete because during evolution the forces that produce change diminish as the need for change decreases. Any attempt to interfere with these awesome natural processes would only worsen the degree of nonadaptation. Abandoning his youthful optimism, and arguing that scientific principles were his only guides, Spencer created a theory of social evolution that was unremittingly harsh, and a vision of society that was narrow and unyielding. His Law of Equal Freedom had been progressively mutilated and ultimately sacrificed to support an increasingly inflexible commitment to an individualism that applied only to adult males. In his retreat from the radical views of *Social Statics* to the gloomy conservatism of his later works, Spencer truly earned the praise that Charles Darwin offered when he called Spencer "a dozen times my superior, even in the master art of wriggling."[14]

Although Gilman paid appropriate homage to Spencer and Darwin as the pioneers and champions of evolutionary thought, Gilman believed that existing human societies were not the inevitable products of biological forces but the result of human ideas, choices, and behaviors. Gilman and other reform Darwinists argued that we must learn to understand and guide human evolution, but we need not wait for complete knowledge of how society works in order to begin to fix it (*Living*, 182).[15] Reform Darwinists believed that with a determined effort at education and management, social conditions could be changed and rather rapidly improved. Indeed, inaction, consciously chosen in accordance with laissez faire gospel, was itself a form of action that was as likely to be deleterious to society as any other choice. Like Spencer, Gilman believed that evolutionary science was indispensable for understanding human nature and ethics. But with an understanding of ethics as the science of social relations, she argued that the ethical laws of human society could not be understood by individualists.

The ancient analogy of the "social organism" was used by both Spencer and Gilman, but their views of its composition and proper mode of behavior could hardly be more dissimilar. Within Spencer's system the individual units of the social organism owed nothing to each other or to the whole. Gilman saw the social organism as the form of life within which, and only within which, human beings could be fully human. Society consists of individual human beings performing interrelated and highly specialized functions that could not have evolved in isolation. The human animal is the constituent basis of humanity, but specifically human qualities only developed through collective and complex transactions. Certainly difficulties were to be expected with such a complex living form; nevertheless, in Gilman's vision of evolutionary theory, the benefits of social evolution must exceed the disadvantages. To the advocate of individualism, human societies might seem to have many disadvantages because of the apparent conflict between self-sufficiency and the interdependency necessitated by specialization, but Gilman argued that increased interdependency was a mark of evolutionary progress. For Gilman, the concept of the social organism was the natural foundation for social ownership, sound management, and cooperative action for the common good (*Human Work*, 99, 95–96, 91).

While brute animal forms could exist separately, independent teachers, physicians, or carpenters were as inconceivable as independent eyes "rolling around and doing business by themselves." Because Gilman's primary commitment was to collectivity instead of individualism, she was less troubled by the use of the concept of the social organism than Spencer. She even claimed that the social organism did not exist merely as a useful analogy or illustration, but as a literal biological fact. The organ and function that caused Spencer the most trouble—the human brain and consciousness—for Gilman was the greatest proof of the value of the concept of the social organism. The human brain could operate effectively only in an interdependent society because human beings were provided with powers useful to society, but unrelated to personal needs. The possession of such traits was inexplicable under any purely individualistic hypothesis, but was perfectly explained in terms of the "social hypothesis."

In urging that the existence of the social organism be accepted as literally true, Gilman argued that the concept of organic life was not to be limited to presently existing forms. When the social organism was properly studied, it revealed the novel pattern of the evolution of systems of relationships. The boundaries of the social organism were determined only by the natural limits of its organic social relations. As human interdependent functions became international, the social organism would evolve to a form limited only by the earth itself. The Spencerian system could not encompass a social organism composed of the entire human race. Because of Spencer's well-known scorn for the study of history, he disregarded the arbitrary and artificial nature of his concept of the state and viewed the state as the natural "organism" of his system.[16] Therefore, he put forth the "struggle for existence" carried out by competing states as the equivalent of the struggle for existence throughout nature.

Like many of the early social evolutionists, Gilman assumed that "evolution" was essentially equivalent to "progress." However, the social analogues of the biological mechanisms of selection and mutation were generally unspecified or uncritically identified with biological processes. She accepted Spencer's theory that evolution must progress according to natural laws of organization from unstable and homogeneous forms to complex, differentiated, and heterogeneous forms. Cells, organisms, and human societies were formed and maintained by the force of economic necessity. Organized beings—aggregates that worked harmoniously—survived while others perished. However, Gilman argued that for the social organism, the collective good represents not simply "altruism" but basic economic necessity. Society, like a gland, secretes specialized products, such as art, music, literature, facilities of travel, and education. If all members of society were allowed free access to such social products, the individual would absorb proper nourishment from society just as the cells of the body absorb their nourishment from the blood (*Women and Economics*, 116–17; *Human Work*, 103, 106–107, 160).

According to Gilman, human beings had entered into a novel and superior process of development that involved mechanisms not possible in physical evolution. To the common biological processes, human beings had added education, a unique social process, which profoundly influenced the whole social environment and the time scale in which improvement of the human condition could be achieved. It had become natural for human beings to build their own world through science and technology. Although both competition and altruism played a role in all evolutionary processes, their relative significance in human evolution had changed. Human evolution had reached a stage where the development of ever better social organs and functions did not take place through combat between individuals, but by a superior process supplanting an inferior process. No essential injury to the individuals making up the social organism need be involved; neither physical "survival" nor "reproductive success" served as the mechanism of social evolution. Obsolete machines and animal species that failed to adapt inevitably faced extinction, but human beings, as all-purpose animals, need not become "unfit" to survive under the new conditions.

In her treatment of the nature of the sexes, Gilman found support in Lester Frank Ward's "Gynecocentric Theory," which she called the most important contribution to the history of thought since evolution itself. While evolutionary theory had changed our concept of human social organization, the "Gynecocentric Theory" proved that the greatest obstacle to social progress was "the inverted relation of the sexes."[17] Once we understood that the female was the "main line of evolution," new truths for human guidance emerged: first, that evolution means growth rather than combat; second, that the human race was open to "measureless improvement"; and most importantly, that the female was the race type and that her natural impulses were more in accordance with the laws of growth than were those of the male. For Gilman, as for Ward, the differences between men and women were real and profound: woman was the natural, patient, tireless worker, the mother. Males were essentially individualistic and competitive. Thus, prevailing assumptions about the nature of the human species and society that reflected only the masculine viewpoint were both wrong and dangerous. The special distinction of the male was not humanity itself, but rather a proclivity for military combat and a failure to realize that warfare was a form of social pathology.

Evolutionary history proved that the female was the race type because reproduction of primitive life forms occurred without fertilization. Spencer had assumed that the appearance of sexual reproduction was due to the impoverishment and declining vigor of asexual reproduction, but according to the Gynecocentric Theory, sex had evolved gradually as a method of promoting the variation and evolution of the species. Asexual reproduction reflected the "life force"; sexual reproduction represented the "improvement force." The male had evolved as a fragile and transient form, a temporary assistant needed only for reproduction. Further evolution had produced species in which the two sexes were more nearly equivalent in terms of species traits.

Like all species, the human race was "gradually modified and developed through heredity and environment," but unlike other species human beings could improve the race by changing the specifically human social environment. Among primitive human beings the male had developed as hunter and warrior, while the female had carried on the role of bearer and caretaker of the young. In the prolonged dependency of the human infant, Gilman saw the development of the special work of the human mother and the beginnings of industry. To the usual tasks of all animal mothers—nurture and defense—were added human inventions in the securing, storing, preparing of food, and the making of things, such as tools, cooking utensils, and storage containers. The increasing value of woman's services led to subjection of the female by the male to ensure himself easy access to economic and sexual services. The human male eventually claimed all modern industry, art, and science as his own, thereby perverting the invaluable lessons of biological evolution for the study of social evolution. The imbalance between the sexes had led to a misunderstanding of evolution in terms of the male preoccupation with combat. The equally natural factors of altruism and mutual aid had been ignored or explained away as blemishes on the universal scheme; and the Darwinian world was seen as a "battlefield" where the natural mode of life for men was to struggle for existence with one another.

Agreeing with Spencer that the female was provided with special energy for reproduction, Gilman rejected his conclusion that it was associated with a lower level of evolution. Instead, she argued that the natural impulses of motherhood were particularly appropriate to social evolution. Becoming increasingly useful, the services performed by human mothers led to the development of conduct that promoted wider social coordination. Whereas egoism was a masculine trait, altruism—in terms of love, service, care, teaching, and improvement of conditions for the sake of the young—was characteristic of the female. Such altruistic traits in the female were not in any danger of conflict with inner impulses of a destructive nature, as they were in the male. Because of the woman's superior adaptation to the service of others, and her "rich fund of surplus energy for such service," her attitude toward life and work was essentially different from that of the male. A female perspective would restore altruism to its proper place in evolutionary science.[18]

Gilman argued that the proper growth of society would be enhanced more by the progress of women than by any previous changes, since specialized, specifically human traits were called forth and developed only by social evolution. But men believed that they were the only truly human creatures, able and entitled to perform the work of the world, while women were merely "female creatures," restricted to maternal functions and domestic duties. Because under the present social organization women are confined to their sex roles, and unable to fully participate in the complex working of the social organism, their interactions with men and children provide a drag and an obstacle to social evolution. Just as biological evolution progressed from "indefinite, incoherent homogeneity to definite, coherent heterogeneity," so too must social evolution proceed.[19] Forcing half the adult population into a rigidly maintained, permanent homogeneity has obstructed social evolution and race progress. Because the role of women had been limited to acting as house servants for adult males, women have failed in their full duty to the child and the race. When women were allowed equal participation in truly human activities, society would benefit not only from their direct works, but also from benefits to children who would finally have two fully human parents.

In Gilman's view of human evolution women played two important roles: as members of the human race, they should participate in all the activities, achievements, and interests that are the measure of social progress. But the special female purpose was to reproduce and improve the race. Women had two means of accomplishing this latter goal: one was through the selection of superior fathers; the other more practical method was to improve the physical and intellectual environment of all children. Improving the material and psychical environment of the young would improve the race more rapidly than "eugenics," or "cattle breeding" for human beings. Because of the unique human faculty for acquiring and transmitting knowledge, education could serve as a "conscious short-cut" that would accomplish more than many thousands of years of natural selection. Education was compassionate as well as efficient; in contrast, Nature's crude way of teaching was "mere wholesale capital punishment."[20] Education, free schools, and libraries improve the rank and file of society so rapidly that improvements could be seen within one generation. This particularly human mechanism of development did not obstruct natural selection but, properly exercised, acted in harmony with it.

Although, like his father, Herbert Spencer had experienced the life of the schoolmaster, for many reasons he had a difficult time finding a comfortable position on education. Of course he opposed compulsory state-supported education as another dangerous example of over-legislation and misguided philanthropy, but he also had peculiar notions about the development of children.[21] His expectation that even ideas and behavior could be inherited by the Lamarckian mechanism was perhaps as significant with respect to his ideas on education as his objection to the extension of state functions.

Unlike Spencer, Gilman did not believe that human evolution entailed the elimination of the "idle and unfit" by natural selection. Nor did she accept the Malthusian preoccupation with the problem of excess fertility among the "unfit" or the concern that the "fit" were not making their proper contribution to reproduction. Especially provoking to her was the notion that women must sacrifice their human potential in order to breed more children. She argued that the Malthusian doctrine was in error in assuming that a given rate of reproduction is fixed and final. Actually, there is a wide variation in the rate of reproduction in both the animal kingdom and the human species. Her authority for this was none other than Herbert Spencer, who had taught her that: "Reproduction is in inverse proportion to individuation. The lower the efficiency of the individual, the more young ones it has."[22] Therefore, the child of unaided, inferior parents would not simply be "shouldered aside" and quietly disappear, but would produce a flock of even more inferior children, a result Spencer seems to have ignored. Would helping the "unfit" encourage degeneracy and hinder evolution? Gilman argued that this fear rested on the erroneous assumption that the better individuals are developed by the "struggle for existence." If we recognized the organic unity of society we would see that development takes place not in direct combat between individuals, but in a superior process supplanting an inferior process. Through the forces of physiology and the science of sociology, families once rejected as irreparably "unfit" could be restored to full human status in a few generations. Finally, increasing specialization and education would bring about a balance of births and deaths. The individuation of woman was the most critical factor in this process, because it was her fertility that was the final determinant of population growth.[23]

Gilman thought that given an understanding of the evolutionary process and the nature of society, we should be able to plan and accelerate its improvement. If society could rapidly reform, why then did it not do so? Why did eminent social philosophers warn us that it was impossible? Gilman believed that our minds and the body politic itself were perverted and enfeebled by the pathological effect of our worst social relations—the low status of women and our notion of work as the contemptible sphere of slaves. Spencer had argued that one could not accelerate social evolution by education or by changing institutions because "character" or "moral sense" evolves too slowly.[24] But a study of changing technologies proved that they led to more rapid social evolution than did the slow processes of nature. Just as technological change could have rapid and far-flung ramifications, so too could institutional changes. Reflecting the view of a younger generation and the experience of America's rapid and profound transition from a rural and agricultural to an urban and industrialized society, Gilman argued that America was itself proof of the fact that such change was possible—even inevitable.

While Spencer's confidence in the rationality of mankind and the possibility of reaching a higher state had deteriorated along with his mental and physical powers, Gilman's faith in evolution, science, and the further improvement of the human race grew ever more certain: understanding evolution, the law of growth, and the link between social evolution, education, and the "natural altruism" of motherhood, would make possible the improvement of the human race. Unfortunately, the mind of man had modified science, just as it had modified religion, so that evolution was perceived as only the "struggle for existence" rather than as growth and action. If we could understand that ideas, especially those derived from science and religion, were the most powerful forces in directing social evolution, we would see that too often human conduct was not governed by the laws of nature, but by our theories about them. Scientists and those who mediated between scientific discoveries and public awareness of scientific theory were key factors in this process. Their responsibility lay in making the public aware that the cause of human misery was not science or natural law, but the misinterpretation and misunderstanding of nature. With such an educated perspective, humanity could look backward to the intellectually liberating achievements of astronomy, geology, history, anthropology, and zoology, and forward to anticipate similar effects flowing from the new sciences of evolution and sociology.[25]

Gilman was correct about the certainty of change, but in error in her optimistic assumption that social evolution led rapidly and inevitably to substantive improvement. In her outlook on science and society she shared many of the prejudices and uncritical assumptions common to those influenced by Spencer and Darwin—especially the logical fallacy of taking analogies for proofs. Unlike Spencer, Gilman never visualized social evolution as a series of steps so small that the generations now living could have no hope for themselves or even their children and grandchildren. Just as human beings took advantage of artificial selection to improve plants and animals with amazing rapidity, so too could we consciously choose to assist the evolution of our own species. "It has taken Mother Nature long, long ages to turn fierce greedy hairy ape-like beasts into such people as we are," Gilman wrote, but she confidently predicted: "It will take us but two or three close-linked generations to make human beings far more superior to us than we are to the apes" (*His Religion*, 140, 175).

Notes

1. Lois N. Magner, "Women and the Scientific Idiom: Textual Episodes from Wollstonecraft, Fuller, Gilman, and Firestone," *SIGNS: Journal of Women in Culture and Society* 4, no. 1 (1978): 61–80.

2. Antoinette Brown Blackwell, *The Sexes Throughout Nature* (1875; repr. Westport: Hyperion Press, 1985), 235; hereafter cited as Blackwell.

3. Edward L. Youmans, comp., *Herbert Spencer on the Americans and the Americans on Herbert Spencer* (1883; repr. New York: Arno Press, 1973), 87.

4. See, for example, James G. Kennedy, *Herbert Spencer* (Boston: Twayne, 1978); Richard Hofstadter, *Social Darwinism in American Thought* (Boston: Beacon Press, 1955); and David Wiltshire, *The Social and Political Thought of Herbert Spencer* (Oxford: Oxford University Press, 1978).

5. See, for example, Mary A. Hill, *Charlotte Perkins Gilman: The Making of a Radical Feminist, 1860–1896.* (Philadelphia: Temple University Press, 1979).

6. Walter Bagehot, "Lady Mary Wortley Montagu," in *The Collected Works of Walter Bagehot* (1862; repr. Cambridge: Harvard University Press, 1965), II, 208.

7.   See, for example, Robert C. Bannister, *Social Darwinism: Science and Myth in Anglo-American Thought* (Philadelphia: Temple University Press, 1979); Cynthia Eagle Russett, *Darwin in America, The Intellectual Response 1865–1912* (San Francisco: W. H. Freeman, 1976).

8.   Charlotte Perkins Gilman, *Women and Economics* (1898; repr. New York: Harper and Row, 1966), 1; hereafter cited as *Women and Economics*.

9.   Charlotte Perkins Gilman, *The Living of Charlotte Perkins Gilman, an Autobiography*. (1935; repr. New York: Arno Press, 1972), 154; hereafter cited as *Living*.

10.   Herbert Spencer, *Social Statics* (1851; repr. New York: Augustus M. Kelley, 1969), v–vi, 16–17, 19–20, 33–34; Hofstadter, *Social Darwinism*, 32; Wiltshire, *Social Thought* (see preface).

11.   Herbert Spencer, *The Works of Herbert Spencer*, 21 vols. (repr. 1880–1907 ed.; Osnabruck: Zeller, 1960); *An Autobiography*, 2 vols., I, 50; hereafter cited as *Autobiography*.

12.   Spencer, *The Principles of Ethics*, in *Works*, II, 192–93, 92, 160; see Walter M. Simon, "Herbert Spencer and the 'Social Organism,' " *Journal of the History of Ideas* 21 (1960): 294–99; F. W. Coker, *Organismic Theories of State: Nineteenth Century Interpretations of the State as Organism or as Person* (1910; repr. New York: AMS Press, 1967).

13.   Herbert Spencer, "The Development Hypothesis" (1852, *Leader*; repr. *Essays* I, 377–83).

14.   Francis Darwin, ed. *The Life and Letters of Charles Darwin*, 3 vols. (London: John Murray, 1887), II, 239.

15.   Gilman, *Human Work* (New York: McClure, Philips, 1904), 6; hereafter cited as *Human Work*.

16.   See Wiltshire, *Political Thought*, 1.

17.   Charlotte Perkins Gilman, *His Religion and Hers: The Faith of Our Fathers and the Work of Our Mothers* (1923; repr. Westport: Hyperion Press, 1976), 56–58, 275; hereafter cited as *His Religion*; Lester Frank Ward, *Pure Sociology: A Treatise on the Origin and Spontaneous Development of Society* (New York: Macmillan, 1903); see also Lester Frank Ward, "Our Better Halves," *The Forum* 6 (1888): 266–75.

18.   Gilman, *His Religion*, 243, 252, 262, 270; see also Petr Kropotkin, *Mutual Aid: A Factor in Evolution* (1902; repr. Boston: Extending Horizons Books, n.d.).

19.   Gilman, *Women and Economics*, 223.

20.   Gilman, *His Religion*, 58–59, 9–11, 242; *Human Work*, 377; Gilman, *The Home: Its Work and Influence* (New York: McClure, Phillips, 1903), 231; Gilman, *Concerning Children* (Boston: Small, Maynard, 1900), 263–64; hereafter cited as *Children*.

21.   Herbert Spencer, *Social Statics Abridged and Revised Together with The Man Versus the State* (New York: D. Appleton, 1892), 88–89.

22.   Gilman, *Human Work*, 378.

23.   Gilman, *Human Work*, 378–379, 142–143, 380; Gilman, *Children*, 4, 269, 297–298.

24.   Spencer, *Principles of Biology*, II, 527; see Kennedy, *Spencer*, 82; Gilman, *His Religion*, 210, 214, 241, 272–73.

25.   Spencer, *Autobiography*, II, 50; Gilman, *His Religion*, 92, 106, 140, 175, 274.

"Begin Again!": The Cutting Social Edge of Charlotte Perkins Gilman's Gentle Religious Optimism

FRANK G. KIRKPATRICK

The religious mood of America has oscillated historically between deep despair over the depravity of the human condition and unbounded optimism about its potential for perfection. Charlotte Perkins Gilman's religious views can only be properly appreciated within the context of this historical oscillation. Writing her only sustained study of religion after the horrors of the First World War, she seems remarkably undaunted by the heavy blow that conflict struck at others' confidence that the human race was evolving steadily toward unfettered happiness. In the light of the postwar themes of despair and anxiety that characterized the neo-orthodox theologies of Karl Barth in Europe and Reinhold Niebuhr in America, Gilman's religion of optimism and confidence might appear naive and hopelessly unrealistic. At the same time, she lays the ground for contemporary feminism's realistic critique of older images of God, which effectively eliminated any notion of the divine as nurturing, compassionate, and relational, and of religion as an experience of organic interrelatedness and the source of empowerment in the struggle for liberation and justice in the social order.

Even if one finds the articulation of her religious ideas to be more reflective of the scientific romanticism of her time than she might have acknowledged herself, Gilman must be recognized as a thinker who had the courage to challenge an image of God that had been drawn primarily from men's experience and to suggest revisions in that image which would be more faithful to the experience of women. In this sense Gilman has much to say to contemporary feminist theologians, as well as to religious communities which are seeking to create more affirmative, supportive centers of mutuality than they perceive many traditional religious institutions to have been.

I would suggest that we can provide the historical context for Gilman's religious outlook by locating it, ironically, within the thought world of late nineteenth century, romantic, liberal theology. This world was, in particular,

This essay was written specifically for this volume and is published here for the first time by permission of the author.

that which her own great uncle, Henry Ward Beecher, did more to exemplify than almost any other major religious leader of the time. While she would have found herself very much at odds with Henry's social views and closer to those of the social gospel, her own religious views are strikingly similar to the romantic, liberal theological outlook which he represented. This is particularly remarkable, inasmuch as she never indicates any debt to his work nor acknowledges that she had read any of it.[1] Instead, she seems far more influenced by the emerging science of sociology, especially that of Lester Ward. When she is inclined to look back on her Beecher past, it is primarily through the eyes of her progressivist views, calling great grandfather Lyman Beecher and his cohorts "Great Adventurers" who displayed "inventive progressiveness".[2]

Much of what she says about her religious development was written fairly late in her career, her autobiography *The Living of Charlotte Perkins Gilman* being published only in 1935. Yet it and her other "mature" works on religion, especially *His Religion and Hers*, published in 1923, leave out much of the personal struggle and conflict of her life before she became famous. Mary A. Hill has written persuasively, movingly, and thoroughly about Gilman's personal life. It seems clear that her public expressions of buoyant optimism and evolutionary confidence were not always reflected in her own private dilemmas and crises, such as those involving her relationships with her first husband, her daughter, her women friends, and especially her father and mother. It surely was a great struggle for Gilman to affirm the progress of the human race and to call for ever renewed efforts to improve its conditions when so much of her own life was subject to depressions, reversals, misery, and disappointments. Her bravado and daring in print never entirely overcame her often bitter internal anguish and despair.

One of the earliest and strongest influences on Gilman's religious ideas was the thought world of Unitarianism. One of her close friends was William F. Channing, the son of the titular theologian of Unitarianism, William Ellery Channing.[3] An even closer confidant was Grace Channing, William Ellery's granddaughter. She also acknowledges the influence, in particular, of Unitarian-Transcendentalist James Freeman Clarke's *Ten Great Religions* on her understanding of the evolution of religion. Clarke had been a Unitarian who was one of the founding members of the Transcendentalist club (Scharnhorst, 38).[4] It is clear that Gilman was far more deeply influenced by their much more generous view of human nature than she was by the gloomy evangelical picture of depravity, corruption, and the necessity of an experience of conversion to a personal, wrathful, but loving God. As Gary Scharnhorst notes, she "had formulated a personal creed akin to Unitarianism, conceiving of God not as a 'heavenly Father' or transcendent patriarch but a rational power or immanent presence" (Scharnhorst, 4).[5]

Reflecting on her own early encounters with traditional religion, Gilman claims (years later) that she soon "realized the importance of religion as a cultural factor, but also the painfully conspicuous absurdities and contradictions of the world's repeated attempts in this line" (*The Living*, 37–38). She was, nonetheless, convinced that there was a universal need for religion, and, already employing the biological imagery that would mark her developed religious thought, she referred to "the functional demand of the brain for a basic theory of life" (*The Living*, 38).

At the heart of that "basic theory of life" was her conviction, which seems never to have altered throughout the remainder of her life, that human beings demand a "conscious and repeated connection with the Central Power, and for 'sailing orders,' a recognized scale of duties" (*The Living*, 38) somehow linked to that Power. Her mature views on religion always centered on a notion of God as the "Central Power" or life-force, and on the moral obligation of the human species to respond to God's reality. She hardly ever used the language and metaphors of her great grandfather's religious tradition to describe this God, however, preferring instead terms that were closer to the austere and somewhat abstract God of Unitarianism and Deism. In this sense, her indebtedness to the progressivism of her Puritan ancestors was, at best, minimal. Ironically, it was this very absence of the evangelical tradition in her religious development that makes her thought so much closer to that of her uncle Henry Ward Beecher, Lyman's son, who had made his own singular break with the inherited orthodoxy of his father's generation.

Her independence of mind revealed itself in her teens when, she claims, she "set about the imperative task of building my own religion, based on knowledge" (*The Living*, 38).[6] Rationality or intellect was the foundation and touchstone of all her later religious thinking. As a good Unitarian might do, she set out "calmly and cheerfully, sure that the greatest truths were the simplest," to see what she could see about reality. Such an approach could not be in starker contrast to the evangelical, neo-Puritan tradition in which the soul, tormented by the anxiety of damnation, waited helplessly for God's loving (but uncertain) saving grace. In this tradition, rationality and self-reliance were corrupt and presumptuous, barriers to a personal openness to receiving God's grace.

Gilman's major study of religion came in 1923 with her book *His Religion and Hers*, though its themes are not new in her published writings. Many of them had been anticipated and at least briefly articulated in *Women and Economics* (1898) and in *The Man-Made World* (1911). By 1898 she had identified human progress as the duty of society and defined it as the maintenance of health and happiness both of the individual and of society. In 1911, she was contrasting masculine "combat" religion with maternal service and nurturing religion. Her autobiography claims that she had formed at least the outlines of her own religion as early as the late 1870s when she set out to build a religion of her own.

She declares that the evident fact on which her religion is based is action, that "this universe is a going concern." And behind this action is "Power . . . Force. Call it God." And this Force is behind a process that "worked all one way—up. . . . This long, irresistible ascent showed a single dominant force. . . . 'Here's God—one God and it Works!' " (*The Living*, 39). Her commitment to the notion of ascent made her open to the doctrine of evolution, which we shall consider shortly. But more immediately, it led her into an almost unbounded confidence in the ability of human beings (the finest product of the ascent to date) to overcome any and all obstacles to further development. She seems to dismiss the traditional interpretation of the problem of evil with a conviction that we make our own evil by erroneous action "and can stop it when we choose" (*The Living*, 41). She even notes in passing that women, specifically mothers, would never associate the "inevitable mistakes of childhood" with the "problem of evil."[7]

Her relatively superficial treatment of evil probably has been the single greatest obstacle to a sustained interest in Gilman's *religious* views. While she is quite perceptive about how the status of evil has been used by male religious authorities to degrade and denigrate human achievement, especially that of women, her solution to the problem seems to many modern ears somewhat simplistic. She claims that human effort, once freed from primitive superstition, can confront evil head-on and virtually eliminate it. Even contemporary feminist theologians, while rightly critical of the exploitation of gender differences by men who defend their actions on the ground that everything humans do is tainted by evil and that, therefore, no real reform is possible, generally do not believe that evil can be overcome by sheer effort of will alone. This may explain why Gilman's attack on androcentrism has survived in cogency and relevance while being stripped away, for the most part, from the religious framework in which she herself tried to embed it.[8]

There is little in Gilman's view of God that suggests any prolonged grappling with the complexities and conundrums it had undergone in the history of Christian theology or even in the atheistic attacks upon it by its cultured despisers. Her concept of God is simply one of "Life," or the force behind or under Life. (Her theological imprecision often results both in her identifying God with Life and in her proclaiming that God is the power undergirding and flowing through Life.) Gilman's God is not conceived as a distinct personality set over against or even in intimate relation to the human race (even if that personality might conceivably be invested with more feminine traits). Because Gilman sees God as ultimately "within us, to be expressed, instead of above us, to be worshipped" (*His Religion*, 292), she holds that you cannot "worship a force within you" (*His Religion*, 51). She claims that although men have invested God with knowledge and power (and generally denied the same qualities to the human race), women envision God as Life itself, as the process of bringing new life into being, "always coming, through motherhood, always growing, always improving through care and teaching!" (*His Religion*, 251). God is "the first Mother, Teacher, Server, Maker," the "Power under all this pouring flood of Life," the "Love behind this ceaseless mother-love," the "Goodness to make Life so good, so full of growing joy" (*His Religion*, 251).

Gilman believed that the notion of God as a powerful, individualized being had been created by men who are afraid of death and who want a superior being to save them from it. Such a God arises out of what Gilman calls "death-based" religions. These religions reflect the warrior and hunter men of primitive ("savage") times. Because death was the inevitable outcome of the slaughter of the hunt, so "man's mind, searching inward, saw in all one red reflection, filled the world with dark religions built on Death" (*His Religion*, "Two," v.).

Connected with the notion of a God who saved the warrior from the death he caused others and therefore feared for himself is the belief that heaven will be a happy hunting ground in which men can go on with their savagery without further fear of its ultimate termination. Since the masculine impulses are generally those of combat and self-expression through struggle, the God that men created not only gave them a heaven where the combat could be continued indefinitely, but even gave Himself an "Adversary."[9] His victories over the Devil also gave God "boundless pride and a thirst for constant praise and prostrate admiration" (*Man-Made World*, 140).

Gilman's formal writing on religion does not explicitly disavow a belief in a life after death, but does object to men's tendency to use that belief to divert attention from the nurture of life here and now.[10] She seems to assume that men's vision of the afterlife necessarily excludes their devotion to making this life better (even if only to enhance the conditions of combat), whereas women's indifference to life after death does not. Perhaps men's death-based religions are so characterized by struggle precisely because of a hatred of the world, which must be subdued by brute force rather than, in birth-based religion, enjoyed by cooperative love.

Men's religion is also faulted because it makes no room for women's pleasure in heaven, even denying in many cases that women have souls (*Herland*, 43).[11] She specifically targets the "guilt of Eve" notion and its derivative concept of the pain of birth as punishment, as reflective of a masculine attitude that demeans women.

But Gilman's chief objection to man-made religion is its preoccupation with death and what she regarded as its consequent obsession with developing and protecting the individual after death, a "posthumous egotism . . . a demand for the eternal extension of personality . . . required to placate the deity or to benefit one's self" (*Herland*, 47). The male in particular is given to individualism or self-expression (*Herland*, 75). The male wants to live through his work, which he regards as a "field of warfare, a process in which to get ahead of one another, by which to seize for one's self what another has made" (*Herland*, 78). Man's heaven, therefore, is pictured as a place where the successful will enjoy the rewards of their self-aggrandizing achievements and his hell as the location where failures will suffer the punishments of their sloth and errors.

Gilman's alternative to death-based religion, women's birth-grounded religion, is not a repudiation of self-expression but rather a balancing of its one-sided development by men. While acknowledging that all persons have a right to legitimate self-expression, Gilman insists that in a birth-oriented religion this right is exercised in service to others, and not just to and for oneself. For a birth-based religion, the overriding concern is " 'What must be done for the child who is born?'—an immediate altruism" (*Herland*, 46). For Gilman everything in such a religion must be concentrated upon the opportunities of the future, not the mistakes of the past. The moral duty inherent in this religion is that of developing the human race to its greatest potential. "It would tell no story of old sins, of anguish and despair, of passionate pleading for forgiveness for the mischief we have made, but would offer always the sunrise of a fresh hope: 'Here is a new baby. Begin again!' " (*Herland*, 50).

Her hopes for the evolving race are virtually without limits. "The race can work toward perfection and approach more closely to it in every generation" (*Herland*, 90). And in the process, it need not succumb to the masculine idea of the "survival of the fittest." Gilman, unlike Darwin, envisions evolution as growth, not as conflict or, as Tennyson wrote, nature "red in tooth and claw." Evolution is also cooperation and the development of different social functions for different persons, all working toward a common end. These social functions may even work against individual advantage in the short run, but without functional differentiation there can be no progress for the race as a whole.

Women, fortunately, have already acquired the disposition to serve others altruistically and thus are able to provide the necessary subordination of self-interest to race-interest, whereas men will be hampered in their ability to do so given their long history of rampant individualism and fear of subordinating their interests to those of others. Women, she declares, are marked by the mother instinct of "unmixed devotion, of love and service, care and defense, *with no self-interest*" (*Herland*, 131; emphasis added). Gilman, in fact, so extols the altruistic, self-giving nature of women that she seems to echo favorably some of the traditional traits that men have attributed to women (usually with the intention of demeaning them). As Polly Wynn Allen-Robinson has pointed out in her study of Gilman's social ethics, her challenge to women to express themselves "was obscured by the theory of woman as innately giving and nurturant. How could she reasonably urge women to self-fulfilling acts when to do so was somehow to question their superior moral virtues?"[12]

Gilman ironically reverses Nietzsche's condemnation of Christianity for appealing to the slave morality of service by noting with appreciation that Christianity appealed to women especially *because* it "called for the essentially motherly attributes of love and service" (*His Religion*, 51). In fact, Gilman seems to exempt much of Christianity, or to be more precise, the religion of Jesus himself, from her condemnation of death-based religions. Jesus, she believes, was a strong advocate of the improvement of the race and of the need for service to it. "He taught unmistakably of God in man, of heaven here, of worship expressed in the love and service of humanity" (*His Religion*, 35). Like many of the Social Gospelists of her era, Gilman struggled to single out the teaching of Jesus (whom she called the "Greatest Sociologist" [Allen-Robinson, 246])[13] from its corruption through ritual and dogma by the ecclesiastical institution (which had historically rested in the hands of men). She seems to believe that if Jesus' ideas had been followed more faithfully, the baneful legacy of death-based religion would have been considerably diminished.

Once birth-based religion had the opportunity to develop, it would, according to Gilman, begin to produce new religious ideas. One would be the recognition that Life needs to be nurtured—that we have the opportunity and the obligation to assist consciously the natural laws of evolution and that we will find joy in doing so. Gilman continually reminds her readers that while the power of God is coursing through nature and its development, human beings have the "supreme distinction" of being able to participate in that development by the power of their ideas (*His Religion*, 100). No matter how grievous the results of our participation might be on occasion, Gilman is confident that in the end the laws of nature are "stronger than all our mistakes" and that we "cannot prevent their ultimate success" (*His Religion*, 238).

There is a curious ambivalence in Gilman's argument here. On the one hand, she wants to emphasize the role that intelligent beings can and should play in evolution, but on the other she wants to eliminate any possibility that they can play that role so destructively as to thwart the powers of Life which undergird and flow through the whole process of cosmic growth. She gives the human being dignity within nature but ultimately keeps nature in a position of dominance, determining the limits of human "interference" and power. This is, perhaps, not so remarkable when we remember that orthodox Christianity has traditionally held that the will of God cannot ultimately be overridden by morally wrong human decisions. Since Gilman essentially substitutes nature for God (or identifies one with the other), it is not unexpected that she simply appends human thought and culture to those underlying forces that determine the progress of the race. What distinguishes human action is its ability to "recognize and promote its own evolution" (*His Religion*, 242) in accord with the laws of nature. Since the forces of evolution are conceived as "calm, slow, friendly,"[14] the traditional conflict of man versus nature is unnecessary. What is particularly distinctive about women's contribution is their awareness that cooperation is more effective than combat in promoting and conforming to the law of growth. The female is the "race type and her natural impulses are more in accordance with the laws of growth than those of the male" (*Women and Economics*, 275).

It is women's particular advantage to be attuned to this progress both through their experience of motherhood and through their efforts at cooperation, nurture, and tenderness toward all that grows. It is precisely this experience that women are now drawing upon to challenge and reform ideas of religion that assume the priority of conflict, competition, and exclusionary moral judgment.

It is clear that Gilman's new religion will be one of *action*. Beliefs, to be relevant, must be applied to life here and now. Gilman is here echoing, at least in part, the Unitarian emphasis on right action in the course of moral development instead of the Puritan/orthodox emphasis on right thought in the defense of doctrinal purity. But if religion is action, and if human action is a reflection of what is distinctive about human beings, namely intelligence, then the only acceptable form of action must be that which is guided by the most intellectually up-to-date understanding of reality. This is the basis for Gilman's fascination with sociology and what she calls the "science of ethics," which is the science of social relation (*Man-Made World*, 126) or "conscious physics" (*The Living*, 238). It is the scientific discipline that will expose the human mind to all the relevant facts about social growth and organization. This explains Gilman's rather thorough dependence on the sociology of Lester Ward.

Ward's views were themselves grounded in an ethical vision that called for an end to ethics understood as a helping hand. While sharing in the ethical concern for the betterment of the human race through the "lessening of pain, the mitigation of suffering, the decrease of misery, and the removal of unhappiness in general,"[15] Ward argued that as human beings gained a greater acquaintance with the laws of nature they would be able to organize their world in such a way as to achieve the greatest happiness (thus eliminating the need for "conventional" ethics). Knowledge put to use is, in effect, the new ethics, and its realization will be "civilization" or "the utilization of the materials and forces of nature . . . which increases the sum total of human happiness . . . an increase in the algebraic sum of pleasure and pain." And sociology is the science that "sets forth the principles and indicates the method for attaining this end" (Commager, 426–28).

Gilman was not as inclined as Ward to "mathematize" the goal of moral progress. She was more attuned than he to the organic rhythms of motherhood and nurture. Nevertheless, she did accept Ward's assumption that only a true science of nature, including that of persons in social organizations, could provide the means to the moral end of human perfection. Thus it was easy for her to apply her Unitarian legacy of trust in the human mind to her search for the appropriate means to achieve human happiness. In this sense, science was ethics and ethics was science. The possibility of the misuse of science for so-called evil ends seems not to have overly concerned her since she was confident that, once women were given their rightful place in the world, and lived out the implications of their birth-based religion, no one would have any reason to want to do "evil."

It should be clear that two crucial assumptions underlie Gilman's religion of birth and ethical action. One is her belief that nature *is* evolving whether we like it or not, and the other is that we have the opportunity to participate in the evolutionary process provided we can get our ideas straight about what is really going on. What is significant about these assumptions is how much they have in common with the optimistic liberal theology of her uncle, Henry Ward Beecher, and of the Social Gospel. Beecher did not, in fact, draw from his openness to evolution the same social lessons that Gilman did, and she did not base her social views—which she shared with the Social Gospelists—on the same Christian foundation they did. But her thought becomes easier to understand if we can see it as standing somewhere between the hearty optimism and social timidity of Beecher's views and the more nuanced optimism and social challenges of the Social Gospel.

Beecher, Gilman, and the Social Gospelists all assumed a warm, sentimental, organic view of developing human life. All were deeply indebted to some version of the theory of evolution; all looked to the future with a confidence that it had to be better than the past, especially through the mediation of human intellectual effort; all tended to see sin as an historical variable, capable at least of diminution if not of outright abolition. What separates them—especially Gilman and the Social Gospel—from Beecher is a rather different assessment of what *kind of social change* would be in line with evolution.

Sharing as she did much of Beecher's theological outlook, why was Gilman able to embrace political and economic views so very different from his? The answer probably lies in the lack of theological precision (i.e., adherence to carefully defined theological tenets or dogmas from which specific social consequences follow in logical order) that tends to characterize liberal theology's embrace of the new theories of evolution. These theories became pliable material onto which one could press the forms of one's primary and more deeply rooted social views. Evolution did not so much suggest a specific form of advance as provide a formless substratum into which one could read one's own social or political agenda. This was as true of Beecher as it was of the Social Gospelists and of Gilman herself.

Henry Ward Beecher was the prototypical preacher of hearty optimism who articulated and symbolized established religion's doctrinal and attitudinal break with its orthodox Puritan past. Having turned his back on a God who punishes people with the fires of hell for their sinfulness, Beecher, calling himself a "cordial Christian evolutionist," embraced the Darwinism of Herbert Spencer, who, he said, gave him a renewed faith in the "Something" whose power has worked the way of the human race upward (like Gilman, Beecher tended to refer to God in highly abstract and impersonal terms).[16] Beecher asserted that there is no inherent sin in mankind. To his congregation he is reported to have said "ye are gods! . . . I behold in each of you an imprisoned angel that is yet to burst forth."[17]

Like Gilman, Beecher believed that one of the most important means for bringing forth the intrinsic divinity of people was science. "Not only would I cast no obstacle in the way of scientific research, but I hail it as the great almoner of God's bounty" (quoted in McLoughlin, 44). This is a logical implication of Beecher's conviction that God was universally present throughout all of Nature, "universally diffused, to such an extent that wherever there is force, there is God (call him "Force" or "Energy," I care not) behind that force . . . and if there be one thing that is to be triumphantly demonstrated by Evolution, it is that the whole life of the world is permeated by the life of God himself" (*Evolution and Religion*, 78). Gilman could have lifted this sentence verbatim into her own texts on religion!

Beecher is quite clear that one should always be striving to make a difference on behalf of humankind. His imagery here is strikingly anticipatory of Gilman's. He says that the ideal of the preacher is "a large nature filled with enthusiasm for God, but even more for man, and caring for men as the chief care of his own life more than for the Church, more than for the law, more than for theology. A true preacher is a man that lives for his fellow-men, caring for them as a mother cares for her babes" (*Evolution and Religion*, 137). There is hardly a suggestion here of what Gilman called death-based religion, and it is noteworthy that the image Beecher evokes of the human ethical ideal is that of a mother and her infant.

Beecher also anticipates Gilman in his willingness to substitute moral conduct for doctrinal purity as the true test of Christianity. It "is to be tested not by creeds but by conduct . . . in the spirit that is developed by it, not in the technical creeds that men have constructed out of it" (*Evolution and Religion*, 301). And the spirit Beecher calls for is one of love, not fear. He rejects any notion of a God who inspires morality by threats of punishment or eternal damnation.

With all this in common, what separates Gilman from Beecher? Is she simply a somewhat later echo of her uncle's views, which she mysteriously failed to read and/or to acknowledge? While she certainly shares with Beecher a profoundly similar grounding in a liberal theological framework, he was distinctly conservative in his social views, whereas she was just as distinctly radical, especially with respect to her hopes for a change in the gender and economic relations between men and women in American society. While Beecher was not strictly a retrograde social thinker, he carefully modulated his social views to conform to the generally accepted views of the wealthier ruling classes upon whose support his ministry and fame depended. As William McLoughlin, Clifford Clark, and Milton Rugoff have all made abundantly clear, Beecher was never ahead of his times but ingeniously always just abreast of them. Beecher never challenged the optimism of his generation. Instead he reflected it through his eloquence and showmanship. He always knew just which causes had become socially acceptable (and which he could therefore adopt) and which remained still beyond the pale of class approval. In speaking about slavery for the first time in 1846, Beecher explained his position by saying: "I have for myself deliberately concluded and acted in my ministry on the conclusion that on subjects upon which society had not yet been instructed, on questions involving much doubtful casuistry—in all secondary truths . . . the success of the cause and truth required a fretful minister to withhold, when speaking would only injure; and to speak only when there seemed a favorable state of soil to receive the seed."[18] While identifying himself as antislavery, he never accepted black persons as the social equals of whites (Clark, 168–69).

He also associated himself with the struggle for women's rights, but only after it was socially acceptable to do so. He became president (in name only) of the American Woman Suffrage Association in the late 1860s (Rugoff, 388), even though he also believed that "generations must pass" before "we should understand" (meaning presumably before men would permit) the right of women to take their place in public as well as in private affairs (Clark, 200). Charlotte, of course, would have rejected Beecher's timidity and caution as indefensible as well as redolent of the male view that women could contribute little to public affairs and, even then, only when men allowed them to do so.

Beecher was perhaps at his most conservative (because his social base would not permit him to be more liberal) on the issues surrounding economic justice in America. Beecher bought into the ethos of the self-made, entrepreneurial, individualistic successful-man theory that underlay the capitalism of his era. Beecher held firmly to the conviction, which he believed was an implication of the law of evolution, that within laissez-faire capitalism the most morally advanced individuals would rise to the top, and having succeeded in doing so would be justified in controlling the society from their acquired positions of power. That these people for the most part were white, Anglo-Saxon males was not a matter of *moral* concern to Beecher. They would, through their wise and moral leadership, eventually bring the lower strata up through the ranks of evolutionary advance. But the progress would be slow, nonconflictual, and guided throughout by the moral wisdom of the already successful.[19] Beecher never really abandoned one of the common myths of his social class, namely that the poor remained poor because they were sinful. He said in 1875, "there may be reasons of poverty which do not involve wrong; but looking comprehensively through city and town and village and country, the general truth will stand, that no man in this land suffers from poverty unless it be more than his fault—unless it be his sin" (quoted in McLoughlin, 150).

In particular, Beecher was wary of laboring men joining forces in organized protest against working conditions and low wages (his fear was stimulated in part by the fact that many of the laborers agitating for unions were "foreigners," not Anglo-Saxon stock). His most famous anti-labor, anti-union sentiment is found in his comment about the union demand for higher pay: "It is said that a dollar a day is not enough for a wife and five or six children. . . . But is not a dollar a day enough to buy bread with? Water costs nothing and a man who cannot live on bread and water is not fit to live" (quoted in Clark, 236). That Beecher himself was reputed to carry uncut diamonds in his pockets and to own a stable full of prime racehorses goes unremarked.

Gilman, though never commenting directly on Beecher's views, may well have understood how he read into his theological beliefs a set of social views very much at odds with her own. She would have seen clearly how invidious his social attitude was to the role of women in the economy. She would have been appalled at his blindness to the economic injustice of a system that rewarded white males while virtually ignoring the economic oppression of women, Beecher's involvement in women's rights notwithstanding. Gilman may also have appreciated the fact that Beecher's religious views tended always to mirror the views of his social class (even when he occasionally chose the more "advanced" views of his class to articulate) without significantly challenging them. She stood in direct opposition to his virtually uncritical defense of capitalism and its relegation of women to secondary and degrading economic status. In the end, her liberal theology justified a totally different conception of the organization of society which could best enhance the development of a cooperative community. She was far more insightful than Beecher as to the oppressive, discriminatory, and unjust effects that capitalism entailed in practice, if not always in theory.

Ironically, however, she failed to distance herself completely from Beecher's fear of foreigners and the "baser-born." She used the evolutionary notion of self-selection to justify her fear of what Allen-Robinson calls "the reproduction of the unfit and the . . . most unpromising" (Allen-Robinson, 86). She could even talk of black people having successfully achieved "our" level of civilization—a sentiment reflective of Beecher's notion of the superiority of the Anglo-Saxon community.

Despite her lapses into the racism and classism of Beecher's social views, Gilman remained steadfastly committed, in a way that he clearly had not, to the elevation of women to the rights and privileges due them by virtue both of their humanity and, especially, of their superior moral and religious attributes. She took the protean ideology of evolutionary progress and embedded in it a secure place for the role of women in the advance of humankind toward immortality. She was, in this respect, a faithful spokesperson for the organic, optimistic, and evolutionary religious credo that characterized liberal theology at the end of the nineteenth century. She was so faithful to its principles, in fact, that even the slaughter of and by men in the most culturally advanced nations of the Western world during the second decade of the new century was unable to qualify her fidelity.

Despite what a later generation might have regarded as her undue optimism about human progress, Gilman's greatest legacy was her keen awareness of how one's social experience informs one's views of religion and of God. By lifting up women's experience of giving birth, nurturing, and cooperating in the development of new life, Gilman began a process of deconstructing an essentially male image of God as death-threatening, avenging, and authoritarian (which reflected men's experience of combat, victory, and defeat). That process is still under way. Those theologians who are today stressing the centrality in religion of mutuality, community, and compassion, and who are challenging traditional male images of God, can find in Charlotte Perkins Gilman's religious views precursors of their own, even as they gently disengage them from the romantic theological liberalism in which they were historically encased.

Notes

1.   It is not clear whether Gilman's reluctance to read or to cite Henry Ward Beecher's views was due to his notoriety (particularly that involving his trial for adultery in 1871, while he was serving as pastor of the Plymouth Congregational Church in Brooklyn Heights, New York). Mary A. Hill indirectly suggests this was not the case when she notes that Charlotte, then twelve years old, responded to the trial with a "lifelong craving for contact with 'movers and shakers' generally" and that Henry "promoted an exalted image of the Beecher birthright which a young ambitious Charlotte would accept fairly early as her own" (*Charlotte Perkins Gilman: The Making of a Radical Feminist, 1860–1896* [Philadelphia: Temple University Press, 1980], 18, 14); hereafter cited as Hill. It may be that much of Charlotte's mature ideas on religion were very much her own despite their general reflection of the liberal theological temper of her times. It may also be that Henry Ward Beecher's conservative social views were so antithetical to her own that she simply dismissed his thought entirely and refused to draw upon any of it, including those parts which, as I will show, foreshadowed so much of her own thinking.

2.   Charlotte Perkins Gilman, *The Living of Charlotte Perkins Gilman: An Autobiography*, foreword by Zona Gale (New York: D. Appleton-Century Company, 1935), 3; hereafter cited as *The Living*.

3.   Gary Scharnhorst, *Charlotte Perkins Gilman* (Boston: Twayne, 1985), 3; hereafter cited as Scharnhorst.

4.   Strangely, Gilman consistently misspells Clarke's name as "Clark" in all of her references to him. Clarke's main ideas included his belief that God is *within* all persons (thus rejecting the traditional dualism that put God "outside" the world) and that we have the capacity to actualize our divine potential. While Clarke moved beyond Unitarianism in the direction of greater stress upon the Transcendentalist idea of the indwelling of God in all persons, he always considered his views part of Unitarianism (see William R. Hutchison, *The Transcendentalist Ministers* [New Haven: Yale University Press, 1959], 189). His *Ten Great Religions*, published over a twelve-year period from 1871 to 1883, was a comparative study that may have provided Gilman the data from which she drew her information regarding death-based religions.

5.   Unitarianism generally held that only those religious doctrines which met the test of reason could be held by rational people. Thus, they rejected the doctrine of the Trinity as irrational, preferring instead to think of God as a single personality whose essential attribute was moral perfection. This attribute was, they believed, shared with human beings, whose nature could become infinitely good by earnest moral effort. Jesus was the moral paradigm for such moral achievement but was not divine (except as all human beings have the divine potential within them). Ultimately, "character was more important than creed" in Unitarianism (see Hutchison, *The Transcendentalist Ministers*, 2–6). Gilman seems to have absorbed this

view completely. One of Charlotte's closest friends was Grace Channing, the granddaughter of Unitarianism's greatest theological expositor, William Ellery Channing. Mary Hill has suggested that Grace may have influenced Charlotte's thinking by informing her of William Ellery's idea that the well-being of a rational person required a strong element of self-affirmation along with a willingness to suffer for others (Hill, 154–55). Both values were part of the self's development of a perfect moral character, and Charlotte seems to have struggled to reconcile them with each other in her own personality.

6. Again, we need to remember that Gilman makes these claims about her own development years later. As Mary Hill reminds us, drawing upon Gilman's diaries and letters from this earlier period, she glosses over or fails to recollect some of the deeper, more painful struggles in her personal life and, we might reasonably assume, also in the development of her religious outlook.

7. Charlotte Perkins Gilman, *His Religion and Hers* (New York: The Century Co., 1923; repr. Westport: Hyperion Press, 1976), 53, hereafter cited as *His Religion*.

8. It may be that while Gilman writes as if evil can be overcome by effort of will, what she intends to say is that *ultimately* the force of Life, or God, is so powerful that evil cannot overwhelm it. As Mary Hill notes, for Gilman, even the laws of evolution justify an optimistic point of view: it is "one of Nature's laws, or God's Laws, that things *shall* grow up and improve. . . . the most important thing for you to remember is that wrong doing is punished and right doing rewarded just as surely as night follows day." But as Hill also observes, "the formula is clear, straightforward, simple" (Hill, 110–11). The simplicity of this view does reveal a deeper level of confidence, which is much closer to orthodoxy than the level that Gilman often tends to express in her writing. At this deeper level, Gilman is evoking a positive vision of the powers-that-be within the universe, which seems closer to many contemporary theologians who are rejecting the orthodox idea of a God who punishes persons for the very sins that God has caused them to commit by engendering original sin in them.

9. Charlotte Perkins Gilman, *The Man-Made World or, Our Androcentric Culture* (New York: Charlton Company, 1911; repr. New York: Johnson Reprint Corporation, 1971), 139; hereafter cited as *Man-Made World*.

10. While not explicitly disavowing a belief in life after death, Gilman's own views on the matter may be revealed in her treatment of the issue in *Herland* (New York: Pantheon Books, 1979; with an introduction by Ann J. Lane), originally published over a series of years in Gilman's monthly magazine *The Forerunner* from 1909 to 1916; hereafter cited as *Herland*. In this feminist utopian novel, one of the protagonists says that she simply does not want to go on and on forever because she finds satisfaction enough in her children and her children's children going on through time. There is, she says, enough of peace and beauty and comfort and love here in this life. A next life seems unnecessary and "singularly foolish" (116).

11. Gilman might have made effective use here of the views of such orthodox and highly influential theologians as Aquinas and Luther, both of whom seemed to regard women as "defective" men.

12. Polly Wynn Allen-Robinson, *The Social Ethics of Charlotte Perkins Gilman* (Ph.D. thesis, Harvard University, Cambridge, Mass., March 1978), 235; hereafter cited as Allen-Robinson. Gilman may have absorbed some of her great-aunt Catherine Beecher's ideas on the importance of women's domesticity as a source of unique values that women could exploit in their demand for power and influence in an essentially male world. See especially Hill, 14; and Kathryn Kish Sklar, *Catherine Beecher: A Study in American Domesticity* (New Haven: Yale University Press, 1973).

13. Interestingly enough, while Gilman's social views were extremely similar to those of the major Social Gospelists, she hardly acknowledges having read or been influenced by them in her writings, even though, according to Mary Hill, she had studied and admired them (Hill, 139). The Social Gospelists held that the essence of Christianity was a vision of society reformed through the work of economic and political justice. The Hebrew prophets had announced this vision, and Jesus had embodied it. But the vision had undergone the

corruptions of ritualism, institutionalism, and individualism. The Social Gospelists attempted to call the Protestant churches to a greater social conscience, especially one in support of working men and women and the trade movement generally. Some embraced socialism, but the majority remained committed to a political progressivism tempered with religious ideals. Ironically, the Social Gospel shared a similar confidence about the latent perfectibility of human nature with the otherwise much more socially conservative theology of Henry Ward Beecher. It is quite possible that Gilman learned some of her economics from one of the major Social Gospelists, Richard Ely, a professor of economics at Wisconsin, who had taught Charlotte's friend and coworker Helen Campbell.

14. Charlotte Perkins Gilman, *Women and Economics*, edited by Carl Degler (New York: Harper Torchbooks, c. 1966), 340 (originally published in 1898 by Small, Maynard and Company, Boston); hereafter cited as *Women and Economics*.

15. Henry Steele Commager, ed., *Lester Ward and the Welfare State* (Indianapolis: Bobbs-Merrill, 1967), 145: hereafter cited as Commager.

16. William McLoughlin, *The Meaning of Henry Ward Beecher: An Essay on the Shifting Values of Mid-Victorian America, 1840–1870* (New York: Alfred A. Knopf, 1970), 50; hereafter cited as McLoughlin. See also Henry Ward Beecher, *Evolution and Religion. Part I. Eight Sermons, Discussing the Bearings of the Evolutionary Philosophy on the Fundamental Doctrines of Evangelical Christianity* (New York: Fords, Howard, & Hulbert, 1886), 430; hereafter cited as *Evolution and Religion*.

17. Milton Rugoff, *The Beechers: An American Family in the Nineteenth Century* (New York: Harper and Row, 1981), 510, 372; hereafter cited as Rugoff.

18. Clifford Clark, Jr., *Henry Ward Beecher: Spokesman for a Middle-Class America* (Urbana: University of Illinois Press, c. 1978), 66; hereafter cited as Clark.

19. See especially William McLoughlin's analysis of Beecher's social philosophy, 139ff.

20. Gilman also endorsed the notion of "race-improvement" through birth control and the sterilization of the "unfit" (Scharnhorst, 65).

"Overwriting" the Rest Cure: Charlotte Perkins Gilman's Literary Escape from S. Weir Mitchell's Fictionalization of Women

Catherine Golden

In 1887 S. Weir Mitchell treated Charlotte Perkins Gilman (then Stetson)[1] for a nervous breakdown following a postpartum depression and forbade her to write.[2] A specialist in women's nervous disorders, Mitchell attended well-known male and female literary figures. George Meredith and Walt Whitman apparently experienced no ill effects from his prescriptions; Jane Addams, Edith Wharton, Charlotte Perkins Gilman, and Virginia Woolf suffered from his Rest Cure treatment.[3] After nearly losing her sanity by rigidly following his parting advice "never [to] touch pen, brush or pencil as long as you live" (*Living*, 96), Gilman defied Mitchell and transformed him into a minor but memorable character in her fiction. In "The Yellow Wallpaper" the nameless narrator, undergoing a three-month Rest Cure for a postpartum depression, protests that her physician/husband John "says if I don't pick up faster he shall send me to Weir Mitchell in the fall."[4] Although Gilman does not discuss her physician in detail in her story, she does name him as well as indict him in this one salient reference, which continues: "But I don't want to go there at all. I had a friend who was in his hands once, and she says he is just like John and my brother, only more so!" (19).

Gilman's introduction of her doctor into a first-person narrative gains interest and complexity when we consider that this foremost nineteenth-century American neurologist had a second career as a novelist. In addition to medical books and essays on the nervous system, mental fatigue, and convalescence, he published several collections of short stories, three volumes of poetry, and nineteen novels between 1884 and 1913.[5] Although virtually unknown today, Mitchell was, in fact, one of the most popular turn-of-the-century American writers; critics compared Mitchell's *Hugh Wynne* (1896) to Thackeray's *Henry Esmond* (1852).[6] Many of his literary efforts incorporated psychiatric themes and doctor-patient relationships informed by his own practice and that of his affluent physician father, John Kearsley Mitchell.

This essay was written specifically for this volume and is published here for the first time by permission of the author.

Supporters of Mitchell's fiction such as David Rein and Ernest Earnest argue that Mitchell "deserves to be restored to the canon of American literature" (Earnest, 235).[7] Rein praises Mitchell as an author, for "in his fictional studies of nervous disorders he stood alone. He was the first novelist in American literature to present such clinically accurate portraits of mentally ill characters. No one else had done it, except Oliver Wendell Holmes. But even Holmes's work lacks much of the merit of Mitchell's" (Rein, 182–83). However, even those who commend Mitchell's fictional studies modeled after his own patients are quick to raise his shortcomings as a novelist. Mitchell's fiction disappoints because it often fails to bring a character vividly to life, to explore the causes of the protagonists' nervous breakdowns, or to show their progressive deterioration into hysteria, as Rein and Jeffrey Berman have noted.[8] Moreover, as a writer, Mitchell sacrifices the plotline of his novels to feature conversations his characters have with one another; as a result, his style is conversational at best.

Mitchell never wrote about Gilman in his fiction exploring abnormal psychology or in his psychiatric books detailing the Weir Mitchell Rest Cure. Nonetheless, his almost forgotten fiction offers insight into why Gilman decided to write "The Yellow Wallpaper"; in her words, "to reach Dr. S. Weir Mitchell, and convince him of the error of his ways" (*Living*, 121). A comparison of the fictional female characters in S. Weir Mitchell's late nineteenth-century novels and Gilman's own protagonist in "The Yellow Wallpaper" (1892) suggests that through his Rest Cure treatment Mitchell tried to reform his patient Charlotte Perkins Gilman along the lines of his fictional female protagonists, many of whom followed a version of his Rest Cure. Mitchell's *Characteristics* (1891), written shortly after Gilman's treatment in Mitchell's sanitarium, demonstrates the physician/author's patriarchal portrayal of the (male) doctor-(female) patient relationship that Gilman revised in "The Yellow Wallpaper" (1892). She defied her doctor in 1890 not only by writing "The Yellow Wallpaper" but also, more specifically, by creating a protagonist who also writes. Her creative life and her fiction reveal that she ultimately "overwrote" Mitchell's efforts to make her more like the ideal female patients predominant in his affluent medical practice and his fiction.

Gilman was twenty-six years old when she traveled to Philadelphia to enter the sanitarium of Dr. S. Weir Mitchell. Like Sigmund Freud, Mitchell was trained as a neurologist, but he earned special recognition as a nerve specialist for women. Only by the end of the century did the medical profession, influenced by the work of Freud, begin to distinguish between diseases of the mind, to be treated by psychiatrists, and diseases of the brain, to be treated by neurologists. Neurology in the mid-to-late nineteenth century explored the relationship between psychology and physiology. Nerves were considered the link between the mind and the body, and the symptoms of mental exhaustion and depression were thought to be somatic in origin.

Aiming to heal the mind by healing the body, Mitchell's Rest Cure attended to the physical symptoms of depression. Although Mitchell is credited with the Rest Cure, he developed it from a number of accepted medical practices. His Rest Cure earned him international acclaim (his work was translated into four languages before his death in 1914). In fact, Freud favorably reviewed Mitchell's first book, *Fat and Blood* (1877), approved of his Rest Cure, and even adapted and used it for a period of time.[9]

Mitchell diagnosed Gilman's condition as "nervous prostration" or "neurasthenia," a breakdown of the nervous system, and prescribed his Rest Cure. Following the birth of her daughter, she had become depressed, spiritless, weak, and hysterical. This psychiatric condition was in no way unique to Gilman or to the female population; men also suffered from it, as had Mitchell himself.[10] Because of the strains on the Victorian woman imposed by the rigid ideals of femininity, debilitating nervous disorders were more common among upper-and middle-class women than men. The causes of neurasthenia were thought to be gender-specific: while men succumbed from overwork, women suffered from too much social activity, sustained or severe domestic trials (e.g., nursing a sick family member), and overexertion brought on by pursuing higher education.

In treating his patients Mitchell demanded obedience and deliberately assumed a detached, stern manner that he believed helpful, especially for patients who had been pampered and indulged by well-intentioned relatives. He was patronizing to women, a trend that characterizes his extensive writings about the Rest Cure, mental fatigue, and convalescence. For instance, in *Doctor and Patient*, Mitchell writes that "there are many kinds of fool, from the mindless fool to the fiend-fool, but for the most entire capacity to make a household wretched there is no more complete human receipt than a silly woman who is to a high degree nervous and feeble, and who craves pity and likes power";[11] in fact, he considered Gilman's involvement in the history of her own case "proved self-conceit" (*Living*, 95). Nonetheless, Mitchell was more liberal than many male physicians of his time. He believed in the legitimacy of and the suffering caused by neurasthenia, validating women's complaints. He openly scorned the abuse of ovariotomies and other forms of commonly prescribed radical gynecological surgery. Mitchell also approved of physical exercise as well as higher education for women in the areas of child care and home management in order to fit women for the domestic sphere.[12]

Although Mitchell's Rest Cure was in accordance with the most advanced neurological thinking of his day, in modern eyes it can be read as an attempt to reorient women to the domestic sphere (and away from influences of their changing world) so that they could fulfill their most important role in society: to bear and rear children. The covert aim of severely enforcing the treatment was so that the patient would feel "surfeited with [rest] and [would] welcome[] a firm order to do the things she once felt she could not do."[13] Typically lasting six to eight weeks, the Rest Cure focused on nutrition and revitalization of the body. It included five components: total, enforced, extended bed rest (the patient was forbidden to sew, converse, move herself in and out of bed, read, write, and, in more extreme cases, even to feed herself); seclusion from family and familiar surroundings (to remove the patient from the pampering of well-meaning relatives would sever hurtful old habits); a carefully controlled diet (overfeeding, the key ingredient being milk and cream to create new energy by increasing body volume); massage; and electricity (the latter two components were introduced to prevent muscular atrophy).[14]

The Rest Cure was not without merits; similar to the spa water cures in fashion in nineteenth-century Europe and America, the Rest Cure removed the individual from the tensions of his or her world and offered a sanctuary for rest. Hundreds of women traveled to Mitchell's sanitarium from around the world to seek his Rest Cure. Many felt relieved that their complaints had been both recognized and treated, and they left satisfied. Nonetheless, to many women, including Gilman, Mitchell's Rest Cure was punitive. Mitchell admitted that his methods of treating women for neurasthenia were harsh: "Rest can be made to help. Rest can also hurt."[15] Despite this admission of what many women feared about his Rest Cure, Mitchell consistently defended his methods as necessary to cure them, allowing them to resume their traditional domestic roles.

Threatened by the direction of the "new woman" emerging in the late nineteenth century, Mitchell clung to the traditional view of the dutiful, protected woman and immortalized her in his fiction. Unlike the women in Gilman's stories, passive heroines abound in Mitchell's writings. Some female characters demonstrate intellectual vigor, such as Alice Leigh in *Characteristics*, or exert strong will, such as Serena Vernon in *A Comedy of Conscience* (1900). Both ultimately put aside their independent notions and follow the advice of strong male characters, taking the opposite course from that of Gilman's protagonists.

At least in the novel's opening, *A Comedy of Conscience* reveals a portrait of a liberated woman. A spinster by choice, Serena is described as a healthy, attractive, strong-willed, and "intelligent, but not intellectual"[16] woman who often asks for but seldom takes advice. Similar to the nameless protagonist in "The Yellow Wallpaper," Serena keeps a diary throughout the novel and has a suitor named John (a common name in Mitchell's fiction).[17] While the nameless protagonist in "The Yellow Wallpaper" defies her husband/physician John, Serena Vernon increasingly relies on her male cousin John Winterbourne, her rejected suitor who remains devoted to her. Serena becomes more dependent upon others for advice after she is robbed—a criminal steals her wallet on the trolley-car (and inadvertently drops a stolen diamond ring into her handbag); although Mitchell does not overtly discuss the robbery as a cause for her change, this event seemingly accounts for Serena's dramatic transformation from self-sufficiency to dependency on the advice of male figures, namely the trusted Doctor Saffron, her rector, and John. Although Serena asks advice of her "nearest female friend" (8) Mrs. Clare regarding what to do with the "stolen" diamond ring and even claims "A woman will see this miserable business from my side" (41), she discounts Mrs. Clare's advice; she listens instead to John, whose hand in marriage she accepts at the very end of the novel (despite her strong convictions not to marry him at the beginning). At this point, Serena's John declares her "nervous" (although we were initially assured that she was rarely ill) and prescribes rest: "Go to bed, dear" (125). When she resists, he calls her a "Dear child!" (127), paternalistic language reminiscent of the nameless protagonist's husband John in "The Yellow Wallpaper."

In an earlier novel, *Roland Blake* (1886), the most interesting character is not the hero Roland, an intelligence officer in the Union army, but a more minor character, Octopia Darnell, a patient similar to those Mitchell describes again and again in *Doctor and Patient* and *Fat and Blood*.[18] Octopia— who shuns the light, constantly complains, and prefers to recline rather than stand—is thin and lacks blood. By giving Octopia an attenuated frame and impoverished blood, Mitchell embodies in his fictional patient two of the outstanding characteristics of the class of nervous women for whom he devised and prescribed his Rest Cure.[19] At the onset of the novel, Octopia is a "settled inmate"[20] in the home of a distant relative, the elderly Mrs. Wynne. The cause of her physical condition, which we are told has no physiological origin, remains unclear until the second third of the novel. Nursing Mrs. Wynne's son, Arthur, during the last week of his life, Octopia witnesses his suicide and immediately proclaims herself ill. She gains power over Mrs. Wynne by declaring that her illness results from the strain of attending Arthur Wynne at his deathbed and by threatening to reveal Arthur's suicide (her recovery would thus diminish her claim on Mrs. Wynne).

Arthur Wynne's daughter, Olivia, comes to live in the home of her paternal grandmother, in which her distant invalid cousin Octopia has earned a permanent residence. With Olivia's arrival, the hysterical Octopia, whom Mitchell describes as "too wicked to die" (62), becomes a scheming chronic invalid who assigns herself to bed but continues to use her invalid status to plague her younger, passive cousin Olivia (e.g., " 'That was rough child. You forget I am an invalid' " [44]); she also tyrannizes Mrs. Wynne (e.g., "She [Octopia] is killing me by inches" [62]), who fears Octopia too much to remove her from her own home. Throughout the novel Olivia defers to her petulant, selfish, and cunning older cousin and becomes nursemaid both to her elderly grandmother and Octopia.

Mitchell does not glorify Octopia's well-meaning "victim" (97) but uses Olivia to make a point in fiction central to his medical writings on the Rest Cure: the overindulgence of well-intentioned relatives can only exacerbate the hysterical patient's condition and weaken the caretaker's health.[21] In

Olivia's case, "the exactions of her nervous, sickly cousin were surely sapping the wholesome life of the younger woman, and as surely lessening her power of self-restraint" (50). The forbearing Olivia, whose health deteriorates, admits that the capricious Octopia is only "half-sick": "what must be the worst evil of half-sick people is the absence of regular work, of set duties— things that must be done" (376). However, Octopia, like many of the hysterically ill women Mitchell treated in his practice, does not know she is cruel to others: "she thought about herself and thought she didn't think about herself" (376). At the end of the novel, Mitchell rewards Olivia with marriage to Roland Blake and frees her from her nursemaid position. Olivia's departure, compounded by Mrs. Wynne's death, leads Octopia to wed Addenda Pennell, who caters to her whims as Olivia once did (e.g., "As for Pennell, he followed her [Octopia] about with a shawl and a scent-bottle, and says he has left the club and prefers the evening tranquility of domestic life" [379]). Mitchell is too much a realist to reform Octopia or to restore her health. Rather, this final twist shows how both sexes can succumb to the tyranny of the kind of "half-sick" patient possessing "the most entire capacity to make a household wretched" that Mitchell bemoans in *Doctor and Patient* and his other medical writings.

An apparent exception to the undermining of women's initiative by male (typically the physician's) authority occurs in *Constance Trescot* (1905). The eponymous heroine avenges the unjust death of her lawyer/husband George Trescot, who was shot by an emotionally unstable lawyer named Greyhurst under the pretense of a duel. Constance's power and authority, however, are only seen to serve male authority: these traits allow her to ruin her husband's murderer and to restore George Trescot's name and reputation. In other respects, Constance behaves like a typical Mitchell hysteric. Predictably, at the scene of the murder, Constance falls "insensible, convulsed, and quivering" at her husband's murderer's feet.[22] Although a physically healthy woman at the opening of the novel, her passionate and obsessive love for her husband (which lies beyond the scope of Mitchell's inquiry) triggers an emotional collapse that leaves her physically wasted and eventually turns her into an anemic, "couch-loving invalid,"[23] rivaling Octopia Darnell. She devotes her life to ruining Greyhurst (who is not found guilty of murder) and uses her disabled status to rule her caretakers (e.g., "Constance relied on her misfortunes and her long illness to insure her an excess of sympathetic affection and unremitting service" [382]). In fact, just as Octopia made Olivia the victim of her demands in *Roland Blake*, Constance expects her well-meaning sister Susan to care for her tirelessly and, like Octopia, seems unaware of her own selfish nature.[24]

Unlike *Roland Blake* and *Constance Trescot*, which offer portraits of tiresome invalids whose conditions worsen due to the indulgence of well-intentioned relatives, *Characteristics* and its sequel, *Dr. North and His Friends* (1900), epitomize the relationship between the (male) doctor and the ideal (female) patient that Mitchell prescribes and Gilman defies in the literary arena.[25] Two parts of the same story, these semiautobiographical novels of conversation contain developed characters but do not have a sustained plot. Both works, narrated by Dr. Owen North, offer veiled self-portraits of Mitchell's own life; this is particularly true of *Characteristics*, which describes North's war injuries (Mitchell himself suffered greatly from the Civil War) and his ambivalence about pursuing medicine (Mitchell battled with his father, who initially objected to his career choice). Both novels feature female patients and offer but one strong female protagonist; Anne Vincent, the wife of Dr. North's best friend, Frederick Vincent, stands out as an intelligent and intrusive social matron, yet her strong role as a female adviser is undermined by Mitchell's frequent references to her unfortunate childless state. Both works offer Mitchell an occasion to present his belief that women can be good patients but not necessarily successful doctors.

In *Fat and Blood*, Mitchell states that women doctors "do not obtain the needed control over those of their own sex" (41). Mitchell questioned whether women doctors could exert the strict, objective manner necessary to manage the class of hysterical invalids that his fictional characters Octopia Darnell and Constance Trescot represent. Of course, in *Fat and Blood* he also admits that the male physician may also experience difficulty with this type of patient, and he does refer in passing to the abilities of women physicians as he qualifies: "it is in these cases that women who are in all other cases capable doctors fail" (41).[26] More than by the issue of competence, Mitchell was disturbed by the personal consequences for women entering medicine. Through the development of Alice Leigh in *Characteristics*, he presents his belief that a "capable" woman doctor would lose her essential femininity.

While the nameless protagonist in "The Yellow Wallpaper" defies her physician/husband John as the story continues, Alice Leigh enters the story as a woman with a mind and will of her own who sacrifices her convictions to follow the ideas of Dr. Owen North, who speaks Mitchell's views. Anne Vincent initially describes Alice as "a woman of unusual force of character . . . and intellect (for she is more than merely intelligent)."[27] Her quality of mind at the outset of the novel surpasses that of Serena Vernon's in *A Comedy of Conscience*. Mrs. Leigh, Alice's mother, turns to the much-respected Dr. North for advice when she discovers the extent of her daughter's ambitions: "Now she [Alice] proposes to . . . it is awful. She wants to study medicine, and, oh, you do not know Alice. She is so determined" (235). Owen North shares Mrs. Leigh's belief that a woman's entrance into the medical profession is "awful." Though initially "determined" to pursue "something which offers an enlarging life" (249), Alice rather quickly abandons her plans to study and practice medicine right after Dr. North prescribes otherwise.

Although Owen does not attend Alice for a physical malady, her plan to be a doctor is referred to as a "disease" (235), and North counsels her as he would his female patients. When she first meets Owen North, the twenty-four-year-old Alice passionately ridicules her mother's suggestions that she sketch, play music, and sew. Spirited Alice argues for the need for "an enlarging life" (249), not for personal ambition but to benefit her society. Owen wins Alice's favor when he professes that "every human being is entitled to any career he or she may please to desire" (251); however, he soon reveals his prejudices. He tells Alice: "I said I did not believe it was best either for the sick or for society for women to be doctors; that, personally, women lose something of the natural charm of their sex in giving themselves either to this or to the other avocations until now in the sole possession of a man" (264). Immediately following their discussion, Alice becomes "quite tranquil" (275) and acquiesces to her mother's plan to leave behind her " 'hunger for imperative duties' " (235) and concentrate on marriage. Unfortunately, Mitchell neither explores nor explains the cause of Alice's sudden transformation, which seems implausible to the contemporary reader.

When Alice suddenly becomes ill (she starts looking pale), Mrs. Leigh attempts to engage Owen North as Alice's physician. He refuses because he has fallen in love with her. Proposing to Alice on the penultimate page of the novel, Owen secures the hand of the once willful Alice, who has become so rattled that she shreds her fan in a dozen bits as she accepts his proposal. Reduced to tears, she "sobbed like a child" and admits defeat: "Owen North, be very good to me. I meant to have done so much" (306). Rather than become a doctor, she marries the man who advises her not to develop her intellect. Mitchell concludes that, Alice, like her mother before her, is "cured" of her ambitions by marriage (235). At the end of the novel, Alice represents the ideals Mitchell prescribes to women through his medical writings and in his fiction. Nonetheless, the tearful state of the obedient Alice testifies to the trauma she experiences in putting aside her desire for a purposeful career only to gain usefulness through her physician/husband's life.

The narrator in "The Yellow Wallpaper" also sobs uncontrollably, although primarily at the beginning of the story.[28] Gilman revises the typical (male) doctor-(female) patient relationship by reversing the heroine's progress: Mitchell's strong-willed Alice is made passive, whereas Gilman's once submissive protagonist gains a forceful sense of self as she acts out of madness. Initially Gilman's nameless protagonist is as obedient to her physician/husband John as Mitchell's Alice Leigh sadly becomes toward her future husband/physician Owen North. Gilman's narrator defers to "Dear John" as well as to what "John says" (16) when he prescribes Mitchell's Rest Cure. Even though her room initially repulses her, she rests in the former nursery because John chose it for her. She stops her writing when she senses John's entry.

In her own text Gilman creates through the characterization of John a physician of "high standing" (10) who is also self-assured ("I am a doctor, dear, and I know" [23]) and thus similar to Owen North and to Mitchell himself. Moreover, John's authority is backed by the protagonist's well-respected physician/brother and by the threat of S. Weir Mitchell "only more so" (19). Unlike Mitchell's Alice, Gilman's heroine becomes aware of her submissiveness and defies her doctor's advice. Referring and deferring less to John as the story continues, the narrator pursues her ambitions: first, to find out the pattern of the wallpaper, then to tear it away, freeing the woman (and that part of herself) trapped behind the pattern. As she creeps along the walls of the sanitarium/prison, her actions move beyond the realm of sanity. Nonetheless, acting out of madness, she defies John and the male-dominated medical profession he represents. She creeps flamboyantly in the daytime as she desires. While Alice Leigh rips her fan to bits and acquiesces to her physician/husband, the nameless protagonist in "The Yellow Wallpaper" creeps over her physician/husband—a crucial reversal. Although her mad state allows her only a dubious victory,[29] in Gilman's story it is the male physician whose force is circumvented and who faints when confronted by the newly claimed autonomy of his female patient.

The behavior of Gilman's narrator also diverges from that of the female protagonists in *Dr. North and His Friends*, the sequel to *Characteristics*. This novel confirms the total submission of Alice Leigh, for whom even a dubious victory never comes. The narrator of *Dr. North and His Friends* refers to the once independent Alice Leigh as Mrs. North or "my wife." Throughout this novel, Alice's voice is silenced as a result of her constant deference to her husband/physician. Now unsure of her intellectual abilities, Alice Leigh relies on her husband to supply her with knowledge and support during social conversations: "I never can express what I mean. Sometimes I think I am clever, but when I talk it out I conclude that I am a fool. Tell me what I mean."[30] Frequently her discussions of social issues are flavored with her husband's paternalistic views. Although she once fervently wished to be a doctor, Alice radically alters her perception of a woman's aptitude for medicine and comes to hold her husband's—and Mitchell's—belief that a woman should solely be educated in the area of domestic duties. Her friend Sibyl Maywood, a memorable invalid in Mitchell's fiction, shares this view and voices Mitchell's belief in a woman doctor's inability to exert control: "I do not think I should like to have a woman doctor. . . . Oh, I should never obey her—never; why, I could not say. I should have no confidence" (127).

Sibyl Maywood enters Dr. North's circle when North's friend Xerxes Claybourne hires his cousin Sibyl as his secretary to aid him in his scholarship. Sibyl has a physical disability that becomes the subject of much conversation throughout the novel. Victor St. Clair, the free-spirited, attractive bachelor artist, says: "She is lame and not quite erect" (34). Claybourne explains apologetically: "She is slightly, very slightly deformed, and halts" (35). Using more graphic, clinical terms, Owen North laments that Sibyl has a "maimed body" (76). One shoulder is slightly higher than the other, and she walks in a halting gait, but "above this crooked frame rose a head of the utmost beauty" (42). Anne Vincent regrets that Sibyl is not also "deformed of face" (35) because her physical beauty makes her attractive to men whereas her "crumpled figure" (65)—a spinal distortion resulting from childbirth—precludes her chances for marriage. Her physical deformity is presented as an impediment to marriage and thus true happiness.

When Sibyl falls in love with St. Clair, Dr. North and his wife worry that she will lose her heart, that her strong romantic nature coupled with her "physical incompleteness" (230) will lead St. Clair to spurn her. Although Sibyl displays a vast amount of knowledge throughout the novel, her intelligence is compromised by her fits of hysterical passion.[31] Her friends Dr. and Mrs. North and Mrs. Vincent overlook her intellect—that she can cite Shakespeare and Goethe—and focus instead on her writing of anonymous poetic love letters to win the love of St. Clair. Alice and Owen North discover these letters, which they regard as dangerous folly because, in their opinion, St. Clair could never love a deformed person. St. Clair's initial rebuff worsens Sibyl's already unstable emotional condition and weakens her physical condition: she becomes nervous and anemic. Quickly intervening, Dr. North treats Sibyl with the Rest Cure and advises that Sibyl stop writing, rest after every meal, and give up her job as a secretary, because he believes that any type of work is too stressful for her. Exerting his power as a physician, he tells Sibyl that in order to become well again she must not become excited. He treats his patient like a child and exhibits a bedside manner similar to the physician/husband in "The Yellow Wallpaper." Eager to cure herself of nervousness and anemia, Sibyl adheres to all the components of the Rest Cure without hesitation: "I am in bed by your orders, sir, at nine; also, I sleep at once and well" (232). She has confidence in Owen North, obeys her male doctor completely, and is miraculously—and implausibly—cured. Sibyl's physical and emotional ailments virtually disappear as a result of her devotion to the Rest Cure ("the halt in her gait is at times hardly visible" [486]), making her fit for marriage to Victor St. Clair.

Dr. John in "The Yellow Wallpaper" attempts to cure the nameless narrator, as Dr. North did Sibyl, but fails to understand her nature. Not a docile patient like Mitchell's Sibyl or readily susceptible to influence like Alice Leigh, Gilman's protagonist at first subverts Dr. John's treatment by writing secretly. Abandoning her timidity, which Sibyl sustains throughout *Dr. North and His Friends*, the protagonist of "The Yellow Wallpaper" "disagrees" with the diagnosis of the male medical authorities (10). Instead of dutifully climbing into bed after every meal as Sibyl Maywood does, Gilman's narrator escapes what she considers to be punitive rest by feigning sleep. She writes covertly, hiding her journal when she hears John approaching because he "hates to have [her] write a word" (13). If we conceive of the narrator and protagonist as one, she continues to defy John merely through the act of writing her story.[32] Ironically, Gilman's narrator ultimately proves the dangerous consequences of her Rest Cure by remaining entrapped within the sanctity of the home. She actively explores the only text allowed to her—the yellow wallpaper in her prison/sanitarium. Her defiance leads her to crawl in madness in front of Dr. John, who faints before his wife. The nameless narrator of "The Yellow Wallpaper" shows the extreme consequences of living in a society in which the sanctified home proves confining to women. Gilman's narrator illuminates the dangers of following a rigid, restrictive therapeutic treatment. The narrator, though mad, defies the doctor's prescription for healthy eating, moderate exercise, and extended rest and chooses literal madness over John's cure for sanity. In defying her physician's attempt to suppress her, she writes herself into a position of power: she defiantly creeps over John but remains trapped within the home from which Gilman freed herself in order to stay "sane."

Had Gilman's fiction followed Mitchell's prescription for female patients, the righteous Dr. John would not have been "floored"; rather, by following the Rest Cure, the narrator, like Alice Leigh, would have been cured of her ambition to develop her intellect. Gilman concludes that had she herself followed Mitchell's advice, her fate would have been similar to her own narrator's: "It was not a choice between going and staying, but between going, sane, and staying, insane" (*Living*, 97).

In "overwriting" his treatment and the choices available to Mitchell's protagonists, Gilman challenges the happy ending that Mitchell envisions for obedient women. The grimness of Gilman's ending calls attention to the compromises that Mitchell's women make even though they seemingly achieve a happy ending. Although Sibyl Maywood becomes physically cured through following Dr. North's rigid prescription, she does not use her intellectual abilities. In *Dr. North and His Friends* Alice Leigh gains social stature and respectability as Mrs. North, but she loses the very spirit that makes her a compelling female character at the beginning of *Characteristics*.

Rejecting Mitchell's advice—" 'And never touch pen, brush or pencil as long as you live' " (96)—Gilman defied Mitchell and the typical behavior he imposed on his female patients both within his medical practice and his fiction. Continuing to revise Mitchell's fictionalization of female patients, she wrote plays, stories, novels, and nonfiction, with *Women and Economics* (1898) bringing her international acclaim. Although she believed that she never fully recovered from the nervous breakdown brought on by the strains of marriage and motherhood, she concluded of her writing: "A brain may lose some faculties and keep others. . . . To write was always as easy to me as to talk. Even my verse, such as it is, flows as smoothly as a letter, is easier in fact" (*Living*, 98–99).[33]

Although only "The Yellow Wallpaper" and *Herland* are well known today, Gilman was as prolific a writer as Mitchell. Like Mitchell's novels, her other fiction is formulaic, but her stock characters and the formula she prescribes diverge radically from his. Typically, through the intervention of an older woman, often a doctor, a young and innocent girl breaks from the restrictions or limitations that endanger her. For example, in "The Girl in the Pink Hat" (1916) a strong, older woman (whose occupation and name are never revealed) helps an innocent, courageous girl escape from the clutches of her criminal boyfriend who has deceived her about his intentions to marry her.

In "Mr. Peebles' Heart" (1914), Gilman's Dr. Joan Bascom appears to be the kind of physician Mitchell's Alice Leigh longed to be. In this story Gilman reverses the typical dynamics of the (male) doctor-(female) patient relationship. Dr. Bascom's brother-in-law suffers from a nervous breakdown that results, in her opinion, from his confining occupation, which proves necessary to support all the women who have clung to him with "tentacles." Dr. Bascom demands the confidence of her male patient, who protests a bit but follows her advice as docilely as Mitchell's female patients do Dr. Owen North. She prescribes a very different cure than S. Weir Mitchell's enforced rest, however—two years of independent travel. Mr. Peebles returns younger, healthier, stimulated. Without her husband to depend upon during his absence, his wife gains independence. Both improve due to the intervention of Dr. Bascom, who serves as a "new woman" and a role model for women readers.

Gilman's commitment to advance the lives of women and her understanding of women's problems engage the reader more than the style of her writing, which sounds hastily crafted at times. Nonetheless, Gilman never lost her faculty to write: literature offered her an opportunity to challenge the restrictions imposed upon women. By writing numerous stories voicing her dedication to improve conditions for women, Gilman defied Mitchell and the ethos he used to describe women in his fiction. To call upon the apt title of one of Gilman's own poems, Mitchell became "An Obstacle"[34] both in real life and fiction, one that Gilman implicated in "The Yellow Wallpaper" and ultimately "overwrote" by touching pen and pencil as long as she lived.[35]

Notes

1. Gilman was then Charlotte Perkins Stetson. She also published "The Yellow Wallpaper" under that name. For consistency, this article refers to her throughout as Gilman.

2. Gilman discusses S. Weir Mitchell's full prescription following her Rest Cure treatment in her autobiography, *The Living of Charlotte Perkins Gilman: An Autobiography* (New York: D. Appleton-Century, 1935), 96; hereafter cited as *Living*.

3. George Meredith was pleased with the results of a buttermilk diet S. Weir Mitchell had recommended, and he was enthusiastic about Mitchell's fiction; he considered *Roland Blake* Mitchell's best novel. Mitchell treated Walt Whitman occasionally and gave him funds to help him to continue writing. Suzanne Poirier notes, however, that "Mitchell's treatment of Jane Addams, Winifred Howells (daughter of William Dean Howells), and Charlotte Perkins Gilman, and the use of his treatment on Virginia Woolf caused cries of protest from all these women and their families" (15). Although Woolf never saw Mitchell, a British neurologist, Dr. Playfair, brought the Weir Mitchell Rest Cure to England in 1880 and encouraged its use. The treatment Woolf's physician, Dr. Savage, prescribed following her second breakdown in 1904 included a milk regimen, rest, and isolation. Although Woolf did not completely reject the treatment, she complained bitterly about it to friends and attacked it through her fiction such as *Mrs. Dalloway* (1925). In 1898 Edith Wharton traveled

to Mitchell's sanitarium in Philadelphia to seek Mitchell's care. Her treatment was more moderate: not hospitalized, she remained in a hotel room and was allowed to write letters; however, she had enforced bed rest and was permitted no visitors for four months. For more information on Mitchell's treatment of male and female literary figures, see Suzanne Poirier, "The Weir Mitchell Rest Cure: Doctor and Patients," *Women's Studies Quarterly* 10, no. 1 (1983): 15–40. For more discussion of Mitchell's relationship with Meredith and Whitman, see Ernest Earnest, *S. Weir Mitchell: Novelist and Physician* (Philadelphia: University of Pennsylvania Press, 1950), 40, 99–100, 115; hereafter cited as Earnest.

4.   Charlotte Perkins Gilman, *The Yellow Wallpaper* (Old Westbury: Feminist Press, 1973), 18; hereafter cited in the text.

5.   The *Definitive Edition* of S. Weir Mitchell's oeuvre amounts to 6500 pages. The exact number of his short story volumes and novels remains unknown because he destroyed several of these works before they were actually published.

6.   *Hugh Wynne* sold over one-half million copies and is often regarded as Mitchell's best book. In the foreword to *S. Weir Mitchell: Novelist and Physician*, Ernest Earnest writes that Mitchell's "*Hugh Wynne* was compared to *Henry Esmond*, his *Ode on a Lycian Tomb* to *Lycidas*." Jeffrey Berman also makes this point in "The Unrestful Cure: Charlotte Perkins Gilman and 'The Yellow Wallpaper,' " *The Talking Cure: Literary Representations of Psychoanalysis* (New York: New York University Press, 1985), 48; hereafter cited as Berman.

7.   David Rein similarly states: "Mitchell's novels should be evaluated anew, for his accomplishments deserve to be recalled more widely and wrought into the tradition of American culture" (*S. Weir Mitchell as a Psychiatric Novelist* [New York: International Universities Press, 1952], 202); hereafter cited as Rein.

8.   See Berman, 45–49, and Rein, 186–202. Berman's essay cites this important connection and discusses the range of Mitchell's fiction; however, his chapter does not explore the relationship between Gilman's fiction and Mitchell's.

9.   Earnest, 227, and Regina Markell Morantz, "The Perils of Feminist History," *Women and Health in America*, ed. Judith Walzer Leavitt (Madison: University of Wisconsin Press, 1984), 239–45. In her criticism of Ann Douglas Wood's essay, " 'The Fashionable Diseases': Women's Complaints and Their Treatment in Nineteenth-Century America," *The Journal of Interdisciplinary History* 4 (1973): 25–52, Morantz offers a much more favorable reading of S. Weir Mitchell than Wood, Poirier, and Gilman's biographer Ann J. Lane, author of *To Herland and Beyond: The Life and Work of Charlotte Perkins Gilman* (New York: Pantheon Books, 1990); hereafter cited as Lane. Perturbed that Mitchell's personality "is so utterly distorted in Wood's characterization" (240), Morantz rebuts specific claims that Wood makes in her essay: that Mitchell believed that women doctors would always be inferior to male doctors, that doctors were gods, and that patients were to be docile children. She presents Mitchell as a neurologist, not a "woman's doctor" as Wood does; she also discusses the effective use of his treatment on soldiers suffering from battle fatigue as well as the praise Mitchell received from Freud.

10.   Although Mitchell initially earned his reputation during the Civil War for his treatment of gunshot victims suffering from paralysis, he came to specialize in nervous diseases, which had plagued him as a young man. His first nervous breakdown occurred just after the Civil War, following the death of his young wife and his affluent Virginia physician father (who had initially opposed his decision to enter medicine); his second breakdown came three years after in 1872, following the death of his mother.

11.   S. Weir Mitchell, *Doctor and Patient* (Philadelphia: Lippincott, 1888), 117.

12.   S. Weir Mitchell, *Wear and Tear* (Philadelphia: Lippincott, 1871), 33.

13.   S. Weir Mitchell, quoted in Lane, 117.

14.   Mitchell did not anticipate that his female patients, under treatment, would continue to question and apply their creative minds as was the case with Gilman, who followed his treatment for one month.

15.   S. Weir Mitchell, "Rest in Nervous Disease: Its Use and Abuse," *A Series of American Clinical Lectures*, ed. E. C. Sequin, M.D., 1 (1875): 102.

16. S. Weir Mitchell, *A Comedy of Conscience* (New York: The Century Co., 1903), 8; hereafter cited in the text.

17. John was also S. Weir Mitchell's father's name and his son's name. Although the choice of name for the male protagonist in Mitchell's and Gilman's fiction may be merely coincidental, *Characteristics* was published prior to "The Yellow Wallpaper."

18. Rein also makes this point and argues, "While the main story [of *Roland Blake*] is about quite normal people, the main attraction is in the abnormal minor characters" (Rein, 190). Octopia, however, is not as minor a character as he implies.

19. Mitchell describes these women in *Fat and Blood* as "nervous women, who as a rule are thin, and lack blood" (Philadelphia: Lippincott, 1878), 7; hereafter cited in the text.

20. S. Weir Mitchell, *Roland Blake* (New York: The Century Co., 1901), 40; hereafter cited in the text.

21. In *Fat and Blood*, Mitchell describes this relationship and concludes "the nurse falls ill, and a new victim is found. I have seen an hysterical, anaemic girl kill in this way three generations of nurses" (30).

22. S. Weir Mitchell, *Constance Trescot* (New York: The Century Co., 1909), 222; hereafter cited in the text.

23. Rein uses this term to describe Octopia Darnell in *Roland Blake*, Constance Trescot in *Constance Trescot*, and Ann Penhallow in *Westways* (1914), Mitchell's last novel. See his chapter "The Couch-Loving Invalids."

24. Susan in *Constance Trescot*, like Olivia in *Roland Blake*, escapes her ministering role through marriage, and Constance goes abroad with a nursemaid.

25. These novels were not as well reviewed as some of Mitchell's other fiction. The *Nation* called *Characteristics* "not very exciting" but recognized that it was "sane and even in tone" ("More Novels," *Nation* 55 [8 December 1892], 437). The style of *Dr. North and His Friends* received more stringent criticism: "Almost everybody who believes himself to be intelligent may be heard, at one time or another, expressing a regret that the age of conversation is past. An attempt to read the conversations between 'Dr. North and His Friends' is likely to stifle such regrets; indeed, to convert them into an ardent prayer that the art may not be revived, at least in our time" ("Recent Novels," *Nation* 72 [28 February 1901], 182). The book was better received by the *Critic*, which called *Dr. North and His Friends* "a book such as only a wise and learned man could write, for it garners the wit and wisdom of a lifetime" ("Fiction," *Critic* 37 [January 1901], 86). For more discussion of these and other works, see Rein, particularly his concluding chapter entitled "Mitchell as a Novelist" (178–202).

26. This point has been much debated between Wood and Morantz; while Wood claims that Mitchell believes "women doctors would always be inferior to male physicians" in " 'The Fashionable Diseases' " (228), Morantz finds no firm support for this claim in *Fat and Blood* or any of Mitchell's writings (240).

27. S. Weir Mitchell, *Characteristics* (New York: The Century Co., 1891), 234; hereafter cited in the text.

28. While Mitchell's females typically cry in front of their physicians, Gilman's narrator conceals her sobbing.

29. The end of Gilman's controversial story invites conflicting interpretations of entrapment and liberation. While many critics read the conclusion as a triumph, some argue that she is defeated, and others assert that she achieves a partial victory. For further reading on this range of interpretations, see *The Captive Imagination: A Casebook on "The Yellow Wallpaper,"* ed. Catherine Golden. (New York: Feminist Press, 1991).

30. S. Weir Mitchell, *Dr. North and His Friends* (New York: Century, 1900), 18; hereafter cited in the text.

31. Sibyl Maywood is described as having a dual personality who carries out passionate acts in a somnambulist state.

32. This issue has recently been raised by Paula Treichler and Richard Feldstein. See Paula A. Treichler, "Escaping the Sentence: Diagnosis and Discourse in 'The Yellow

Wallpaper,' " *Tulsa Studies in Women's Literature* 3 (1984): 61–77; Richard Feldstein, "Reader, Text, and Ambiguous Referentiality in 'The Yellow Wallpaper,' " *Feminism and Psychoanalysis*, eds. Richard Feldstein and Judith Roof (Ithaca and London: Cornell University Press, 1989), 269–79.

33.   Gilman mentions in her autobiography that she lost the ability to read for longer than a short period of time. She also had trouble learning languages and following indexes.

34.   In her foreword to *The Living of Charlotte Perkins Gilman*, Zona Gale includes this poem along with "Similar Cases" as an indication of Gilman's constant preoccupation with the advance of women (xxxiii–xxxiv).

35.   This essay grew out of a Collaborative Student-Faculty Research Grant funded by Skidmore College during the summer of 1990. Erin Senack, now Assistant to the Editor of *Woman of Power* magazine, was instrumental in the research involved in this project.

Looking Backward: From *Herland* to *Gulliver's Travels*

Elizabeth Keyser

Most utopias are born of utopias, however pretentious the claims to complete novelty may be.

Utopian fantasies are as book-ridden as philosophical arguments, dependent upon an eternal dialogue with forerunners.[1]

In *Reinventing Womanhood* Carolyn G. Heilbrun explains how literary works that purport to deal with "the nature of man" but in fact deal only with men can be reinterpreted so as to serve as models for women.[2] Charlotte Perkins Gilman's feminist utopia, *Herland*, published in 1915, can be viewed as such a reinterpretation of *Gulliver's Travels*, especially of the Fourth Voyage. In *Herland* Gilman uses Swift's satire on human pride in general as a model for her attack on male pride in particular, offers an explanation for the Yahoo in human nature, and, finally, suggests how that Yahoo can be eradicated.

The complete *Gulliver's Travels* and *Herland*, together with its sequel, *With Her in Ourland* (1916), share a common preoccupation or theme. When in *Ourland* Ellador, a native of Herland, visits the United States, she compares the country to Gulliver imprisoned by the Lilliputians:

> "Here you are, a democracy—free—the power in the hands of the people. You let that group of conservatives saddle you with a constitution which has so interfered with free action that you've forgotten you had it. In this ridiculous helplessness—like poor old Gulliver—bound by the Lilliputians—you have sat open-eyed, not moving a finger, and allowed individuals—mere private persons—to help themselves to the biggest, richest, best things in the country. . . . What can we think of a Democracy, a huge, strong, young Democracy, allowing itself to become infested with such parasites as these?"[3]

Like Swift, Gilman is concerned with the way in which people fail to recognize their own strength, allow themselves to be enslaved, and then pride themselves on their identification with the individuals and institutions

Reprinted from *Studies in American Fiction* 11, no. 1 (1983): 31–46, with the permission of the journal.

that enslave them. In *Herland*, however, Gilman follows Swift even more closely to show how women in the early twentieth century are little more than beasts of burden, a theme she anticipates in *Women and Economics* (1899). There Gilman draws an analogy between the horse in captivity and women; they both work, but their exertions "bear no direct relation to [their] living."[4] Both are dependent economically on the wills of their masters. She then goes on to compare women's work in the home and caring for children with the work of a horse; their labors enable men to produce more than would be otherwise possible—they are economic factors but not economically independent (p. 13). Like Gulliver and the economically oppressed citizens of a democracy, both horses and women, through a combination of their own servility and the tyranny of others, have become so "saddled" as to have forgotten their freedom.

In *Herland* Gilman does with the sexes what Swift does with the reversal of stations and perspectives. In *Herland* the supposedly superior sex becomes the inferior or disadvantaged just as Gulliver in the first two voyages perceives himself first as the giant, then as the dwarf, and in the Fourth Voyage first as the higher, then as the lower animal.[5] At the beginning of *Herland* three young male scientists hear rumors of a highly civilized country populated only by women. Van, a sociologist, is intellectually fascinated by the idea of a state administered by women. Jeff, a physician and botanist with a poetic temperament, finds the idea of a nation of women romantically appealing. And Terry, a geographer by training but a wealthy playboy in practice, imagines an unlimited opportunity for sexual conquest. On entering Herland, however, the three suddenly find themselves as powerless as Gulliver in Brobdingnag or Houyhnhnmland. Once convinced that they cannot escape, the men cooperate with their captors, master the language, and are eventually freed, though they remain under the supervision of three middle-aged mentors. Finally they are allowed to meet the younger women, and all three fall in love. But when, after much deliberation, the Herlanders permit them to marry, they find themselves in the position of women in their own country—that of having to adjust to their partners and deny their own needs. In fact, their position is worse in that they have not, like the women of their own country, been conditioned for generations to accept it but have been conditioned to expect the opposite. At the book's end Jeff, like Gulliver among the Houyhnhnms, has come to acknowledge the superiority of his new country's social system; Van is still undergoing the painful process of reassessment; and Terry, who has been expelled for attempting to rape his wife, is completely unregenerate.

Van, Gilman's first-person male narrator, together with his two companions, serves many of the satiric functions performed by Gulliver. Like Gulliver, the three men have mistaken notions about the country they are entering and inappropriate strategies for dealing with the natives. Because Gilman's travellers arrive in Herland by design rather than by accident, they formulate much more elaborate theories, but these, like Gulliver's simpler ones, are comically disproved. Terry, the stereotypical male chauvinist, cannot conceive of a progressive, well-run country without men: "We mustn't look for inventions and progress; it'll be awfully primitive."[6] Significantly, he does not envision finding mature women, "just Girls and Girls and Girls" (p. 7). Jeff, a gentle idealist, expects to find a combination nunnery ("a peaceful, harmonious sisterhood") and nursery. Van, the social scientist, "held a middle ground, highly scientific, of course, and used to argue learnedly about the physiological limitations of the sex" (p. 9). He is convinced they will find men there even if the country is "built on a sort of matriarchal principle" (p. 7). When on landing they discover it to be a beautifully cultivated, obviously civilized country, they are certain of the presence of men. The presence of men suggests a need for protection as the presence of women alone would not. Thus "we saw to it that each of us had a good stock of cartridges" (p. 13). The three proceed cautiously until they hear the sounds of suppressed laughter. Van warns "look out for a poisoned arrow in your eye," but Terry, glimpsing three girls in a tree, retorts "in my heart, more likely" (p. 14). Pursuing the girls up the tree, Terry decides he will "have to use bait." "He produced from an inner pocket a little box of purple velvet . . . and out of it he drew a long sparkling thing, a neckless of big varicolored stones that would have been worth a million if real ones." The girl nearest him eyes it curiously but not like "a girl lured by an ornament" (p. 16). Amid shrieks of laughter she snatches it from him, drops to the ground, and, followed by her companions, swiftly proceeds to outrace the men. Terry's disgruntled comment is that "the men of this country must be good sprinters" (p. 17).

The parallels between the initial encounter with the Herlanders and Gulliver's with the Houyhnhnms are obvious. Gulliver too assumes that the inhabitants are men and their nature warlike. He walks "very circumspectly for fear of being surprised, or suddenly shot with an Arrow."[7] But he realizes that his trusty hanger will not defend him against a whole tribe, so he comes prepared to "purchase my Life from them by some Bracelets, Glass Rings, and other Toys, which Sailors usually provide themselves with" (p. 192). When, instead of savages, he encounters a Houyhnhnm, he attempts, like Terry, to treat it like an ordinary member of the species he is familiar with: "At last I took the Boldness, to reach my Hand towards his Neck, with a Design to stroak it; using the common Style and Whistle of Jockies when they are going to handle a strange Horse" (p. 194). But this horse is no more like the horses Gulliver is accustomed to than the Herlanders resemble Terry's previous conquests. The Houyhnhnm repels his "Civilities with Disdain" and altogether conducts himself in such a way that Gulliver is forced to conclude "that if the Inhabitants of this Country were endued with a proportionable Degree of Reason, they must needs be the wisest People upon Earth" (p. 195). But neither Terry nor Gulliver learns immediately that the natives are too intelligent and disinterested to be bribed by baubles. When surrounded by a band of middle-aged Herlanders, Terry presents their leader with a scarf and a circlet of rhinestones. Gulliver, believing the Houyhnhnm to be a magician in disguise, tries to barter a knife and a bracelet for a ride to the nearest village. Neither Herlander nor Houyhnhnm is much impressed with the offer.

In the opening chapters Gulliver expects to find primitive men, "savages," and assumes them to be both warlike and easily dazzled by cheap finery; Gilman's travellers expect to find either primitive women against whom they would need no defense other than a few trinkets or somewhat more civilized men against whom they would need to use weapons. Instead, Gulliver encounters the wise and peaceable Houyhnhnms, who protect him from the slings if not the arrows of the belligerent Yahoos, and Gilman's travellers encounter the "vigilance committee" of unarmed but unyielding Herlanders. But whereas Gulliver must learn that European warfare is just an advanced form of Yahoo savagery and that his assumption about primitive man's treacherous nature holds true for the rest of mankind, Gilman's travellers must learn that women are capable of cooperating for their own protection and that they can do so without resorting to male violence.

In retrospect, Van can laugh at their naive assumption "that if there were men we could fight them, and if there were only women—why, they would be no obstacles at all" (p. 21). But first he and his comrades must undergo a process of humiliation rather like what Gulliver undergoes in Lilliput, Brobdingnag, and the country of the Houyhnhnms. As they try to break through the solid mass of Herlanders, they are "lifted like children, straddling helpless children, and borne onward, wriggling indeed, but most ineffectually." They are "borne inside, struggling manfully, but held secure most womanfully" (p. 23). The adverb "manfully" in this context is ironic as the men's struggles have already been compared to those of willful children, thus suggesting the childish nature of many male heroics. The adverb "womanfully," on the other hand, points to a major theme of Gilman's work, what "we call masculine traits are simply human traits, which have been denied to women and are thereby assumed to belong to men: traits such as courage, strength, creativity, generosity, and integrity."[8] Women, too, possess power, though the absence of a feminine equivalent of "manfully" suggests how they have been persuaded to relinquish it.

Without men to accuse them of lacking femininity, the Herlanders have developed desirable human traits normally attributed to males. Van notes with surprise, "never, anywhere before, had I seen women of precisely this quality. Fishwives and market women might show similar strength, but it was coarse and heavy. These were merely athletic—light and powerful. College professors, teachers, writers—many women showed similar intelligence but often wore a strained nervous look, while these were as calm as cows, for all their evident intellect" (p. 22). But while Van is intellectually curious and Jeff openly admiring, Terry's overt response represents society's often more subtle one. He can "almost find them feminine" only when they knit. Otherwise "the Colonels," as he calls the middle-aged Herlanders, are woefully inadequate as women: "They've no modesty . . . no patience, no submissiveness, none of that natural yielding which is a woman's greatest charm" (p. 98). In short, they have few of the traits considered natural and desirable in women. Van, reflecting on Terry's response, which in part he shares, finally concludes that "those 'feminine charms' we are so fond of are not feminine at all, but mere reflected masculinity—developed to please us because they had to please us" (p. 59).

The middle chapters of *Herland*, in which Gilman's travellers settle down to learn the language and to instruct, and be instructed by, the Herlanders, correspond to those in which Gulliver instructs and is instructed by his Houyhnhnm master. One of their first questions, naturally enough, is how, if there are no men, the Herlanders reproduce themselves. The answer, they learn, is by parthenogenesis or, as Terry calls it, virgin birth. But just as in Houyhnhnmland "Power, Government, War, Law, Punishment, and a Thousand other Things had no Terms, wherein that Language could express them" (p. 211), so the word "virgin" is unknown to the Herlanders. Thus Jeff, like Gulliver conversing with his Houyhnhnm master, must resort to circumlocution and explains that "among mating animals, the term *virgin* is applied to the female who has not mated." But the Herlanders are even more puzzled: "And does it apply to the male also? Or is there a different term for him?" Jeff "passed over this rather hurriedly, saying that the same term would apply, but was seldom used" (p. 45). The unequal application of the term "virgin," like the lack of female equivalents for such words as "manfully," exposes the double standard. Just as Gulliver becomes more conscious and condemning of European vice as a result of having to explain it to the Houyhnhnms, so Jeff and Van, if not the incorrigible Terry, become conscious of sex bias in their society.

Like Gulliver in the second and fourth voyages of *Gulliver's Travels*, Gilman's travellers are confident at first that their society is more advanced than the one they are visiting. But as in *Gulliver's Travels* the naive natives either react with a shock which exposes the more sophisticated society or, as Van comments, "their lines of interrogation would gradually surround us in till we found ourselves up against some admissions we did not want to make" (p. 50). For example, the Herlanders are astonished when Terry boasts that women are not allowed to work in America; instead they are cherished, idolized, kept in the home (another concept unknown to the Herlanders). Gradually, through questioning, the Herlanders learn that one-third of the women, "the poorer sort," actually do work and that these, as Jeff admits, tend to produce more children. But Van hastens to explain that "in our economic struggle . . . there was always plenty of opportunity for the fittest to reach the top." Instead of questioning Van's Social Darwinism, however, his interrogator, by thoughtfully repeating "about one-third, then, belong to the poorest class" (p. 63), shifts the emphasis from where Van put it, on the many who rise to the top, to the significant number who fall to the bottom. Terry's mentor, Moadine, without being the least satirical, points up the incongruity of wealthy, idle women kept in the home to care for one or two children while poor women work outside to support many.

The women are aided in their investigations by Jeff, who translates Terry's self-approving and Van's evasive or euphemistic answers so as to give them a realistic picture of conditions in his country. Jeff, who has always idealized women, finds it easier than the others to give the Herlanders his unqualified admiration and respect. Like Gulliver in the land of the Houyhnhnms, he soon "began to view the Actions and Passions of Man [men] in a very different Light; and to think the Honour of my own kind [sex] not worth managing" (p. 224). Terry, on the other hand, like Gulliver in Brobdingnag, persists in attempting to puff up himself and his kind even while laboring at a tremendous disadvantage. The women, however, are unlike the Brobdingnagian king and the Houyhnhnm master in that they have a naive faith that the travellers' world, despite evidence to the contrary, must be better. Unlike the Brobdingnagians and Houyhnhnms, they see their geographical isolation as a limitation and feel that a more heterogeneous world must be preferable to such a homogeneous one: "We want so much to know—you have the whole world to tell us of, and we have only our little land! And there are two of you—the two sexes—to love and help one another. It must be such a rich and wonderful world" (p. 60). By making the women insist on their limitations, on their being only half a people, Gilman makes explicit what Swift and other utopian satirists have left implicit: that if a deprived or less than fully human race (or half the human race) can accomplish this much, a richly endowed, fully human race (or the entire race) ought to be able to accomplish much more.

The Herlanders' civilization is superior to a male-dominated one because, like that of the Houyhnhnms, "the most salient quality in all their institutions was reasonableness" (p. 76). Reason prevents both races from succumbing to vices, including those, such as masculine aggressiveness and female submissiveness, that commonly parade as virtues. The Herlanders are economical, inventive, far-seeing, and peaceable. They "thought in terms of the community. As such, their time-sense was not limited to the hopes and ambitions of an individual life" (p. 79). Like the Houyhnhnms, and unlike the Gulliver so enamored of the Struldbruggs, they have no use for the notion of immortality. Because their individual identities are bound up with that of the race, they have no desire for individual self-perpetuation. For this reason, the Herlanders have no surnames. As Van comments, "the element of personal pride seemed strangely lacking" (p. 75). Yet for all their community spirit, they have no word for patriotism, for such chauvinism, as Van comes to admit, "is largely pride, and very largely combativeness" (p. 94). Similarly, they have no word for family because, like the Houyhnhnms, who prize universal friendship and benevolence, "they loved one another with a practically universal affection, rising to exquisite and unbroken friendships, and broadening to a devotion to their country and people" (p. 94).

When, after generations of parthenogenesis, Herland was threatened by overpopulation, reason enabled the country not only to survive but to flourish. Rather than resigning themselves to a " 'struggle for existence' which would result in an everlasting writhing mass of underbred people trying to get ahead of one another" (p. 68), the Herlanders decided voluntarily to defer childbirth: "When that deep inner demand for a child began to be felt [a woman] would deliberately engage in the most active work, physical and mental; and even more important, would solace her longing by the direct care and service of the babies we already had" (p. 70). It became an honor for a woman to be chosen an "over-mother," one whose distinction conferred on her the privilege of being allowed to produce children over the limit of one per woman. In their practice of birth control the Herlanders are like the Houyhnhnms, for "when the Matron Houyhnhnms have produced one of each Sex, they no longer accompany with their Consorts" (p. 234). True, birth control is easier for both races to practice in that procreation is not accompanied in either case by sexual passion and pleasure.[9] The fact remains, however, that the Herlanders "were Mothers, not in our sense of helpless involuntary fecundity . . . but in the sense of Conscious Makers of People" (p. 68).

When after much deliberation the Herlanders decide to make "the Great Change" to bisexual reproduction, their lack of sex-tradition allows Gilman her most telling ironies. Permitted at last to court the women of their choice, Terry, Van, and Jeff find that their mode of courtship fails to work. Because the three young foresters they have selected are already self-sufficient—well-established in their careers and enjoying their communal way of life—they cannot appreciate the advantage of a "home" and someone to provide for them. And because the Herlanders' sex drive has lain dormant for generations, they do not look forward to marriage as a source of sexual pleasure; neither do they need husbands in order to have children. They have no notion of masculine chivalry or feminine coquetry, and, having no vanity, they cannot be flattered or won by gifts. As Van comes to realize, the women stand outside the tradition that would have made them easy prey:

> You see, if a man loves a girl who is in the first place young and inexperienced; who in the second place is educated with a background of caveman tradition, a middle-ground of poetry and romance, and a foreground of unspoken hope and interest all centering upon the one Event; and who has, furthermore, absolutely no hope or interest worthy of the name—why, it is a comparatively easy matter to sweep her off her feet with a dashing attack (p. 93).

Jeff and Van abandon their unsuccessful tactics, but Terry continues to try to convince Alima that he is conferring a favor and that she should reciprocate by utterly abandoning herself to him. Even after Alima, who seems to retain a vestige of the sex drive that has been so successfully sublimated by the other Herlanders, marries him, she cannot submit to the mastery Terry is used to asserting.

Although Van is much more willing to compromise than Terry, even he resents the position he finds himself in after his marriage to Ellador, a position similar to that of many married women. Reflecting on the difference between his expectations and the reality of his marriage, he begins to recognize that when most engaged couples discuss "the conditions of the Great Adventure," "there are some things one takes for granted, supposes are mutually understood, and to which both parties may repeatedly refer without ever meaning the same thing" (p. 121). Different educations give rise to different expectations, but Van now realizes that, once married, the man "generally carries out his own views of the case. The woman may have imagined the conditions of married life to be different; but what she imagined, was ignorant of, or might have preferred, did not seriously matter" (p. 121). Lacking the long tradition in which the woman accommodates herself to the man in marriage and having no "idea of that *solitude à deux* we are so fond of," the Herlanders naturally expect to continue their careers and to retain their personal privacy. To the males' chagrin, life goes on much as it did before marriage: "We had, as it were, all the pleasures of courtship carried right on; but we had no sense of—perhaps it may be called possession" (p. 125).

Of course, the males' greatest deprivation is sexual. Whereas the woman in marriage traditionally has had to have sex whenever her husband desired it, now the men can have sex only if their wives allow it. The Herlanders cannot understand the use of sex except for procreation and wish to postpone the consummation of their marriages until they are ready to have children. Each of the three males responds differently to sexual deprivation. Gentle, androgynous Jeff seems to have the least trouble moderating his sexual desires. Perhaps because he is less demanding, his wife, Celis, is less resistant, and it is clear by the end of the book that she is bearing their child. Van, during a longer probationary period, begins to realize that "what I had honestly supposed to be a physiological necessity was a psychological necessity" (p. 128). Ellador, by giving him a little too much of her company rather than withdrawing so that he will want her more, tends to defuse his sex drive: "Here was I, with an Ideal in mind, for which I hotly longed, and here was she, deliberately obtruding in the foreground of my consciousness a Fact. . . . I see now clearly enough why a certain kind of man . . . resents the professional development of women. It gets in the way of the sex ideal; it temporarily covers and excludes femininity" (p. 130). Meanwhile, however, a deep and lasting friendship with Ellador is growing, a friendship not dependent on sex.

But while Jeff and Van manage to cope with sexual frustration, Terry continues to try to master Alima. When his desperate attempt to rape her is thwarted, he receives what is by now for him a welcome sentence: "You must go home." When Ellador refers to Terry's "crime," Van attempts to argue that "after all, Alima was his wife" (p. 139). But Ellador, "for all her wide intellectual grasp, and the broad sympathy in which their religion trained them, could not make allowance for such—to her—sacrilegious brutality" (p. 139). Just as the repulsive Yahoos, hard as it is for Gulliver and the reader to identify with them, mirror the most loathsome human qualities, so Terry is a caricature of existing social prejudice and the irrational violence to which it can give rise. But extremists like Terry are not the only victims of social conditioning. That the much more moderate Van can view Ellador's indignation as a failure of tolerance reminds one of the "narrow Principles and short Views" which led the Brobdingnagian king to refuse Gulliver's offer of gun powder and suggests how pervasive are the beliefs in male prerogative and female duty.

While it is easy enough for the reader to dissociate herself—or even himself—from Terry's chauvinism, some of his criticisms of Herland seem convincing. Herland, like the land of the Houyhnhnms and most utopias, seems at best limited, incomplete, and, at worst, inhuman. Lewis Mumford's objections to utopias in general would undoubtedly extend to Herland: "Isolation, stratification, fixation, regimentation, standardization, militarization—one or more of these attributes enter into the conception of the utopian city."[10] Herland, despite its inhabitants' concern for the future, is, as Terry complains, a static society. Van in part agrees: "The years of pioneering lay far behind them. Theirs was a civilization in which untroubled peace, the unmeasured plenty, the steady health, the large good will and smooth management which ordered everything, left nothing to overcome" (p. 99). Yet after observing their children and young people Van begins to see "the folly of that common notion of ours—that if life was smooth and happy, people would not enjoy it" (p. 103). Van here anticipates the position of Northrop Frye, who, in countering readers' objections to utopias, makes the point that what appear to be constraints would "carry with them a sense of freedom" were the reader to experience them from inside a utopia.[11]

Life is smooth and happy for the Herlanders because their reason, like that of the Houyhnhnms, "is not mingled, obscured, or discoloured by Passion and Interest" (p. 233). But it is just this that Terry objects to: "They've neither the vices of men, nor the virtues of women—they're neuters!" Terry's remark is interesting for the suggestion that men's vices and women's virtues are somehow connected. Translated, Terry's objection seems to be that the Herlanders are without lust themselves and unwilling to be the objects of others' lust. Jeff's response to Terry, that "these women have the virtue of humanity, with less of its faults than any folks I ever saw" (p. 98), reinforces the idea that the "virtues of women," the so-called feminine virtues, are not virtues at all. Still, Jeff's defense of the Herlanders is more troubling to the reader than Terry's attack on them, for it leads one to ask whether they can really possess "the virtues of humanity" while lacking passion. It is one thing to have a mind unclouded by passion; it is another to be incapable of feeling it.

In having Van continue his courtship of Ellador after marriage,[12] Gilman seems very close to advocating what the Houyhnhnms in fact practice, sex for the sole purpose of procreation. Surely she makes Van appear foolish in his attempt to convince Ellador that "there were other, and as we proudly said 'higher,' uses in this [sex] relation than what Terry called 'mere parentage.'" "In the highest terms," Van attempts to explain that "all the power of beautiful permanent mated love" comes through sexual expression, which also provides an impetus to creative work (pp. 125–27). But Van is embarrassed when Ellador asks if in his country he has found "high and lasting affection appearing in proportion to this indulgence," and he feels still more uncomfortable when she naively believes, on the basis of his claims, that "you have a world full of continuous lovers, ardent, happy, mutually devoted," producing "floods, oceans of such work, blossoming from this intense happiness of every married pair!" (pp. 126–27). When she falls silent thinking, so does Van, presumably of the difference between his self-serving vision of sexual love and the reality he knows all too well.

Although this dialogue ironically implies that sexual indulgence can destroy happiness and stifle creativity rather than promote them, reflection suggest that Gilman is not actually recommending passionless unions between the sexes. Instead, she is doing what Northrop Frye sees most utopian writers as doing—establishing a standard by which to judge existing society (p. 31). As Gulliver says halfway through his Fourth Voyage, "the many Virtues of those excellent Quadrupeds placed in opposite View to human Corruptions, had so far opened my Eyes, and enlarged my Understanding, that I began to view the Actions and Passions of Man in a very different Light" (p. 224). By having Van argue the ennobling effects of sexual love, and by having Ellador question him as to those effects, Gilman not only exposes the delusions that are suffered and encouraged about sex; she suggests the effects it might have were people more discriminating. Were everyone, like Gulliver, to see the "Passions of Man [or men] in a very different Light"; were they, like Jeff and Van, to recognize the spurious quality of much sexual provocation, that "very much, of what [was] honestly supposed to be a physiological necessity was a psychological necessity" arising from overdeveloped sex differences (pp. 128–29); and were they to establish sexual relationships on the broader base of respect and friendship, as Jeff and Van are forced to do, then sex might indeed become a "climactic expression . . . specialized to higher, purer, nobler uses" (p. 127). When intimacy produces the conditions Ellador naively assumes it must, then it will be more than a "beautiful idea"; it will be a beautiful reality.

According to Frank and Fritzie Manuel, utopias provide a "leap into a new state of being in which contemporary values in at least one area—the critical one for the utopian—are totally transformed or turned upside down" (p. 8). Gilman, by concentrating on the one area of sex roles, may seem limited and superficial where Swift is sweeping and profound. And surely no one would argue that *Herland* is a literary masterpiece comparable to *Gulliver's Travels*. But *Herland* (illuminated by *Women and Economics*) can be said to repair a significant omission in Swift's anatomy of human nature by tracing a main source of human self-alienation to the division between the sexes. And by appropriating Swift's form in order to amend his analysis, Gilman provides an example of the collaboration possible between men and women.

In *Women and Economics* Gilman argues that, in most species, both sexes adapt to their environment through the process of natural selection. Although they also develop secondary sex characteristics that distinguish them from each other, natural selection keeps sexual selection under control. In the human race, however, Gilman sees a Darwinian version of Milton's "hee for God only, shee for God in him" for the male by making the female economically dependent on him, interposed between her and the environment. Thus in the human female natural selection, which would make her more like the male, is checked, and sexual selection, the process by which she acquires complementary or contrasting qualities in order to attract the male, runs rampant. Yet as every human being is the product of both parents' genetic make-up, the entire race suffers attenuation (pp. 34–39).

Because a woman's "economic profit comes through the power of sex-attraction," she must make some kind of bargain with the opposite sex, whether it be the short-term bargain of prostitution, for which she is denigrated, or the long-term bargain of marriage, on which she is congratulated. Her need to bargain with her sexuality "keeps alive in us the instincts of savage individualism" (p. 121) and impedes "the tendency of social progress to develope co-operation in its place" (p. 110). Like other feminists, such as Mary Wollstonecraft, Gilman feels most women, because of their economic dependence, tend to be egocentric—wrapped up in themselves, their homes, their children—and thus less likely than men to rise to the level of disinterested benevolence. But women's overdevelopment of and obsession with the single art of pleasing men takes its toll on men as well. As Gilman writes in *The Home: Its Work and Influence*, "the woman is narrowed by the home and the man is narrowed by the woman."[13] Most men remain economic individualists and, kept in a state of constant titillation, their reason is, as Swift observed, "mingled, obscured, or discoloured by Passion and Interest." Van, in Herland, remembers how "we were always criticizing *our* women for *being* so personal" (p. 126), but he and Terry miss that exclusive preoccupation with husband and home. In the world they are used to, economic individualism bred of dependence makes it impossible for women to transcend the merely personal or egocentric, and their insistence on the personal drags down men as well.

Women's inferiority of status and often character makes unequal matches inevitable, and the progeny are "hybrids," torn between selfish impulses and a yearning for virtue. Swift, too, presents man as a product of what Gilman in *Women and Economics* calls "moral miscegenation" (p. 339): Gulliver's capacity for reason allies him with the Houyhnhnms, but his passions ally him with the Yahoos. Gilman argues that at one time the instinct of savage individualism, as well as pronounced sex differences, was necessary to the survival of the race. But because of women's economic dependence, the savage instinct has long outlasted its usefulness. Swift seems to suggest something similar when he has the Houyhnhnm master point out how Gulliver lacks the sharp nails and physical agility of the Yahoo even though, according to Gulliver's account, civilized human beings are just as rapacious. Whether imperfectly evolved or "fallen," however, humanity, both authors believe, is cursed with a divided nature. In *Women and Economics* Gilman argues that man has long blamed woman for his plight, but his attempts to punish her have only worsened it (pp. 332–33). Man has also thwarted his own and the race's progress by insisting that the development of woman's talents would be injurious to motherhood. But the more woman is limited "to sex-functions only, cut off from all economic use and made wholly dependent on the sex-relation as means of livelihood, the more pathological does her motherhood become" (p. 182). On this point Swift would agree, for Gulliver's "Master thought it monstrous in us to give the Females a different kind of Education from the Males . . . whereby, as he truly observed, one Half of our Natives were good for nothing but bringing Children into the World: And to trust the Care of their Children to such useless Animals, he said was yet a greater Instance of Brutality" (p. 235). Man cannot promote his own development by placing restrictions on that of woman. Under constraint she becomes still less like him, her difference gives rise to violent passions, and the cycle of mismatches and improper nurture is perpetuated.

Swift, like Gilman, seems to believe that rational cooperation as opposed to irrational aggression cannot take place while people are blinded by passion and that people would be less its prey were there greater similarity and equality between the sexes. But Swift, unlike Gilman, holds out little hope for humanity. Gilman, in her appropriation of the Fourth Voyage as a model, seems to be agreeing with Swift's analysis of human nature, but she also seems to be offering an explanation and solution for it. Unlike Swift, Gilman in *Women and Economics* envisions a time when "a general Disposition to all Virtues" might be as natural to us at it is to the Houyhnhnms. Once women are freed from their socio-economic bondage, "we shall no longer conceive of ethical progress as something outside of and against nature, but as the most natural thing in the world. Where now we strive and agonize after impossible virtues, we shall then grow naturally and easily into those very qualities; and we shall [again like the Houyhnhnms] not even think of them as especially commendable" (p. 340). "The largest and most radical effect of restoring women to economic independence" will be wholeness; individualism in the sense of selfish striving will give place to individuality or the integration of the self. Then "we shall be able to feel simply, to see clearly, to agree with ourselves, to be one person and master of our own lives, instead of wrestling in such hopeless perplexity with what we have called 'man's dual nature' " (p. 332).

In the final chapter of *Herland* Van sees the drama of human history as enacted by men and excluding women. But he also sees that for the Herlanders an equivalent drama has been enacted solely by women. The Herlander's historic panorama is more impressive than the male-dominated one—it has the same constructive elements and none of the destructive ones. But it is nonetheless partial, incomplete, as Ellador realizes. Thus she and Van choose to leave utopia, unlike Terry and Gulliver who are exiled from it. Whereas Terry was impervious to utopian values and Gulliver made despairing by them, Van and Ellador hope somehow to translate them into action. Gilman's utopia is more optimistic than its model, just as there may be more hope for man in the collective sense of men and women than there is for man in the sense of men alone.

Notes

1. Frank E. Manuel and Fritzie P. Manuel, *Utopian Thought in the Western World* (Cambridge: Belknap Press, 1979), pp. 13, 110.

2. Carolyn G. Heilbrun, *Reinventing Womanhood* (New York: Norton, 1979).

3. Charlotte Perkins Gilman, *With Her in Ourland*, serialized in *The Forerunner*, 7 (1916), 184.

4. Charlotte Perkins Stetson, *Women and Economics: A Study of the Economic Relation Between Men and Women as a Factor in Social Evolution* (Boston: Small, Maynard, 1899), p. 7.

5. Esme Dodderidge in *The New Gulliver: Or the Adventures of Lemuel Gulliver, Jr. in Capovolta* (New York: Taplinger, 1978) seems to have taken her cue from both Swift and Gilman. Her "new Gulliver," finding himself in Capovolta, where the sex roles are reversed, has to submit to various humiliations such as sexual harrassment at his secretarial job and the loss of his executive wife to a shallow male beauty. When his wife deserts him, he is torn between his need to stay home with the children and his need to work in order to supplement his wife's meager child-support checks. Despite the fact that Dodderidge refers explicitly to Swift and has her Gulliver imitate his prose style, she does not, like Swift and Gilman, present a superior society by which to evaluate our own.

6. Charlotte Perkins Gilman, *Herland*, introd. Ann J. Lane (1915; rpt. New York: Pantheon Books, 1979), p. 8. All further references will be to this edition and will appear in the text.

7. Jonathan Swift, *Gulliver's Travels*, ed. Robert A. Greenberg (New York: Norton Critical Editions, 1970), p. 193. All further references will be to this edition and will appear in the text.

8. Lane, "Introduction," *Herland*, p. xi. Thus Gilman anticipates a 1970 study which found that both men and women social scientists, when asked to identify desirable masculine, feminine, and, finally, adult traits, tended to identify the same traits as masculine and adult

but different and even opposing traits as feminine. See Inge K. Broverman, et al., "Sex-role Stereotypes and Clinical Judgments of Mental Health," *Readings on the Psychology of Women*, ed. Judith M. Bardwick (New York: Harper and Row, 1972), pp. 320–24. According to the Broverman study, women are placed "in the conflictual position of having to decide whether to exhibit those positive characteristics considered desirable for men and adults, and thus have their 'femininity' questioned, that is be deviant in terms of being a woman; or to behave in the prescribed feminine manner, accept second-class adult status, and possibly live a lie to boot" (p. 324).

9. I suspect that Gilman, in having the Herlanders reproduce by parthenogenesis, was advocating that procreation be dissociated from sexual pleasure. As Carolyn Heilbrun argues in *Reinventing Womanhood*, "the birth of a child must come to be seen universally as a profound event: not the distant result, often accidental, of sexuality. We shall probably come to recognize before too long the essential rightness of those earlier peoples who denied or ignored the relation between sex and childbirth. That children should arrive in the world, unwelcome and unprepared for, as a consequence of lust or sexual pleasure, is no longer supportable as an ideal except by the most retrograde theories of human behavior" (pp. 194–95). A recent feminist utopian novel, *Woman on the Edge of Time*, by Marge Piercy (New York: Fawcett Crest, 1976), also presents a society in which sex is wholly divorced from procreation. In fact, her women no longer bear children "cause as long as we were biologically enchained, we'd never be equal. And males never would be humanized to be loving and tender" (p. 105). Instead, children are produced in laboratories, and both male and females can become mothers.

10. Lewis Mumford, "Utopia, The City and The Machine," *Utopias and Utopian Thought*, ed. Frank E. Manuel (Boston: Beacon, 1967), p. 9.

11. Northrop Frye, "Varieties of Literary Utopias," *Utopias*, p. 31.

12. In chapter 8 of *Ourland* we learn that Van's marriage to Ellador is still unconsummated, although he has "the dear hope of a further fulfillment" (p. 210). This hope has been realized by the end of the book, for the last line reads "and in due time a son was born to us" (p. 325).

13. Charlotte Perkins Gilman. *The Home: Its Work and Influence* (New York: McClure, Phillips, 1903), p. 277.

Victorian Daughters: The Lives and Feminism of Charlotte Perkins Gilman and Olive Schreiner

BARBARA SCOTT WINKLER

In the period before World War I, when most feminists in Britain and America were preoccupied with the struggle to gain the vote, two women addressed instead the social and economic roots of women's oppression, Charlotte Perkins Gilman and Olive Schreiner. Both were recognized as powerful feminist voices by their contemporaries. Gilman's most important work, *Women and Economics*, was acclaimed in the United States and England as an articulate argument for women's economic freedom.[1] Schreiner, a South African novelist, explored the theme of women's subjection in her fiction, most notably in "Three Dreams in a Desert" and *The Story of an African Farm*, as well as in her theoretical *Woman and Labor*, which was hailed as "the Bible of the British Women's Movement."[2]

The writings of these two women are not only of historical interest as statements of nineteenth century feminism but also raise issues of enduring significance. Both Schreiner and Gilman examined the reasons for and ramifications of women's exclusion from the public sphere, the psychological effects of women's economic dependence upon men, and the relationship between patriarchy and capitalism. They argued for women's participation in all walks of life, the elimination of the economic motive from marriage, and, in Schreiner's case, the sexual freedom of women.

Yet both women must be understood in the context of their time. Schreiner, born in 1855, grew up on the colonial frontier of South Africa in a remote section of the British Cape Colony. Gilman, born in 1860, was raised in New England. Despite these differences in their childhood environments, they had the Anglo-American culture of Victorianism in common and were raised according to the precepts of Victorian womanhood.[3] While their brothers were trained for careers, they were expected to become the pious and dependent helpmeets of men and to subordinate their own desires to the needs of their families. While Schreiner and Gilman rebelled against

Reprinted from *Michigan Occasional Papers in Women's Studies* 13 (Winter 1980), 1–73, with the permission of the publisher.

this submissive and domestic model of womanhood, they assimilated the requirement of service to others. Their feminism was as much influenced by concern for the moral good of society as it was shaped by desire for justice for women.

Parallels in both the lives and feminism of Schreiner and Gilman emerge from their struggle with the Victorian feminine role. . . . The first signs of assertiveness against the restrictions placed upon them as females can be seen in their rebellion against the moral and religious codes of their families. Skepticism, the critical spirit, and rejection of religious authority were not unknown to other Victorians, male as well as female. But for Schreiner and Gilman, the religious and moral struggle was connected with their struggle against the submissiveness, dependency, and suppression of self inherent in the Victorian conception of femininity. For both, this moral struggle involved conflict with their mothers who attempted to raise them in accordance with the prevailing social norms.

Conflict with the social norms also affected Schreiner's and Gilman's ideas about and experience of marriage and motherhood. Yet as each woman painfully fought for a more egalitarian relationship between the sexes, neither was able to escape entirely from the Victorian conception of femininity, and, as we shall see, it subtly affected their ideas about womens' roles in the past, present, and future.

. . . The relationship between mother and daughter was a highly charged one for Schreiner. Although she was able to empathize with her mother elsewhere, Schreiner's fictional images of female grotesques and petty tyrants expressed her rage against Rebecca [Lyndall Schreiner].[4] Although Schreiner recognized that women internalize their oppression, she created split images of women as powerful evil accomplices of men or victims and their sacrificial protectors that caricatures but does not elucidate the mother-daughter bond under patriarchy. This triple image of women enabled her to enshrine the principle of motherhood in her spiritual thinking, even as she denied that women were the moral superiors of men. . . . Schreiner, however, later admitted that men could be nurturant figures and that women could be cruel. Although she denied women were the moral superiors of men, Schreiner, by idealizing motherhood, showed the extent to which the Victorian concept of womanhood still influenced nineteenth century feminist opponents of the woman's sphere.[5] . . .

Like Schreiner, Gilman also rebelled against her mother's authority and the culturally dominant image of proper feminine behavior. And like Schreiner, Gilman's rebellion was acted out in the context of religion and ethics. However, the religious context in which Gilman's struggle took place was not orthodox evangelical Protestantism, but rather Swedenborgianism. . . .

. . . While Gilman never identified with her mother's religion, she assimilated the Swedenborgian message of love and service to collective humanity. She later acknowledged the extent to which her mother's attempts to mold her nature had succeeded: she admitted to having inherited her mother's "profound religious tendency" as well as her "implacable sense of duty."[6] Like Schreiner, Gilman abandoned the notion of a personal patriarchal deity and redefined God as an underlying presence and power, an ordering or unifying principle, upon which human beings could rely in order to infuse the universe and their own lives with meaning. This unity was present in the solidarity of the human community and one's responsibility to it.[7]

. . . On the other hand, Gilman's rebellion against her mother's attempts to completely control and mold her was later translated into her chief criticism of religion. All religions, according to Gilman, were marred by the demand for unquestioning obedience, the origin of which was ultimately to be found in obedience to parental authority.[8] Like Schreiner's, Gilman's first experience of the tyranny of the powerful over the weak was at the hands of another woman, her mother. Yet Gilman was also aware of her mother's own relative powerlessness, her inability to control the circumstances of her life. Impoverished by her husband's desertion, given the lack of economic opportunities for women, Mary Perkins was dependent on the bounty of others. Submissiveness, even if imposed upon women by other women was, according to Gilman, the mark of a subject class to which all women belonged.[9] Religion, in Gilman's experience and estimation, had been a major cultural agent in the enforcement of that subjugation.

Gilman criticized the effects of women's economic and psychological dependence in ethical terms. While women's subordination had fostered "self-indulgent habits" and "irresponsible dominance" in men, it encouraged "blind submission an unthinkable [sic] acceptance of authority" and prevented "the growth of self-control" in women.[10] Relinquishing self-control and submitting to the control of others was a kind of ethical paralysis.[11] This was the lesson of her rebellion against her mother's demand for complete obedience.

Both Schreiner and Gilman engaged in early struggles for self-definition. Schreiner's rebellion was the more explicitly religious struggle. Schreiner had been brought up as a believer in the evangelical Protestantism that she finally repudiated, while Gilman never overtly identified with her mother's Swedenborgianism. Yet both Schreiner and Gilman later expressed their struggle against obedience to authority in religious terms. In the pre-Freudian nineteenth century the internal life was an affair of the spirit and defined in a religious context.

The rebellions of Schreiner and Gilman also implied struggle against the feminine role and repudiation of the submissiveness required of them as females. They recognized this and their struggle against maternal authority led them to later question authoritarian social relations, especially the hierarchical relations of the sexes in which women were subordinate to men. Yet neither Schreiner nor Gilman were entirely able to free themselves from the Victorian definition of womanhood. They struggled with the conflict between selflessness and self-concerned behavior. Even as they attacked the confinement of women to the domestic sphere, they employed the rhetoric of motherhood and upheld the moral requirement of service to others as an originally, if not exclusively, feminine virtue. The Victorian ideal of womanhood not only influenced their theoretical conceptions of woman's role in society but shaped their personal experience as well.

The Victorian feminine role required the suppression of one's own needs in favor of service to other individuals, especially one's family members. A woman's identity was almost exclusively defined by roles that implied connection with other individuals within the family: as daughter, wife, mother. Inability or unwillingness to confine one's identity to the interpersonal demands of these roles could be censured as selfishness. For example, Gilman's mother condemned her as "thoughtless" because she did not "think of other people."[12] Both Gilman and Schreiner were sufficiently influenced by this ideal that marriage became a difficult problem for them. As girls they had asserted themselves, bringing them into conflict with their families. They initially interpreted marriage as loss of newly won freedom, as requiring subordination and self-suppression.[13] Yet both did marry and eventually struggled toward a more egalitarian vision of marriage.[14]

. . . [Like Gilman,] Schreiner did not reject marriage; she wanted to reform or purify it so that it no longer entailed the subordination of women that she herself had feared, but rather was an intimacy of equals.

Schreiner therefore struggled toward a more egalitarian vision of relations between the sexes, even as she was fascinated by the image of sacrificial womanhood. However, Schreiner's critique of marriage was confined to psychic compatibility and economic independence and did not extend to sex roles. Schreiner assumed that women would continue to be the primary caretakers of children. Like most Victorians, she was impressed with the power of mothers to shape future generations. She felt that "one woman better fitted to be a mother means a whole generation starting with a greater vantage in life."[15] However, unlike most Victorians, Schreiner believed that women were ill-prepared to do a good job as mothers precisely because of their confinement to the domestic sphere. (Gilman concurred in this opinion.)

. . . While Schreiner maintained that women were poor mothers because their confinement to the domestic sphere narrowed their interests and crippled their abilities, Gilman went further. . . . Since domestic work kept women out of the world, which Gilman saw as the arena of progress in contrast to the static home, the development of the human race was necessarily retarded. . . . Gilman's attack on "matriolatry" and the position of women as domestic servants within the family can be seen as undermining both the material and ideological bases for the sentimental idealization of women as saintly givers who devote themselves to the needs of others. Nevertheless, Gilman continued to be influenced by this Victorian ideal and it shaped her explanation of the origin of women's oppression. . . . In words reminiscent of Schreiner's image of motherhood as the underlying principle of life, she declared that "service and love and doing good are the spirit of motherhood, and the essence of human life."[16]

. . . Service to society was the lifelong ethos Gilman adopted as a compromise between the demand that she subordinate her needs to the needs of others and her own conviction that women had a wider role to play in the world. This ethos justified both women's struggle for liberation and their past subordination as socially necessary and eliminated the need for conflict. Gilman's evolutionary model is teleological. She justified the past subjugation of women as socially necessary because, for her, evolution was essentially progressive, even if the action of evolution was circumscribed by human error and ignorance. Although Gilman maintained that relations between the sexes were the result of patriarchy, she denied the need for even temporary struggle between men and women. Instead she maintained that "progress," the greater good of society, mandated the entrance of women into the labor force and that this action would inevitably liberate them.

Gilman's model is also ahistorical. Her description of the position of woman throughout history is a projection of that role of the nineteenth century middle-class woman, as defined by the cult of domesticity, backward in time. Furthermore, by defining the public sphere as the arena of progress, Gilman removed women from history. There is the tendency in her argument to see women as victims, not participants, and their role as unchanging and to devalue their experience as not part of civilization.

Gilman ultimately attributed the characteristics of capitalism to the sex-linked natures of men and women fostered by women's economic dependence. The modern industrial world was characterized by "the brutal ferocity of excessive male energy struggling in the market place as in a battlefield and the unnatural greed generated by the perverted condition of female energy."[17] Gilman, therefore, believed that the entrance of women into the labor force would not only bring about the liberation of women, but also an end to the capitalist system as she knew it.

> We shall not move from the isolated home to the sordid shop and back again, in a world torn and disserved by the selfish production of one sex and the selfish consumption of the other; but we shall live in a world of men and women humanly related, as well as sexually related, working together, as they were meant to do, for the common good of all.[18]

To Gilman, women's economic dependence and social isolation in the home is the single villain. She therefore took one aspect of the social relations under capitalism as almost the whole of her analysis.[19] Gilman's language is as much moral as it is political and scientific—"greed" and "selfishness" are the antisocial effects of the "perverted" relations between men and women. Gilman valued the liberation of women primarily because it would promote the common good. At times she seems to succumb to blaming the victim in the heat of her argument because she is intent upon emphasizing the pernicious effects of oppression. Thus women become "social idiots" with "low-grade intelligence," the "selfish consumers" who hinder progress.[20]

Service to society was also the main focus of Schreiner's analysis of women's oppression. Economic dependence, which she like Gilman identified as the single most important feature of women's subjugation, came about as a result of their declining usefulness to society. According to Schreiner's more historical analysis, industrialization was the culprit. Before industrialization, women's labor was essential and valued. Women were the first farmers. When men took this work for themselves, women remained productive laborers since they processed raw materials into finished goods for their households. Women also raised and educated numerous children and nursed the sick and wounded with home-made remedies. But industrialization brought an end to the home workshop, and what was once women's work became the province of men when it was removed to the factory. Women's duties as the bearers and educators of children also diminished. Whereas, at one time many children were needed as potential workers, this was no longer the case, since mechanical invention had lessened the need for masses of untrained workers. A failing [sic] infant mortality rate also contributed toward decreasing the number of years women spent in childbearing. The establishment of schools largely stripped women of their function as educators of the young. The shrinking away of women's traditional functions, according to Schreiner, was the main cause of the women's movement, as women sought new areas of labor and expression.

With certain important exceptions, Schreiner did not believe that women were the equals of men in the pre-industrial period. She recalled a moving conversation she had with a Bantu woman who impressed upon her the subjection of women to men in tribal society and by analogy in primitive times. Like Gilman, Schreiner concluded that the past subordination of women had been necessary.

> It was this conversation which first forced upon me the fact, which I have since come to regard as axiomatic, that the women of no race or class will ever rise in revolt or attempt to bring about a revolutionary readjustment of their relation to society, however intense their suffering and however clear their perception of it, while the welfare and persistence of their society requires their submission.[21]

The fact that women were seeking to "adjust their position" in modern times was proof that "women's acquiescence was no longer necessary or desirable."[22]

Schreiner enlisted both the course of history and evolution in behalf of the woman's movement. Like Gilman, Schreiner maintained that the subordination of women inevitably circumscribed the progress of which men were capable through the action of heredity:

. . . While modern Europeans could not go back to the stable relations of the Boer, they could learn from the respected usefulness of Boer women. The main impulse behind the modern women's movement was the desire to replicate that usefulness within the new conditions of industrial society. Thus Schreiner cleared feminists of the charge of frivolity and self-seeking, that under the guise of work they sought "only increased means of pleasure and self-indulgence . . . new means of self-advertisement and parasitic success."[23] In contrast, Schreiner asserted

> The Woman's Movement is essentially a movement based on woman's determination to stand where she has always stood beside man as his co-labourer. And the moral fervour which is the general accompaniment of this movement rises from woman's conviction that in attempting to readjust herself to the new conditions of life and retain her hold on the social labours of her race, she is benefiting not herself only, but humanity.[24]

Schreiner, like Gilman, argued for equal access to work on the basis of service as well as justice; woman's participation in the labor force would lead to further progress. Schreiner emphasized that women's economically dependent relationship with men, which she called "sex-parasitism," was only a broader form of prostitution.[25]

. . . Schreiner thus shared with the purity reformers who fought the regulation of prostitution the belief that sexual corruption was the greatest blight on society.[26] Gilman also believed that sexual impurity was one of society's foremost problems. As she wrote in *Women and Economics*, women were unnaturally modified toward sexuality and frequent sexual indulgence was an unnatural excrescence that would disappear when relations between the sexes moved toward equality. Gilman, like many other American and British feminists, upheld a single standard of purity and praised monogamy as the highest form of sexual union.[27] While Schreiner also condemned the use of women as "passive tools of . . . sexual indulgence,"[28] and praised monogamy in *Woman and Labor*, she prophesied a time when sexuality would come into its own, when women became the equals and co-workers of men. "So far from the economic and social independence of the woman exterminating sexual love between man and woman, it would for the first time fully enfranchise it."[29] While Schreiner felt that the ideal of monogamy had not yet been fulfilled by most men and women, someday it, too, would be superseded. Schreiner shared her recognition of female sexuality with [Havelock] Ellis, a leading theorist of sexual modernism,[30] and their mutual friend Edward Carpenter, utopian socialist and defender of homosexuality who, in his book *Love's Coming of Age*, argued that "only when the free woman is honored will the prostitute cease to exist."[31]

Schreiner made a distinction between the corruption or "impurity" of prostituted relations and the beauty of the sexual instinct in and of itself. As she wrote in 1907: "I always feel that the sexual instinct pure and simple is much maligned; that the worst and meanest vices of life do *not* arise from sexual passion pure and simple."[32] Unlike the purity reformers, who preached that immoderate sexual indulgence was at the bottom of other corruptions in society, Schreiner maintained that it was

> brutality and selfishness that degrades and tarnishes the divinity of sex . . . Sex intercourse is the great sacrament of life—he that eateth and drinketh unworthily eateth and drinketh damnation to himself, but it may be the most beautiful sacrament between two souls without any thought of children.[33]

Schreiner, therefore, differed from Gilman in her more positive evaluation of sexuality, although they both agreed that only equality between men and women could produce "pure," i.e., undegraded sexual relations.[34]

While Schreiner, like Gilman, maintained that such equality could never be achieved until women entered the labor force, she did not believe that capitalism would be transformed thereby. Gilman held that feminism and the labor movement were "parts of the same pressure, the same world-progress. An economic democracy must rest on a free womanhood; and a free womanhood inevitably leads to an economic democracy."[35] In contrast, while Schreiner felt that both movements arose from the same material conditions and should be fought "co-extensively," they were essentially distinct and separate fights. Schreiner warned that women could not rely on the "male labor movement" to free them: Male trade unionists, especially, actively fought against women's entrance into their fields of labor.[36] A more equitable distribution of wealth among only male workers might even "open up exactly those conditions which made parasitism possible to millions of women today leading healthy and active lives."[37]

Schreiner maintained that women would have to free themselves, nobody else could do it for them. She emphasized the *process* of struggle. Both Schreiner and Gilman felt that women needed to be transformed, but while Gilman assumed that their entrance into industry would eventually achieve this transformation, Schreiner repeatedly stressed that the fight for their rights would help women discard their internal shackles. The goal of suffrage was less important to Schreiner than the moral education women achieved in the process of fighting for the vote.

> I am not so anxious for women to get the vote as they should keep in fighting for it—it is the struggle that educates. A degraded and subject class or race gains much more by a fight for freedom than by having it given them. The great thing one wants for women after their long ages of subjection is that they should be *mentally* and spiritually free, and hold freedom the dearest thing on Earth. *Giving* them the franchise is of value because it will educate them to demand freedom in all things; but the fact that they fight for it and win it shows at least that body of women are free![38]

Like Gilman, Schreiner stressed that women's fight was *not* with men: "It is not against man we have to fight but against *ourselves* within ourselves."[39] Both feminists felt sure that women's economic freedom would only improve relations between the sexes by removing the corrupting element of barter from love and marriage and using women's untapped potential in service to the world. . . .

Notes

1. See Carl Degler, "Charlotte Perkins Gilman on the Theory and Practice of Feminism," *American Quarterly* VIII (Spring, 1956):21, 22.

2. See Vera Brittain, "The Influence of Olive Schreiner," in *Until the Heart Changes, A Garland for Olive Schreiner*, ed. Zelda Friedlander (South Africa: Tafelberg-Uitgewers, 1967), 125 (hereafter cited as "Friedlander").

3. On American Victorianism as a culture and its similarities with and differences from British Victorianism, see Daniel Walker Howe, "American Victorianism as a Culture," *American Quarterly*, Vol. XXVII, no. 5 (Dec. 1975). While Schreiner and Gilman lived toward the end of the Victorian era, they were nevertheless shaped by its image of womanhood.

4. See Samuel Cron Cronwright-Schreiner, *The Life of Olive Schreiner* (London: T. Fisher Unwin Ltd., 1924), 11 (hereafter cited as "*The Life of Olive Schreiner*").

5. The British "cult of the lady" differs from its American counterpart, the "Cult of True Womanhood," insofar as it is a more explicitly aristocratic ideal. Although Patricia Branca demonstrates that the majority of British middle-class families could not afford to live up to this ideal, the Lyndall family prepared Rebecca for it. While the ornamental leisured aspect of the British "lady" was inappropriate to the frontier conditions of South Africa, Rebecca Schreiner attempted to inculcate the other elements of the feminine ideal in her daughters. Both the British and American images of femininity stress submissiveness and piety and assume that women's activities are confined to the domestic sphere. See Patricia Branca, *The Silent Sisterhood, Middle Class Women in the Victorian Home* (London: Croom Helm Ltd., 1975) and Barbara Welter, "The Cult of True Womanhood," in *Our American Sisters: Women in American Life and Thought*, eds. Jean E. Friedman and William G. Shade (Boston: Allyn and Bacon, Inc., 1973). On the "cult of the lady," see Martha Vicinus's introduction to *Suffer and Be Still, Women in the Victorian Age*, ed. Martha Vicinus (Bloomington and London: Indiana University Press, 1973).

6. Charlotte Perkins Gilman, *The Living of Charlotte Perkins Gilman* (New York: Harper Colophon Books, 1975), 44 (hereafter cited as "*The Living of Charlotte Perkins Gilman*").

7. See Charlotte Perkins Gilman, *The Forerunner*, Vol. III, no. 5 (May, 1912):118 (hereafter cited as "*The Forerunner*").

8. See *The Forerunner*, Vol. V, no. 3 (March, 1914):80 and Vol. V, no. 7 (July, 1914:188–89).

9. See Charlotte Perkins Gilman, *His Religion and Hers* (New York and London: The Century Co., 1923), 134 (hereafter cited as "*His Religion and Hers*").

10. *The Forerunner*, Vol V, no. 7 (July, 1914):191–2.

11. *The Forerunner*, Vol V, no. 8 (August, 1914):218.

12. *The Living of Charlotte Perkins Gilman*, 57.

13. This is not to imply that Gilman's or Schreiner's expectation that marriage was inconducive to freedom (to do one's work, to assert one's opinions) was an illusion; both popular sentiment and institutional discrimination favored confinement of married women to the domestic sphere. However, Gilman's and Schreiner's initial belief that marriage required self-suppression of women contrasts with the markedly different expectations of earlier feminists such as the American reformer-abolitionists of the 1830s and 1840s who, even while they extolled domesticity, saw their work in the world as an extension of their home responsi-

bilities and had radically egalitarian marriages for their time. See Blanche Glassman Hersh, " 'A Partnership of Equals': Feminist Marriages in Nineteenth Century America," in *University of Michigan Papers in Women's Studies*, Vol. II, no. 3 (1977):39–62. Gilman and Schreiner were ignorant of such alternatives. Gilman did not start reading feminist literature until the year of her separation from her first husband. Schreiner was also comparatively ignorant of explicitly feminist works. Although she had read John Stuart Mill and was deeply influenced by his philosophy, she was unfamiliar with *On the Subjection of Women*. The only feminist statement that influenced Schreiner's thinking was Mary Wollstonecraft's *A Vindication of the Rights of Woman*, which she read in 1888. Schreiner planned to write an introduction to this classic but never completed it.

14. [Editor's note, based on Winkler's text, 21–31]. Like Gilman, Schreiner initially resisted marriage; she did not accept a proposal until she was thirty-nine. Her husband, Samuel Cronwright, "was a South African farmer-politician who combined physical prowess with intellectual curiosity" (24). Although strongly attracted to him, the prospect of a dependent union unnerved her to the extent that she left Africa for Europe. A lengthy correspondence worked out her resistance, but ambivalence remained. This ambivalence, like Gilman's, expressed itself physically: "her asthma worsened and . . . four months before the ceremony, she had an attack of hysterical paralysis that affected her speech" (25). After the marriage took place, another attack of asthma prevented her from living at Cronwright's farm. Schreiner (who convinced her husband to accept the joint married name "Cronwright Schreiner") suggested that they separate, but he refused. Like Walter Stetson, Cronwright attempted to make the transition to married life more bearable by helping with the housework. Although she never lost her ambivalence about the married state, Schreiner's marriage to Cronwright more closely resembles Gilman's stable second marriage to Houghton Gilman (also undertaken when Gilman was in her late thirties) than Gilman's turbulent first marriage to Stetson.

15. *The Life of Olive Schreiner*, 244.

16. Charlotte Perkins Gilman, *The Man-Made World or Our Androcentric Culture* (New York: Charlton Co., 1914), 202. (hereafter cited as *"The Man-Made World"*). This book was first published in Volume I of *The Forerunner* in 1910 and then reissued in book form in 1911.

17. Charlotte Perkins Gilman, *Women and Economics* (New York: Harper Torchbook, 1966), 119 (hereafter cited as *"Women and Economics"*). Peter Gabriel Filene describes Gilman's reforms as a socialist scheme of cooperative housekeeping. See Peter Gabriel Filene, *Him/Her/Self, Sex Roles in Modern America* (New York: New American Library, Mentor Books, 1976), 57. However, while Gilman was a socialist, she was very clear that her "domestic factory" was in no way cooperative housekeeping, the sharing of domestic tasks, but rather the professionalization of domestic industry analogous to other capitalist industry. Housework would be socialized, that is, brought into the public sphere, but it could operate on a purely capitalist basis, the services sold as commodities. Such a scheme is illustrated in Gilman's "novel" "What Diantha Did" in *The Forerunner*, Vol. I. Gilman essentially wanted to rationalize housework. She did, however, hope that increased social organization would result in the peaceful elimination of private industry. See *Women and Economics*, 242–247, and *The Home*, Chapter XVI.

18. *Ibid.*, 313.

19. In *Human Work*, Gilman also criticized the idea that people would not work unless motivated by want. This belief, Gilman asserted, arose from a disdain for work inherited from the past when labor was performed by slaves. However, even the "want theory" can ultimately be traced to relations between the sexes since women were the first enslaved. See *Human Work*, (New York: McClure, Phillips and Company, 1904), Chapter Four.

20. *Women and Economics*, 315, 240.

21. Olive Schreiner, *Women and Labor* (New York and London: Johnson Reprint Corporation, 1972), 6–7 (hereafter cited as *"Woman and Labor"*).

22. *Ibid.*, 7.

23. *Ibid.*, 151.

24. Olive Schreiner, *Thoughts on South Africa* (New York: Frederick A. Stokes Co., 1923), 216–217.

25. *Woman and Labor*, 252.

26. Schreiner may also have been influenced by her reading of Mary Wollstonecraft's *A Vindication of the Rights of Woman*, since Wollstonecraft asserted that prostitution was a logical outgrowth of woman's education in idleness and economic dependence on men. See Mary Wollstonecraft, *A Vindication of the Rights of Woman* (New York: W. W. Norton and Co., Inc., 1967), 120.

27. See *Women and Economics*, 30. Gilman also held that sexual intercourse should mainly be for procreative purposes. See *The Forerunner*, Vol. 6, no. 7 (July, 1915): 179–180. However, as Linda Gordon points out, it would be wrong to see Gilman simply as a sexual prude. Gilman preached moderation and warned that sexual liberation was illusory when women were still oppressed in other areas since social power was indivisible. See Linda Gordon, *Woman's Body, Woman's Right, A Social History of Birth Control in America* (New York: Penguin Books, 1977), 238–239. David Pivar sees the sympathy of some of Gilman's ideas with those of the purity reformers. For example, Gilman, like advocates of purity reform, stressed self-control, transformation of religious values into social ethics and faith in professional expertise. However, Gilman was less enamored of obedience to rules and regulations. See Pivar, 164–165, 226, and 274.

28. *Woman and Labor*, 116.

29. *Ibid.*, 258.

30. The phrase belongs to Paul Robinson. See Paul Robinson, *The Modernization of Sex, Havelock Ellis, Alfred Kinsey, William Masters and Virginia Johnson* (New York: Harper Colophon Books, 1977), p. 2. Robinson is incorrect, however, in assuming that the Victorians denied women a sexual existence. See Carl Degler, "What Ought to be and What Was: Women's Sexuality in the Nineteenth Century," in *The American Family in Social-Historical Perspective*, second edition, ed. Michael Gordon (New York: St. Martin's Press, 1978), 403–425.

31. See Edward Carpenter, *Love's Coming of Age* (New York and London: Mitchell Kennerley, 1911), 67.

32. *The Letters of Olive Schreiner*, 262 (Jan. 20, 1907).

33. *Ibid.*, 313 (Aug. 7, 1912) and 303 (Dec., 1911).

34. It would be wrong, however, to exaggerate the extent to which Schreiner was a sexual radical. She still held conventional views on the roles of men and women in love and sex. In her story, "The Buddhist Priest's Wife" she wrote, "If a man loves a woman, he has a right to try to make her love him because he can do it openly, directly, without bending. There need be no subtlety, no indirectness. With a woman, it's not so; she can take no love that is not laid openly, simply at her feet. Nature ordains that she should never show what she feels. . . . That is the true difference between a man and a woman." See Olive Schreiner, "The Buddhist Priest's Wife," in *Stories, Dreams and Allegories* (New York: Frederick A. Stokes Co., 1923), 69–70.

35. *The Man-Made World*, 260. Of course, Gilman did not argue that women should wait for the coming of socialism before fighting for their own liberation any more than Schreiner. But she did see the two movements as inextricable, while Schreiner did not. Although a socialist, Schreiner never addressed herself to what a socialist society would look like. Gilman assumed that women's nurturant qualities would help transform capitalism by ending competition. However, she did not spell out how power relations in the workplace would be transformed.

36. *Woman and Labor*, 122–123.

37. *Ibid.*, 120.

38. *The Letters of Olive Schreiner*, 314.

39. *Ibid.*, 151. Emphasis in original.

On the Diaries of Charles Walter Stetson

MARY ARMFIELD HILL

In 1912, a large memorial exhibit of the paintings of Charles Walter Stetson began an extended American tour. They were powerfully "original," wrote artist Sydney Burleigh, "stamped with his personality, and marked by that distinction which comes from a strong artistic temperament working by its own methods to achieve its own end."[1]

According to most contemporary critics, Stetson's greatest strength lay in the range and vision of his color. "So far as I have seen," wrote Lydia Coonley Ward, "there is to-day in the world of Art no color comparable to his in splendor and beauty." Or, as the editor for the Boston *Evening Transcript* put it, "It is a bold statement, but scarcely a challengeable one that there is no other American painter now living who is Stetson's superior as a colorist." Through color, he wanted to express "love in life," not because it is "indispensable," but because "it imparts to living its supremest interest, its heavenliest hope, its most enduring recommendation." "What is an artist but a lover?" Stetson queried. "And what am I but both?"[2]

Unfortunately, however, it was Stetson's fate to experience a grim and debilitating love. His choice, romantic and unwise, was the beautiful, bright, vivacious Charlotte Anna Perkins. She seemed perfect to him—so energetic, so earnestly ambitious, so rebelliously unlike other women that he knew. But that precisely was the problem, for she was so rebellious she rejected what he thought were ideal women's roles. At first her rebellion was self-destructive. It manifested itself in agonizing ambivalence, suicidal depressions, hysteria, and "madness." But when finally she translated rage into constructive action, Charlotte Anna Perkins emerged as Charlotte Perkins Gilman, the "Marx and Veblen" of the women's movement, though also an exasperatingly complicated human being. According to one critic, she was "the leading intellectual in the women's movement during the first two decades of the twentieth century." Suffragist organizer Carrie Chapman Catt called her the "most original and challenging mind which the movement produced." *Women and Economics* (1898), one of her major works, would be

This is a shortened version of the Introduction to *Endure: The Diaries of Charles Walter Stetson*, edited by Mary Armfield Hill (Philadelphia: Temple University Press, 1989), i–xxi, reprinted with the permission of the author and publisher.

translated into at least six languages, go through more than half a dozen printings, and serve as a bible for suffragists and feminists for years.[3]

But all that was the achievement of Charlotte Gilman in her later years, after her divorce from Walter Stetson, after the tale this diary tells. In this volume (covering the years 1881–1888), we see Charlotte Perkins at a different stage, agonizing through courtship, marriage, and motherhood, with Walter patiently trying to endure. And although Gilman later would document the story more professionally and analytically—in her impressive fiction (most particularly "The Yellow Wall-paper"), in her hard-hitting poetry ("it was written to drive nails with"), and also in some pathbreaking full-length books—Walter's diaries have a special interest because they describe it in the raw.[4]

Admittedly, it was my interest in Charlotte Gilman's life and work that first led me to Walter Stetson. When writing my biography of Gilman, I never came to know him fully, though I read his letters in scattered manuscript collections, interviewed his daughter Katharine Stetson Chamberlin and his granddaughter Dorothy Chamberlin, and talked with relatives and friends. But I had never read his diaries. The beginning of my friendship with the late David Goodale marked the turning point. Art lover, Whitman scholar, close friend of the Stetson family, Goodale had acquired the Stetson diaries in the mid-1960s and for a number of years had planned to write a Stetson biography himself. In 1980, however, his health was failing, his progress was painfully slow, and he decided to offer his Stetson materials to me: not only the diaries, but also photograph albums, early sketchbooks, family letters, and scrapbooks of Stetson essays and reviews. Without question, my commitment to this project was inspired first by David Goodale: by his affection, generosity, and confidence, by his intellectual rigor and excitement, by his passion for the world of literature and art.

While David Goodale served as an early and enthusiastic collector and admirer, recently Stetson has again attracted national attention. In 1982, there was a travelling exhibit of Stetson's paintings (sponsored by the Spencer Museum of Art, the University of Kansas, and the National Endowment for the Arts). Charles Eldredge, Director of the National Museum of American Art, prepared an unusually detailed exhibition biography and catalogue. And in the early 1980s Marian Bowater, of the Bowater Art Gallery in Los Angeles, purchased and restored a large collection of Stetson works. I hope that the publication of these diaries will not only augment his artistic reputation, but also, through his private musings, reveal him as a fascinating and impressive human being.

Of course Stetson never dreamed his diary would be published. It is so totally his private work—his "comfort," his "refuge," his "old friend," or, as he also wrote, a "system of drainage or sewage for this microcosm," his "anodyne for over excited organs." It is "my one place of outpouring that replies nothing," "God pity whoever reads and misjudges."[5]

Although Stetson kept his diary as a tool for private living—trying to clarify his focus, to control his feelings, to claim importance for himself—along the way he became a master in the nineteenth-century art of diary-writing. Articulate, well-read, eloquent, he was perceptive, keenly attuned to dramatic fluctuations of feeling in himself and others, and also remarkably generous in sharing his perceptions. Many diary entries are depressing, to be sure. Creating a persona or alter ego, Walter sometimes tried to control or even stamp out "inappropriate emotions," or used self-flagellating tactics to mold himself according to "manly," "noble" ideals. He was determined to be earnest and hard-working, to be patient, loving, and forgiving always, to "endure" despite the cost. But what is remarkable is that he would succeed so grandly, not in crushing out troublesome emotions, but in sustaining energy and drive. "God is leading me," he wrote. "The spirit that pervades all is developing my soul. I have every reason to believe that in the end I shall be a master."[6]

Born in Tiverton Four Corners, Rhode Island, on March 25, 1858, Walter Stetson never knew a happy home. Uprooted constantly, his family faced agonizing economic worries, repeated illnesses, and an atmosphere of "crushed ambition" and cheerless defeat.

For one thing, his mother, Rebecca Steere Stetson, was habitually ailing. She had a "naturally sensitive" and "affectionate bright nature." She was "wonderfully patient and good," but she was also "warped and embittered by poverty and dark struggle." As far back as Walter could remember, she grimly and "calmly" accepted "woman's lot," always "doing the same things, seeing the same things, and I know not but thinking the same things from year's end to year's end."[7]

Although Stetson's drive and confidence by no means came directly from his parents, perhaps their misery inspired him, or their disappointments left him straining for opportunities they missed. His father, the Reverend Joshua Stetson, had been a Freewill Baptist minister during the Civil War years; then he briefly studied medicine; and by the time the family moved to Providence (in his mid-fifties) he was developing and selling herbal cures and patent medicines. But never quite successfully. He was a man of "eminently good parts," in Walter's view. He could have had an "honorable large place" as a "powerful and famous" preacher. Or, had he been where art was cared for, he might have been a painter. But since he had almost no encouragement or opportunity, his talents were "overgrown with . . . weeds" instead, and with family cares and worries. He was "trodden down by what he *could* not throw off," Walter wrote; "his feeling of duty to his children silenced all that he wanted for himself." Besides, his father was so "impractical." He had "beautiful sentiments" and "unusual brains," but "because of his ideality," his "fear of hurting someone," his generosity and "lack of business ability," "he accomplished nothing."

No wonder Stetson admired his father and yet resisted his example. Stetson, Sr., was so "eminently Christian," so "pitiful," "so patient." "My heart aches for him," Walter wrote, but "I am wondering if my life is to be a counterpart or likeness" of his. "Crushed ambitions," "dwarfed acquirements," family burdens and incessant debts—"God No! If I grow maddened Hell shall revisit earth once more—I shall grow mad if my end is not accomplished."[8]

Yet the young Stetson had no money, not even enough for food, much less for paint, canvas, or models, or leisure time to learn his craft. And he had virtually no formal schooling either, nor art school training, nor drawing lessons. Yet by age 19 he had started painting to sell. Stark necessity compelled him. No wonder lack of money was at first his diary's most persistent theme. "Money! I hate it," he wrote resentfully, the "shame" of trafficking in art, groveling to sell a painting, begging for loans. He did not dream, of course, that paintings even of these early years would later hang in the Smithsonian and other significant collections. What he resented, and what for the moment mattered more, was that the city of Providence—one of the richest of its size in the country—cared more for industry and profit than it did for art. Even "Raphael would be unknown" in "this stupid little town," he quipped.

> Here people are calves and wolves & sheep. They have no love of art, no feeling for it, no knowledge of it, and even do not take interest enough in it to persecute one. It is a damnable place for a fellow like me, that's sure. And here are men too with hundreds of thousands who might almost be Lorenzo de Medici, and by demand inspire us anew and keep us up to a high enthusiasm, make this city famous and beautiful, and get glory to God and themselves. They are too content with their dinners and cotton. And I doubt if it will ever be much different. It comes of the blood.[9]

Although Stetson hated businessmen's scrambling for profit, he nonetheless usually respected and admired wealth. Moreover, he didn't like reformers, especially "moral meddlers" in matters of "political economy" or "affairs of state." He enjoyed discussing aesthetic questions, or reflecting on the work of literary giants—Shakespeare, Milton, Dante Gabriel Rossetti. But he had little patience for the kind of dead-end questions political reformers raise: why some have wealth to spare while others scrape along in poverty, why some have rich cultural exposure while others have to work before they have a chance to learn. Such questions have no answers, Stetson argued. One endures, regardless.

Actually, in his more despairing moods, Stetson tried to shape some answers for himself, and not all of them stressed patience and submission. Occasionally he attributed inequalities to unpredictable and higher powers, to an accident of fate, to God's design. But far more frequently, he felt that failure or success was personally deserved. One must be a "Man," he thought, hard working and nobly earnest, as though good men were necessarily rewarded, and as though he really thought Horatio Alger myths were true. It wouldn't be the first time, of course, that political perspectives had shaped a personality and character; the American Dream, the work-ethic promises, seem so beautifully attractive for the economically successful, and so cruelly crushing for those who fail. No wonder Stetson took himself so seriously, fearing idleness, fearing failure, fearing joy. And no wonder too that he was prematurely middle-aged. If, as one art critic observed, he was "born a young old master," he was also born a young old man. "Ah, to have boyhood's bounding spirit and wide golden visions of a near future! And I am but twenty-five! I—twenty five and feeling so aged that I must cry for past spirit."[10]

While Stetson's duty-oriented ethic repeatedly inspired some heavy-hearted grimness, it had its compensations, especially since he actually assumed that he was on the winning side. In fact, he seemed to use his agonies and burdens as a proof of manhood. That led to arrogance at times, to isolation, occasionally to a grim intolerance for the "uninspired." It also helped solidify determination and sustain his drive. For whether by choice or temperament, Stetson remained startlingly ambitious to untangle life's complexities, to see clearly, to love fully, to thrust his vision into art. Isolated and aloof though he sometimes was, he tried to be an artist according to his own ideal. "The real artist," he wrote, "is a soul of fire in a form of marble. *Within must be intensest passion, without, profoundest calm,—the result of will. This alone makes creation possible.*"[11] . . .

On October 6, 1881, Stetson started working on these diaries: reflecting on artistic aspirations, on colleagues' efforts, on books in vogue. And only three months later, on January 14, 1882, he began to emphasize another theme as well, his evolving love for Charlotte Anna Perkins. Later she would be Charlotte Perkins Gilman, best-selling author, pungent lecturer, flamboyant wit. But for now, she was Walter's choice as the embodiment of feminine ideals. The incongruities are striking: a charismatic national celebrity linked to a man who didn't like reformers; a "radical feminist" committed to an artist whose images of womanhood conformed exactly to those she later would condemn. Why this tragic combination? And from what mistaken motives did these vastly different personalities converge?

In some respects, Charlotte Anna Perkins and Charles Walter Stetson had a lot in common. Both were hard-working and ambitious. Both were self-educated and well-read. And because both also came from miserably unhappy families, they lacked sufficient tenderness in childhood, assumed adult responsibilities at an unusually early age, and thus very likely turned to one another with unhealthy if complementary needs. In any case, Walter sensed, and it was no doubt true, that in Charlotte he had met a woman very like himself. "Were you made a man you were not much different from Charles Stetson."[12]

Charlotte *was*, of course, in some respects "masculine" according to the conventions of the time. And no wonder. She was born into a family for whom conventional sex-role expectations didn't fit. She was a Beecher. Whereas most nineteenth-century women were taught "true womanhood" ideals—to be pious and pure in self-sacrificing service to their families— Charlotte was taught, by example anyway, to be a self-assertive reformer instead. Among her relatives, calmness and conformity were the exception, innovative eccentricity the norm. Harriet Beecher Stowe, best-selling novelist, was Charlotte's great aunt, as were nationally known suffragist crusader Isabella Beecher Hooker and authoritative writer Catherine Beecher. Thus Charlotte's female models were fiery abolitionists when women were expected to be peaceful; physical fitness enthusiasts when they were supposed to faint; and prolific public writers when most women occupied themselves at home.

Charlotte's parents were clearly less successful than her famed Beecher aunts and uncles, but they were no less eccentric by the standards of the times. Charlotte's father, Frederick Beecher Perkins, was a drifter. He loved brandishing ideas, but hated formal schooling. He attended Yale, but never graduated. He studied law, but never practiced it. Finally, he tried teaching for a while, then wrote some essays and short stories glorifying home and family life. Yet, when problems with his own wife and children mounted— unpaid debts, crying dying babies, endless domestic chores—he insisted on his "right" to leave. For women he preached self-sacrifice and duty, but for himself he proclaimed an "instinct" to be free. [13]

Charlotte's mother, Mary Westcott Perkins, was thus a rebel by default. Forced to raise two children by herself, to move from relative to relative, to worry about money, about her future, about contemporaries' scorn, she was understandably cheerless, hard-working, and stern. No wonder Charlotte's childhood years were ones of deprivation, discipline, and coldness. She was never cuddled or loved enough by her busy disapproving mother, probably because Mary, like Walter's parents, was so miserably depressed herself.

Although Mary Perkins faced her troubles with unbending toughness, her daughter—to judge from early diaries and letters (1876–1880)—energetically resisted her mother's heavy-hearted style. She learned to "fight fire with fire," "to seek perfection in everything," to become so competent, in fact, so independent and precocious, that she removed herself even further from the cuddling and protective love she craved.

Moreover, since her father was distant and her brother unsupportive, Charlotte sometimes felt compelled to give her mother both financial and emotional support. Having studied briefly at the Rhode Island School of Design, she painted advertisements and greeting cards to sell occasionally, and gave art lessons to younger women. She ran a small day school for "young scholars" with her mother, to say nothing of helping Mary with domestic work. Despite recurrent mother/daughter warfare, Charlotte often felt responsible for Mary, and pitied rather than respected her. The pressures were painful, to be sure—an adolescent taking on adult responsibilities—but the experience confirmed a sense of self-sufficiency that in later years she was reluctant to surrender.

In some respects, the harsh realities of Charlotte's family situation were very like her future husband's. But there were fundamental differences, particularly in the style of their response: whereas Walter tended to absorb misery and grimness into the very structure of his personality, Charlotte usually managed to ward them off with humor and *joie de vivre*. "Have taken a fancy to work hard and be very smart," she wrote. "Let us call good reading solid food; novels candy, poetry fruit—and nonsense the peanuts of life." Also she enjoyed calls and callers, delighted in the local sleigh-ride parties, romped flirtatiously up and down the hills of Providence with "kissing cousins" and perspicacious friends.[14]

Whereas Walter was a loner, easily intimidated by the prominent and wealthy, Charlotte, while remaining economically impoverished, was perfectly comfortable with the upper middle class. One of her closest friends was Grace Channing, granddaughter of the famed Transcendentalist and Unitarian clergyman William Ellery Channing. (Grace would later be Stetson's second wife.) Another was Ada Blake, daughter of Brown University physics professor Eli Whitney Blake. And a third was the "gentle, lovely, intellectual" Martha Luther. In the spring of 1881, Charlotte and Martha entered a "compact of mutual understanding." They agreed never to " 'put on' any pretense of feeling," never to allow "the slightest falsehood or deceit," and then—just before Martha left Providence for the summer holidays— they gave each other "lovely little red bracelets with gold across," to be worn as a "badge, ornament, bond of amour." For the next few months Charlotte wrote her almost daily, sometimes ten-, fifteen-, twenty-page letters at a time. "Can't you cuddle me a little? My pet! Fancy me strong and unassailable to all the world beside, and then coming down and truckling to you like a half-fed amiable kitten!"[15]

To Charlotte, as to so many nineteenth-century women, there was a basic equality in female friendships that relationships with men so often lacked. Hugging, kissing, commiserating, sleeping unashamedly in one another's beds, they enjoyed what Carroll Smith-Rosenberg has called a "Female World of Love and Ritual," an essential source of "integrity and dignity which grew out of women's shared experiences and mutual affection."[16] Or, as Charlotte put it, "The freedom of it! The deliciousness! The utter absence of 'how will he take it?'! Never again will I admit that women are incapable of friendship." In fact, to compare the letters Charlotte wrote to Martha with later ones to Walter, the differences are striking. The Martha letters have a cheerful energy, an openness, a consistent confidence which in retrospect seem understandable: for, with Martha, Charlotte didn't have to compromise ambition, blunt her "masculine" assertiveness, or assume the burdens of a nineteenth-century wife.

The close phase of their relationship ended in the winter of 1881 when

Martha became engaged to Charles A. Lane. Charlotte later said that the pain of losing Martha was the longest-lasting, the deepest she had ever known. Her diary entry at the year's end reads:

> A year of steady work. A quiet year and a hard one. . . . A year in which I knew the sweetness of a perfect friendship and have lost it forever. . . . Most of all I have learned what pain is, [and] have learned the need of human sympathy by the unfilled want of it. . . .[17]

In facing her burdens, Charlotte tried turning to her standard sources of support: her self-improvement projects, her physical fitness programs, her reading. In the past, she had experienced occasional depressions, to be sure. But almost always she had managed to control them, rarely thinking, as Walter did, that suffering was God's way of testing, or misery the road to strength. By the winter of 1881, however, her mood fundamentally had changed: she had lost her confidence that ambition was compatible with happiness.

In part it was because both Charlotte Perkins and Walter Stetson were so miserably unhappy—both trying to cope with insecurities and disappointments, both needing friendship and support—that at this juncture their two unhappy lives converged. In early January 1882, just after they first had met, Walter already felt the magnetic force of love. She is "original," "eccentric," and "unconventional," he exclaimed, and also "moral, intellectual and beautiful." "She has a form like a young Greek & a face also resembling a cameo. She is an athlete—strong, vivacious, with plenty of bounding blood. She is an indefatigable worker—but I shall see some of her." A week later, Charlotte also recorded her reaction, but with more reserve. "Mr. Stetson calls. We are left alone, and have a nice talk. I introduce myself as fully as possible, and he does the same. We shake hands on it, and are in a fair way to be good friends."[18]

Walter Stetson's diaries were fundamentally shaped by his relationship with Charlotte. They begin only months before he first met her, and they end roughly at the time of separation. Walter the artist, Charlotte the writer and reformer, both struggled with their work commitments and their inordinately ambitious private goals. They worked so conscientiously toward ideal family images, Walter hoping to succeed as the protector and provider, Charlotte as the proper wife. It was almost as though they applied "work ethic" determination to their most intimate relationships, so energetically did they embrace the elevated, romantic imagery common to their generation, so keenly did both aspire to "Victorian" masculine and feminine ideals. If only people were rewarded for their good intentions, surely they would have been a prize-winning pair.

From the very outset, however, Walter was more passionate and eager, Charlotte more doubtful and restrained. Only seventeen days after their first meeting she recorded in her diary, "I have this day been asked the one great question in a woman's life and have refused." Two days later she wrote "An Anchor to Windward."

> This is for me to hold to if, as I fore-fear, the force of passion should at any time cloud my reason, and prevent or benumb my will.
> Now that my head is cool and clear, now before I give myself in any sense to another; let me write down my Reasons for living single.
> In the first place I am fonder of freedom than anything else. . . .
> I like to have my own unaided will in all my surroundings—in *dress, habits, diet, hours, behavior, speech,* and *thought.* . . .
> I like to be *able* and *free* to help any and everyone, as I never could be if my time and thoughts were taken up by that extended self—a family.
> If I were bound to a few I should grow so fond of them, and so busied with them that I should have no room for the thousand and one helpful works which the world needs. . . .
> I am cool, fearless, and strong; and have powers which can do good service in proper circumstances if I can only trust in them and coming opportunity. . . .
> For reasons many and good, reasons of slow growth and careful consideration, more reasons than I now can remember; I decide to *Live*—Alone.
> God help me!¹⁹

Charlotte's independent outlook, which spelled trouble from the start, reappeared sporadically for years: through courtship, then marriage and motherhood, until finally it led to separation and divorce. But at least she never kept her reservations secret. She told Walter bluntly, in letters as well as face to face, that she thought herself too self-directing and ambitious to be capable of marriage. At times Walter seemed to hear her, to respect her ambitions, to accept her right to choose. But gradually he began formulating ways to change her mind. From his point of view, she was "burdened" by "unnatural" and utterly unnecessary conflicts. "Yielding and rebellious," she suffered from that "curious, passionate mixture . . . of tender love and selfish struggle."[20]

It was almost as though Walter used the diaries to claim Charlotte, and also to control her. Clearly he meant that she should read them. For by describing his perspectives, by copying her letters and then drafting a response, he could guide her thinking, correct "indelicate" behavior, even direct her to the "proper" books to read. And another motive was emerging half-consciously as well: to preserve a written record of her progress toward his goal. "If our love letters could be printed verbatim, and side by side," he wrote, "there would be a novel of great truth and philosophical worth. It would give the exact relation of the whole minded of both sexes. I would not be at all surprised to know that Malloch's philosophical novels were actual experiences of someone—either himself or another."[21]

Although the diaries, with Charlotte's copied letters interspersed, provide a fiction-like portrait of a remarkable relationship, they by no means do so according to Walter's intent. He hoped, of course, that they would show the truth and beauty of the friendship. But they show some glaring blind spots as well: his anti-woman bias, his sexual double standard, his failure to tolerate in Charlotte attitudes he assumed were essential for himself. In fact, the diaries show a full-scale battle—Walter trying to impose standard lessons of Victorian morality, Charlotte resisting with every ounce of strength.

Take the issue of combining work successfully with marriage: Walter knew perfectly well, for himself, that love and work were both central to his happiness. But what if someday he were forced to choose? Impossible, he wrote. "I feel my whole essence tremble" at the "unwise economy" of a man sacrificing either. A woman's needs, however, were different. Surely "anything that takes woman away from the beautifying and sanctifying of home and the bearing of children must be sin," he wrote. "Every one knows that I believe in the utmost freedom for women but that freedom is false which makes them rebel against the ties of love and home." Charlotte's ambitions thus reflected such a "deep selfishness," he decided, that he must "stop her on her road for fame and 'freedom' . . . [and] show her what a miserable mess of pottage she was exchanging for her birthright."[22]

Moreover, Stetson showed his double-standard expectations on matters of love and sexuality. From his perspective, men necessarily were the mentors and protectors, while women naturally were inexperienced and pure. He didn't want Charlotte to attend the Museum of Anatomy in Providence, "that vile show of monstrosities and sin." Nor did he think it appropriate for women to be "contaminated" by male physicians: "I shuddered to think of any physician (male) using an instrument of any sort in my love's holy place." And finally, he did not want her reading freely or finding information for herself. He wanted to be perfectly sure she read about the "holiness" of sexual relations, and not, he insisted, about "the odor of its perspiration, the action of its phallus, the hairiness of sweating breasts"—or any other "delicacies" such as one would find in Whitman's *Leaves of Grass*.[23]

Whatever the nature of Stetson's sexual prejudices or preferences, he was strikingly blunt about the importance of human sexuality itself, and about the force of his own needs: "much of my energy is consumed in trying to subdue the desires thereof—most innocent and sweet desires, in themselves, but most inconvenient and embarrassing when a mate is lacking." Unfortunately, however, someone in the Stetson family—was it Charlotte? or Katharine? or Grace?—felt that Stetson was too blunt. For whatever the reasons, whether because of disapproval, or respect for loved ones' privacy, or simply shock that "Victorians" weren't as tight-laced as is sometimes assumed, the diaries' anonymous censor took pen and ink and repeatedly deleted the "offending" passages, sometimes even taking scissors and cutting entire pages out.[24]

It would be such an irony—this deleting, this crossing out and cutting up of Stetson's diaries—if a loved one deemed them too earthy, too sexually explicit, and thus degrading to human sexuality and love. Instead Walter was trying so earnestly to celebrate and glorify the "soul delight" and "god-like joy" of sex. It did not occur to him that by idealizing women he might be objectifying and thus denigrating them. From his point of view he worshipped Woman as the model of perfection, "the shape of the soul's form," destined "to lead man back to the dignity so sadly lost." Never mind some nagging personal confusions—that Charlotte didn't fit the image, or that nude models for his paintings usually were "damsels of the demi-monde." He still viewed Woman as man's central inspiration: to impel his genius, to love, honor, and serve him in his life and work. "Wherefore should man be so needy of woman?" he wrote. "Is not Art enough? Is not gold enough? Is not sight enough? But what is sight, or gold, or Art when love is not?" In actuality, Stetson's goal was to secure Love and Woman both, to express not only "the loveliness of womanhood & the purity of the sexual relation," but also to solidify the bond between his love life and his art. The secret of "great painters," he wrote, is their "association with beautiful women."[25]

. . . In art, as in love and life, Stetson was the idealist *par excellence.* Viewing women as models of perfection and art the means to find one's God, he preferred image to reality, the conceptual to the perceptual, the "purer and more perfect states of existence" to the tangles of daily life. Stetson wanted to enjoy his "quietude," his "mind and memory" pleasures, his "silent days and moonlit nights." But tragically, he married Charlotte Perkins Gilman instead. Later to become one of America's most dynamic and charismatic women's movement leaders, she was hardly the patient or peaceful type. For a time, she tried conforming to the standard "True Womanhood" ideals. It very nearly killed her. But in her later years she reversed her efforts, and began to attack vigorously the very notions of wife, home, and motherhood that Stetson and his generation so passionately cherished. At the time, most women did not even recognize their problems: a lack of economic independence, a frequent anger and frustration with full-time domestic chores, a tendency toward self-hatred psychologically and sexually. Yet Charlotte Gilman integrated these problems into an impressive feminist philosophy; and each she presented with a clip and style and drama that had a broad appeal. For instance, on women's economic dependence, she wrote:

We have not as a class awakened to the fact that we have no money of our own.

[W]hatever the economic value of the domestic industry of women is, they do not get it. The women who do the most work get the least money, and the women who have the most money do the least work.

Or on women's domestic service:

If each man did for himself the work he expects of his woman, there would be no wealth in the world; only millions and millions of poor tired men, sweeping, dusting, scrubbing, cleaning, serving, mending, cooking, washing, ironing—and dying for lack of food.

Or on the female personality:

Of women especially have been required the convenient virtues of a subject class: obedience, patience, endurance, contentment, humility, resignation, temperance, prudence, industry, kindness, cheerfulness, modesty, gratitude, thrift, and unselfishness.

Or on "love" as woman's first priority:

We have been told so long that
"Love is of a man's life a thing apart,
Tis woman's whole existence,"
That we have believed it. . . . Our whole existence was carefully limited to this field; we were dressed and educated to grace it; we were bloomed out into a brief and glorious career while under inspection and selection before our final surrender, and then we pursued the rest of our lives with varying devotion and satisfaction in this one department of life.[26]

Charlotte had learned some facts of life the hard way: that romantic goals can be poisonous and sometimes fatal, that purportedly respectful ideals too often map out things a woman should and shouldn't do, like earning money, or having a job, or establishing some independence. As in Stetson's painting of the ideal nude, she was to be an object of adoration: beautiful, innocent, and pure, but also starkly prone and passive, impotent, utterly bored with pedestal life. By romanticizing and idealizing women, Stetson was defining them according to his own fantasies rather than according to their interests and needs.

Almost instinctively, Charlotte seemed to recognize the problem long before it came to pass: that "ideal" marriage required capitulation, and she wasn't of the capitulating kind. Repeatedly she warned him, as much "as I love you I love WORK better, & I cannot make the two compatible."[27]

Walter's diaries, peppered with Charlotte's letters, stand as a blow-by-blow account of Charlotte's struggle for survival and Stetson's maneuvers for control. At times he thought she simply was too "selfish" to be thoughtful, too "daring and independent" to consider his "wants and needs." But at other times, he was ecstatically pleased with his results: "Ah! how different from the triumphant conqueror's look of some time ago!" he wrote. "O how that spirit is broken. The false pride is melting before love rapidly." "She wants to be treated more as a child now than a woman."[28]

Unfortunately, the more child-like Charlotte felt with Walter, the more hatred she directed toward herself. "There is no limit to her self-denunciation," Stetson wrote just months before their marriage; "a great spasm of self-abnegation seems to have come over her. She talked of dying until my heart ached." Yet her psychological deterioration continued, as did their wedding plans. The result was Charlotte's descent into madness, "spasms of horror," and "hysteria," which "The Yellow Wall-paper" grimly and starkly describes.[29]

As readers follow Stetson's daily trials with Charlotte, they almost certainly will sympathize with him. They will respect his helpfulness and patience; very likely they will sometimes see Charlotte as the shrew. But also surely they will see Walter's culpability in the equation: his double-standard expectations, his reactions to her illness, his benevolent but condescending and controlling style. For however helpful, patient, generous, kind, and loving Walter clearly was, he nonetheless assumed that Charlotte's break-down resulted from unnatural inclinations, from her "old ambitious 'free-dom'-loving nature rising in rebellion against the 'weakness' of tenderness and love." In retrospect, the double standard seems so obvious. Walter was acutely aware of his own professional frustrations, yet starkly oblivious to reasons for the anger in his wife. It was wrong to be "wasting" his "energy" on household tasks, he wrote, or to misuse the "power" he needed for his art: "Oh how I long to do my work, and how heavy a burden I bear that gnaws so that I cannot do it!" "If it seems to last very long I must hire help . . . for I cannot afford, nor would it be right for me, to give up all my time and strength to such things." Yet when Charlotte expressed parallel frustrations, Stetson decided she must be mad. She was afraid "that her whole usefulness & real life was crushed out of her by marriage and the care of the baby," he wrote. Her "fierce rebellion at the existing state of things" must be symptomatic of her "brain disease."

> It calls for tremendous patience and tact. She still rushes in her mind from all our sweet life to try to go out into the world to rid it at one fell swoop of all evil, pain and the like. Strange and terrible how such ideas can take possession of one's brain. She forgets that she could do good right at hand, even in our family. Of what account is that to her! She would convert the world.[30]

Without question, Charlotte was impossible at times. And Walter heroically tried to fill the model husband role. He arranged for a maid, sent for her mother, and did many of the household chores himself. Always he was conscientious; in fact, too much so at times, probing for helpful clues in literature and art and poetry, eagerly absorbing the message—rooted in the very subconsciousness of the culture itself—that would so complicate his life. For Walter as well as Charlotte was a victim of destructive sex-based images. His tormented sense of loyalty and guilt and duty, his conscientious response to three generations' needs, his struggle for professional success, to say nothing of his fatherly concern for Charlotte, all resulted from his misdirected efforts to live according to the standard nineteenth-century tenets for the ideal male. Even his weaknesses—his selfishness, arrogance, and self-serving faith—fit comfortably with the Victorian image of the proper husband-father. And while in retrospect these may seem offensive, their sources often lie outside the private man himself, beyond his own control. In any case, Stetson deserves our admiration. Despite all the gnawing problems in his marriage, all the assaults on his ego, all the costs to his career, he still kept faith in Art and Love. "Years ago," he wrote,

> my mind was full of pictures which I did not hesitate to try to paint. But now if ideas come as they will at times, I say—How can I? Every cent I get now has to pay bills and must be spent to distract Charlotte from her brooding. I cannot hire models. I cannot buy any of the accessories that I need. I am become in duty bound a mere supporter of a family.[31]

In the fall of 1888, Charlotte and Walter separated. Charlotte left for California with their daughter Katharine, and Walter stayed in Providence to continue with his work. In early December 1888, after holding an auction to sell his paintings (some 101 watercolors and oils), Stetson joined Charlotte in Pasadena to attempt a reconciliation, but by early 1890 it was clear that they would be divorced.

Out of all this agony, however, there was one strangely pleasant, almost bizarre development: Walter's growing affection for Grace Channing, Charlotte's closest confidante for years. Grace and Charlotte had written short stories and drafted plays together. It was to Grace's home in Pasadena that Charlotte first fled the trials of motherhood and marriage in the winter of 1885–86. In the summer of 1888, Grace again served as Charlotte's main support by dismantling the Stetson household, tackling practical responsibilities, and responding to emotional needs. Grace must have been a remarkably sensitive and tactful person, for despite the tensions, she managed not only to remain the confidante of both Stetsons, but also to win Charlotte's blessing after deciding to be Walter's second wife. Walter Stetson married Grace Channing on June 11, 1896; four years later, on June 11, 1900, Charlotte Stetson married Houghton Gilman, providing in each case a relatively happy ending to this complicated tale.

What is particularly striking about this triangular relationship is that it continued to be warm despite some powerfully disruptive tensions: from delays and complications in the divorce proceedings, from the scandal reporters tried to cause, from financial responsibilities for their daughter Katharine and where Kate would finally live. There were some inevitable resentments, as will shortly be apparent. But for the most part, they worked them through with remarkable good will. Katharine lived alternately and amicably with both parents, and Grace and Charlotte—sharing a husband and a child—remained life-long friends. After Walter died, on July 20, 1911, Grace and Charlotte became close New York neighbors. And in 1935, when Charlotte was dying of cancer, Grace came to California to share her last few months of life.[32]

. . . The first attempt to edit and annotate Walter's diaries was begun years ago, in May 1912, by Grace Channing-Stetson. She started the project rather casually, almost accidentally, less than a year after Walter's death. As she was reading the diaries, she began sharing her reactions in a series of letters to a mutual friend, Dr. E. B. Knight—family physician, art patron, and Stetson's confidant for years. Knight was "woven all through" the diaries, Grace told him, and by describing them and quoting them, she wanted to give him a "foretaste" of what she hoped to publish later as a book. "There is so much that is inspiring and of profound interest," she wrote, "not because you and I loved him, but because he was a wonderful human being and because destiny . . . moulded all his days in strange and unusual ways." "Will it not make a book for everybody—can you not see already the *human* quality in it—which only very rare souls are ever able to transmit, for themselves?" "But it is *he*—what he *was* that makes the book so great a human document."[33] . . .

> New York—Thursday (the 23rd)
> [May, 1912]

Dear Brother:

I am so glad you continue to enjoy the extracts and I purpose mailing more today. You say it will make a book which will interest many; before I have done with it—it will make a book which will *enthrall everybody*! It will be a wonderful book. It will embrace two continents and include many interesting people, and the material I have to draw upon is so rich. . . .

. . . The thing which first fascinated and drew me irresistably to Walter was a kind of wonderful purity in his attitude toward life and love and every day facts, which he somehow transfigured into ideal things. It was purity like that of fire—vivid and beautiful, and I recognized then and reverenced ever after in him a quality which was all his own and which seemed only to grow brighter and brighter with the years of his life. Surely if anyone knows him,— I do; and I know that with him the ideal *was* the real, and that he did actually attain the things his early records show him striving so ardently for. His frankness was without limit; he was purely Pagan in a multitude of ways; and he was exquisite and lovely in the smallest details as in the largest facts and acts of his life. More and more I grow to have the feeling that he died—partly because Life had no more to do for him. We do not see how he could have become more beautiful, more courageous, more selfless and serene than he was in the latter years. And we always had, and frequently put into words, our feeling that he was really living chiefly in some other world—some higher world than the rest of us, even while with us. . . .

We always send our love to you all.

> Grace E.C.S.[34]

As Grace wrote these letters, she was preparing a travelling exhibition of Walter's paintings, collecting and sorting through his major works, and also, of course, mourning deeply. Her sympathetic, respectful, and at times eulogistic response to the diaries is understandable and moving. But what of her reactions to her late husband's love for Charlotte Gilman? What of her thoughts about this national celebrity and long-time friend? Grace must have felt some powerfully conflicting loyalties as she read of Walter's passion, or of the traumas that earlier she had witnessed from Charlotte's side. Clearly she respected Charlotte's public efforts, her theoretical achievements, her long-term fight for women's rights. And certainly she felt Charlotte was among her closest friends. But she felt some deep ambivalence as well, which, despite disclaimers, could not be disguised.

> No one who loves him ought to be able to help loving Charlotte. At the very moment when he so needed a companion and inspiration—she was both to him. He had never known a woman so fine and so capable of nobility and understanding, and through all the ups and downs of the years that followed, before their marriage, which were alternate heaven and hell to him, as she decided she could not live without him or could not live with him (and she changed her mind constantly) yet she remained to him steadily a flame of purity, and however faultful or capricious, was never anything but noble, honest and right-meaning. It is impossible to guess—even though she martyr-ised him,—what she may have saved him from of worse, with that sensitive imagination, his great need of loving *something*, and only the barren field of Providence (the city) to draw from. She furnished to him constantly a noble ideal and a steadfast purpose, just when both were so necessary to him; and if she very nearly killed him by inches afterwards, still that was not her fault.[35]

Grace Channing's account of this ill-fated friendship is sometimes eulo-gistic, but also it is often factually sound. Charlotte *was* "faultful" and "capricious." Also, as Grace rightly claimed, Charlotte rarely understood the pain that women's freedom sometimes causes men. And yet it was almost as though Grace had forgotten some fundamental differences in situation. Grace had been a journalist, a novelist, a professional—all before she married Walter. Equally important, she had learned from first-marriage mistakes. As she reviewed the written record, Grace attempted to be sympathetic and supportive. Here were "two such wonderful young people" entering "a new heaven on earth," she wrote. "He had found out that she was both 'wonderful and good,' and she can't have discovered less; they had begun that 'perfect friendship' of which each had dreamed, and which was to mould all their lives—and that of others." And yet in part because Grace had managed to hold her own with Walter, to love him without threatening either her career or her identity, she unrealistically concluded that Charlotte foolishly had thrown away "an earthly paradise," an "ideal love" and marriage. It was almost as though Grace Channing allowed idealism to come full circle. Like Walter Stetson, she apparently believed that the "ideal *was* the real." For while her letters provide fascinating insights on the Perkins-Stetson marriage, they also demonstrate, once again, why the rebellious and complicated Charlotte Gilman felt compelled to direct such a rigorous attention to fighting off and understanding the "madness" of her private life.

> Of all the people in this world,—I pity Charlotte most! She had—actually *had* in her very hands, heaven on earth, and threw it away. With youth, beauty, an ideal love who had already made an almost story-book success (the first Boston exhibition was over)—a perfect child,—what had all the world to offer her or any woman more. I love Charlotte very much, and I blame her not at all—as he never blamed her—but I look at her now, when she comes here, still beautiful and full of her own work and interests, and I pity her from the depths of my soul. She was fairly *within* an earthly paradise—once. She was not in the least to blame—not in the very least; but she nearly killed him. And the miracle is that she did not kill his art. That however was indestructible; in the worst of times it still flamed on. The strangest thing is that Charlotte has gone through life with a conviction that *she* was nearly wrecked by that marriage, and without even a passing suspicion that he suffered in any way whatever from it! This is fact.[36]

Notes

1. George W. Whitaker and Sydney R. Burleigh, "An Appreciation of the Late Charles Walter Stetson," *Providence Sunday Journal*, July 23, 1911, p. 10.

2. L[ydia] A[very] C[oonley] W[ard], "Charles Walter Stetson: An Appreciation," 1912, Stetson Scrapbook; "The Fine Arts: Mr. Stetson's Pictures in Chicago," reprinted from the *Chicago Record-Herald* in the *Boston Evening Transcript*, March 14, 1902, p. 8; Diaries, April 21, 1883.

3. Andrew Sinclair, *The Emancipation of American Women* (New York: Harper and Row, 1965), p. 272; Alice Rossi, ed., *The Feminist Papers: From Adams to de Beauvoir* (New York: Bantam, 1978; 1st pub., 1973), p. 568; Mary Gray Peck, *Carrie Chapman Catt: A Biography* (New York: H. W. Wilson, 1944), p. 454.

4. "The Yellow Wallpaper" was first published in 1892 as "The Yellow Wall-paper." An interview with CPS, quoted in the *Topeka State Journal*, June 18, 1890.

5. Quotations in the diaries are taken from April 27, 1886; Oct. 9, 1885; June 16, 1883; April 27, 1886; April 16, 1883.

6. Diaries, Nov. 15, 1881.

7. Diary quotations about Rebecca Steere Stetson are from Jan. 19, 1887; Feb. 12, 1883; Feb. 2, 1882.

8. Diary quotations about the Reverend Joshua Stetson are from May 13, 1882; Jan. 18, 1885; Aug. 14, 1882; May 13, 1882; Feb. 12, 1883; Sept. 9, 1885; Jan. 19, 1887.

9. Diaries, July 21, Oct. 27, 1883; Jan. 14, 1887; July 10, 1883.

10. "Art Modernity," *Philadelphia Record*, Jan. 5, 1913, Stetson Scrapbook; Diaries, Aug. 8, 1883.

11. CWS, "The Price of a Picture," A. E. Club Lectures, Club Papers no. 118, June 19, 1890, p. 2, RIHS.

12. Diaries, Jan. 29, 1882.

13. Frederick Beecher Perkins' attitudes are apparent in his own writings. See, for example, Frederick Beecher Perkins, "Childhood: A Study," in *Devil Puzzlers, and Other Studies* (New York: G. P. Putnam's Sons, 1877), pp. 130–140. Frederick and Mary Perkins had

two children who survived infancy, Thomas Adie Perkins (b. May 9, 1859) and Charlotte Anna Perkins (b. July 3, 1860). Thomas Henry Perkins was born on March 15, 1858, and died in April that same year. Julia de Wolf Perkins was born January 29, 1866, and died the following September.

For discussion of Charlotte's relationship with her mother, see CPG, *The Living of Charlotte Perkins Gilman: An Autobiography* (New York: Harper & Row, 1975; 1st pub., 1935), pp. 51–69. See also Mary A. Hill, *Charlotte Perkins Gilman: The Making of a Radical Feminist, 1860–1896* (Philadelphia: Temple University Press, 1980).

14. CAP, Diaries, March 26, 1887, AESL.

15. CPG, *Living*, p. 48; CPG, unpublished autobiography, ca. 1920, p. 54, AESL; CAP, Diaries, May 14, 1881, AESL; CAP to Martha Luther, Aug. 1, 1881, RIHS.

16. Carroll Smith-Rosenberg, "The Female World of Love and Ritual: Relations Between Women in Nineteenth-Century America," *Signs* 1, no. 1 (Autumn 1975), pp. 9–10; CAP to Martha Luther, Aug. 13, 1881, RIHS.

17. CAP, Diaries, Dec. 31, 1881, AESL.

18. Diaries, Jan. 14, 1882; CAP, Diaries, Jan. 22, 1882, AESL.

19. CAP, Diaries, Jan. 29 and Jan. 31, 1882, AESL.

20. Diaries, March 22, 1882.

21. Diaries, May 20, 1882.

22. Diaries, July 21, March 28, March 22, April 9, and March 28, 1883.

23. Diaries, June 25, July 14, and June 23, 1883.

24. Diaries, April 5, 1883. Obviously I cannot be sure of the contents of deleted sections, but the context suggests they are similar to other diary reflections, though more vivid and explicit.

25. Diaries, April 12, 1882; CWS, "The Nude in Art," A. E. Club Lectures, Club Papers no. 19, Feb. 19, 1886, p. 7, RIHS; Diaries, Aug. 19, 1882; April 23, March 24, and March 22, 1883.

26. CPG, "Her Own Money: Is a Wife Entitled to the Money She Earns?" *Mother's Magazine* 7 (Feb. 1912), p. 7; CPG, *Women and Economics: A Study of the Economic Relation Between Men and Women as a Factor in Social Evolution* (New York: Harper and Row rept., 1966), pp. 14–15; CPG, "How Home Conditions React Upon the Family," *American Journal of Sociology* 14 (March 1909), p. 598; CPG, *His Religion and Hers: A Study of the Faith of Our Fathers and the Work of Our Mothers* (New York: Century, 1923), p. 134; CPG, "Love Stories and Life Stories," *Woman's Journal* 35 (May 7, 1904), p. 146.

27. Quotation from an undated letter, CAP to CWS, Diaries, March 22, 1882.

28. Diaries, March 21, May 20, 1882; and Jan. 19, 1883.

29. Diaries, Dec. 3, 1883.

30. Diaries, Nov. 26, 1883; Jan. 25, 1885; Oct. 3, 1887; Jan. 25, and Aug. 24, 1885.

31. Diaries, Aug. 6, 1887.

32. The papers of Grace Ellery Channing-Stetson have recently been purchased by the Arthur and Elizabeth Schlesinger Library at Radcliffe College, and are now available for research.

33. GEC to EBK, May 16, 1912, p. 49; May 19, 1912, p. 66–67; May 16, 1912, pp. 49–50.

34. GEC to EBK, May 23, 1912, p. 70.

35. GEC to EBK, May 23, 1912, pp. 77–78.

36. GEC to EBK, May 6, 1912, p. 32.

When the Marriage of True Minds Admits Impediments: Charlotte Perkins Gilman and William Dean Howells

Joanne B. Karpinski

At first glance, the intellectual minuet between Charlotte Perkins Gilman and William Dean Howells seems vulnerable to Gertrude Stein's complaint about Gilman's onetime home of Oakland, California: "There isn't any *there*, there." Unlike the Larcom-Whittier relationship, for example, this one lacks an elaborate prior myth to deconstruct.[1] Nor is there a complex text of correspondence to (mis)-read, as in the case of Dickinson and Higginson. But postmodern criticism alerts us to the heuristic value of absence, allowing us to focus on Howell's cautious fulfillment of the mentorial role he had initiated with such rhetorical fervor. Sincere but correct, Howells was not suited by temperament or conviction to become the passionate champion that Gilman had hoped for.

Gilman's first major poem, "Similar Cases," was published in the April 1890 issue of the socialist periodical the *Nationalist*, where it attracted the appreciative attention of William Dean Howells. Gilman recorded his "unforgettable letter" and her reaction to it in her autobiography:

> DEAR MADAM,
>
> I have been wishing ever since I first read it—and I've read it many times with unfailing joy—to thank you for your poem in the April *Nationalist*. We have had nothing since the Biglow Papers half so good for a good cause as "Similar Cases."
>
> And just now I've read in *The Woman's Journal* your "Women of To-day." It is as good almost as the other, and dreadfully true.
>
> > Yours sincerely,
> > Wm. Dean Howells
>
> That was a joy indeed. . . . There was no man in the country whose good opinion I would rather have had. I felt like a real "author" at last.[2]

Gilman's enthusiastic response to Howells's letter may seem overdone to twentieth-century readers for whom Howell's reputation has been eclipsed,

Reprinted from *Patrons and Protégées: Gender, Friendship, and Writing in Nineteenth-Century America*, edited by Shirley Marchalonis (New Brunswick: Rutgers University Press, 1988), 212—34, with the permission of the author and the publisher.

but in 1890 Howells was a name to conjure with. As editor of the prestigious *Atlantic Monthly*, as a contributor of fiction and reviews to such significant periodicals as the *Century* and *Scribner's*, and as writer of "The Editor's Easy Chair" column for *Harper's Monthly*, he was "in a position of greater prestige and authority than any other reformer of his time."[3] Thus, Gilman had good reason to be pleased. As fellow socialist Edward Bellamy wrote to Howells in thanks for his praise of *Dr. Heidenhoff's Process*, notice from such an august quarter was "as refreshing to me as you may suppose a note from Hawthorne in recommendation of one of your earlier efforts would have been to you."[4]

The esteem in which Howells held Gilman's writing receives forceful expression in his 1899 article, "The New Poetry," published in the *North American Review*:

> Her civic satire is of a form which she herself invented; it recalls the work of no one else; you can say of it (and I have said this before), that since the Biglow Papers there has been no satire approaching it in the wit flashing from profound conviction . . . but the time has not yet come when we desire to have the Original Socialists for our ancestors, and I am afraid that the acceptance of Mrs. Stetson's [Gilman's first married name] satire is mostly confined to fanatics, philanthropists and other Dangerous Persons. But that need not keep us from owning its brilliancy.[5]

As Gloria Martin points out in her dissertation on women in Howell's criticism and fiction, the irony of Howells's assessment might seem at first to be directed against Gilman, but is in fact directed at his audience, "implying that only when the country has accepted the humane theories of socialism will Stetson's work become as respectable as Lowell's famous satire has now become." Martin characterizes this passage as "a rare acceptance of another author by Howells into the privacy of the editorial tone."[6]

Personal similarities and political sympathies disposed Howells to be appreciative of Gilman and her work. Both writers experienced financially insecure childhoods, with their mothers marshaling the family struggle for economic security. Each fought with recurring depression from adolescence until late in life. Gilman's affiliation with socialism came early and enthusiastically, while Howells embraced the same social philosophy later in life and more gradually. Never the ardent feminist that Gilman was, Howells nevertheless supported the cause of women's equality with a vigor unusual for a man of his times.

With so much in common, it would seem inevitable for the dean of American letters to foster the professional fortunes of the young woman whose work he praised so highly. Instead, Howells temporized, using his influence to get her work brought out by other publishers than those with which he was directly associated. Why did the budding mentorial relationship not flourish? Apparently, it suffered from a residual timorousness on

Howells' part about the bitterness of Gilman's social indictment, even at its most humorous. Moreover, Howells' relationship with his oldest daughter and with the female writers whose work he did promote suggest a patriarchal temperament poorly suited both to Gilman's emotional needs and to her style of writing.

Gilman's father, Frederick Beecher Perkins, held a variety of editorial and library jobs while trying unsuccessfully to establish himself as a fiction writer. He left the family when Charlotte was nine, after increasingly lengthy periods of separation during which he left his family (four children, of whom only Charlotte and her older brother, Thomas, survived infancy) in the care of relatives. After his departure from the family scene, Charlotte's mother supported the household by taking in boarders or by acting as companion to invalid relations, since Frederick's contributions were both meager and irregular. Periodically, Gilman would attempt to reestablish contact with her absent father, but found him emotionally as well as physically distant.[7]

Howells's praise of her poetry and political opinions thus satisfied a deep thirst for something like paternal approval. However, Gilman could no more rephrase her polemics to please Howell's sense of decorum than she could retract the impolitic kiss she once offered her father in the Boston Public Library.

Like Gilman, Howells had spent his childhood wandering nomadically on the frontiers of respectable poverty. His father, William Cooper Howells, began married life as an itinerant printer. He moved rapidly into the editorial office, where radical opinions in both religion and politics often irritated his subscribers. His outspoken support of abolition and the Free-Soil party lost him several positions at newspapers run by the Whig party in Ohio, while his ardor for the mystical doctrines of Emanuel Swedenborg outstripped even the New Church loyalists of that state. The senior Howells had "the heroic superiority to mere events and shifts of fortune which was in keeping with his religion and his temperament as an idealist,"[8] but the loss of income and alienation from community life were more difficult for his wife and family to bear.

Staunchly loyal to her husband, Mary Dean Howells undertook the financial management of their affairs to protect the family from the consequences of his principled indifference to money. Like Mary Perkins, she took in boarders. When Howells again found editorial work in a more congenial political climate, she had title to the business and the property placed in her name and that of her oldest son.

These mothers, forced into roles of unusual self-reliance, were deeply influential on Gilman and Howells. Neither woman particularly liked the autonomy that was thrust upon her: Gilman's mother cast herself as the victim of fate, while Howells's steeled herself to endure what she could not cure. The frictions produced between their dislike of their new roles and their competence in pursuing them greatly affected their children.

Gilman alternately blamed her mother's smothering affection for driving her father away, admired her as a tower of strength in adversity, and resented the severity and irritability that her mother's overwhelming responsibilities had engendered. Howells idolized his father's principles, but keenly felt the consequences of his honoring them. As a result, his naturally lively affection for his mother grew into an attachment so fervent and idealized that it became unbearable for him to leave her, even for a brief period. Several times in his adolescence he was humiliated by having to return home from a job because of homesickness.

Ironically, Howells adopted toward his own family the role of Victorian paterfamilias despite the opportunity afforded by his upbringing to evade this stereotype, since his wife and oldest daughter suffered debilitating health conditions. His acquiescence to the prevailing mythology of gender had tragic consequences for the family. Convinced by the doctors he consulted that his daughter Winifred's reluctance to eat was psychological rather than physical in origin, Howells committed her to a variety of therapeutic regimes, and regarded her resistance to these as a contest of wills.[9] When a postmortem examination revealed an organic cause for her pain, Howells was devastated by remorse, although he accepted the doctors' reassurance that the problem could not have been discovered by the diagnostic procedures then available.[10] Even after her death, however, Howells continued to associate Winifred's symptoms with a level of intellectual activity deemed excessive for a woman.[11]

This inability of a loving and compassionate father to comprehend his intellectual daughter's illness seems the more poignant in that Howells himself periodically suffered from bouts of an acute but obscure malaise that left him unable to work or study. He recovered his health by resorting to the type of nature cure imposed on his daughter Winifred, but these breakdowns permanently dimmed the optimism of his earlier character.

Gilman's physical and emotional makeup, so similar to his own, might have disturbed Howells by its likeness to Winifred's as he understood it. Gilman's adult life alternated between periods of exultant productivity and paralyzing depression. Already at age fifteen she wrote to her long-absent father for "a good strong dose of advice" on this issue:

> "Unstable as water, thou shalt not excel" said the patriarch to his son. The words often ring in my ears, and I sometimes feel, as if there was not hope, and the irrevocable Word of the Lord had pronounced my doom. That is in my intervals of depression; few and far between you may think, but it is not so. I often feel hopelessly despairing, at my total inability to *work*. [Emphasis in the original][12]

Adolescent hyperbole aside, this preoccupation with the necessity of useful work and the emotional obstacles to accomplishing it satisfactorily reappears in Gilman's letters and journal entries ever after. "Useful work" for Gilman always meant something creative or done for the public good. The traditional work of women exacerbated her depression, particularly after her marriage to Walter Stetson and the birth of their only child, Katherine.

Paradoxically, these depressions spurred her literary career. Her poem "The Answer," an outcry against the "work that brainless slaves might do" that ultimately kills an optimistic bride, won first prize for the year from the *Woman's Journal*: more important, it strengthened her affiliation with the American Woman Suffrage Organization, which sponsored the journal.[13] Also, Gilman's struggle with the misdirected therapy prescribed for her depression formed the anecdote for "The Yellow Wallpaper," the story for which she is best known today.

Unable to endure the tension between growing public success and domestic misery, Gilman sought professional help. Dr. S. Weir Mitchell, who had treated several of Gilman's Beecher relatives for "nervous ailments," prescribed his six-week "rest cure": bed rest, massage, lots of food, and complete avoidance of mental stimulation. Gilman followed the regimen under Mitchell's supervision, but once she returned home, his admonition— "live as domestic a life as possible. Have your child with you all the time. Have but two hours intellectual life a day. And never touch pen, brush or pencil as long as you live"[14]—drove her to the brink of mental collapse. In desperation, Gilman abandoned the regime and her household. The separation from Stetson became permanent; divorce followed soon after.

Curiously, this emancipation from traditional womanliness did not put an end to Gilman's depressive episodes. Any protracted contact with domesticity—her own or others'—tended to bring one on. She visited Jane Addams at Hull House and was so impressed by the "useful work" done there that she intended to stay on, but soon the drudgery and dreary climate overcame her. After an enthusiastic beginning, a trip to England to participate in the socialist experiments of the Fabians came to a similar end.

Gilman wrote in her memoir that "Mr. Howells told me that I was the only optimist reformer he ever met,"[15] but for much of his life this evaluation was true of Howells himself. Brought up in the golden age of American rural egalitarianism, Howells increasingly saw the values of that era sacrificed to the rampant acquisitiveness of the industrial Gilded Age. Two major influences on this altered point of view were the Haymarket bombing and Howells's introduction to the Christian Socialism of Tolstoy.

Howells was one of the few opinion leaders of the era to defend the Haymarket anarchists in print, and he was pilloried in the press for it. Although Howells vacillated for weeks after writing to the anarchists' defense attorney that he believed the defendants to be innocent, he ultimately acted courageously on the attorney's advice that Howells initiate a press campaign in their behalf. Thus it appears that fear of controversy alone cannot account for Howells's holding back in his mentorial relationship with Gilman.

Just at the time that he was forced to confront the accumulated shortcomings of his beloved Republic, Howells "became interested in the creed of Socialism," in which "the greatest influence . . . came to me through Tolstoy."[16] Tolstoy's repudiation of industrial society, based as it was on the Christian tenets Howells had imbibed as a youth, revived Howells' optimism by redirecting it:

> Tolstoy gave me heart to hope that the world may yet be made over in the image of Him who died for it. . . . He gave me new criterions, new principles.[17]

Howells acted on his new convictions both in his own fiction and in the editorial support he gave to other writers of similar persuasions. He gave an enthusiastic review to Edward Bellamy's utopian novel *Looking Backward*, which reversed the trend of mixed reviews and poor sales that had initially greeted the book. Hamlin Garland credited Howells's favorable review of *Main-Travelled Roads* with winning it a place in the east. Thorstein Veblen's biographer noted that Howells's two laudatory columns on *The Theory of the Leisure Class* "helped to make the book a sensation."[18] And, at various times, Howells published his admiration of Charlotte Perkins Gilman. Late in his career he praised her work as "witty and courageous," adding that "the best things that have been said about woman suffrage in our time have been said by Charlotte Perkins Gilman."[19]

When Gilman received Howells's compliments on "Similar Cases," she sent a copy of his letter to her friend Martha Lane, with the following comments:

> I'm glad you thought my poem funny. I herein boastfully enclose a copy of a letter showing it was thought rather more of by some!
> . . . Isn't that a delightful letter? I am so pleased too to find the man thinks well of Nationalism in spite of its "flabby apostle."[20]

The "apostle" was Edward Bellamy, whose novel was helped to prominence by Howells's favorable review.

Gilman was prepared by nature and education to embrace the Nationalist creed, which expounded the necessity of the government's taking complete control of the means of production in order to eradicate the panoply of evils generated by laissez-faire economics. Like Howells, Gilman had grown up in a family atmosphere suffused with belief in progress. Her maternal relatives, the Nonconformist Beecher preachers, extended from the spiritual to the social sphere their conviction that the individual could improve his own life with the help of grace. Reading lists compiled by her father nurtured this conviction into support for the theories of the Reform Darwinists, who saw evolutionary progress as the collective right and duty of the entire enlightened human species.

This linking of social progress to natural law appealed to Gilman's personal tendency toward rational optimism and preference for provable over revealed truth. For Gilman, the "will of God" meant "health, intelligence, normal development, beauty, joyous fulfillment of all life's processes," and she believed that "economic measures which promote such things must be in accordance with it."[21] As Howells had also done, Gilman rejected sectarian Christianity in favor of a God-ordered universe in which Christian ethics assisted the laws of evolution to pursue the perfection intended by the Creator. Both authors linked social responsibility to religious tenets rather than political ideology.

The family environment also oriented Gilman toward feminism. Her great-aunts included the novelist Harriet Beecher Stowe, Catharine Beecher (the architect of "domestic feminism"), and suffrage worker Isabella Beecher Hooker. Gilman came to know these women and their convictions during the extended family visits brought about by her father's lapses in financial support. From them she learned that women could have a stimulating intellectual and social life of their own, without standing in the shadow of husband or father, yet without sacrificing womanliness.

She also learned that exposing men's exploitation of women to public criticism would bring a storm of recrimination around a woman's head, but that a strong woman could survive it. Harriet Beecher Stowe provoked a considerable scandal when she insisted on publishing Lady Byron's accusation that her husband had seduced his half sister. Isabella Beecher Hooker caused a major rift in family relations by supporting fellow suffragist Victoria Woodhull's right to publish the story of Henry Ward Beecher's many lapses from the sexual propriety expected of a minister. These role models undoubtedly assisted Gilman in managing the spiteful publicity generated by her divorce as well as reinforcing her outspoken opinions about women's rights. Nationalism and feminism worked together, in Gilman's view: nationalism was "the most practical form of human development," but equality of the sexes was "the most essential condition of that development."[22]

For both Gilman and Howells, the political rights of women were founded on their equality with men. Howells was frequently misunderstood on this topic, because his fiction treats women evenhandedly rather than idealistically: *Dr. Breen's Practice*, for example, deals with the setbacks experienced by a female homeopathic doctor in her encounters with the male-dominant allopathic medical establishment; *A Woman's Reason* looks at the limited economic options open to a woman lacking a male protector; and *A Modern Instance* charts the catastrophic effects of the stigma of divorce on a woman's life. In his "Editor's Easy Chair" column, Howells argued that women had the duties of citizens, and therefore should have citizens' rights as well. Since women lived within the State, they ought to be able to vote on its practices, and since they had to pay taxes, the principle of "no taxation without representation" ought to entitle women to suffrage.[23]

Howells wrote on women's issues as part of a general commitment to social reform. Gilman did the reverse: she committed herself to a general reform of "masculinist" social order as a precondition to the achievement of equality for women. Her monumental study of *Women and Economics* (1898) won her international recognition. It was followed by *Concerning Children* (1900), *The Home: Its Work and Influence* (1903), *Human Work* (1904), *Man Made World: or, Our Androcentric Culture* (1911), and *His Religion and Hers: A Study of the Faith of Our Fathers and the Work of Our Mothers* (1923). For seven years (1909–1916), she published a quarterly journal called the *Forerunner*, writing all the columns, fiction, poetry, and even the advertisements herself. She supported this endeavor by lecturing and contributing to other publications. The *Forerunner* addressed feminist issues great and small: suffrage; dress reform; sexual autonomy and family planning; the efficient management of housework, cooking, and child care by experts; men's oppression of women and women's oppression of themselves.

The quarterly serialized Gilman's utopian novel, *Herland*, which pictures the successful operation of a society entirely without men. Miraculously endowed with the power to reproduce by parthenogenesis when a catastrophe permanently isolates the women at home from the men who have gone off to war, the female citizens of Herland put the stamp of nurture on traditionally male domains. When a trio of male adventurers stumbles upon this sanctuary, their efforts to comprehend its extraordinary environment and to explain the workings of their own society produce a humorous and satirical indictment of sex-specific divisions in human activity. Thus, this utopia avoids the usual pitfall of the genre, namely ponderous didacticism, a fault that mars its sequel, *With Her in Ourland*.

Howells, too, used the utopian genre to envision a society based on gender equality. His Altrurian romances assume that an enlightened proletariat would use the democratic process to ensure that men and women have not only equal opportunities but equal obligations in the economic, political, and domestic spheres. With women freed from the pressure of supporting the entire family unit, both sexes of Altrurians are able to achieve their full human potential. Curiously, the American woman who travels to Altruria and marries there follows a career path not unlike Gilman's; she becomes a traveling lecturer, combining intellectual work and domestic chores through a communal housekeeping arrangement. This heroine's name, Eveleth Strange, brings together the female archetypes of Eve and Lilith without reference to the sanctified, pedestaled archetype of the Virgin.

More important to the cause of gender equality than Howells's fiction, however, was his editorial support of women writers. In "Recollections of an *Atlantic* Editorship," Howells lists nineteen women whose work appeared during his tenure and adds that he does not know whether he published more men or women,

> but if any one were to prove that there were more women than men I should not be surprised. . . . For in our beloved republic of letters the citizenship is not reserved solely to males of twenty-one and over.[24]

As Ann Douglas Wood points out, Howells held up for special praise several representatives of the local-color school, finding that their "directness and simplicity" is of a piece with "the best modern work everywhere."[25] While the high quality of the local colorists' literary achievement and the sincerity of Howells's support for them are incontestable, these women's motives and methods are so different from Gilman's that it is easy to see why Howells, admiring the former, would be disconcerted by the latter.

The qualities of style that Howells praised in the work of the local colorists were on the whole foreign to Gilman's. While the local colorists wrote in the realistic mode, Gilman's fiction and poetry were unabashedly romantic in the intensity and extravagance of her expression. In general, Howells disparaged the romance genre for presenting women with unwholesomely exaggerated role models, and for making it possible for them to take refuge from their real problems in a world of fictional triumphs. Gilman's utopian novels and serial fiction could be seen as vulnerable to such a critique, but oddly enough in this context, the Gilman short story that Howells elected to anthologize belongs to the Gothic tradition. Even when Howells writes about Gilman's poems, which do not exhibit the presumed defects of the romance genre, a consistent motif of his letters to Gilman is enthusiasm for her convictions tempered by genteel consternation over her verbal deportment.

The restraint that differentiated the local colorists' literary style from Gilman's extended to their professional styles as well. Contrasting them to the assertively professional women of the earlier sentimentalist school, Wood notes that the local colorists tended to be reclusive "pure artists," neither subscribing to the cult of domesticity nor competing in the male-dominated marketplace. While the former quality places their writings in the artistic and social vanguard, the latter preserved their personal aura of conventional femininity. That both qualities figured centrally in Howells' esteem of these women can be seen in his correspondence with and about them.

In an 1885 letter to Edmund Gosse, for example, Howells expresses his astonishment that "Charles Egbert Craddock" turns out to be a woman writer in terms that revere her feminine weakness:

> We are just now in an excitement as great as the Gosse boom at its wildest, about Charles Egbert Craddock, the author of the Tennessee mountain stories, who has turned up in Boston, a little *girl-cripple* [emphasis in original], not so big as Pilla. . . . She has a most manful and womanly soul in her poor, twisted little body. Her stories are extraordinary; but I dare say you know them.[26]

A similar emphasis appears in a fulsome but domesticated compliment to Sarah Orne Jewett:

> You have a precious gift, and you must know it, and can be none the worse for your knowledge. We all have a tender pleasure in your work, which there

is no name for but love. I think *no* one [emphasis in original] has shown finer art in a way, than you, and that something which is so much better than art, besides. Your voice is like a thrush's in the din of all the literary noises that stun us so.[27]

It is hard to recognize in this rhetorical throwback to the "sweet singer" that stereotyped an earlier generation of literary women the same stylist whom Howells had praised in the *Cosmopolitan Magazine* for "the perfect artistic restraint, the truly Greek temperance" of her prose.[28]

In several respects. Gilman's career differed from those of the local colorists whom Howells deservedly placed on a critical pedestal. Gilman made her living by writing, while of that group "only Freeman and Stuart supported themselves by their pens."[29] In addition, she earned money from public speaking, still a daring occupation for a female at the turn of the century. She wrote and spoke explicitly about the invidious way "in which the sexuo-economic relation has operated in our species,"[30] while the local colorists' frequent focus on female protagonists living independently from men only implicitly addressed the material price paid for this autonomy. Neither in their person nor in their work did the local colorists challenge conventionally imposed standards of feminine virtue, while Gilman did both.

These differences are significant because Howells indulged in the unfortunate habit of impugning the femininity of women writers with whom he disagreed. He once wrote to Henry James about his unpleasant meeting with "a certain celebrated lady novelist, who once turned to criticism long enough to devote me to execration" that "I find I don't take these things Pickwickianly; but she avenged me by the way she dressed and the way she talked. I wish I could present you with the whole scene, but I mustn't."[31]

It should be noted that Howell's admiration for Gilman's writing evidently did not extend to appreciation for her unconventional domestic arrangements: her divorce from Walter Stetson and relinquishment of their daughter's custody to him and his new wife, who happened to be Gilman's best friend and her housemate during her year of separation (Hill asserts that Gilman encouraged Stetson to court her friend).[32] He attached the following acidulous biographical account to an 1898 letter from Gilman recommending some stories written by her "friend and co-mother," Grace Ellery Channing:

Mrs. Stetson's "co-mother" is married to Mrs. Stetson's divorced husband. Mrs. S. attended the wedding and gave her young daughter to her "co-mother" as a wedding present.[33]

The scandalous "abandonment" of her five-year-old daughter, Katherine, to the child's father and stepmother on the undoubtedly accurate grounds that they were better suited both temperamentally and economically to take care of her haunted Gilman's career as a writer and lecturer for years: however, Howells's privately expressed opinion did not prevent him, or his wife and daughter, from socializing with Gilman. He attended her lectures—indeed, on one occasion she substituted for him on the lecture platform when he was unable to keep a speaking engagement—and she visited Howells's family at home. Gilman regarded this friendship as a "special pleasure."[34]

Howells could offer unqualified enthusiasm for Gilman's "Similar Cases" because it satirized resistance to social change without going into embarrassing particulars. Written in the "thump and swack" meter popular to nineteenth-century oratorical verse, the poem's three "cases" represent stages in evolutionary development: the Eohippus, the Anthropoidal Ape, and the Neolithic Man. Each of these announces to his coeval creatures his vision of his future greatness, but is hooted down by them on the basis of his present unprepossessing status. "You would have to change your nature," argue the soon-to-be evolutionary castoffs against the aspirations of the progressive species.

The best verse of the poem shows the Neolithic Man's unfazed awareness that civilization will have its pitfalls as well as peaks:

> We are going to live in cities!
> We are going to fight in wars!
> We are going to eat three times a day
> Without the natural cause! . . .
> We are going to have Diseases!
> And Accomplishments!! And Sins!!![35]

This irony within an irony is typical of Gilman's satire at its sharpest. The barb seems at first somewhat softened by the fact that the "similar cases" under discussion have come to view from the pre-societal past, but a missing case is clearly implied by the "you would have to change your nature" refrain—that of women, whose efforts to evolve into fully human dignity and competence were regularly condemned as "unnatural" in Gilman's era.

In his letter congratulating Gilman on the appearance of "Similar Cases," Howells also complimented her poem "Women of Today" (that Howells read it in the *Woman's Journal*, sponsored by the American Woman Suffrage Association, testifies to his sympathetic interest in this issue). This short work chastises the "women of today who fear so much/The women of the future," and who proudly cling to the traditional roles of mother, wife, and housekeeper. The poet questions whether the "woman of today" indeed fulfills these roles: as a housekeeper, unlike her ancestors, she only keeps servants, and she cannot even keep them in service for long; as a wife, who in principle holds the key to her husband's heart, she must fear the consequences of the prevailing sexual double standard; and as a mother, she must suffer the grievous knowledge that half of the children born in the nineteenth century were doomed to die in infancy. The jeremiad predicts that the "woman of today" will never improve her blighted lot unless she can recognize her contentment as an unenlightened sham:

And still the wailing babies come and go,
And homes are waste, and husband's hearts fly far,
There is no hope until you dare to know
The thing you are![36]

Howells somewhat overstated the case when he told Gilman that this poem "is as good almost as the other"—it lacks the lash of wit to give it energy, and tries to supply the missing verve with exclamation points—but he was no doubt correct in calling it "dreadfully true." However, as will be seen more strongly in his response to "The Yellow Wallpaper," the word "dreadfully" and its synonyms apparently cut two ways in Howells's lexicon: the production of dread in the reader may be a worthy aesthetic goal, yet not be worthwhile as a publisher's risk.

Six months after his first paean, Howells again wrote to Gilman, this time on letterhead from the *Cosmopolitan Magazine*'s editorial department:

Do you think you could send me for this magazine something as good and wicked as *Similar Cases*, and of the like destructive tendency? And could you send it "in liking?"[37]

Gilman sent him "The Amoeboid Cell," which recounts a conversation between an amoeboid cell and a specialized one, in which the latter urges the advantages of development upon the former.

The amoeba resists the motion, unwilling to lose its personal freedom. The specialized cell retorts that in its present state the amoeba is just a "speck in the slime at the birthday of time," subject to mass death at the whim of nature. In contrast, the specialized cell enjoys the fruits of cooperation, while retaining the pleasures of diversity's "limitless range."

In the last stanza, the amoeba appears to get its just deserts, but the smugness of the specialized cell is also undermined by the final line of the poem:

Just then came a frost and the Amoeboid Cell
    Died out by the billion again:
        But the Specialized Cell
        In the body felt well
    And rejoiced in his place in the brain!
    The dead level of life with a brain![38]

Howells's letter of response to this offering giveth with one hand and taketh away with the other, as do many of his assessments of Gilman's writing:

The Amoeboid Cell is so good that I think it deserves working over more carefully, and condensing a good deal. I don't like any part of the joke that's in the spelling, like "individualitee" and "anybodee," and I think your moral is a little too sharply pointed. Couldn't it be incidental, somehow? Perhaps I am over-particular, but then I always think I am worth pleasing, as an admirer of your gifts.[39]

The available correspondence does not indicate whether Gilman made the effort to please the "admirer of her gifts," but "The Amoeboid Cell" never appeared in the *Cosmopolitan Magazine*.

Gilman's and Howells's estimates vary about his role in the publication of "The Yellow Wallpaper." By Gilman's description, Howells was an ineffective advocate for the story:

This ["The Yellow Wallpaper"] I sent to Mr. Howells, and he tried to have the *Atlantic Monthly* print it, but Mr. Scudder, then the editor, sent it back with this brief card:

Dear Madam:
Mr. Howells has handed me this story. I could not forgive myself if I made others as miserable as I have made myself![40]

After lamenting Scudder's lapse of perception ("I suppose he would have sent back one of Poe's on the same ground"), Gilman notes that she then put the story in the hands of a commercial agent, who placed it with the *New England Journal*. The agent never transmitted the *Journal*'s stipend to the author.

In "A Reminiscent Introduction" to the anthology in which Howells finally reprinted "The Yellow Wallpaper," however, he credits himself with assuring the story's first appearance in print:

It wanted at least two generations [after Poe] to freeze our young blood with Mrs. Perkins Gilman's story of *The Yellow Wallpaper*, which Horace Scudder (then of *The Atlantic*) said in refusing it that it was so terribly good that it ought never to be printed. But terrible and too wholly dire as it was. I could not rest until I had corrupted the editor of *The New England Magazine* into publishing it. Now that I have got it into my collection here, I shiver over it as much as I did when I first read it in manuscript, though I agree with the editor of *The Atlantic* of the time that it was too terribly good to be printed.[41]

While Gilman could scarcely blame Howells for Scudder's refusal to print "The Yellow Wallpaper" in the *Atlantic Monthly*, she either did not know about Howells' efforts to "corrupt" the editor of the *New England Journal* or did not appreciate them sufficiently to take note of them in her memoir, where she records only the activities of the tightfisted commercial agent.

In addition to accounting himself more active in the publication of "The Yellow Wallpaper" than Gilman acknowledged, Howells's introductory assessment of the piece in his anthology suggests—by its repetition of the adjective "terrible"—the grounds for his reluctance to press Scudder more assertively for the story's publication. During his own tenure as editor of the *Atlantic Monthly*, Howells had a taste of the consequences that could attend the publication of material "too wholly dire" for the public taste.

In September 1869, Howells brought out Harriet Beecher Stowe's "True Story of Lady Byron's Life," which included Lady Byron's accusation that her husband had committed incest with his half sister. The content of the charge was moral indignation about the things a married woman must endure with patience, but public indignation with the *Atlantic Monthly* for putting such shocking material in print cost the magazine 15,000 subscribers. Since Stowe was absolutely determined to publish her exposé somewhere, and since Howells wanted to keep her contributing to the *Atlantic Monthly* despite his reservations about any particular article, he could hardly have refused to print it. This episode, however—the third publication scandal to plague the magazine during Howells's association with it, although the only one for which he was accountable—made Howells somewhat more chary of offending the subscribers' sense of decency. This hard-earned editorial caution would have led Howells to respect Scudder's decision not to "make others miserable" by publishing "The Yellow Wallpaper."

Gilman was not unaware of Howells's aesthetically if not politically conservative tastes. Although she valued his praise, his writing was

> never a favorite of mine you know. His work is exquisite, painfully exquisite, but save for that Chinese delicacy of workmanship it seems to me of small artistic value. And its truth is that of the elaborate medical chart, the scientific photograph.[43]

On the other hand, she apparently was not aware of the painful personal connection that Howells had had with the rest-cure regimen lambasted by "The Yellow Wallpaper."

S. Weir Mitchell, who had supervised Gilman's disastrous rest cure, was a personal friend and artistic discovery of Howells, who published some of the doctor's fiction in the *Atlantic Monthly*. Mitchell had also prescribed this treatment for Winifred Howells, who gained physical strength but died of "a sudden failure of the heart" while under his care.

It is unclear whether Howells understood that Mitchell's methods were the particular target of Gilman's wrath in "The Yellow Wallpaper" at the time that she sent it to him for the *Atlantic Monthly*. Not until her letter to Howells accepting his invitation to anthologize the story in 1919 does Gilman make this explicit:

> Did you know that one piece of "literature" of mine was pure propaganda? I was under Dr. Weir Mitchell's treatment, at 27. . . . I tried it one summer, and went as near lunacy as one can, and come back. So I wrote this, and sent

him a copy. He made no response, but years after some one told me that he had told a friend "I have completely altered my treatment of neurasthenia since reading "The Yellow Wallpaper." Triumph![44]

Gilman's failure to credit Howells with facilitating the initial appearance of "The Yellow Wallpaper" in print follows a pattern of denying the actual contributions of those who, in Gilman's opinion, ought to have done more. Her correspondence with Lester Ward, the father of American sociology, shows a similar reaction.[45]

In 1893, the year following the publication of "The Yellow Wallpaper," Gilman brought out a volume of her collected poetry, entitled *In This Our World*. Again, Howells sent Gilman a letter praising the poems and their author in the warmest terms:

I am ashamed not to have said long ago how much pleasure we have all taken in your book of poems. They are the wittiest and wisest things that have been written this many a long day and year. You are not only the prophetess of the new religion (in the new conception of religion) but you speak with a tongue like a two-edged sword.

Once again, however, Howells's reservations begin to appear even as he praises:

I rejoice in your gift *fearfully* [emphasis added], and wonder how much more you will do with it. I can see how far and deep you have thought about the things at hand, and I have my bourgeois moments when I could have wished you for success's sake to have been less frank. But of course you know that you stand in your own way![46]

Thus it comes as no surprise that Howells graciously declines the opportunity to escort any more of Gilman's poems into print:

I like your Immortality, but I can understand why magazines would not. As to the volume of poetry, I suggest your sending it by Ripley Hitchcock, the literary man of Appletons, who have just brought out Bellamy's book. He will give it intelligent attention, and I beg you to quote me as cordially in its favor as your self respect will allow. I will tell him you are going to send it.[47]

The poem that magazines would not like depicts a conscious being in various stages of evolution: as grass, ape, man, and immortal soul. In its earliest avatars, the conscious being passively endured its fate or futilely rebelled against it. As man, it self-consciously gloried in its existence and learned to aspire to immortality. So far so good, in terms of conventional Christian evolution. The penultimate stanza, however, attacks the vision of the afterlife's reward as "hypothetical" as well as egotistical ("In this an endless, boundless bliss I see,—/ Eternal me!"), while the final verse contradicts the idea of divine providence with a perspective supremely indifferent to human events:

> When I was a man, no doubt I used to care
> About the little things that happened there,
> And fret to see the years keep going by,
> And nations, families, and persons die.[48]

The bromidic concluding couplet—"I didn't much appreciate life's plan / When I was a man"—can hardly counteract the acid tone of the poem as a whole.

Since Gilman published only the one collection of poetry, it is not clear whether Howells' letter refers to a projected second volume or to the 1898 reprint of *In This Our World*. In either case, Gilman's self-respect apparently would not allow her to quote Howells cordially enough to "the literary man at Appletons": no second volume ever appeared, and the copyright to the 1898 reprint was entered by Small, Maynard and Company of Boston.

Except for including "The Yellow Wallpaper" in *The Great Modern American Stories*, Howells's mentorial efforts for Gilman did not operate on the practical level: however, he never ceased to offer her sweeping moral support on the order of "when the gods really wake up and begin to behave justly you will have no cause to complain."[49] Why did Howells prefer to leave Gilman's career in the lap of the gods when he took other women writers under his own wing? The evidence suggests that while Howells held in high esteem Gilman's passionate defense of principles he, too, held sacred, he could not espouse her rhetorical and personal flamboyance. From childhood on, the ideal of the gracious lady exercised a powerful attraction over him. As Edwin H. Cady notes:

> His recollections of their drawing rooms and conservatories in *Years of My Youth* is almost a hymn to the ladyhood he learned to worship in Columbus. In later life he became disenchanted of almost all his other romanticisms. But he never entirely sloughed off his worship of the lady, though by means of it he gained deep insights into the nature of the civilized woman.[50]

Even on the issue of women's suffrage, about which Howells believed Gilman to have been the best and wisest exponent, his approach is genteel where Gilman's is wryly impatient. Howells believed that suffrage would come to women (in some unspecified, spontaneous manner) when women themselves sufficiently wanted this right. Gilman gleefully satirized this point of view in a poem entitled "Women Do Not Want It":

> What women want has never been a strongly acting cause
> When women has been wronged by man in churches, customs, laws:
> Why should he find this preference so largely in his way
> When he himself admits the right of what we ask to-day?[51]

Perhaps, too, Gilman sought a mentorial relationship with Howells at a level of emotional intensity to which he was not prepared to respond. Her letters of compliment to him are couched in no more exaggerated terms than his to her, but women of that period were expected to express themselves to men more circumspectly; apparently even Walter Stetson felt that his wife's demonstrations of emotional need were a little too frank.[52] Their correspondence indicates that Gilman initiated all the meetings that took place between them, with Howells occasionally (though graciously) demurring on the grounds of his own or his family's ill health.

Certainly her need for his assistance was great, since she published almost all of her works at her own expense, but the directness of her appeal may have put off a man accustomed to being the patriarch in such situations—he wrote to Lucy Larcom, for example. "You take rejection so sweetly that I have scarcely the heart to accept anything of yours."[53]

In the letter that thanks Howells for wishing to include "The Yellow Wallpaper" in his anthology, Gilman anxiously seeks his approval of her magazine:

> Please—did you ever receive either one of the bound volumes of the first year of my precious *Forerunner?* . . . I did want you to notice *my baby*, and tried twice, letter and book.[54]

Howell's one-line reply simply regrets that he never received her book, ignoring her plea for reassurance.

Summing up the successes and failures of her efforts to place work in magazines other than the *Forerunner*, Gilman made a list of those who were "good friends among editors." Howells's name is not among them, although she claims to have had so many that she can "by no means remember them all."[55] Recalling Theodore Dreiser's gloomy advice to "consider more what the editors want," Gilman explains the reason she ignored his counsel:

> There are those who write as artists, real ones; they often find it difficult to consider what the editor wants. There are those who write to earn a living, who if they succeed, *must* please his purchasers, the public, so we have this great trade of literary catering. But if one writes to express important truths, needed yet unpopular, the market is necessarily limited.[56]

Taking into account its defensively self-congratulatory tone, this explanation seems essentially valid with respect to Howells's unwillingness to publish

Gilman's work himself or to strongly advocate its publication by his powerful friends.

It was undoubtedly easier for Howells to praise Gilman's opinions than to take responsibility for them. Nevertheless, Howells's public votes of confidence in Gilman's writing enhanced its credibility and gave it a broader forum than it had achieved on its own. Despite his reservations, Howells kept faith with Gilman—in his fashion.

Notes

1. The Howells biographies I consulted (see below) simply do not mention the Gilman connection, probably because the major ones were written before interest in her work was revived in the early 1960s. Hill's biography of Gilman (see below) merely refers to Howells's enthusiasm for Gilman's "Similar Cases" and *In This Our World*, and notes his socialist sympathies. Hill only goes up to 1896 in this volume, so perhaps she will have more to say in a subsequent installment. In her introduction to Gilman's *Herland* (New York: Pantheon, 1979), vii. Ann J. Lane says that Howells "did much to sustain her career," but does not go into detail. So far as I know, the present study is the first treatment of the Gilman-Howells relationship.

2. Charlotte Perkins Gilman, *The Living of Charlotte Perkins Gilman: An Autobiography* (1935, repr. New York: Arno Press, 1972), 113.

3. Robert L. Hough, *The Quiet Rebel: William Dean Howells as Social Commentator* (1959; reprint, Hamden, Conn.: Archon Books, 1968), 4.

4. Edwin H. Cady, *The Road to Realism: The Early Years (1837–1885) of William Dean Howells* (Syracuse, N.Y.: Syracuse University Press, 1956), 173. Bellamy probably did not know how close to the mark his compliment came. When Howells first arrived in New England, he achieved an audience with Nathaniel Hawthorne. Upon learning that Howells intended next to visit Ralph Waldo Emerson, Hawthorne gave Howells one of his visiting cards to take to Emerson: the card bore the message, "I find this young man worthy" (Hough, *Quiet Rebel*, 1).

5. William Dean Howells, "The New Poetry," *North American Review* 168 (May 1899):589–590.

6. Gloria M. Martin, "Women in the Criticism and Fiction of William Dean Howells" (Ph.D. diss., University of Wisconsin, 1982), 170.

7. Mary A. Hill, *Charlotte Perkins Gilman: The Making of a Radical Feminist, 1860–1896* (Philadelphia: Temple University Press, 1980), 38–41, and passim.

8. Cady, *Road to Realism*, 28–39.

9. William Dean Howells to his father, 18 November 1888, 30 November 1888, and 6 January 1889, in *Selected Letters of W. D. Howells*, ed. George Arms, Don L. Cook, Christopher K. Lohman, and David J. Nordloh, 6 vols. (Boston: Twayne, 1980), vol. 3. *1882–1891*, ed. Robert C. Leity III. 235, 243.

10. Howells to his father, 17 March 1889, and Howells to S. Weir Mitchell, 7 March 1889, in ibid., 3:249, 247.

11. Ibid., 3:53.

12. Hill, *Gilman*, 39, quoting a letter from Gilman to her father, undated (probably after 1875); quoted by permission of the Arthur and Elizabeth Schlessinger Library, Radcliffe College, Cambridge, Mass.

13. Hill, *Gilman*, 136.

14. Gilman to Howells, 17 October 1919: quoted by permission of the Houghton Library, Harvard University, Cambridge, Mass.

15. Gilman, *Living*, 182.

16. Hough, *Quiet Rebel*, 29, quoting Gilman, "Mr. Howells' Socialism," *American Fabian* 4 (February 1898):2.

17. William Dean Howells, *Criticism and Fiction* (New York: Harper's, 1910), 183–184.

18. Hough, *Quiet Rebel*, 112–113.

19. Joyce Kilmer, "War Stops Literature, Says William Dean Howells," *New York Times*, 16 December 1914.

20. Hill, *Gilman*, 176.

21. Gilman, "A Socialist Prayer," *Forerunner* 2 (May 1911):124.

22. Gilman, unpublished lectures given on 20 and 21 December 1890, quoted by Hill, *Gilman*, 182.

23. Howells, "Editor's Easy Chair," *Harper's Monthly* 111 (October 1905):796: and 118 (May 1909):967.

24. Howells, "Recollections of an *Atlantic* Editorship," quoted by Martin, "Women in Howells," 186.

25. Ann Douglas Wood, "The Literature of Impoverishment: The Women Local Colorists in America, 1865–1914," *Women's Studies* 1 (1972):4, quoting Howells, *Criticism and Fiction* (1910; reprint, New York: Hill and Wang, 1967), 134, 168–169.

26. *Selected Letters*, 3:117.

27. Ibid., 3:305.

28. "Editor's Study" (April 1891), 804–805.

29. Wood, "Literature of Impoverishment," 15.

30. Charlotte Perkins Stetson [Gilman], *Women and Economics* (Boston: Small, Maynard, 1898), 75.

31. *Selected Letters*, 4:305.

32. Hill, *Gilman*, 158.

33. Gilman to Howells, 8 March 1898: quoted by permission of the Houghton Library.

34. Gilman, *Living*, 222.

35. Gilman, "Similar Cases," in *In This Our World*, 3d ed. (Boston: Small, Maynard, 1898), 99–100.

36. Gilman, *Our World*, 128–129.

37. Howells to Gilman, 10 December 1891: quoted by permission of the Schlesinger Library.

38. Gilman, *Our World*, 205–208.

39. Howells to Gilman, *AESL*, 31 January 1892: quoted by permission of the Schlesinger Library.

40. Gilman, *Living*, 119.

41. Howells, "A Reminiscent Introduction," in *The Great Modern American Stories* (New York: Boni and Liveright, 1920), vii.

42. Cady, *Road to Realism*, 136.

43. Gilman to Martha Lane, 27 July 1890, Rhode Island Historical Society, quoted by Hill, *Gilman*, 176.

44. Gilman to Howells, 17 October 1919: quoted by permission of the Houghton Library.

45. Gilman was much impressed with Ward's gynecocentric theory of evolution (which held that in most species the female controlled both selection of the mate and reproduction, making her rather than the male the dominant partner), and did much to popularize it in her own writing. When Ward complained that his theory had not received the attention it deserved, Gilman wrote several letters reminding him of her appreciative efforts in its behalf. When no acknowledgment of her reminders appeared, she sent him a copy of her book *Human Work* and expressed the hope that she would someday have the time to read some more of his

writing: "So far—except for the Phylogenic forces in Pure Sociology; and some of the shorter papers—. . . I have not really read you at all." Thus prodded, Ward finally produced the desired tribute:

> I have read your book. I could hear my own voice all the time. But of course, it was not an echo. It is pitched much higher than I can strike and differs also entirely in *timbre*. (See Hill, *Gilman*, 266–267)

46. Howells to Gilman, 11 July 1894: quoted by permission of the Schlesinger Library.

47. Howells to Gilman, 25 June 1897: quoted by permission of the Houghton Library.

48. Gilman, *Our World*, 62–63.

49. Howells to Gilman, 8 May 1911: quoted by permission of the Schlesinger Library.

50. Cady, *Road to Realism*, 74.

51. Gilman, *Our World*, 156–157.

52. Hill, *Gilman*, 123.

53. Cady, *Road to Realism*, 242, quoting Daniel Dulany Addison, *Lucy Larcom: Life, Letters, and Diary* (Boston: Houghton Mifflin, 1894), 189.

54. Gilman to Howells, 17 October 1919 (emphasis added), quoted by permission of the Houghton Library.

55. Gilman, *Living*, 302–303.

56. Ibid., 304.

"Out at Last"? "The Yellow Wallpaper" after Two Decades of Feminist Criticism

Elaine R. Hedges

"I've got out at last," said I . . . "And I've pulled off most of the paper, so you can't put me back!"

Since 1973, when I wrote the Afterword to the Feminist Press edition, "The Yellow Wallpaper" has become the Press' best-selling volume and one of the best-selling works of fiction by university presses in the United States. It has been reprinted in England, France, Spain, the Netherlands, Germany, Sweden and Iceland, and it has inspired several film and dramatic versions, a television adaptation and even an opera. It is of course regularly assigned in women's studies and literature courses and is by now firmly established in the literary canon, appearing in all of the major anthologies. Together with *The Awakening* it is probably the most well-known rediscovered work by a nineteenth-century American woman.

Since the story's republication, there have been more than two dozen critical studies of it, including biographical, genre, reader response, discourse theory, psychoanalytic, and new historicist and cultural studies readings. Collectively they offer a dazzling and significantly disparate array of interpretations. The wallpaper, as the story's key metaphor, has been read as inscribing the medical, marital, maternal, psychological, sexual, sociocultural, political and linguistic situation of its narrator-protagonist; as an image of the situation of the woman writer and hence a way of understanding the dilemmas of female authorship; as revealing the relations between gender and reading and gender and writing; and as a description of the problems of female self-representation within both the Lacanian world of the Symbolic and the capitalist world of the United States in the late nineteenth century. Analyses of the story's formal and stylistic features have variously argued for it as a realistic story, a feminist Gothic tale, and one of the earliest modernist texts. The endlessly debated ending has been interpeted as the narrator's

This essay was presented in a briefer version at the Modern Language Association convention in Washington, D.C., in December 1989. It also appears in *The Captive Imagination: A Casebook on "The Yellow Wallpaper,"* edited by Catherine Golden (New York: Feminist Press, 1992), 319–338, and is reprinted by permission of the author.

triumph and/or her defeat, with positions ranging along a spectrum that, at one end, sees her madness as a higher form of sanity and her search for meaning in the paper as successful and liberating, to the other end, that sees her as fatally retreating to a condition of childishness, or infantilism, or animalhood, or even inanimateness. Her crawling, thus, is either a sign of rebirth or of regression; and her husband's fainting proof either that she has outwitted him or that, by becoming unconscious, he's outwitted her, by refusing to listen to her. Finally, critics have argued that Gilman's contemporaries could not read the story because they lacked the necessary reading conventions, and, on the other hand, that they in fact had such conventions but would not read it, for very fear of discovering what it really said.

Such a synopsis might suggest that "The Yellow Wallpaper" has become our white whale, or, as some recent critics would have it, our feminist albatross, for by now not only the story's once roughly agreed-upon meaning, but its privileged status as an exemplary text and a feminist critical touchstone are being challenged. At the same time, however, the story has been adopted by new historicist critics as one of *their* exemplary texts, so that its continuing visibility and critical viability seem assured. This would seem, then, to be a good moment for a backward glance and a reconnoitering. What do the story's changing interpretations, and the recent challenges to the earliest interpretations, tell us about the trajectory of literary criticism, and particularly of feminist literary criticism, over the last twenty years?

The earliest studies of the story—and I'm referring to four that are frequently grouped together—my Afterword,[1] Sandra Gilbert and Susan Gubar's treatment in *The Madwoman in the Attic*,[2] Annette Kolodny's "A Map for Rereading: or, Gender and the Interpretation of Literary Texts,"[3] and Jean Kennard's "Convention Coverage, or How to Read Your Own Life"[4]—read it, sympathetically, as the narrative of a woman's efforts to free herself from the confining social and psychic structures of her world, with the wallpaper interpreted as encoding those oppressive structures. The extent to which she was seen as succeeding was moot, with my arguing that she achieves temporary insight but is at the end defeated, totally mad, and Kolodny similarly concluding that she manages only to re-encode her own unacceptable reality within herself. The readings of Gilbert and Gubar and Kennard showed the greatest investment in the narrator's success, with the former seeing her as "mad" only by society's standards but in fact moving into "the open spaces of . . . [her] own authority"[5] and the latter arguing that her madness could be seen as a higher form of sanity or truth. Other early, briefer, analyses were similarly split, with Loralee MacPike[6] and Beate Schöpp-Schilling[7] describing the narrator's insanity as, respectively, a creative act and a successful defiance, and Mary Beth Pringle on the other hand arguing that all she accomplishes is to shape the wallpaper into "the only thing she knows: a cage."[8] Despite what is roughly a fifty-fifty division here, the idea that its earliest critics saw an essentially or largely triumphant conclusion to the story, a victory for the narrator, has prevailed, with critical consequences that will be apparent later.

Although these studies, from 1973 to 1981, tended to read the wallpaper primarily in terms of the narrator's social situation, broadly defined, interest in describing her dilemma through reference to issues of textuality, language, and discourse was early evident, since, of course, the narrator in the story is crucially engaged both in writing—she tries to record her experience in her journal—and in reading—she tries to decipher the patterns in the paper. However, whose text she was reading—whether her own or her husband's—and how she read it, soon became as problematical as the degree of her success or failure. For Gilbert and Gubar, concerned as they were in *The Madwoman in the Attic* with the anxiety of female authorship, the wallpaper was "the facade of the patriarchal text,"[9] which, by releasing the woman inside it, the narrator escapes, becoming ready to author her own. But for Kolodny the wallpaper was the narrator's own text, the text of herself, which could not get read or recorded. In 1985 Paula Treichler approached the story as a struggle over woman's right to author her own sentences, in opposition to her doctor-husband's medical "sentencing" of her, and found that the narrator did so, at least temporarily, through an "impertinent" language that defied male control, and through her relation to the wallpaper, which Treichler saw as a metaphor for women's discourse, "thick with life, expression, and suffering."[10] The following year Judith Fetterley,[11] also concerned with male control of textuality—of the scripts or stories through which women must try to define and understand themselves—found the narrator temporarily achieving the authority of her own script, but the wallpaper, as patriarchal text, eventually strangling the women who try to get through—a conclusion with which two other critics, Karen Ford[12] and Carol Neely,[13] who had written brief rejoinders to Treichler, generally agreed.[14]

By 1986 this approach to the story, in terms of textuality and language, was producing readings that seemed to offer less and less autonomous or expressive space to the narrator. Two articles appeared that year that read the wallpaper, in Lacanian psychoanalytic terms, as the site of the narrator's struggle with self-representation through language. In "Monumental Feminism and Literature's Ancestral House: Another Look at 'The Yellow Wallpaper,' "[15] Janice Haney-Peritz, arguing, as Treichler had, that the story should be approached not in terms of oppressive social structures, as earlier interpretations had approached it, but in terms of the oppressive structures of male discourse, could find less room for even the partial victory that Treichler and Fetterley, like most earlier critics, had tried to negotiate. For Haney-Peritz, once the narrator perceives a *real* woman as opposed to the *symbol* of a woman in the paper, she has surrendered all access to the Symbolic realm, the linguistic realm in which her identity as a speaking and writing subject must be constructed, and retreated into the realm of the pre-Oedipal Imaginary, where she becomes infantilized and hopelessly encrypted in fantasy. And Mary Jacobus, in her book, *Reading Woman*,[16] by focusing on the narrator as an hysteric, saw her as engaged in a process of figuration, an hysterical overreading of the wallpaper, that trapped her in a maze of signs, where she becomes totally lost.

These readings, and especially Haney-Peritz's, were in turn given additional currency in a 1988 article by Diane Herndl, for whom the narrator is also an hysteric who, after failing in the Symbolic realm to find self-representation, retreats to the hallucinatory realm of the Imaginary. When, in that hallucinatory realm, she endows the wallpaper with life, she becomes herself an object, "just another of the indecipherable furnishings in her husband's house."[17] Although in 1988 in *Writing Beyond the Ending* Rachel Blau DuPlessis could suggest both possibilities—that the narrator's madness might be seen as "divinest Sense" or, from the "perspective of normalcy," as irrational and delusive behavior;[18] and in 1989, in volume two of *No Man's Land*, Gilbert and Gubar could envision the narrator not only out on the garden paths beyond the house but "fleeing towards the . . . gardens of *Herland*,"[19] Gilman's utopian world of liberated women, it was apparent that a new critical period had begun.

The new readings depended to a significant degree on foregrounding elements in the story that, Jacobus argued, earlier critics had left unexamined: the disturbing yellow color of the wallpaper, and its smell. In her interpretation Jacobus had importantly relied on these elements, reading the yellow "stain" and the odor that the narrator ascribes to the paper as symbols of her repressed sexuality, denied representation by her culture. Embodied in her hysteric posture and erupting in her defensive and anxiety-induced overreading of the paper, this repression reduces her, at the story's end, to a creeping animal, "all body," repugnant and terrifying to her fainting husband.[20]

By the time of Jacobus's essay the wallpaper's yellow color and smell had in fact already begun to be examined, by Juliann Fleenor in 1983, and Jeffrey Berman in 1985. Both of these critics had also read the yellow color and smell as representing the narrator's sexuality, specifically her sexual fear and disgust. For Fleenor, the yellow color implied "something strange and terrible about . . . female procreation, and about female physiology,"[21] and for Berman the color and the smell also suggested fears of "uncontrolled reproduction" and "sexual defilement."[22] Three more recent readings have concurred. In 1988 William Veeder associated the yellow color and smell with the narrator's inability to handle adult sexuality;[23] in 1989 Marianne deKoven saw the paper as "bloated" with denied sexual desire, its "waddling," "sprawling," "wallowing" qualities as well as its smell, symbolizing the narrator's sexual self-disgust;[24] and in the same year Linda Wagner-Martin also found the story conveying the "disgust . . . [the narrator] feels for herself as a sexual, procreative woman."[25]

As the quotations from Fleenor, Berman, and Wagner-Martin suggest, critics were also relating the narrator's sexual difficulties to her experience and attitudes as a new mother—another aspect of the story that its earliest critics had not extensively explored. Berman, who offered a Freudian interpretation of the story based on Gilman's own life—her unsatisfactory first marriage and her troubled childhood relationship to her parents—emphasized the narrator's fascination with the wallpaper's frightening ability to sprout into uncontrolled new growths—toadstools, seaweed, fungi—and found her projecting on to the paper her morbid fears of motherhood and reproduction. Veeder, reading the story in the light of psychological models taken from boundary and object relations theory and also using the facts of Gilman's own life, similarly found the narrator unable to deal with motherhood and, as a result, retreating to an infantile state, with the paper's repugnant yellow stain and smell becoming the infant's urine.

Meanwhile, the interpretations of Haney-Peritz and Jacobus not only disputed what they saw as the hegemonic reading of the story in my Afterword, and in Gilbert and Gubar, Kolodny, and Kennard; they also importantly challenged the interpretive practices on which those readings were based. Early interpretations, Haney-Peritz charged, citing especially Gilbert and Gubar's and Kolodny's, were essentialist: generalizing from the situation of one nineteenth-century woman, they read the story as "the" woman's story, as having some essential " 'female meaning' "; and, she also argued, by encouraging readers to identify with the narrator, especially through a belief in the possibilities of her liberation, the critics had created and perpetuated an erroneous feminist critical assumption—namely, that women's literature contains "a really distinctive body" of meaning that can be discovered through such identification (123). Questioning whether we should identify with a narrator who may be reading her husband's text rather than her own, she therefore also warned against the assumption that such identification is necessarily liberating.

In 1990, in "Feminist Criticism, 'The Yellow Wallpaper,' and the Politics of Color in America," Susan Lanser reiterated and extended these charges. She, too, questioned the story's canonical status, the essentialist readings of some of its earliest critics, and their encouragement of reader identification with the narrator, while adding the observation that its interpreters have all been white academics, who have perhaps simply repeated the reading practice of the story's narrator, pursuing and finding in the text, as the narrator does in the wallpaper, only our own image reflected back. Emphasizing that both the story and its author are the products of their culture, Lanser urged us to recognize that not only men's writings, as feminist critics have long recognized, but women's, and feminist criticism as well, are all "collusive with ideology,"[27] likely, that is, to embody and reflect the biases and prejudices of their times. In the light, especially, of current concern with differences among women, she therefore reads—or as she admits, provocatively overreads—the wallpaper, not, or not only, as either the patriarchal text or the woman's text, but as the culture's text. The result is that she finds in the paper's yellow color and smell and in its imagery a reflection of the nation's obsession, at the turn of the century, with issues of race, due to the massive immigration at the time from southern and eastern Europe and from Asia, an obsession which Gilman, as shown in her nonfictional writings, shared, and one which, according to Lanser, the word "yellow" came to convey, as connoting strangeness, ugliness, uncleanness, and inferiority. Where the wallpaper, for Jacobus, was the site of the sexual unconscious, it is now the site of the "political unconscious,"[28] and what is found there is equally unsettling.[29]

But if some recent feminist critics are rejecting "The Yellow Wallpaper" as a paradigmatic or exemplary text, preferring to see it as at best a "minor classic of female Gothic"[30] and at worst a "memento mori,"[31] it seems to have found a new home among the new historicists, who, moreover, like Lanser, are interested in the text's complicitousness with ideology.[32] Two new historicist studies of the story that appeared in 1987 focus, as Jacobus and Herndl do, on the narrator's hysteria, but with hysteria now seen as a disease of capitalism. Walter Benn Michaels uses the story as the introduction to his study of the relation of late-nineteenth-century literary texts to American capitalism, *The Gold Standard and the Logic of Naturalism*, explicitly calling it his exemplary text.[33] What it exemplifies now is the genesis of the marketplace, or the birth of the culture of consumption. In Michaels's reading, which is based on the Derridean idea of the self as an effect of writing, the narrator's nervous breakdown is "a function of her involvement in a certain political economy of selfhood." Determined to produce herself through writing, she consumes herself in the process—a turn of affairs that of course undermines the gospel of production that Gilman preached, but that makes the narrator, as combined producer and consumer, the "efficient scene of [market] circulation." Michaels's reading is extended and refined by Gillian Brown in "The Empire of Agoraphobia,"[35] which similarly sees the narrator as engaged in circulation—in, out, and around the walls of her room. But for Brown, such circulation, in both parodying that of the marketplace and protesting the immobility of domestic confinement, succeeds in making the story a feminist critique, one that anticipates Gilman's feminist redefinition of the home and women's role in her later, nonfictional works.

Where, then, are we, after almost two decades of reading "The Yellow Wallpaper," with its narrator described now as a "post-partum psychotic" or "schizophrenic,"[36] a child or infant, a disgusting body, a dead object; or, what may not be much better, a politically compromised but quite efficient member of the world of capitalism? To state the critical situation thus is of course to overstate it, since most of the newer critical interpretations still read the story as a feminist text. But it highlights what has been a major shift: the diminishment or even disavowal of the narrator's status as a feminist heroine.

What accounts for this shift are of course changes in the intellectual and critical climate since the story's first republication in the early 1970s. In her 1981 essay Kennard ably described much of that climate out of which the earliest readings emerged, especially the literary and extraliterary circumstances that enabled and encouraged us to read madness as a kind of sanity, or insight; to see the narrator as on a quest for her identity, or, as I described her, as "fighting for some sense of independent self" (51); and to see her husband as representing the patriarchal forces with which she had to contend. I should like now simply to elaborate a bit on what Kennard said, to talk in somewhat more detail about a few aspects of that intellectual climate.

Certainly the prior rediscovery and publication of Kate Chopin's *The Awakening* centrally mattered. The story of a woman who was questioning marriage and motherhood in the interest of her need for some greater fulfillment, its thematic appeal was strong at a time when we were posing the same questions about our own lives. "The Yellow Wallpaper" carried the same theme, with its important additional emphasis on the narrator's yearning for what she calls "congenial work."[37] And both stories, of course, posed similarly problematic endings: whether the narrator's madness, like Edna Pontellier's drowning, was to be read as a victory or a defeat. To the extent that there was an early critical investment in finding some degree of triumph in the endings of both works, it was, I think, due not only to the textual clues that could support such readings, but also to our concern, in those years when the history of women's lives was being newly recovered, that that history not be read merely as one of victimization, the passive acceptance of subordination and suffering. As Elaine Showalter has noted, the image of "awakening" carried special resonance for women at the time, and so the narrator's growing awareness of her situation, her efforts to decipher, understand, and then question it—quite apart from the degree of her ultimate success or failure in changing it—were given important thematic weight. Kennard found "a sort of triumph" in the narrator's "understanding of her situation," and I found her "heroism" residing "in her perceptivity and in her resistance."[38]

To a significant degree that resistance took the form of anger, as expressed for example in her defying both her husband's and the housekeeper's orders, or in tearing the paper, and this was important at a time when we were discovering, and wondering how to deal with, our own. Two years before the republication of "The Yellow Wallpaper" the poet Adrienne Rich had delivered a talk that would become one of her most influential pieces of writing. In "When We Dead Awaken: Writing as Re-Vision"—and the title's use of the image of awakening is of course further proof of its power in the early 1970s—she had linked women's anger to their victimization, encouraging its release into creative expression, thus validating what was considered an "unfeminine" emotion and supporting its discovery in women's texts.[39]

In "The Yellow Wallpaper" the narrator's husband is also a doctor, important of course in many interpretations of the work; here was yet another aspect of the story that in the 1970s carried a special force, as we absorbed the implications of the discoveries then being made about the medical profession's treatment of women in the nineteenth century. Those reactions were best captured in the title of a later work on nineteenth-century medical attitudes towards women, G. J. Barker-Benfield's *The Horrors of the Half-Known Life* (1976). The work of researchers like Barbara Ehrenreich and Deidre English in *Complaints and Disorders: The Sexual Politics of Sickness* and of Ann Douglas Wood in " 'The Fashionable Diseases': Women's Complaints and Their Treatment in Nineteenth-Century America," both published the same year as The Feminist Press edition of "The Yellow Wallpaper," provided a context that further committed us to the story's narrator in her struggle against a husband who could be seen as a doubly powerful antagonist. In the words of the title of the book published in 1971 by the Boston Women's Health Book Collective, at the beginning of the women's health movement, we, like the narrator, were trying to reclaim "our bodies, ourselves."[40]

Finally, one cannot discount the political climate of the time. The year that saw the republication of "The Yellow Wallpaper" was the year of the *Roe v. Wade* Supreme Court decision, which climaxed a decade of legislative victories for women, from the Equal Pay Act of 1963 to Title VII of the Civil Rights Act to Title IX of the Education Act. This record of accomplishment created a sense of hope and expectation that could infuse the reading of women's texts, since their recovery, after years, decades and sometimes centuries of silence and neglect, was itself a "political" achievement. As Rich said in 1971, and as we believed, "hearing our wordless or negated experiences affirmed" in literature could have "visible effects on women's lives."[41]

In August 1973, shortly after The Feminist Press edition of "The Yellow Wallpaper" was published, I received a letter from writer Joanna Russ that described her experience teaching the story to her students. "I found myself emphasizing to the class (I'm not sure why) that although the protagonist is, of course, defeated at the end . . . some really extraordinary kind of positive things come out at the same time. Rage is one of them. And that lovely statement, 'Life is much more exciting now than it used to be.' And a genuinely eerie, ironic over-playing of her role into caricature, acting out (almost) the kind of questions her husband keeps asking her: But darling, what's *wrong*? Do be sensible! Her behavior in the last scene is a marvellously witty, wicked, loony way of doing the same to him, with its mock naivete, its addressing him as 'young man' (silly goose) and its triumphantly ghastly question, 'Now why should that man have fainted?' "[42]

In asking why, in 1973, she found herself emphasizing the comic-triumphant aspects of "The Yellow Wallpaper," and clearly rooting for its heroine, Joanna wondered if it was "just a matter of temperament." I think it was more: our living in a historical moment when, as Kennard recognized, there was a community of readers sharing the same literary conventions, the same expectations of women's literature, and, I would add, the same political hopes. So Joanna found the story "wonderful to teach and the class loved it."

The newer interpretations of "The Yellow Wallpaper" come out of a drastically changed intellectual and political climate and out of a myriad of new schools of critical thought whose methods and governing assumptions importantly differ, as Haney-Peritz, Jacobus, and Lanser make clear, from those that informed the story's earliest readings. If my Afterword appeared in the same year as *Roe v. Wade*, recent interpretations are appearing in the years that have seen increasing attacks on that decision, the failure of the Equal Rights Amendment, the erosion of affirmative action, and renewed, virulent racism, all leading to a skepticism or disillusionment about women's power to create and sustain significant political and social change, or at least to the recognition that change will be slower and more difficult to achieve. The new schools of critical thought are consonant with, although not the direct outgrowth of, this climate of reduced expectations. Post-structuralist, deconstructionist, psychoanalytic, and cultural studies critical theories—all of which have been brought to bear on "The Yellow Wallpaper"—newly problematize terms or concepts that were important to the thinking of the story's earliest critics and to the political activism of the time, such as "identity," "autonomy," and "liberation." Especially in retheorizing "identity"—seeing it as culturally or linguistically or textually constructed, and as fragmented and alienated from itself, even as fictitious—and in focusing on the narrator's unconscious, the new theories, from a pre-poststructuralist point of view, diminish her potential for understanding her situation, displace her from the heroic center of her tale, and drastically reduce the extent to which she can be seen as in control of the telling. Unconscious feelings, be they sexual, maternal, or racial, damage or even destroy her; her efforts to find her identity or subjectivity within the masculine signifying system of the Symbolic, the male realm of language, are almost always, given the sheer difficulty for all women of inserting themselves into that realm, likely to fail; and the story she tells unconsciously reveals meanings of which she is unaware, and which undermine faith in what Kennard had called the "triumph" of her understanding.

The story continues to be read as a feminist text. Many of its critics continue to find its narrator achieving a temporary insight into the nature of her oppression or a momentary victory over it; indeed, this tension between the degree of her success or her failure, dramatically unresolved in the narrative, continues to be the dynamic propelling many of the new readings. And in interpretations that see the narrator as defeated, the text itself still triumphs, makes its feminist point. For Jacobus, for example, the narrator's hysteria, and for Veeder her infantilization, are to be read as compelling critiques of her society's sexual or marital arrangements. For Jacobus the repugnant body to which the narrator is reduced becomes a figure for the repressions imposed both on representations of sexuality and on women's writing in the Victorian period; for Veeder, the story is a feminist cautionary tale that brilliantly exposes the inadequacies and infantilization of both men and women in Victorian marriage. While we may have lost a feminist heroine, we have retained a feminist text.[43]

To say that in their diminishment of the protagonist these new feminist readings are less empowering than earlier ones would probably be to misplace the locus of concern, implying that newer readings of the story should do for their time what our earlier readings did for ours. Critics like Haney-Peritz, for example, or Lanser, in warning against the tendency of earlier critics to identify with a narrator whom they see as seriously flawed or embedded in fantasy, are concerned, still, with the need for political and social change. Haney-Peritz's concluding argument is that only radical changes in "the material conditions of social life" will ultimately liberate the delusioned protagonist; and Lanser's caveat against assuming that the situation of one white woman can stand for the situation of all women reflects the greater sensitivity to issues of racial and ethnic diversity that has characterized the women's movement in the last decade, as well as her sense that feminism's identity today is more "precarious and conflicted" than it was in the 1970s.

But warnings against essentializing the story of "The Yellow Wallpaper" and against identifying with its protagonist—if indeed she is allowed an identity to identify with—can also run the risk of depoliticizing it, stripping it of some of its imaginative—and political—power. Current suspicion or rejection of "essentializing" or "totalizing" words like "woman," as others have observed, seriously risks denying the existence of commonalities among women and of their group identity, rooted in subordination, whose recognition is essential to political action.[46] "The Yellow Wallpaper" is a story about a nineteenth-century white, middle-class woman, but it addresses "woman's" situation in so far as women as a group must still contend with male power in medicine, marriage, and indeed most, if not all, of culture. In so far as its earliest critics "identified," we identified, I believe, with that situation. As Diana Fuss has recently observed, the poststructuralist project to problematize and displace identity is difficult to reconcile with the feminist project to reclaim it.[47] Whether newer readings of "The Yellow Wallpaper," as they continue to nuance both its narrator and her story, may help achieve that reconciliation remains to be seen.

Notes

1. Elaine Hedges, "Afterword," *The Yellow Wallpaper* (New York: The Feminist Press, 1973).

2. Sandra Gilbert and Susan Gubar, *The Madwoman in the Attic: The Woman Writer and the Nineteenth-Century Literary Imagination* (New Haven, Conn.: Yale University Press, 1979), 89–92.

3. Annette Kolodny, "A Map for Rereading: or, Gender and the Interpretation of Literary Texts," *New Literary History* 11, no.3 (1980), 451–67.

4. Jean E. Kennard, "Convention Coverage: or, How to Read Your Own Life," *New Literary History* 13 (Autumn 1981), 69–88.

5. Gilbert and Gubar, *Madwoman*, 91.

6. Loralee MacPike, "Environment as Psychopathological Symbolism in 'The Yellow Wallpaper,' " *American Literary Realism 1870–1910* 8 (Summer 1975): 286–88.

7. Beate Schöpp-Schilling, " 'The Yellow Wallpaper': A Rediscovered 'Realistic' Story," *American Literary Realism 1870–1910* 8 (Summer 1975): 284–86.

8. Mary Beth Pringle, " 'La Poetique de L'Éspace' in Charlotte Perkins Gilman's 'The Yellow Wallpaper,' " *The French American Review* 3 (1978) :21.

9. Gilbert and Gubar, *Madwoman*, 90.

10. Paula Treichler, "Escaping the Sentence: Diagnosis and Discourse in 'The Yellow Wallpaper,' " *Tulsa Studies in Women's Literature* 3 (1984): 75, 73.

11. Judith Fetterley, "Reading About Reading: 'A Jury of Her Peers,' 'The Murders in the Rue Morgue,' and 'The Yellow Wallpaper,' " in Elizabeth A. Flynn and Patrocinio P. Schweickart, eds., *Gender and Reading: Essays on Readers, Texts, and Contexts* (Baltimore, Md.: Johns Hopkins University Press, 1986), 158–64.

12. Karen Ford, " 'The Yellow Wallpaper' and Women's Discourse," *Tulsa Studies in Women's Literature* 4 (Fall 1985): 309–14.

13. Carol Thomas Neely, "Alternative Women's Discourse," *Tulsa Studies in Women's Literature* 4 (Fall 1985): 315–22.

14. Paula Treichler, "The Wall Behind the Yellow Wallpaper: Response to Carol Neely and Karen Ford," *Tulsa Studies in Women's Literature* 4 (Fall 1984–5): 323–30.

15. Janice Haney-Peritz, "Monumental Feminism and Literature's Ancestral House: Another Look at 'The Yellow Wallpaper,' " *Women's Studies* 12, no. 2 (1986): 113–28.

16. Mary Jacobus, "An Unnecessary Maze of Sign-Reading," in *Reading Women: Essays in Feminist Criticism* (New York: Columbia University Press, 1986), 229–48.

17. Diane Herndl, "The Writing Cure: Charlotte Perkins Gilman, Anna O., and 'Hysterical Writing,' " *NWSA Journal* 1, no. 1 (1988): 52–74.

18. Rachel Blau Du Plessis, *Writing Beyond the Ending: Narrative Strategies of Twentieth-Century Women* (Bloomington, Ind.: Indiana University Press, 1985), 92–93.

19. Sandra Gilbert and Susan Gubar, *No Man's Land: The Place of the Woman Writer in the Twentieth Century*, vol. 2 (New Haven, Conn.: Yale University Press, 1989), 77.

20. Jacobus, 241.

21. Juliann Evans Fleenor, "The Gothic Prism: Charlotte Perkins Gilman's Gothic Stories and Her Autobiography," in Sheryl L. Meyering, ed., *Charlotte Perkins Gilman: The Woman and Her Work* (Ann Arbor, Mich.: UMI Research Press, 1989), 123.

22. Jeffrey Berman, "The Unrestful Cure: Charlotte Perkins Gilman and 'The Yellow Wallpaper,' " in *The Talking Cure: Literary Representations of Psychoanalysis* (New York: New York University Press, 1985), 56.

23. William Veeder, "Who is Jane? The Intricate Feminism of Charlotte Perkins Gilman," *Arizona Quarterly* 44 (1988): 40–79.

24. Marianne DeKoven, "Gendered Doubleness and the 'Origins' of Modernist Form," *Tulsa Studies in Women's Literature* 8, no. 1 (Spring 1989): 31, 32.

25. Linda Wagner-Martin, " 'The Yellow Wallpaper': A Centenary," in Sheryl L. Meyering, ed., *Charlotte Perkins Gilman: The Woman and Her Work* (Ann Arbor, Mich.: UMI Research Press, 1989), 60.

26. Haney-Peritz, 121, 122.

27. Susan S. Lanser, "Feminist Criticism, 'The Yellow Wallpaper,' and the Politics of Color in America," *Feminist Studies* 15, no. 3 (Fall 1989): 422.

28. Jacobus, 429.

29. Barbara Johnson, "Is Female to Male as Ground Is to Figure?" in Richard Feldstein and Judith Roof, eds., *Feminism and Psychoanalysis* (Ithaca, N.Y.: Cornell University Press, 1989), 255–68, also deals briefly with the race and class aspects of the story, arguing that "[t]he very equation of the woman's body with the blank page implies that the woman's body

is white," and noting that "there are many other invisible men and women trapped in the wallpaper of the Western canon . . . that neither psychoanalytic nor feminist theory has taken sufficiently into account. . . " (267, 268).

30. Jacobus, 235.

31. Haney-Peritz, 123.

32. For Veeder, the story is still a major text, "one of the premier women's texts" (40).

33. Walter Benn Michaels, *The Gold Standard and the Logic of Naturalism* (Berkeley: University of California Press, 1987), 27.

34. Michaels, 13.

35. Gillian Brown, "The Empire of Agoraphobia," *Representations* 20 (Fall 1987): 134–57.

36. Veeder, 63, 64.

37. Hedges, 10.

38. Elaine Showalter, "Women's Time, Women's Space: Writing the History of Feminist Criticism," in Shari Benstock, ed., *Feminist Issues in Literary Scholarship* (Bloomington Ind: Indiana University Press, 1985), 40, 77, 53.

39. Adrienne Rich, "When We Dead Awaken: Writing As Re-Vision," in *The Norton Anthology of Literature by Women*, ed. Sandra M. Gilbert and Susan Gubar (New York: W. W. Norton & Company, 1985), 2044–2055.

40. Boston Women's Health Book Collective, *Our Bodies, Ourselves: A Book by and for Women* (New York: Simon and Schuster, 1971).

41. Rich, 2045.

42. Quoted by permission of the author.

43. Michaels would be an exception. In arguing that the narrator's commitment to work produces her madness he is not reading the story as a feminist text but seems, as a reviewer of his book has observed, "treacherously close to blaming a victim." Christopher P. Wilson, "Containing Multitudes: Realism, Historicism, American Studies," *American Quarterly* 41; no. 3 (September 1989): 475. Richard Feldstein, on the other hand, argues for retrieving the protagonist as a feminist heroine by reading her regression ironically, as a "cunning craziness, a militant, politicized madness" but he notes that this is, by then, a minority view. Richard Feldstein, "Reader, Text, and Ambiguous Referentiality in 'The Yellow Wall-Paper,' " in Richard Feldstein and Judith Roof, eds., *Feminism and Psychoanalysis* (Ithaca, N.Y.: Cornell University Press, 1989), 273.

44. Haney-Peritz, 124.

45. Lanser, 425.

46. For an excellent discussion of this and related issues, see, for example Susan Bordo, "Feminism, Postmodernism, and Gender-Skepticism," in Linda J. Nicholson, ed., *Feminism/Postmodernism* (New York: Routledge, 1990).

47. Diana Fuss, *Essentially Speaking: Feminism, Nature and Difference* (New York: Routledge, 1989), 70.

"Making a Change": Strategies of Subversion in Gilman's Journalism and Short Fiction

SHELLEY FISHER FISHKIN

In October 1894 Charlotte Perkins Gilman, editor of *The Impress*, ran the following note under the headline "The Woman's Exchange": "It was asked of the editor, eagerly, if *The Impress* could be written to about matters of special interest to women and women's clubs; if it was to be a medium for exchange of thought on such subjects. That is one of the things *The Impress* is for," Gilman wrote. But, she continued, only those letters "dealing with matters of real importance will be answered. No inquiries as to what is good to remove freckles, and whether a lady should take a gentleman's arm or he hers, or what color goes with the kind of dress you want to make over will be answered here."[1] In this brief and blunt response, Gilman lays out her agenda as a journalist and editor: her central motivating goal will be helping women to learn to claim as their "special interest" matters, as she put it, "of real importance."

It would not be an easy task. Gilman knew that many women were accustomed to allowing their own agendas to be set by publications that felt that freckle removal was a problem worthy of serious attention. Yet publications directed to women were not the only problem: newspapers in general and their definition of news were culpable as well. In another article in that same issue of the *Impress* titled "Do We Get 'The News'?" Gilman lambasts the press as a whole for managing to consistently miss or belittle the really important news of the day. "These clamorous papers," she writes, "give us from day to day great masses of 'facts' in no sense news, and other masses of 'facts,' new indeed, but of no earthly importance. Meanwhile the vital incidents of the day—the era-making events, are sometimes passed over and sometimes so buried in unimportant details as to command no attention."[2]

In popular fiction as well, Gilman saw conventions that artificially constricted the sphere of women's interests, and the scope of their aspirations. "Ninety per cent. of fiction," Gilman wrote in the *Forerunner*, is preoccupied with the "Love Story. . . . Love and love and love—from 'first sight' to marriage. There it stops—just the fluttering ribbon of announcement, 'and

This essay was written specifically for this volume and is published here for the first time by permission of the author.

234

lived happily every after.' Is that kind of fiction any sort of picture of a woman's life?" Gilman asks (or of a man's for that matter?). For Gilman, the answer is clearly no.[3]

In her work as a journalist and as a writer of fiction, then, Gilman saw herself as writer consciously trying to subvert the conventions of genre in order to expand the horizons of gender.

From the early 1880s through the early 1930s, Gilman's journalism ran in publications including *Providence Journal, Alpha, Woman's Journal, Pacific Review, Pacific Monthly, California Nationalist, Weekly Nationalist, Kate Field's Washington, Christian Register, Pacific Rural Press, Stockton Mail, San Francisco Call, Worthington's Illustrated, American Fabian, New Nation, Coming Nation, Saturday Evening Post, Cosmopolitan, Puritan, Independent, Harper's Bazar, Success, Truth, Woman's Home Companion, Good Housekeeping, Harper's Weekly, Boston Globe, Collier's, New Idea Woman's Magazine, Physical Culture, Century, Forum,* the *North American Review, Ainslee's,* the *Birth Control Review,* the *Nation,* the *Louisville Herald,* the *Baltimore Sun,* and the *Buffalo Evening News.*[4] However, it is in the *Impress* and the *Forerunner,* both journals that Gilman edited herself, that some of her most memorable journalism can be found. During these years Gilman also published short fiction in publications including *Alpha, Kate Field's Washington, Pacific Monthly, New England Magazine, Impress, Woman's Home Companion, Success,* and *Physical Culture*; the vast majority of her short stories, however, appeared in the *Forerunner.*[5]

Indeed, it was the limited nature of the market for the kinds of articles and stories Gilman wanted to write that prompted her to start the *Forerunner* in the first place. By 1909 Gilman found her pile of rejection slips growing at an alarming rate. While she was convinced more and more of the importance of her work, editors seemed to be convinced less and less of their market value.[6] As Theodore Dreiser, then editor of the *Delineator,* admonished, "You should consider more what the editors want" (*Living,* 304). Gilman resisted. As she put it in her autobiography:

> Of course I should have, if I had been a competent professional writer. There are those who write as artists, real ones; they often find it difficult to consider what the editor wants. There are those who must write to earn a living, they, if they succeed, *must* please the editor. The editor, having his living to earn, must please his purchasers, the public, so we have this great trade of literary catering. But if one writes to express important truths, needed yet unpopular, the market is necessarily limited. As all my principal topics were in direct contravention of established views, beliefs and emotions, it is a wonder that so many editors took so much of my work for so long.
>
> —*Living,* 304

Gilman resolved, "If the editors and publishers will not bring out my work, I will!" Thus was born the magazine in which Gilman would publish much of her most memorable journalism and short fiction.

Journalism and fiction for Gilman were two distinct but related tools in her efforts to dismantle the seemingly a priori assumptions of patriarchy. Ann Lane has characterized the premise underlying the lecture series Gilman often gave as follows: "All our sufferings are preventable if we apply our human intelligence to their resolution, because human beings are capable of reshaping their social environments; unlike other creatures, human beings are not simply passive agents of evolution but are capable of controlling the evolutionary process."[7] This assumption held true of Gilman's journalism, as well, which was often closely connected with her lectures. But recognizing that imagination combined with analysis could yield the most potent persuasive force of all, Gilman refused to rely on logic alone to make her case. Journalism allowed her to launch frontal attacks on an exploitative ideology; it allowed her to anatomize with impressively cold clear reason the absurdity of a society that—mentally as well as physically—locked half its population in the kitchen. Fiction gave Gilman the chance to delineate alternative ways of organizing the world, of women and men playing out new roles in new ways, creating a world in which human needs—not rigid conventions of male and female behavior—form the engine that drives society. It was in her fiction that Gilman could explore dimensions of human experience that elude logic and reason—such as dreams, fears, insecurities, passions, fantasies, jealousies, and joys, and could marshall those dimensions in the service of social change. It was also in her fiction that Gilman could resolve neatly and buoyantly painful conflicts that defied easy solutions in life. Didactic to the core, both journalism and fiction were for Gilman what she once called "writing for a purpose."[8]

Gilman was not oblivious to contemporary writers and precursors who were engaged in endeavors similar to her own. Indeed, her early journalism owes much to the example set by more experienced contributors to publications for which she wrote, such as *Woman's Journal*; she was also familiar with earlier women journalists who wrote on substantive as opposed to frivolous issues, such as Anne Royall and Margaret Fuller. As a fiction writer, too, Gilman was probably aware of precursors who challenged the dominance of the overbearing "love plot" as she did.[9] Seen in this larger context, Gilman's journalism and fiction may seem more conventional and less subversive; but it is important to remember that these counter-traditions were themselves highly subversive, and the dominant paradigms they challenged a generation before Gilman wrote remained the dominant paradigms in her day as well. The Anne Royalls and Margaret Fullers were not only few and far between, but were likely to be vilified, belittled, or forgotten within their lifetimes or soon after their deaths.[10]

Gilman's rhetorical stance, when she defined her project as a journalist and as a fiction writer, was that of an iconoclast staking out positions that "were in direct contravention of established views, beliefs and emotions" (*Living*, 304). In the bold, clear-eyed, commonsense stance she takes toward the problems she tackles, writing as if no one had ever examined them before, Gilman sets herself squarely in that peculiar tradition F. O. Matthiessen called "the frequent American need to begin all over again from scratch."[11] No matter that Margaret Fuller had challenged the dominant paradigm a generation before: the dominant paradigm stood in as great need as it ever had of being challenged once again.

One of Gilman's most fruitful strategies as a journalist involved revising and reclaiming familiar subjects in daringly new and unfamiliar ways. The women's pages whose myopia she deplored were filled with articles on house-cleaning, kitchens, and childcare. Gilman's own journalism focused intently on these subjects as well, but with a subversive twist: "Mind Cleaning" would be a typical Gilman headline, or "Kitchen-Mindedness," or "Teaching the Mother."[12] Gilman's images start out small, then gradually open out until, by the end of a piece, she is addressing nothing less than the transformation of human consciousness—the subject that was always her real subject, no matter where she started out.

In an article called "Kitchen-Mindedness," for example, Gilman takes as her starting point the then largely incontrovertible fact that most women were destined to spend the lion's portion of their lives in the kitchen.[13] Like Fanny Fern a generation before her, and like Tillie Olsen a generation after her, Gilman takes a clear, fresh look at what Olsen calls the "hard, everyday essential work of maintaining human life."[14] Gilman attacks the family kitchen as unsanitary, inefficient, and stultifying. But it is not just the wasteful labor of the contemporary single family kitchen that is her target. Rather, what Gilman really wants to probe is the intellectual and moral consequences of spending one's life, and raising one's children, in this environment. "Kitchen-bred men born of kitchen-bred mothers" continue the "narrowness of vision," "petty self-interest," and hedonistic short-sightedness Gilman deplores. From the simple, familiar, and seemingly sacrosanct tableau of the mother serving her family at the kitchen table, Gilman extracts a chilling and accurate analysis of the warped values of a society fueled by "self-interest" and "habituated to consider only personal gain, personal good and personal evil, because we are kitchen-minded."[15]

Some of Gilman's alternatives to "kitchen-mindedness" appear in the "Reasonable Resolutions" column with which *The Forerunner* ushers in the new year in 1910. "Let us collectively resolve," Gilman urges, "That we will stop wasting our soil and our forests and our labor! That we will stop poisoning and clogging our rivers and harbors. . . . That we will now—this year—begin in good earnest to prevent all preventable diseases; That we will do our duty by our children and young people, as a wise Society should, and cut off the crop of criminals by not making them."[16] Such are the serious matters that can claim the attention of those who transcend "kitchen-mindedness."

But if Gilman is attuned to the negative aspects of a kitchen-bred consciousness, she is also attuned to the positive dimensions of a kitchen-bred heart. A mother, she notes, "does not set her children to compete for their dinner—does not give most to the strongest and leave the weakest to go to the wall. . . . Her attitude is one of seeking to administer a common fund for the common good"—a habit of mind much more suited to exercising civic responsibility and political power than those habits of mind generally preferred by competitive, individualistic men. "This world is ours as much as man's," Gilman writes. "We have not only a right to half its management but a duty to half its service. It is our duty as human beings to help make the world better—quickly."[17]

As a journalist Gilman sought to prepare women to exercise this duty by helping them conceive of their world—and their role in it—in new ways—ways that transcended conventions. Gilman never shirked the task of walking a tightrope over the complexities of sameness versus difference, for example. In an article in the *Forerunner* called "The Humanness of Women," Gilman laid out clearly and bluntly the grand scam that had victimized women since time immemorial—the worldview that defined "male" as "human" and "female," as Gilman puts it, as "Female—and nothing else." Gilman peels off the veils of civility that mask this scam and reclaims the "human" as the birthright of women as well as men:

> The New Woman is Human first, last and always. Incidentally she is female; as man is male. As a male he has done his small share in the old physical process of reproduction; but as a Human Creature he has done practically all in the new Social processes which make civilization. He has been Male—and Human:—She has been Female—and nothing else;—that is, in our old idea. Holding this idea; absurd, erroneous, and mischievous to a terrible degree; we strove to carry it out in our behavior; and human history so far is the history of a wholly masculine world, competing and fighting as males must, forever seeking and serving the female as males must; yet building this our world as best they could alone. Theirs is the credit—and the shame—of the world behind us, the world around us; but the world before us has a new element—the Humanness of Woman.
>
> —"Humanness of Women," 14

Yet her hard-hitting, straight-shooting rhetoric—marshalled in defense of "sameness" on this occasion—will be marshalled in defense of "difference" at other times. For while Gilman recognizes the "sameness" that characterizes women's and men's aspirations and potential in the abstract, she also never loses sight of the "difference" that characterizes their lived experience in the concrete. Her analysis prefigures that which political philosophers will use half a century later as an image of the hollowness of certain brands of presumed "equality."[18] In an *Impress* column titled "Women as a Class," for example, Gilman attacks those who "hold that men and women are, one as it were, . . . and that it is illegitimate to so much as discuss them separately. . . . Here is a vast number of people who for uncounted centuries have been denied equal opportunities with other people of the same age and station, and who, therefore, have been denied the same development," Gilman writes. "For a man and a woman to-day to do the same work is a much more remarkable thing for her than for him."[19] (Despite her sensitivity to differences shaped by gender, we might add, Gilman was largely blind to other forms of difference, such as those shaped by race, ethnicity, and class. Gilman had trouble envisioning and empathizing with women not like herself. The "woman today" to whom Gilman addressed herself, and toward whom she directs her efforts at reform, is white, middle-class, and close to Gilman herself in terms of education and background.)

Gilman is also concerned about the tendency of women who have "made it" to reject those who haven't. Every woman should: "be proud to add her special strength to the growing power of women; to let her gain be theirs and to count in the average—she should not run ahead to join those already ahead, and object to be classed with women's enormous struggle upward" ("Woman As a Class," 3). Whether reassuring women that they are up to all that men can achieve, or castigating women for not allowing the achievement of each to reflect well on all, Gilman keeps her eye on the ball: the game is reclaiming human endeavor for males and females alike.

In the short fiction Gilman published in the *Forerunner* alongside her nonfiction essays and analyses, and in several other publications, she had the chance to play out some alternative visions of gender relations and social organization. At the *Forerunner* her options were limited only by her imagination, since as sole editor, publisher, and monetary backer, she had only herself to please in the choices she made. As a journalist Gilman had deplored the omnipresence of one plot and one plot only in literature: the love story. Did she overstate the case about the overwhelming pervasiveness of this plot? Probably not. As William Dean Howells saw it, "a love intrigue of some sort" is "all but essential to the popularity of any fiction."[20] Given Howells's central role in the literary world at this time, his comment takes on additional weight.

The women in Gilman's fiction, by way of contrast, play out many other plots indeed. The narrator of "When I Was a Witch" makes those who abuse animals feel the pain they inflict themselves. The narrator of "The Girl in the Pink Hat" helps a woman escape from a man who has duped her into eloping, but who doesn't intend to marry her. Mrs. Main, the heroine of "An Honest Woman," manages a successful boardinghouse and resists a former partner's efforts to blackmail her. Esther Greenwood in "The Unnatural Mother" heroically saves the inhabitants of three towns. Celia and Julia Gordins in "Making a Change" found a day care center. Women, in Gilman's short fiction, do a great deal more than fall in love and live happily ever after.[21] (On those occasions when a Gilman heroine *does* choose matrimony, she does so from a sense of personal empowerment at odds with conventional gender expectations.)

As she casts women in these fresh and interesting roles, Gilman has a

chance to explore in highly imaginative ways issues that she limned analytically in her journalism. In an article on "The Dress of Women," for example,
Gilman probes the iconography of male and female dress in painstaking
detail, giving special attention to the roots of "a totally different costume
for men and for women":

> The clothing of women is most modified by psychic conditions. As they were
> restricted to a very limited field of activity, and as their personal comfort was
> of no importance to anyone, it was possible to maintain in their dress the
> influence of primitive conditions long outgrown by men. And as, while men
> have varied widely in the manifold relations of our later economic and political
> growth, women have remained for the most part all in one relation—that of
> sex; we see at once why the dress of men has developed along lines of practical
> efficiency and general human distinction, while the dress of women is still
> most modified by the various phases of sex distinction.[22]

But while Gilman's analysis of gendered dress codes remains rather abstract
in the journalism, it jumps off the page in living color in the short story,
"If I Were a Man," which appeared in *Physical Culture* in 1914. In this story
Mollie Matthewson, who unexpectedly finds herself inhabiting her husband's
body and clothes, incredulously lets her toes spread out in her shoes: "Never
before, since her early school days, had she felt such freedom and comfort as
to feet—they were firm and solid on the ground when she walked; quick,
springy, safe."[23]

Even more shocking for Molly than comfortable shoes, is the heady
exhilaration of *pockets*.

> These pockets came as a revelation. Of course she had known they were there,
> had counted them, made fun of them, mended them, even envied them; but
> she never had dreamed of how it *felt* to have pockets. Behind her newspaper
> she let her consciousness, that odd mingled consciousness, rove from pocket
> to pocket, realizing the armored assurance of having all those things at hand,
> instantly get-at-able, ready to meet emergencies. The cigar case gave her a
> warm feeling of comfort—it was full; the firmly held fountain pen, safe
> unless she stood on her head; the keys, pencils, letters, documents, notebook,
> checkbook, bill folder.
>
> —Lane, *Reader*, 33–34

If Gilman's story "If I Were a Man" should strike a reader today as
outdated or antiquarian, the results of the "pocket census" I conduct every
time I teach the story will prove instructive. The men in the class add up
the total number of pockets on the clothing they are wearing, and take the
average; the women do the same. Despite all the proverbial unisex dressing
of the nineties, the men always end up substantially ahead. I then ask how
many women have had their purses snatched and how many men have had

their *pockets* picked. The results add up to what one might call a gender-based index of vulnerability.

As Gilman recasts the abstract theories of her journalism into vivid concrete images, emotional encounters, and dramatic events in her fiction, something else sneaks in as well: parts of herself that she otherwise kept under wraps. Ann Lane has suggested that "by participating in reform efforts, [Gilman] could hope to find some way to manage her own private demons . . ." (Lane, 159). One might also say that writing fiction served this function as well. There were tensions, conflicts, failures, misunderstandings, withdrawals of affection, frustrations of every stripe that followed Gilman in her personal life throughout her long career. Contentment proved elusive, satisfaction fugitive, tranquility almost too much to hope for. How could she persuade people of the value of her social program when her own life (as all the world could see, her private woes constantly being paraded across the pages of the press) was clearly no unequivocally rosy advertisement for it? Gilman used her short fiction to mitigate the power of that stark gap between her normative formulas for a better world and the actual contours of her personal life. The "private demons" that periodically drew her to desperation, depression, or despair were reduced, in the short fiction, to quickly forgotten transient moments. They were, in short, "managed"—managed more firmly, efficiently, and cheerfully in her fiction than they ever were in her life. A process that must have been highly therapeutic for Gilman was, in turn, pleasantly reassuring for her reader.

A brief story titled "Two Storks," for example, reads like a parable of Gilman's relationship with her first husband—until its end, when the storks come out ahead:

Two storks were nesting.
He was a young stork—and narrow-minded. Before he married he had consorted mainly with striplings of his own kind, and had given no thought to the ladies, maid or matron. After he married his attention was concentrated upon his All-Satisfying Wife; upon that Triumph of Art, Labor, and Love—their Nest. . . . The happy days flew by, fair Spring, sweet Summer—gentle Autumn. . . . Then the days grew shorter, the sky greyer, the wind colder; there was large hunting and small success. In his dreams he began to see sunshine, broad, burning sunshine day after day; skies of limitless blue; dark, deep, yet full of fire; and stretches of bright water, shallow, warm, fringed with tall reeds and rushes, teeming with fat frogs. They were in her dreams too, but he did not know that. He stretched his wings and flew farther every day; but his wings were not satisfied. In his dreams came a sense of vast heights and boundless spaces of the earth streaming away beneath him; black water and white land, grey water and brown land, blue water and green land, all flowing backward from day to day, while the cold lessened and the warmth grew. . . . This was in her dreams too, but he did not know that.[24]

The father stork takes off, "for the Passion of Wings was upon him," and says good-bye to his wife and children. He is shocked when she cries, "I am ready! Come!":

> "Why, my Dear!" he said, "How preposterous! You cannot go on the Great Flight! Your wings are for brooding tender little ones! Your body is . . . not for days and nights of ceaseless soaring! You cannot go!"
>
> —"Two Storks," 12

His wife does not heed him: instead she spreads her wings and takes off and soars. She had been practicing, and she'd strengthened her wings to be up to the task; she also taught her children how to soar as well. The father stork, dumbfounded, can't quite assimilate what is happening as the rest of his family flies off with him:

> "But you are a Mother!" he panted, as he caught up with them. "Yes!" she cried joyously, "but I was a Stork before I was A Mother! and afterward!— and All the Time!" And the Storks were Flying.
>
> —"Two Storks," 13

It is a joyfully affirmative ending—a sharp contrast to the denouement of Gilman's first marriage. Gilman may have strengthened her wings and learned to soar—but not alongside her husband and her child. The storks manage to "have it all"—as Gilman undoubtedly hoped a number of her readers would, as well.

Yet another story in which deep personal pain becomes transmuted into a heartwarming happy ending is "The Artist," a story reminiscent, once again, of Gilman's first marriage. Myra Marne is an artist, as both Charlotte and Walter Stetson were. She marries Bruce Kirby, a writer:

> . . . they were married, and lived happily, yes, blissfully, together for almost a year. And then? Nothing especial happened, nothing dramatic, no rift in the lute big enough to be mended; but the inequalities and incongruities of Myra's disposition began to assert themselves, and the equalities and determinations of Bruce's began to assert themselves, as was to be expected. In the many-faceted complexity of our modern personalities it is an extremely difficult thing to be completely married.[25]

Bruce's work goes well. But there is never a question of Myra earning a living: "his pride of work was not so strong as his pride of being a man, of supporting his wife. He put his neck in the collar and pulled, pulled hard and strong, doing excellent work, useful work, well-paid work and building a reputation which would have satisfied some men. . . . Myra painted and did not sell her pictures" (170).

The familiar assymetry takes its toll. But then a friend of her husband arrives—a German-speaking composer who appreciates her art and who engages Myra in extended, animated, intense discussions about it. Myra's husband, vaguely discomfited by their relationship, secretly learns German to understand what it is that transpires between them. In the process he comes to better understand his wife:

> In the light of this other man's approach to Myra, he, her husband, understood her better. He saw her underlying principles, showing like half-submerged rocks under a washing sea of current ideas, quotations, scraps of philosophy. He saw how eager she was in the mere sport of discussion, and remembered quite vividly how they used to so discuss and how he had wholly discontinued the habit—he used his brain in working hours, handling words and ideas; at home he wanted love and rest. . . . He saw how this man showed an appreciative interest in her painting, looked at her pictures, studied them, praised and blamed them, urged an exhibition, said she had it in her to do great work, but she must have some recognition. Also he saw how constantly the musician talked of his own work, his temperament, his hopes and difficulties. This seemed to Bruce mere babbling megalomania, till he remembered the he too had once spread his life out before her, and that she had liked it. . . . It became painfully clear to him, presently, that he was losing, if he had not lost, his wife.
>
> (171)

But Bruce Kirby rises to the occasion and wins her back. It takes effort, energy, and imagination—but he exerts them all. Gilman only alludes to the breadth of these efforts (she claims "this story would have been a novel if it had lived to grow up" [169])—but the long and short of it is that he makes nurturing his wife's confidence and career his central object in life. And he does so while trying "with ceaseless patience to understand *her*— just what she really felt and tried to do, and, to his unexpected delight he found at length that his interest was more than affectionate, his admiration more than personal. He began to see not only the woman he loved, who was his, a soft and lovely thing; but the artist, who was not his, a strong fierce spirit, winged, rising, not his nor any man's" (172). As if this marvelous transformation itself were not quite enough, Gilman tacks on a surprise ending that is hardly plausible as fact, but that brings the fantasy to a perfect end. The perfect husband exceeds even his own herculean prior efforts at being supportive and loving. It is the domestic utopia to beat all domestic utopias.

The conflict between "marriage" and "career" (or, if you will, between "staying in the nest" and "soaring") that the male and female characters in these two stories resolve so successfully proved disastrous for Gilman during her marriage to Walter Stetson, and contributed to the breakdown she would chronicle in "The Yellow Wallpaper." During that period Gilman addressed these kinds of issues in columns she wrote for the Providence weekly newspaper *People* with deft, hard-hitting prose.[26] In her personal life, however, these same issues were tearing her apart. As Mary Hill has noted, "confident and intellectually excited when she approached women's problems in the abstract, Charlotte still resorted to crying fits when she confronted daily tasks at home" (Hill, 143). It was in her fiction, not in her lived experience, that these conflicts resolved themselves painlessly. Interestingly, Gilman comments in her autobiography, "Of all those childish years the most important step was this, I learned the use of a constructive imagination. . . . I could make a world to suit me. . . . It speaks volumes for the lack of happiness in my own actual life that I should so industriously construct it in imagination." (*Living*, 19–20, 23).

While Gilman does not discuss the therapeutic function of fantasy in adult life, clearly the "constructive imagination" she cultivated in her unhappy childhood stood her in good stead as a writer of fiction. In the worlds her imagination constructed, other problems that plagued her in real life resolved themselves with admirable grace as well. Despite her frequent exhortation to women to earn their way in the world, for example, Gilman bemoaned her own lack of business sense and ascribes the demise of *The Forerunner* to it.[27] In her fiction, however, women characters who try their hand at business—Diantha, in "What Diantha Did," or Mrs. Main in "An Honest Woman"—are shrewd, talented, and successful.

If one took away the upbeat exhortations to work for social change, and if one took away the pleasure of Gilman's quick wit, Gilman's journalism, with its methodical analysis of society's shortcomings, would be unrelievedly grim. Her fiction, on the other hand, often has a playful insouciant quality. Problems that might seem genuinely insurmountable when faced squarely, seem to melt away effortlessly in Gilman's didactic fantasies. Much of Gilman's short fiction appears to minimize the pain involved in creating a new social order as time and time again, men recognize that it is in their own self-interest to give their blessing to their wife's new role. While Gilman may have believed that people could reshape their social environments if they properly understood their problems, she probably also suspected that rational understanding might not be enough to *motivate* them to make those changes. On the other hand, however, the vivid image of a domestic utopia, of a family unit in which the whole is aglow with joy and the parts are fulfilled and delighted as well, could be highly persuasive. It was to harness this power of persuasion that Gilman kept producing her didactic fiction.

"Making a Change," for example, opens with a wailing baby, a depressed wife, a frustrated grandmother, and an unhappy father. Everyone is fulfilling a socially prescribed role when the story begins, and everyone is totally miserable. The wife's suicide attempt is the catalyst that prompts the grandmother to take action: changes start to happen. The grandmother, who adores children and is superb with them, opens a day care center on the roof of their apartment house. With her child happy for several hours a day in his grandmother's establishment, the young mother is free to return to that which she finds most satisfying, giving piano lessons. The added income from the two enterprises results in an impressively well-stocked pantry and the wherewithal to hire a new cook. The father—oblivious to the changes that have gone on by day in his own home—is the envy of all his peers. When someone taunts the husband for letting his wife work, he is so surprised and angry he leaves his business and goes home early one afternoon. The moment of truth comes when he finds his mother cheerfully surrounded by fifteen happy babies on the roof. The wife and grandmother confess their secret ventures. The father's response is heartwarming:

> "If it makes you as happy as that," he said, "I guess I can stand it." And in after years he was heard to remark, "This being married and bringing up children is as easy as can be—when you learn how!"[28]

While this story may not be typical for Gilman, it represents an important and often overlooked dimension of her approach to subverting the social order. Gilman may have felt most in her element when limning, in her journalism and fiction, bold new domestic models—kitchenless houses, partnerships in which husband and wife share the cooking, or professionalization of domestic tasks (i.e., home-cleaning services, take-out food, and inexpensive catering). But Gilman may have suspected that such brave, new worlds might meet resistance; she was open to less radical, less dramatic, more pragmatic and perhaps more tactically effective means of bringing about change, as well. The strategy the wife and grandmother adopt in "Making a Change" is the same strategy of conspiratorial evasion that Peg Bracken developed with great élan in 1960 when she wrote the *I Hate to Cook Book*.[29] Apostles of this approach would claim that as long as dinner is on the table at six (and, of course, is hot and tasty to boot), you can do whatever you want with your life. Once men realize that their own lifestyle will remain unthreatened, Bracken and Gilman (in "Making a Change," at least) seem to suggest, they will embrace with enthusiasm these new changes in the lives of their wives and mothers. Is this approach too easy—for men? Is it too hard—for women? Probably.

On the one hand, both as a journalist and as a short story writer, Gilman wanted to paper over nothing—the pain, the absurdity, the betrayal involved in all of the small and large ignominies women suffered daily under patriarchy. On the other hand, she wanted to paper over everything by minimizing the zero-sum dimensions of the problem. While a part of her (probably the bigger part) wanted to pull apart the family kitchen board by board and build out of those boards something totally new, another part of her recognized an interim stage, a way station along the road to these dramatic transformations. This part of her was willing to reassure men that dinner would still be on the table on time, and would be tasty and hot—even if their wives hadn't cooked it; that they would continue to feel as secure and unthreatened as ever under the "new regime"; that freeing their wives to fulfill themselves and to find themselves wouldn't interfere with their own happiness and wellbeing. In short, she wanted to convince men that they could "have it all"—the privileges of patriarchy without its compromised moral position, their existing lifestyle—but with a happy wife.

But if some of Gilman's fiction minimizes the pain involved in creating a new social order, overall she is far from consistent in her estimation of the cost of social change. In other short fiction like "The Unnatural Mother," she delineates with biting satire and bitter humor the pain and rejection in store for the woman who questions or violates social norms even if she does so for unselfish reasons.

Surely one of the most perplexing and intriguing ironies of American literary history is that the "Unnatural Mother" in Gilman's story of that title has the same name as the protagonist of Sylvia Plath's novel, *The Bell Jar*: Esther Greenwood. Plath's Esther Greenwood has more in common with the narrator of "The Yellow Wallpaper," however, than she does with the Esther Greenwood of "The Unnatural Mother." Madness and mental breakdown on the one hand ("The Yellow Wallpaper") and martyrdom and rejection on the other ("The Unnatural Mother") are two extremes Gilman is willing to face up to. By limning in her fiction both these, and a wide range of other possible fates for her heroines as well, Gilman projects a panoply of possible outcomes for her reader. Somewhere between the extremes of madness and martyrdom, Gilman suggests, there are new ways of living we can wholeheartedly embrace and explore. The majority of the heroines in Gilman's short fiction are neither mad nor martyred. Most of them emerge at the end of the story with a stronger sense of self than they had at the start, and with a greater sense of efficacy, potential, and control. Most manage to change the consciousness of those nearest to them in some profound ways. And some manage to create new models of domestic and communal life predicated on mutual respect, honesty, equality, and affection.

As a journalist and as a short story writer, Gilman anatomized the sources and dimensions of women's oppression in all their diversity and complexity. She saw connections that would not be made by other writers in many cases for more than two generations to come. She understood in remarkably prescient ways the linkages that add up to a constricted horizon of expectations for women *and* men under patriarchy. The changes she advocated involved much more than the simple readjustment of power relations: they involved transforming society's conception of what it means to be male or female, and what it means to be human. Many of her ideas have become realities in the 1990s—these include the concept of day care, take-out food, home-cleaning services, and child care professionals. Others—such as the notion of equal pay for equal work, wages for housework, and a society that faces up to the consequences of the ways it treats its children—are only a little less utopian today than they were in her day.

As she subverted the conventions of genre to expand the horizons of gender, Gilman provided future generations—and especially our own—with an incredibly fertile model of how one might go about exploring in print— as Gilman put it, "matters of real importance."

Notes

1. Charlotte Perkins Gilman, "The Woman's Exchange," *Impress*, 6 October 1894, 4.

2. Charlotte Perkins Gilman, "Do We Get 'The News?' " *Impress*, 20 October 1894, 2–3.

3. Charlotte Perkins Gilman, "Masculine Literature" ("Our Androcentric Culture, or The Man-Made World") *Forerunner* 1 (March 1910), 21.

4. Gilman's articles for the New York Tribune syndicate from 1919 to 1920 ran in papers including the *Baltimore Sun*, the *Buffalo Evening News*, and the *Louisville Herald*. For complete citations of the nearly fifteen hundred articles Gilman published in newspapers and magazines see Gary Scharnhorst, *Charlotte Perkins Gilman: A Bibliography* (Metuchen, N.J.: Scarecrow Press, 1985).

5. See Scharnhorst's bibliography for citations for the nearly two hundred short stories Gilman published in periodicals.

6. Charlotte Perkins Gilman, *The Living of Charlotte Perkins Gilman* (1935, repr. New York: Arno Press, 1972), 303; hereafter cited in the text as *Living*.

7. Ann J. Lane, *To Herland and Beyond: The Life and Works of Charlotte Perkins Gilman* (New York: Pantheon Books, 1990), 163; hereafter cited as Lane.

8. Gilman quoted in Lane, 186.

9. One writer who departed from the basic love plot was, of course, one of Gilman's favorite great-aunts, Harriet Beecher Stowe. Gilman was also aware of Elizabeth Stuart Phelps, for example, who had written a domestic utopia of a sort in 1883, *Beyond the Gates*. As Carol Farley Kessler describes this novel, "The domestication of heavenly 'mansions' shows a father housekeeping while awaiting the arrival of the rest of his family." Carol Farley Kessler, ed., *Daring to Dream: Utopian Stories by United States Women: 1836–1919* (Boston: Pandora Press, 1984), 239. (It is not clear whether Gilman had read this particular novel.) There is no indication that Gilman was familiar with the work of Sara Willis Parton ("Fanny Fern"), who, a generation before Gilman, explored many of Gilman's key issues in both her journalism and her fiction (particularly in her satires on sexism that ran in the New York *Ledger*, and in her 1855 novel, *Ruth Hall*). After her death in 1872, Parton's work quickly fell into neglect despite the fact that she had been the highest-paid journalist in America in the nineteenth century. Although Parton had had a Hartford childhood and had attended Catherine Beecher's seminary as a girl, Gilman does not seem to have come across her work. Gilman was likely to have been familiar with stories by Sara Orne Jewett, which focused on plots other than the "love plot."

10. Gilman made occasional reference to Margaret Fuller (see Lane, 214, for example). In the *Forerunner* in 1909 she celebrated the career of the early nineteenth-century journalist Anne Royall, noting that:

> there are not so many, either men or women, of this mind, that we can afford to overlook this sturdy pioneer "new woman." . . . Left a widow at the age of forty-four, and, after ten years of travel and experience, defrauded of the property left to her by her husband, she began to live a brave self-supporting independent life at an age when most of the women of her years were white-capped grandmothers. Instead of sinking into the position of a dependent female relative, she insisted on earning her own living.

This she did as so many women do to-day, by the use of her pen, a rarer profession in those times. . . . Anne Royall . . . was unique in that she kept in view the general situation of her country, political, economic, geographical and educational, and wrote steadily for thirty-one years on matters of national importance (*Forerunner* 1, December 1909).

In addition to those magazines in which she herself published, Gilman was also familiar with contemporary feminist journals including *The Englishwoman, The Common Cause, The Progressive Woman,* and *Woman's Era,* and ran advertisements for them in the *Forerunner (Forerunner* 1, October 1910).

11.   F. O. Matthiessen, *Theodore Dreiser,* Men of Letters Series (Toronto: George J. McCleod, 1951), 59–60.

12.   Charlotte Perkins Gilman, "Mind Cleaning," *Forerunner* 3 (Jan. 1912):5–6; "Kitchen-Mindedness," *Forerunner* 1 (Feb. 1910):7–11; "Teaching the Mothers," *Forerunner* 3 (March 1912):73–75.

13.   Gilman, "Kitchen-Mindedness," *Forerunner* 1 (Feb. 1910):7–11.

14.   Tillie Olsen, *Silences* (New York: Dell—A Laurel Seymour Lawrence Book, 1983), preface.

15.   Gilman, "Kitchen-Mindedness," 11.

16.   Gilman, "Reasonable Resolutions," *Forerunner* 1 (Jan. 1910):1.

17.   Gilman, "The Humanness of Women," *Forerunner* 1 (Jan. 1910):14.

18.   See James S. Fishkin, *Justice, Equal Opportunity, and the Family* (New Haven: Yale University Press, 1983), 30–32, and Bernard Williams, "The Idea of Equality," in Peter Laslett and W.G. Runciman, eds., *Philosophy, Politics and Society,* second series (Oxford: Basil Blackwell, 1962), 126.

19.   Gilman, "Women as a Class," *Impress,* 17 November 1894, 2–3.

20.   William Dean Howells, *"Criticism and Fiction" and Other Essays,* ed. and with introductions and notes by Clara Marburg Kirk and Rudolf Kirk (New York: New York University Press, 1959), 71, quoted in Carol Klimick Cyganowski, *Magazine Editors and Professional Authors in Nineteenth-Century America: The Genteel Tradition and the American Dream* (New York: Garland, 1988), 89.

21.   Gilman, "When I Was a Witch," *Forerunner* 1 (May 1910): 1–6, repr. Ann J. Lane, ed., *The Charlotte Perkins Gilman Reader* (New York: Pantheon Books, 1980), 21–31; Gilman, "The Girl in the Pink Hat," *Forerunner* (Feb. 1916):29–33 (repr. Lane, *Reader,* 39–46); Gilman, "The Unnatural Mother," *Forerunner* (Nov. 1916):281–285 (repr. Lane, *Reader,* 57–65); Gilman, "Making a Change," *Forerunner* (Dec. 1911):311–15 (repr. Lane, *Reader,* 66–74).

22.   Gilman, "The Dress of Women," *Forerunner* 6 (Jan. 1915):23.

23.   Gilman, "If I Were a Man," *Physical Culture* (July. 1914):31–34 (repr. Lane, *Reader,* 32–38): Lane, *Reader,* 33.

24.   Gilman, "Two Storks," *Forerunner* 1 (February 1910):12.

25.   Gilman, "The Artist," *Forerunner* (July 1916):170.

26.   Mary A. Hill, *Charlotte Perkins Gilman: The Making of a Radical Feminist 1860–1896* (Philadelphia: Temple University Press, 1980), 142; hereafter cited as Hill.

27.   "The cost of publishing this work was $3,000 a year; its price, a dollar. If I could have achieved three thousand subscribers then I would cheerfully have done the work for nothing, but I never had sense enough—business sense, that is, to get them." Charlotte Perkins Gilman, *Living,* 305.

28.   Gilman, "Making a Change," (repr. Lane, *Reader*), 74.

29.   Peg Bracken, *I Hate To Cook Book* (New York: Fawcett Crest, 1960).

Reconstructing *Here Also*: On the Later Poetry of Charlotte Perkins Gilman

GARY SCHARNHORST

"Poetry was always a delight to me," Charlotte Perkins Gilman wrote in her autobiography.[1] Though she is well-known today as a sociologist who authored the treatise *Women and Economics*, and though her story "The Yellow Wallpaper" has been increasingly anthologized in recent years, Gilman in fact began her public career as a poet and her first book was a collection of verse. W. D. Howells ranked her lyric "Similar Cases" and the other "civic satire" in her volume *In This Our World*, first published in 1893, with Lowell's "Biglow Papers."[2]

On her part, Gilman tended to disparage if not to deny the artistry of her verse. She preferred to emphasize its didactic purpose, telling an interviewer in 1896 that she did not consider *In This Our World* "a book of poems. I call it a tool box. It was written to drive nails with."[3] Still, when she visited England a few weeks later she found she had "a far higher reputation [there] than at home, based on the little book of poems" (*Living*, 201).

Her lyrics enjoyed something of a cult following in later years, particularly among socialists in the United States and England. In 1913, Floyd Dell called her "first of all, a poet, an idealist," the author of "the best satirical verses of modern times."[4] Two years later Upton Sinclair hailed her as "America's most brilliant woman poet and critic."[5] No less a luminary than George Bernard Shaw quoted her light verse in his correspondence;[6] Lester Ward cited it in his essays;[7] and figures as different as Eugene V. Debs and Woodrow Wilson were known to recite her lyrics aloud.[8] Gilman continued to publish poetry to the end of her life in such magazines as *Life* and the *Saturday Review of Literature*, though the only essay to date devoted to her verse focuses upon a slender selection of her early work.[9] In all, she published nearly five hundred poems during her career, though only 168 of them are collected in the various editions of *In This Our World*.[10]

Shortly before her death in August 1935, Gilman arranged for the posthumous publication of two books: her autobiography, issued in that same year by Appleton-Century, and a new anthology of her verse, to be

This essay was specifically written for this volume and is published here for the first time by permission of the author.

249

edited by her friend Amy Wellington. In the "Author's Note" to *The Living of Charlotte Perkins Gilman* she refers to Wellington as the "keen and gentle critic" who "has arranged my second book of poems, *Here Also*" (*Living*, ix). As Wellington wrote Gilman in May 1935, "There is no doubt about the power and beauty—and the *timeliness* of this second volume of your poems."[11]

Lamentably, Wellington was unable to place the manuscript with a publisher before her own death thirteen years later. However, a tentative list in Gilman's hand of the poems she wished to collect in this edition, dated 12 February 1935, survives in folder 185 of her papers at Radcliffe College (see appendix). Several of Wellington's letters to Gilman outlining her plans for the volume are also extant. By referring to the list and these letters, the contents of the stillborn collection may be largely reconstructed.

The new anthology apparently was to include a total of 148 poems, about a third of them previously unpublished, virtually all of them written since the last edition of *In This Our World* appeared in 1898. Many of these lyrics betray the influence of Whitman, whom Gilman described in 1933 as one of the "greatest" of all Americans.[12] Wellington planned to divide the poetry into three sections that mirrored the tripartite structure of the first collection. Gilman had grouped the poems in the earlier volume under the headings "The World," "The Woman," and "The March"—basically nature verse, suffrage anthems and other poems on feminist themes, and social satires and allegories. Wellington proposed to organize the new collection into sections entitled "The Satirist," "The Philosopher," and "The Artist," thus retaining three clear divisions among the poems.[13] "Somehow it satisfied my sense of the fitting," she explained, "to put the philosophy between those dynamic satires and all the loveliness."[14]

To be sure, it is now impossible to know for a certainty which poems on Gilman's list Wellington planned to assign to each category. She continually rearranged the order of works within each section, it seems, and she indicated to Gilman that "there is so much diversity in your poems that it is quite a little feat to place them all together without sharp or awkward changes."[15] Still, she detailed at least some of her plans in her letters. "I placed 'Up and Down' as the opening poem," she explained in her last note to the poet, dated 5 August 1935—only two weeks before Gilman's death. "It has true grandeur, and makes a most impressive opening of the second book."[16] Originally printed in the *Arena* in October 1898, reprinted in the *Public* in 1908 and in Gilman's own magazine the *Forerunner* in 1912, these stanzas with their idiosyncratic rhyme and irregular scansion vaguely recall the transcendental Whitman of "Out of the Cradle Endlessly Rocking":

> Up, up, up! On and out and away
> From the little beast I live in,
> Through the sweet home life I give in,
> With its dear, close love;

Out of that fragrant gloom,
With its crowding fruit and bloom,
    Into the wide clear day;
    Into the world above.

Out, where the soul can spread
    Into the lives of many—
Feeling the joy and pain,
The peace, the toil, the strain
    That is not spared to any;
Feeling and working as one;
So is our life begun—
    The life that can never grow
    Till it has widened so.—
The neighborless soul is dead.

On—with a sharp-caught breath,
    Into the space beyond—
Wonderful white-blue space
Where you feel through shifting time
The slow-formed life sublime
Of a yet unconscious race.
Where you live beyond all years
And the flickering screen of death
    Shows God's face calm and fond.

Even—a moment's dream—
    A flash that lifts and flies—
Even beyond our brothers
To a day when the full-born soul,
World-circling, conscious, whole,
    Shall taste the world's full worth—
    Shall feel the swing of the earth—
Feel what life will seem
    When we walk the thronging skies
And the earth shall sing with the others!

Down, down, down! Back and in and
    home!
    Circling softly through
    The spaces vast and blue;
The centuries' whirling spokes
    Settling back again
    To time-marks clear and plain,
As we count the separate strokes.
    The race lifelong and free
    Narrowed to what we see,
Our own set hope and power

In the history of the hour—
Back to our time we come.

In, where the Soul is warm
    With the clinging, lingering touch
    Of those we love so much,
And the daring wings can rest;
    Back, where the task is small,
    Easy and plain to all,
The life that most hold best—
Humanity's first form.

Down! If we fail of this;
    Down to the very base—
    The Universe, the Race,
Country and Friends and Home—
Here at the end we come
    To the first gift that was given,
    The little beast we live in!
Rest and be happy, soul!
This was an age-long goal,
This too you may nobly love—
Failing of aught above;
Feeling that, even here,
Life is as true, as near,
    As one with the will of God
    As sky, or sea, or sod
Of aught of the world that is.[17]

In this lyric Gilman expressed several of her most characteristic ideas: the importance of creative work outside the paradoxically "fragrant gloom" of the home; the promise of a millennial or evolutionary ideal, the inevitability of a heaven on earth; and the immortality, not of the individual soul, but of the race. Structurally, the poem describes a kind of curve, flying ecstatically "up" and "out" and "into the space beyond" in the first three stanzas, pausing at the apogee in stanza four, then hurtling "down" and "in" in stanzas five through seven. "Up and Down" was to be followed, according to Wellington, by "A Central Sun" and "Worship," two odes to the "constant Power" or purpose each of us orbit in "swift obedient utmost flight."[18] These prefatory poems trace, in effect, the same parabola as the poems they introduce: a plunge through topical satire, then an ascent into the more ethereal realms of philosophy and beauty.

I

The satirical verses Wellington planned to include in the first section of the volume are technically comparable to Gilman's earlier work. Indeed, Gilman wrote most of her poetical satires in quatrains of iambic pentameter, often rhyming the even-numbered lines. For example, she had used this formula to lampoon conservative Darwinism in her early poem "Similar Cases":

There was once a little animal,
  No bigger than a fox,
And on five toes he scampered
  Over Tertiary rocks.
They called hlim Eohippus,
  And they called him very small,
And they thought of him of no value—
  When they thought of him at all.[19]

Gilman's most popular late satire, to judge from the frequency with which it was reprinted, was "Child Labor," nine similar stanzas of caustic comment on the economic exploitation of the young. As Gilman explained, child labor represents a fundamental violation of natural law:

No fledgling feeds the father-bird!
No chicken feeds the hen!
  No kitten mouses for the cat—
  This glory is for men.

We are the Wisest, Strongest Race—
  Loud may our praise be sung!—
The only animal alive
  That lives upon its young![20]

Many of Gilman's late satirical poems tend to be more topical than "Child Labor," aiming at such particular targets as recent books on the so-called Woman Question, the psychoanalysis fad, and the sexually discriminatory policies of the New York City school board. If the tone of these poems is more strident, however, their target is more pointed.

    Gilman also wrote at least four satirical poems about the embalmed meat scandal ignited by Sinclair's novel *The Jungle* early in the century, all of them listed nearly thirty years later among the works to appear in *Here Also*. Even before passage of the Pure Food and Drug Act, she ridiculed the packinghouse owners in a poem first published in the *Independent* in 1906:

"I Would Fain Die a Dry Death"

The American public is patient,
  The American public is slow,
The American public will stand as much
  As any public I know.
We submit to be killed by our railroads,

We submit to be fooled by our press,
We can stand as much Government scandal
As any folks going, I guess.
We can bear bad air in the subway,
We can bear quick death in the street,
But we are a little particular
About the food we eat.

It is not so much that it kills us—
We are used to being killed;
But we like to know what fills us
When we pay for being filled.
When we pay the Beef Trust prices—
As we must, or go without—
It is not that we grudge the money,
But we grudge the horrid doubt.
Is it ham or trichinosis?
Can a label command belief?
Is it pork we have purchased, or poison?
Is it tuberculosis or beef?

There is really a choice of diseases
To any one, little or big;
And no man really pleases
To die of a long-dead pig.
We take our risks as we're able,
On elevator and train,
But to sit in peace at the table
And be seized with sudden pain
When we are at home and happy,
Is really against the grain.

And besides—admitting the poison—
Admitting we all must die—
Accepting the second-hand sickness
From a cholera-smitten stye;
Patiently bearing the murder,
Amiable, meek, inert—
We do rise up and remonstrate
Against the Packingtown dirt!
Let there be death in the dinner,
Subtle and unforeseen,
But O, Mr. Packer, in packing our death,
Won't you please to pack it clean![21]

Like Sinclair, Gilman believed the focus of the scandal had been misplaced; that is, rather than advocating governmental reform to save the meat industry, she believed the sale of adulterated food was symptomatic of an unjust economic system that privileged profits above the public health. A socialist by conviction, she identified the more systemic problem in a hitherto unpublished poem:

How About the Man?

We have seen the picture of Packingtown
Painted in blood-red, black and brown
    As only Sinclair can;
We have heard the story long and sweet
Of how they prepare the food we eat
We are hearing a plenty about the meat—
    But how about the man?

Somebody did it. Somebody knew.
Somebody excellent profits drew
    From this public poisoning plan;
They are pushing a Bill to finish the fun,—
But think of the mischief that has been done!—
Is there no blame coming to any one?
    How about the man?

He has killed out competition, honest but small,
He's grown rich on the money that came from us all
    For his death-dealing package and can.
We pay him for meat, but he finds pleasant ways
To feed us on filth, to shorten our days
With ptomaines—and also the prices to raise—
    Now how about the man?[22]

Similarly, in "The Gunman" (1915), one of the poems Wellington assigned to the satire section of *Here Also*, [23] Gilman compared the petty criminal to the capitalist "robber baron" or social atavist à la Rockefeller and Carnegie:

Prowling in the alley, loafing in the bar,
Chancing his swift "get-away" in a stolen car;
Vermin of the city, whose bite is sure to kill,
Hired by wiser villains to work vicarious ill,
Not for hate or vengeance or quarrel of his own,
In sordid risk and danger this savage strikes alone.
Life to him is merchandise, crime he sneers away,
Carelessly he murders for a little pay;
Killing, for his profit, a man he never saw—
Thug—assassin—gunman—laughing at the law.

Honored and defended by church and bench and bar,
Proud in his park and palace, steam yacht and private car;

> Giver to school and college, to charitable care,
> Patron of art and science, a multi-millionaire.
> He makes the guns and sells them; again and yet again
> There die, to his advantage, our armies of young men.
> Not for hate or vengeance, or quarrel of his own
> He kills, but for business—for profit his alone.
> Murderer of millions, by him our wars are made;
> Thug—assassin—gunman—thriving at his trade.[24]

Obviously, Gilman had by this time abandoned her early notion, borrowed from Edward Bellamy,[25] that crime was but a pathology that could be treated medically like any other disease.

Indeed, Gilman grew more politically reactionary over the years. A pacifist, as "The Gunman" suggests, on the eve of the First World War, she had compromised her pacifism, however reluctantly, by 1916 and endorsed the prosecution of the conflict as a necessary evil. She "had little tolerance for those who opposed" American entry into the war, according to George Middletown.[26] "[A]fter having preached all her life the unity of man and the need for human growth," as her friend Zona Gale later remarked, "she sided unconditionally with the allies and spoke of the German nation as criminally insane." It was "an utter contradiction of thought,"[27] a reversal of views so sudden and unexpected it probably alienated some subscribers and so led, if only indirectly, to the demise of the *Forerunner* in 1917. Though she had lectured throughout central Europe in 1905, and though several of her works, including *Women and Economics* and *The Home*, had been translated into German, Gilman came to scorn Germany as "a very Frankenstein among the nations."[28] She derided the reticence of American leaders to enlist the nation on the side of the European allies in "Why? To the United States of America 1915–16," published in the *Forerunner* for January 1916. Each of the three stanzas in this poem opens with a version of the same question (e.g., "Why does America sit so still, / Watching all Europe die?" and "Why does America stain her hands / With blood that will never dry?" and "Why does American turn away / From Europe's bitter cry?").[29] Shortly after the war, in an unpublished poem also listed in the tentative table of contents for *Here Also*, Gilman reiterated her disdain for Germany in unambiguous terms:

On Germany

> At last they had the ruffian downed
> And his spent captors stood around,
> Bleeding and torn in every limb,
> To think what they should do with him;
> What punishment, and for what time,
> Could expiate his hideous crime;
> What fine, how long enforced and paid,
> Could mend the ruin he had made;

And some who called him manic sure,
Sought how to best restrain and cure.

But others who had held it wrong
To struggle with the villain strong;
Claiming that it was *never* right,
No matter what the cause, to fight;
Plead with the judges, lest their dealings
Might somehow hurt the prisoners' feelings.

They said "More honor must be lent
To this so brave belligerent."
"If you should make too sore your sentence
It might postpone his true repentance."
"If you inflict too heavy pain
He may be led to strike again."
"If you, by fines, your wealth regained,
His wife and children would be pained.
Surely, Oh surely you would scorn
So to impoverish the unborn!"

The victors might have answered thus:
"He's no belligerent, this cuss,
But a plain criminal in fact,
And caught redhanded in the act.
He strike again if we do more?
Without offense he struck before,
And doubtless so will strike again
If we let any chance remain.
And for his feelings—Holy Powers!
Suppose you give a thought to ours.
As to his family—'tis true,
But we have wives and children too,
By him impoverished. Please explain
Why his alone should not have pain?
All the unborn the loss must bear,
We propose his shall have their share."

They might have answered thus, or longer,
They might have answered even stronger.
They might, but it seemed too protracted,
The court was sitting, and it acted.

Lest the point of this poem seem too ambiguous, Gilman penciled a note on the typescript after the rise to power of the Nazis in 1933: "O if we had only had the sense to march three armies into Berlin!"[30] Obviously, after the war her satires betray a much darker tone and a more bitter edge.

A longtime proponent of "negative eugenics" to eliminate pernicious character traits and to control population growth, Gilman also betrayed an increasing xenophobia in her late writings. She moved to rural Connecticut in 1922 after living in Manhattan for over two decades, and in such essays as "Is America Too Hospitable?" (1923) she argued the case for restricted immigration. Even in her autobiography she bitterly disparaged New York, that "multiforeign city, that abnormally enlarged city, swollen rather than grown" with new immigrants, where "every one is an exile, none more so than the American (*Living*, 316–17).[31] Her nativist bias is no less apparent in her satirical fable "The Melting Pot," which also was to be printed for the first time in *Here Also*:

> A melting pot has to be made
> With particular care;
> And carefully sampled and weighed
> As to nature, proportion and grade
> Are the ores mingled there.
>
> Let the metaphor change in your mind
> To an effort to bake,
> Of eggs, butter and flour you will find,
> With milk, sugar and raisins combined,
> You compose a good cake.
>
> Or, taking salt pepper and meat,
> With an onion or two,
> Tomatoes, and maybe a beet,
> Fine herbs and some celery sweet,
> A good soup you may brew.
>
> But if all these ingredients here
> Should commingle at will,
> Neither cake nor yet soup will appear,
> There's one name for a mixture so queer—
> That is swill.[32]

Wellington's failure to find a publisher for the new collection of Gilman's poems may, in the end, be explained simply by the radically discordant tones among them, especially the differences between those liberal and tolerant satires written before and the more acerbic and culturally chauvinistic ones written after the outbreak of the Great War.

II

"Your philosophic poems are sometimes didactic and the didacticism is always philosophic, so I had no trouble in classifying here," Wellington wrote Gilman in July 1935.[33] Gilman's ostensibly "philosophical" poems are sometimes little more than witty apothegms like "Queer People" (1899):

> The people people work with best are often very queer;
> The people people own by birth quite shock your first idea;
> The people people choose for friends your common sense appall,
> But the people people marry are the queerest folks of all.[34]

The slant-rhyme of the first couplet here is no doubt the result of Gilman's New England accent—Emily Dickinson, after all, had once rhymed "Judea" and "too near." These "philosophical" poems are among Gilman's most conventional works, and several of them read like textbook examples of the pathetic fallacy. In the unpublished "Patient Truth," for example, she personified Truth as an infinitely patient woman—the "race-type," as the reform-Darwinist Lester Ward had suggested,[35] or the biologically-superior, original form of the species:

> Truth sat around, undated,
>   A million years ago;
> Sat and yawned and waited
> To be appreciated;
> Offered the facts and waited,
>   Waited for us to know.
> But we filled our minds with tradition
>   From the days of our savage youth;
> We worshipped in superstition,
> And murdered the brain's ambition
> That questioned our superstitition—
>   What did we care for Truth?
>
> And still we sit here contented,
>   Sure that the first is last;
> So far as it can be prevented
> We oppose the unprece[de]nted,
> All progress that can be prevented
>   We prevent, preferring the past.
> But Truth is not in a hurry,
>   Truth does not seem to care.
> She does not grieve nor worry
> At our dullness sloth or flurry,
> She does not have to worry—
>   Just keeps on being there.[36]

In "The Oyster and the Starfish" (1925), similarly, Gilman wrote of an anthropomorphic scavenger that "in no haste and with no doubt" cracks open and devours "a fat and juicy" shellfish—a parable of Darwinian struggle for existence reminiscent of the battle of the lobster and squid that young Frank Cowperwood observes in the first chapter of Dreiser's *The Financier*.[37]

Over the years Gilman had often written a type of philosophical verse in dialogue (e.g., "The Pig and the Pearl," "The 'Anti' and the Fly," "The Socialist and the Suffragist," "The Clam and the Lark"). When "the spirit of Philosophy descended" upon the animals in "The Rabbit, the Rhinoceros and I" (1912), for example, a rabbit wished for stronger legs and longer teeth to ward off predators, a rhino preached a sort of stoic resignation to the law of the jungle, but the poet "became a little lighter hearted, / I saw a heaven in sight and wanted some."[38] In 1935, Gilman sent Wellington another unpublished poem in the same vein with the handwritten instruction "be sure it goes in!" The piece illustrates her unwavering faith in the inevitability of progress:

> The Fatalist and the Sailorman.
>
> Said the Fatalist to the Sailorman
>   "Vain are your efforts, vain,
>   To cross the windswept main,
> For the wind blows where it listeth
> And drives you forward and back,
> You are but a chip that twisteth
> Among currents strong and black.
>   The wind is the breath of Fate—
>   Lie in your berth and wait."
>
> Said the Sailorman to the Fatalist
>   "You're right about the wind,
>   But why should I stay behind?
> The wind blows where it listeth
> To drive me forward or back,
> But the art of sailing consisteth
> Largely in learning to tack.
>   Why should I loaf and wait?
>   I know how to tack, on Fate."[39]

This traditional style of verse, with its straining for effect and such precious constructions as "listeth" and "twisteth," may strike modern readers as anachronistic if not downright frivolous. Wellington may have failed to place the manuscript with a publisher, despite her faith in the "timeliness" of these poems, simply because Gilman's style of verse was no longer fashionable.

III

Because she chose to subordinate the formal devices of poetry to her didactic message, Gilman self-consciously resisted the innovations associated with modern poetry; indeed, she repudiated the experimentation associated generally with modernism in the arts. She savaged the Armory exhibition—the so-called Ash Can school of painting—in the *Forerunner* in 1913, for example, in a remarkable denunciation of the *avant-garde*: "In a world that hungers continually for beauty, that bitterly needs truth and hope and enlightenment, it is more than pitiful that the Great Service of Art should be so profaned by these poor little morbid ones, suffering from an inflamed egotism, from elephantiasis of the soul."[40] She elsewhere observed that art "became unpopular when the artist forgot his service and thought only of 'expressing' himself."[41] A true artist, as she suggested in a late poem, "is the intermediate lens / Of God, and so best gives him to the world, / Intensified, interpreted, to us."[42]

Gilman best expressed her attitude toward arcane symbolism and obscure diction in modern poetry in another late poem which concludes:

> Time was when fearless heart and brain
> Used words as common as the rain,
>   And through that veil of lingual light
>   Shone Truth and Hope and Beauty bright;
> But weird, wild words small thoughts enchain,
>   In modern verse.[43]

"The Artist," the final section of *Here Also*, was to consist largely of poems that would stick in the throat of "the 'art for art's sake' people," as Wellington explained.[44]

Many of the poems in this section are brief odes to nature, punctuated with frequent exclamation marks, such as the Whitmanesque free verse "Little Leafy Brothers" (1908), first published by Whitman's disciple Horace Traubel in *The Conservator*; "Out of Doors" (1905), a celebration of "the soft sweet scent of happy growing things";[45] the unpublished "Santa Barbara to San Jose"; and "In Alabama Woods" (1904), a proto-Imagist poem written during one of Gilman's lecture tours through the South early in the century:

> The wet, dark woods—monotonous tall pines,
> The heavy velvet mat of brown below,
> And straight shafts rising, sodden black with rain,
> In clean, long lines.
> From stem to stem, a high-hung solemn pall,
> Thick clouds of blue-green needles cover all;
> But see, across the gloom, again! again!
> The dogwood's flame of snow![46]

Wellington planned to end *Here Also* with a similar, though longer nature poem, "California Colors" (1915).[47]

Gilman also instructed her editor to include the unpublished "To Isadora Duncan" in the collection. Given her antipathy to modernism in the arts, her selection of an improvisational dancer as the subject of a poem may seem paradoxical. However, the explanation is simple enough: Gilman had seen Duncan perform at the Metropolitan Opera House in New York in February 1915 and was impressed, not by her mode of "self-expression," but by the classicism of her art. Duncan, she wrote, "has revived the old Greek use of the dance, a thing intensely serious" and "gravely beautiful."[48]

To Isadora Duncan

> I have seen ballets. Hard-legged women
> Hopping on stiffly distorted ugly foot-pegs;
> Spinning like toy tops; whirling senseless petticoats,
> Short and conventional, graceless as powder-puffs,
> With the hard legs thrusting forth from the center.
> ....
> I have seen Isadora. I have seen dancing.
> She, loving, motherly, utterly gracious,
> Grave in her suave folded robes; and around her
> Blossomed the maidens, budded the children.
> Lovely young maids with their light limbs leaping,
> Arms tossing wide in the grace of young gladness,
> Joy in their movement, joy in their faces.
>
> I have seen dancing; soft-footed music;
> Free naked feet, with each step a caressing,
> White knees uplifting, white arms outwaving,
> Fair growing maids and the fairy wee children,
> Light as the flowers are, light as the snow-flake.
> Leaping as the heart leaps—Springtime! Morning!
>
> All blossom free from the heart of Isadora,
> Mother of music, of melody in motion;
> She, recreator of long-vanished wonder,
> Mother of happiness! Mother of beauty!

Unlike so many of Gilman's other odes, this poem has evidently been carefully crafted. The harsh consonants and tortured meter of the first stanza, particularly the second line, mimic the awkward ballet. The easy turns of phrase and pauses in the next three stanzas simulate Duncan's dance in "folded robes" and flowing draperies. Unfortunately, as Gilman glossed in the margin of the typescript of the poem, she had "Sent a copy to [Duncan] and she never even said thank you."[49]

Gilman's late verse usually elicited little response, in part because it was largely unread. As she complained to her friend Alice Stone Blackwell in 1930, "These very young readers, editors, & critics have no use for writers over thirty."[50] In the ongoing revival of interest in her life and work, her late poetry merits closer scrutiny than it has received to date. "I am tremendously enthusiastic about this collection of the Poems," Amy Wellington had declared unequivocally in 1935.[51] She was, regrettably, the only person ever to record an opinion of the collection.

APPENDIX

Listed below are titles of the poems that appear in the tentative table of contents of *Here Also* which Gilman prepared for Amy Wellington and which survives in folder 185 of the Gilman Papers in the Schlesinger Library at Radcliffe College. The titles appear in the order in which they appear in the document, not the order in which Wellington planned to print them. I have silently deleted duplicate titles, and I indicate with an asterisk the poems that were apparently unpublished. Publication dates for the others are noted in my bibliography of Gilman's works. This is *not* a final list, and other titles that were to appear in the collection (e.g., "Worship," "Closed Doors," "In Alabama Woods," and "California Colors") are identified in Wellington's letters to Gilman.

   1. Some Nordics
   2. Happiness
  *3. Hyenas
   4. A Psalm of "Lives"
   5. The Gunman
  *6. River Windows
   7. The Oyster and the Starfish
  *8. Religious Toleration
  *9. The Powdered Nose
  10. Twigs
  11. The Front Wave
 *12. The Pious Pawn
  13. Out of Doors
  14. The Departing Housemaid
 *15. The Son of Both
 *16. The Fatalist and the Sailorman
  17. Why? To the United States of America 1915–16
 *18. To Isadora Duncan
  19. Our World

Notes

1. *The Living of Charlotte Perkins Gilman* (New York and London: Appleton-Century, 1935), 28; hereafter cited as *Living*.

2. William Dean Howells, "Life and Letters," *Harper's Weekly*, 25 January 1895, 79; "The New Poetry," *North American Review*, 168 (May 1899), 589–90.

3. *Topeka State Journal*, 15 June 1896.

4. Floyd Dell, *Women as World Builders* (Chicago: Forbes, 1913), 24.

5. *The Cry for Justice*, ed. Upton Sinclair (Philadelphia: Winston, 1915), 662.

6. *Bernard Shaw's Collected Letters 1898–1910*, ed. Dan H. Laurence (New York: Dodd, Mead, 1972), 346.

7. Lester Ward, *Glimpses of the Cosmos* (New York and London: Putnam's, 1917), V, 336–39.

8. *Palo Alto Times*, 17 April 1930; *The Papers of Woodrow Wilson*, ed. Arthur S. Link (Princeton: Princeton University Press, 1979), vol. 30, 22.

9. Carol Farley Kessler, "Brittle Jars and Bitter Jangles: Light Verse by Charlotte Perkins Gilman," *Regionalism and the Female Imagination* 4 (Winter 1979); repr. in *Charlotte Perkins Gilman: The Woman and Her Work*, ed. Sheryl L. Meyering (Ann Arbor, Mich., and London: UMI Research Press, 1989), 133–43.

10. See Gary Scharnhorst, *Charlotte Perkins Gilman: A Bibliography* (Metuchen, N.J., and London: Scarecrow Press, 1985), 1–58.

11. Amy Wellington to Gilman, 5 May 1935, folder 125, Gilman Papers, Schlesinger Library, Radcliffe College. Quoted by permission.

12. Cited in *Amerikanische Turnzeitung*, 8 December 1935, 9. See also Joann P. Krieg, "Charlotte Perkins Gilman and the Whitman Connection," in *Charlotte Perkins Gilman: The Woman and Her Work*, 145–49.

13. Amy Wellington to Gilman, 12 June 1935, 5 August 1935, folder 125, Gilman Papers, Schlesinger Library, Radcliffe College.

14. Amy Wellington to Gilman, 3 July 1935, folder 125, Gilman Papers, Schlesinger Library, Radcliffe College. Quoted by permission.

15. Amy Wellington to Gilman, 5 August 1935, folder 125, Gilman Papers, Schlesinger Library, Radcliffe College. Quoted by permission.

16. Amy Wellington to Gilman, 5 August 1935, folder 125, Gilman Papers, Schlesinger Library, Radcliffe College. Quoted by permission.

17. *Arena* 20 (October 1898): 478–479; *Public*, 18 January 1908, 998–99; *Forerunner* 3 (January 1912): 17–18.

18. Amy Wellington to Gilman, 5 August 1935, folder 125, Gilman Papers, Schlesinger Library, Radcliffe College; "A Central Sun," *Forerunner* 1 (January 1910): i; "Worship," *Forerunner* 1 (November 1910): i.

19. Charlotte Perkins Stetson [Gilman], *In This Our World* (Boston: Small, Maynard & Co., 1898), 95.

20. Charlotte Perkins Gilman, *Forerunner* 1 (December 1909): 10. For a list of reprintings, see Scharnhorst's bibliography, 39–40.

21. Charlotte Perkins Gilman, *Independent*, 14 June 1906, 1401.

22. Manuscript copy in folder 188, Gilman Papers, Schlesinger Library, Radcliffe College. Quoted by permission.

23. Amy Wellington to Gilman, 3 July 1935, folder 125, Gilman Papers, Schlesinger Library, Radcliffe College.

24. *Forerunner* 6 (January 1915), 11.

25. Charlotte Perkins Gilman, *The Man-Made World* (New York: Charlton Co., 1911), 189–90. See also my *Charlotte Perkins Gilman* (Boston: Twayne, 1985), 20–31, 78.

26. Judith Schwartz, *Radical Feminists of Heterodoxy: Greenwich Village, 1912–1940* (Lebanon, N.H.: New Victoria, 1982), 34.

27. Zona Gale, "Foreword" to *Living*, xxxi.

28. Gilman, "Studies in Social Pathology," *Forerunner* 7 (May 1916): 120.

29. Gilman, *Forerunner* 7 (January 1916): 5.

30. Typescript copy in folder 189, Gilman Papers, Schlesinger Library, Radcliffe College. Quoted by permission.

31. See also Scharnhorst, *Charlotte Perkins Gilman*, 108–109; and Ann J. Lane, *To "Herland" and Beyond: The Life and Works of Charlotte Perkins Gilman* (New York: Pantheon, 1990), 337.

32. Typescript copy in folder 189, Gilman Papers, Schlesinger Library, Radcliffe College. Quoted by permission.

33. Amy Wellington to Gilman, 3 July 1935, folder 125, Gilman Papers, Schlesinger Library, Radcliffe College. Quoted by permission.

34. Gilman, *Cosmopolitan* 27 (June 1899): 172.

35. Lester Ward, *Pure Sociology* (New York: Macmillan, 1903), 325. See also Scharnhorst, *Charlotte Perkins Gilman*, 46–47.

36. Typescript copy in folder 188, Gilman Papers, Schlesinger Library, Radcliffe College. Quoted by permission.

37. Gilman, *Forum* 74 (October 1925): 629. Gilman wrote for the *Delineator* while Dreiser was its editor (*Living*, 304), though she later panned his fiction (*Forerunner* 7 [July 1916]: 193–96). The episode in *The Financier* may also have inspired Gilman's satire of yellow journalism, entitled "The Daily Squid," in the *Forerunner* 6 (August 1915): 206:

> The Squid he has no implements
> To fight or run or think;
> He has no fins, no wings, no feet,
> To swim, fly, run, or sink;
> When he's attacked he can but hate
> In self-emitted ink.

38. Gilman, *Forerunner* 3 (March 1912): 83.

39. Typescript copy in folder 186, Gilman Papers, Schlesinger Library, Radcliffe College. Quoted by permission.

40. Gilman, "On Some Recent 'Art,' " *Forerunner* 4 (April 1913): 112. Gilman reiterated that "egoism" is "that disease of modern art" in "Painting via Literature," *Forerunner* 7 (July 1916): 186.

41. Gilman, "Why is 'Art' Unpopular?" *Louisville Herald*, 16 June 1919, 7:4–5; *Baltimore Sun*, 16 June 1919, 12:4–5.

42. Gilman, "The Artist," *Forerunner* 2 (May 1911): 126.

43. Gilman, "In Modern Verse," *Forerunner* 3 (November 1912): 287.

44. Amy Wellington to Gilman, 5 May 1935, folder 125, Gilman Papers, Schlesinger Library, Radcliffe College. Quoted by permission.

45. Gilman, *Cosmopolitan* 39 (May 1905): 2–3.

46. Gilman, *Woman's Journal*, 25 June 1904, 201; repr. in *Forerunner* 4 (November 1913): 284.

47. Amy Wellington to Gilman, 3 July 1935, folder 125, Gilman Papers, Schlesinger Library, Radcliffe College.

48. Gilman, "The Dancing of Isadora Duncan," *Forerunner* 6 (April 1915): 101.

49. Typescript copy in folder 186, Gilman Papers, Schlesinger Library, Radcliffe College. Quoted by permission.

50. Gilman to Alice Stone Blackwell, 24 October 1930, Papers of the National American Women's Suffrage Association, carton 12, Library of Congress.

51. Amy Wellington to Gilman, July 1935, folder 125, Gilman Papers, Schlesinger Library, Radcliffe College. Quoted by permission.

Index

◆